The Private Self

The Private Self

Theory and Practice of Women's
Autobiographical Writings

❖❖❖❖❖❖❖❖❖❖❖❖❖❖❖❖❖❖❖❖❖❖

Edited by Shari Benstock

The University of North Carolina Press

Chapel Hill & London

The paper in this book meets the guidelines for
permanence and durability of the
Committee on Production Guidelines for Book Longevity
of the Council on Library Resources.

92 91 90 89   5 4 3 2

Library of Congress Cataloging-in-Publication Data

The Private self.

Includes bibliographies and index.
1. English prose literature—Women authors—History
and criticism. 2. Autobiography. 3. American prose
literature—Women authors—History and criticism.
4. Women—Great Britain—Biography—History and
criticism. 5. Women—United States—Biography—
History and criticism. 6. Women authors, English
—Biography—History and criticism. 7. Women
authors, American—Biography—History and criticism.
8. Women and literature. I. Benstock, Shari, 1944–
PR756.A9P75   1988   809'.93592'088042   88-1282
ISBN 0-8078-1791-9 (alk. paper)
ISBN 0-8078-4218-4 (pbk.: alk. paper)

"Charlotte Forten Grimké and the Search for a Public Voice," from *The Tie That Binds*, by
Joanne M. Braxton. Copyright © 1988 by Rutgers, The State University. An extended
version of this essay will appear in *Autobiography by Black American Women: A Tradition
within a Tradition*, by Joanne M. Braxton, forthcoming from Temple University Press.

Portions of Elizabeth Fox-Genovese's essay, "My Statue, My Self," appeared in *Feminist
Issues in Literary Scholarship*, edited by Shari Benstock, Indiana University Press, 1987.

CONTENTS

ACKNOWLEDGMENTS

The idea for a collection of essays on the theory and practice of women's autobiographical writings came about during a graduate seminar I taught at the University of Tulsa in spring 1984. My thanks to students in that seminar for their lively interest in the full range of issues raised by this topic, and with special appreciation to Jan Calloway, Regina Haslinger, Frances Kerr, Celia Patterson, and Ruth Weston for their bibliographic research. A portion of the manuscript preparation costs was underwritten by support from the University of Tulsa Faculty Research Program.

This book is dedicated to students at the former Tulsa Center for the Study of Women's Literature, whose friendship, feminist humor, and commitment to research on women's issues supported me through some very difficult times.

Belle Isle, Miami Beach
June 1987

INTRODUCTION

The Private Self: Theory and Practice of Women's Autobiographical Writings.
In one way or another each of these concepts—privacy, self, theory,
practice, women, autobiography, writing—is examined in the essays
that comprise this collection. What is it about autobiographical writing
that raises issues of the "private" in terms of the "self," and how is the
"self" opened to question in the self-positioning act of writing? How
does "private" situate itself in terms of the "public"? Are private and
public selves forever opposed to each other? Does "self" position the
subject in the singular? Is "autobiographical writing" a genre? If so, how
do "women" redefine the properties of the autobiographical? What roles
do "theory" and "practice" play in such a grouping?

At the outset, I confess that the choice of title—*The Private Self*—
purposely puts into question its own terms, and the dozen essays that
follow, different as they often are from each other, follow the questioning of these mutually reinforcing terms, the "self" and its "private"
status. Each of these terms plays a role with respect to "theory" and
"practice," because it is a theory of selfhood that is always under examination in analyses of autobiographical writings, whether or not this
analysis overtly raises questions as to how selfhood—and in this case,
female selfhood—is defined. The "private" suggests a scene of writing
that invites the female, a separate space at the very limits of the generic
divide between the autobiographical and other kinds of writings and
the gender divide between the masculine and the feminine. Absent from
the title, but nevertheless of concern to this volume, is that which we
might categorize as the "feminist"—feminist theories and practices that
open the way to writing about women's autobiographical writings. This
volume, like others recently published, testifies to a certain kind of
legitimacy both of autobiographical forms and of women's writing, a
legitimacy that has been purchased against whatever efforts have been
made on behalf of the autobiographical *as such* in critical theory and
practice. Although gender is the overriding concern of these essays, it
situates itself in a field of allied interests: race, class, religion, and
historical and political conditions.

Most problematic, perhaps, are the terms *theory* and *practice*, which divide the volume as signposts to what one might assume to be monolithic and mutually exclusive domains. In general, these terms suggest not only a division of the spoils but also a hierarchical ranking in which theory takes precedence over practice and sets the boundaries within which practice can take place. The word *theory* brings to mind the specters of European philosophy that haunt American criticism at this point in our history and the rhetorical excesses and self-indulgent practices of several prominent theoreticians who compete for academic audiences. But theory has also been acknowledged recently as a field of interacting and competing concerns within feminist practice, a way of restating and rethinking the practical level of archival scholarship and the reclamation of lost writers that is so identified with American feminism. To theorize women's writing practices has become a way of addressing feminist criticism to the theoretical claims of what I might call a traditionally patriarchal criticism. This criticism has appeared in various guises, from the biographical-centered criticism of the nineteenth century, for instance, to the once "New" criticism of the first half of the twentieth century. To be able to theorize women's writing practices, including women's critical writing practices, is to make women's writing somehow legitimate within the academy. The costs of such a legitimacy are always an issue when discussing forms that have traditionally been considered illegitimate, as have autobiographical writings—especially diary, letter, and memoir writing.

This enthrallment to theory often jeopardizes the site of writing and the relation of the text to its author. When writing locates itself at the margins of genre or outside the limits of defined genre, or if the author is also marginalized (that is, if the writer is female, working class, black, Hispanic, lesbian), it serves as a kind of "limit case." Writing that works the borders of definitional boundaries bears witness both to repressive inscription under the law of genre and to the freedom and dispossession of existence outside the law. Such cases—and women's autobiographical writings are exemplary in this—are difficult to define in terms of "theory." As a result, the problems they pose are often avoided altogether, or the writing is submitted to the violence of a theory that merely registers its effects through a sample set of quotations—wrenched from writing and reading contexts—illustrating the "problem." Such writing may fare the worst in both worlds: it is overlooked or misrepresented by "theoretical" critics and denied careful attention to thematic and formal properties by "practical" ones. The exemplary writing used to illustrate theoretical propositions is submitted to a *practice* that advertises the status of *theory* as a superior kind of writing. In the realm of autobiographical writings, then, the suggestion is that only a theoretical criticism of autobiography can justify *analysis* of autobiographical texts. Or, the only autobiographical texts worth our attention are those that claim our interest because of the importance of the life they delineate. Either way, women's autobiographical writings are vulnerable.

Why, then, repeat this gesture by dividing a collection of essays into a section on theory and one on practice, repeating even the priority of theory over practice? In part, because I think that recent work on autobiography has fallen into the theoretical trap in which American criticism now finds itself—that is, this gesture suggests that theory and practice are separate from each other, each with clearly defined interests and borders, and that when they come together (as in the clichéd coupling "theory and practice") theory always takes precedence as that which can make clear the implications of a blinded practice. For auto-biography, this blind enthrallment to theory has serious (and for the most part overlooked) implications; it assumes that autobiographical writings can only be taken seriously when they are taken theoretically to mean something more than a critical practice can elucidate. And it often means that the implications of theory for certain practitioners (women, blacks, working classes, the nonliterary) are deadly: theory is taken up and added on to practice without a rigorous (that is, a theoretical) examination of the effects of that theory. The study of autobiographical writings has often repeated the worst sins of academic criticism in order to legitimate the autobiographical.

One of the first misunderstandings of the relation between theory and practice rests on this notion of "relation," which is often the first casualty of a discussion that insists that the two remain distinct. This "separate and opposed" claim is, in fact, a misreading of theory. Theory and practice are not separate from each other, nor are they necessarily opposed, nor is it certain that practice must bow to the claims of theory or that theory comes first in some kind of ontological reading of the histories of theory and practice. Practice always implies theory of some kind (whether acknowledged or articulated), and theory does not ap-pear in a vacuum—it cannot exist without practice. The arbitrary divi-sion between theory and practice attempts to clarify that which is vague and fragmentary. But the relationship between theory and practice is often vague and fragmentary *by definition*, its articulation a shifting one,

its boundaries never entirely clear or its premises secure. Like auto/
bio/graphical writing, "theory" and "practice" are defined in relation to
each other, and these definitions change depending upon the subject of
the discourse. The interrelation of theory and practice in analysis of epic
poetry or the modern novel is quite different from the relation when
letters and the epistolary novel or film *noir* and the "woman's film" are
under examination.

My sense of the collective work now underway on women's autobiographical writings—and there is an immense amount of work in progress—is that no one is taking the old definitions of genre and gender,
theory and practice for granted. No one adopts a theoretical stance
without a close look at the implications of that stance. Often, various
theories are brought into play with each other (and this has been a
defining feature of feminist theory all along) so as to measure the
usefulness and truthfulness of these theories in relation to each other,
with special attention to questions at hand: gender, race, social class,
religious affiliation, sexual preference, historical and cultural contexts.
If the existing scholarship in women's autobiographical writing has
been more practical than theoretical (the discovery and publication of
hitherto unknown or ignored works preceding a writing about the
effects of such discoveries), no theory about women's autobiography
operates apart from an awareness of the disparateness of such discoveries. Women's writings are as individual as women themselves, and they
often resist easy classification, thus posing problems for theory from the
first. We need to remind ourselves that the discovery and printing of
such writings is ongoing, even as critical analysis of these writings
continues to develop. Neither the subject matter nor the critical practice
is a "given." Their relationship, like that of theory and practice, is
developing, changing as the terrain changes, each adjusting to the
other.

The essays in this volume illustrate the complexity of the relations
between theory and practice, the impossibility of dividing each into a
separate camp and expecting them to stay "within their boundaries." In
other words, the division of this text is arbitrary and announces itself as
arbitrary. The order of the essays defeats an ordering process, as did
their initial selection. Chronologically, the essays begin in the twentieth
century, work back to the eighteenth, start again in the eighteenth and
come back to the twentieth. But that ordering does not take precedence
over other kinds of orderings that resist "advancement," either of an
argument or of a historical development. These essays—which can

be read in any order—trace and retrace certain forms of writing and the concerns special to those forms. In doing so, they take up the old Western divisions: male/female, soul/body, public/private, gender/ genre, letters/literature. They take up these divisions to question them, even when the questioning goes on through a practice that seems to rigidly enforce precisely the divisions in question or to avoid them altogether.

The essays that openly address theory, that try to imagine and re-imagine its limits, avoid giving in to theory, letting it situate the horizons of writing practice. In the essays that hypothesize a specific subject under consideration, the careful attention to the writing practice makes it impossible to imagine the construction of a "theory" that could be sweepingly applied elsewhere. Inductive and deductive reasoning are questioned. In general, most of the essays show a mistrust of naming, of fixing limits and definitions, especially theoretical definitions. I have therefore resisted the temptation to frame the individual essays according to theoretical approaches or reading practices and to fit them into slots labeled "reader response," "deconstruction," "new historicism," "psychoanalysis," and so forth. As with the autobiographical writings they address, these essays do not allow easy categorization or a comfortable and orderly process. By resisting the old frameworks, they call for subtle and carefully attentive evaluations.

These essays speak perhaps less individually and to each other than all at once, simultaneously, setting up a polyphony of readings that repeat, overlap, contradict, and digress from each other. They include the expected "subjects" of women's autobiography: women situated within conflicting and mutually constricting roles (wife, mother, daughter, sister, lover); women placed in societies that make rigid distinctions between "man's world" and "woman's domain," between the public sector and the domestic; black women writing under the power of the dominant white culture; middle-class women seeking freedom from bourgeois definitions of woman's intellectual and imaginative abilities; public women defying patriarchal definitions to open new avenues of professional and personal experiences for women; women who find through autobiographical writing a means to survive childbirth, illness, the deaths of spouses and children, loss of cultural identity and personal regard, fear of failure, aging, death, loss of beauty and physical strength. Such writings serve as a means by which to create images of "self" through the writing act, a way by which to find a "voice"— whether private or public—through which to express that which cannot be expressed in other forms. Autobiographical writing for women has traditionally served all these needs and taken all these forms. But there are some surprises here as well: women whose autobiographical writings explore the relations between philosophic discourse and the autobiographical, between pedagogy and the autobiographical, between discourses of mediocrity and enormous personal success.

P A R T   I

Theories of Autobiography

Essays in this section open the question of definition under the sign of autobiography. What forms are included under the autobiographical? Where does authority rest for writing "autobiography"? How do women of differing races, social classes, nationalities, religions, sexual preferences, professions, and historical time periods and places define the terms of autobiographical writing? These essays assume the woman's signature to the autobiographical writings examined here, but the implications of woman's signature for individual texts and the ways in which her subjecthood is delineated through those texts is a central concern of each.

My own essay, "Authorizing the Autobiographical," begins by examining the reigning attitudes toward autobiography in theories and practices that often do not take women into account as writers of "autobiography," or that do so in terms that leave out of the account the most crucial features of "womanhood": how woman is situated under patriarchy; how metaphors of self and writing write her out of the account; where she is placed with regard to the subjectivity—the "I"—that structures autobiographical accounts. Tracing the split of the "je" and "moi" that in Jacques Lacan's work defines subjectivity, I examine the relation of genre to gender, unconscious to conscious, self to writing.

The next essay, "Women's Autobiographical Selves: Theory and Practice," by Susan Stanford Friedman, carries the questioning further through a resistance against the "individualistic concept of the autobiographical self" and a reversal of the standard definitions of autobiography. Friedman argues that, for the "marginalized cultures of women," a definition that stresses interdependent identifications within community is a starting place for any analysis of women's autobiographical writings. Thinking the autobiographical through the work of Sheila Rowbotham and Nancy Chodorow, Friedman argues that, rather than being a "negative" of the dominant individualistic paradigm of male-authored autobiographical texts, this "collective identity" is a "source of strength and transformation."

In "My Statue, My Self: Autobiographical Writings of Afro-American Women," Elizabeth Fox-Genovese examines the tradition of autobiographical writings with reference to a particular ethnic group to illuminate the definitional problems in placing these writings. Definitions assign these writers to two oppressed groups: black/woman. But, as Fox-Genovese demonstrates, "simple addition does not add up to a new theoretical category." From the double perspectives of historical and cultural analysis, she argues that this kind of thinking eliminates the ways in which writing is mediated by cultural experience and reading is mediated by political categories and commitments. According to Fox-Genovese, a crucial question remains for those who would define the boundaries of the autobiographical in terms of black women: "Why do we find it so much more acceptable to perceive ourselves as members of a sex or a race than as members of a gender or, even more, of a class?"

Kathleen Woodward's essay, "Simone de Beauvoir: Aging and Its Discontents," situates Beauvoir's autobiographical writings within the context of Beauvoir's own theoretical work on aging. Reading both sets of texts through recent work in psychoanalysis and gerontology, Woodward argues for a rethinking of certain kinds of autobiographical writings; she suggests that women's writings often proceed from anxiety rather than desire and are written under the sign of melancholia rather than mourning. These differences—which mark in a general sense a difference between male and female writing—give rise to a specially marked form of writing, one that situates the loss that is the spur to creation not in the past (as Freud and Lacan theorized) but rather in the future, reading its possibilities through the aging process itself.

Jane Marcus, in "Invincible Mediocrity: The Private Selves of Public Women," argues that the mediocrity of the "genre" of women's autobiographical writings, in terms of patriarchal definitions of superior forms and literary subjects, allowed these generic forms to continue in existence, overlooked by the patriarchy as unworthy of notice. Working through theoretical assumptions about narrative construction and the relations of writer to reader, she examines the need of four famous women—an actress, a mathematician, a composer, and an anthropologist—to write in autobiographical forms. Marcus concludes that these women consciously "re/signed" from public discourse, "enacting a deliberate resignation from the public world and patriarchal history which had already or was expected to erase their names and the works," to "re/sign their private lives into domestic discourse." Further, she suggests that autobiography is a "rehearsal for other art forms," a rehearsal that makes the writer a reader of culture, so that the reader "re/signs" herself from the "author's signature."

Felicity Nussbaum's essay, "Eighteenth-Century Women's Autobiographical Commonplaces," emphasizes the situation of women's autobiographical writings, which constitute "the common places of discourse"—places where "subject positions" meet, where subject matter is itself "common place." She suggests that women of this time period were denied a "space of self" and used "diary and journal writing . . . to carve out a space outside of the conscious subject." This space existed for eighteenth-century women writers between the "cultural assignments of gender and the individual's translation of assignments into text." The negotiation of spaces in the effort to find a place, a site, from which to construct a self is crucial to an understanding of these writings, situated in what Nussbaum defines as "particular and local instances of history" in an avoidance of a theory or practice that would "contribute to an oppression based on gender."

The women whose writings and experiences help construct the network of "theories of autobiography" in this set of essays include: Maya Angelou, Paula Gunn Allen, E. M. Broner, Gwendolyn Brooks, Simone de Beauvoir, Hilda Doolittle, Charlotte Perkins Gilman, Nikki Giovanni, Mattie Griffith, Jane Harrison, Zora Neale Hurston, Harriet Jacobs, Maxine Hong Kingston, Sophie Kovalevsky, Isabella Leitner, Audre Lorde, Paule Marshall, Anaïs Nin, Elizabeth Robins, Ntozake Shange, Ethel Smyth, Hester Thrale, Harriet Wilson, and Virginia Woolf. Such a listing brings with it shocks of re-cognition: of the diversity and divisions among these women; of the shifts of particular and general historical situations; of differences in race, religion, social class, language, upbringing, education, and nationality. The effort to theorize a paradigm of self that would include each of these women is revealed as naive and critically self-serving. The writing moment that promises to seal the self and to heal a divided subject instead opens a seam in the autobiographical text exposing what Felicity Nussbaum has termed a "fissure of female discontinuity" that escapes the boundaries of any given theory of selfhood or writing practice.

CHAPTER ONE

Authorizing the Autobiographical

Shari Benstock

I suggest that one could understand the life around which autobiography forms itself in a number of other ways besides the
perfectly legitimate one of "individual history and narrative": we
can understand it as the vital impulse—the impulse of life—that is
transformed by being lived through the *unique medium of the individual* and *the individual's special, peculiar psychic configuration*; we
can understand it as *consciousness, pure and simple, consciousness
referring to no objects outside itself, to no events, and to no other lives*;
we can understand it as *participation in an absolute existence* far
transcending the shifting, changing unrealities of mundane life; we
can understand it as the *moral tenor of the individual's being.* Life in
all these latter senses does not stretch back across time but extends
down to the roots of individual being; *it is atemporal, committed to a
vertical thrust from consciousness down into the unconscious rather
than to a horizontal thrust from the present into the past.*
—James Olney, "Some Versions of Memory" (emphasis added)

In this extended definition of "the life around which autobiography
forms itself," James Olney has accounted for nearly all the concerns
addressed by the essays in this book. In one way or another each
contributor has taken up the issues enumerated here: the assertion that
autobiography is "transformed by being lived through the unique medium of the individual"; the assumption that the individual bears a
"special, peculiar psychic configuration"; the belief that autobiography
represents "consciousness, pure and simple . . . referring to no objects
outside itself, to no events, and to no others" and that it transcends "the
shifting, changing unrealities of mundane life"; the supposition that

"life . . . does not stretch back across time but extends down to the roots of individual being," moving in "a vertical thrust from consciousness down into the unconscious rather than to a horizontal thrust from the present to the past." These essays take up such premises in order to revise them, to rethink the very coincidence of "ontology" and "autobiography." That each of these premises should prove an "issue" in the essays that follow derives, I think, from the primary contexts of their writing—the concerns with gender, race, class, and historical and political conditions in the theory and practice of women's autobiographical writings.

How does writing mediate the space between "self" and "life" that the autobiography would traverse and transgress? One definition of autobiography suggests that it is an effort to recapture the self—in Hegel's claim, to know the self through "consciousness" (Gusdorf 38). Such a claim presumes that there is such a thing as the "self" and that it is "knowable." This coming-to-knowledge of the self constitutes both the desire that initiates the autobiographical act and the goal toward which autobiography directs itself. By means of writing, such desire presumably can be fulfilled. Thus the place to begin our investigation of autobiography might be at the crossroads of "writing" and "selfhood."[1]

Initiating Autobiography

> The autobiographical perspective has . . . to do with taking oneself
> up and bringing oneself to language.
> —Janet Varner Gunn, *Autobiography*

If the autobiographical moment prepares for a meeting of "writing" and "selfhood," a coming together of method and subject matter, this destiny—like the retrospective glance that presumably initiates autobiography—is always deferred. Autobiography reveals gaps, and not only gaps in time and space or between the individual and the social, but also a widening divergence between the manner and matter of its discourse. That is, autobiography reveals the impossibility of its own dream: what begins on the presumption of self-knowledge ends in the creation of a fiction that covers over the premises of its construction. Georges Gusdorf has argued that "the appearance of autobiography implies a new spiritual revolution: the artist and model coincide, the historian tackles himself as object" (31). But in point of fact, the "coincidence" of artist and model is an illusion. As Jacques Lacan has noted, the "mirror stage" of psychic development that initiates the child into the social community and brings it under the law of the Symbolic (the law of language as constituted through society) serves up a false image of the child's unified "self." This unity is imposed from the outside (in the mirror reflection) and is, in Ellie Ragland-Sullivan's words, "asymmetrical, fictional, and artificial." As Ragland-Sullivan continues, the "mirror stage must, therefore, be understood as a metaphor for the vision of harmony of a subject essentially in discord" (26–27). The "discord" that gives the lie to a unified, identifiable, coterminous self has been built up out of the images, sounds, and sensory responses available to the child during the first six months or so of its life; it is called the unconscious, or that which derives from an experience of "self" as fragmented, partial, segmented, and different. The developing child drives toward fusion and homogeneity in the construction of a "self" (the *moi* of Lacan's terminology) against the effects of division and dissolution. The unconscious is thus not the lower depths of the conscious (as in Olney's description of it) but rather an inner seam, a space between "inside" and "outside"—it is the space of difference, the gap that the drive toward unity of self can never entirely close. It is also the space of writing, which bears the marks and registers the alienating effects of the false symmetry of the mirror stage.

[Here I bracket some considerations about a developing self with particular reference to divisions between the soma and psyche and to mirrors.

In Virginia Woolf's "A Sketch of the Past," her effort at writing her own memoirs, she comments at length on her relation to mirrors, remembering crucial events from her childhood in which mirrors played some part:

> There was a small looking-glass in the hall at Talland House. It had, I remember, a ledge with a brush on it. By standing on tiptoe I could see my face in the glass. When I was six or seven perhaps, I got into the habit of looking at my face in the glass. But I only did this if I was sure that I was alone. I was ashamed of it. A strong feeling of guilt seemed naturally attached to it. (*Moments of Being* 67–68)

Woolf lists various reasons for this shame—that she and Vanessa were "tomboys" and that "to have been found looking in the glass would have been against our tomboy code" (68); or that she inherited "a streak of the puritan," which made her feel shame at self-regard or narcissistic behavior. From a readerly perspective, neither of these reasons seems adequate to the kind of shame she clearly felt before the looking glass, a shame that lasted her entire life. Further on in this memoir, she continues her commentary on female beauty: "My mother's beauty, Stella's beauty, gave me as early as I can remember, pride and pleasure" (68). She declares that her "natural love for beauty was checked by some ancestral dread," then clarifies and qualifies her perceptions: "Yet this did not prevent me from feeling ecstasies and raptures spontaneously and intensely and without any shame or the least sense of guilt, so long as they *were disconnected with my own body*" (68; emphasis added).

Slowly, as though with dread, Woolf comes to "another element in the shame which I had in being caught looking at myself in the glass in the hall" (68). She declares that she was "ashamed or afraid" of her own body. The memory of the hallway with its looking glass is overlaid by another memory of that same hallway, a scene that may well have been reflected for her in the very looking glass of which she speaks. This memory is of Gerald Duckworth raising her onto the slab outside the dining room and "there he began to explore my body":

> I can remember the feel of his hand going under my clothes; going firmly and steadily lower and lower. I remember how I hoped that he would stop; how I stiffened and wriggled as his hand approached my private parts. But it did not stop. His hand explored my private parts too. I remember resenting, disliking it—what is the word for so dumb and mixed a feeling? It must have been strong, since I still recall it. This seems to show that a feeling about certain parts of the body; how they must not be touched; how it is wrong to allow them to be touched; must be instinctive. (69)

Sexual abuse adds itself to the shame of looking at the face in the mirror. Or perhaps sexual abuse actually preceded the shame of looking in the glass. Woolf's memories, as we shall see, do not announce their sequence; their timing always contradicts the logical sequence of conscious thought and action, escaping the dating of calendars and clocks. In recounting the scene with Gerald Duckworth, Woolf does not claim to have discovered the reason for her shame at looking at her own face, she admits to having "only been able to discover some possible reasons; there may be others; I do not suppose that I have got at the truth; yet this is a simple incident; and it happened to me personally; and I have no motive for lying about it" (69). The layers of conscious recall and justification overlap each other, their movement inexorably marked by the semicolons of these clauses that march her back to the moment in the hallway, just as her circuitous "tunneling" method of finding her way back to the past had brought her to the scene with Gerald Duckworth from another direction—from the reflection of her own face in the mirror.

Woolf has one more comment on the "mirror stage" of her own sexual and psychic development:

> Let me add a dream; for it may refer to the incident of the looking-glass. I dreamt that I was looking in a glass when a horrible face—the face of an animal—suddenly showed over my shoulder. I cannot be sure if this was a dream, or if it happened. Was I looking in the glass one day when something in the background moved, and seemed to me alive? I cannot be sure. But I have always remembered the other face in the glass, whether it was a dream or a fact, and that it frightened me. (69)

Two things presumably occur at the mirror stage: a realization (even if it cannot yet be verbalized) of wholeness, completeness, in an image that contradicts the intuited understanding that the child is still fragmented, uncoordinated, and not yet experiencing bodily reactions through a kind of psychic "wholeness"; and a shock of awareness that the image (which may be seen not in a mirror, but rather in a parent's or a sibling's face) is that of an *other*—someone or something unlike and unconnected to the infant. The mirror stage marks a differentiation that is potentially frightening, a moment that cannot be recaptured through memory as such, a moment that hangs in a space that is neither dream nor fact, but both. The mirror stage marks both the exceptional and the common; it is a stage common to us all, but within our experience—and this experience exists outside and beyond memory—this stage marks us as exceptional, differentiated. What should be communicated in this moment is a wholeness, an integration that is present in the image but not yet apparent in experience. For Woolf such an experience—really an aftershock of trauma—recorded both differentiation and a psychic/somatic split. A mysterious, frightening, unknown shame clouds the mirror; the other face in the mirror marks dread.]

In a definition of the autobiographical act that strikingly recapitulates the effects of Lacan's mirror stage, Georges Gusdorf has written: "Autobiography . . . requires a man to take a distance with regard to himself in order to reconstitute himself in the focus of his special unity and identity across time" (35). The effect of such a distancing and reconstituting is precisely the effect of the mirror stage: a recognition of the alienating force within the specular (the "regard") that leads to the desperate shoring-up of the reflected image against disintegration and division. What is reinforced in this effort is the *moi*, the ego; what is pushed aside (or driven into the darkened realms of the repressed) is the split in the subject (who both "is" and "is not" the reflected image) that language effects and cannot deny. Man enforces a "unity and identity across time" by "reconstituting" the ego as a bulwark against disintegration; that is, man denies the very effects of having internalized the alienating world order. One such "denial" is autobiography itself, at least as it is defined by Gusdorf, who would place random reflections on self and society, such as diaries, journals, and letters, in a category separate from (and prior to—the sources for) the *self-conscious* autobiography in which the writer "calls himself as witness for himself" (29).

For Gusdorf, autobiography "is the mirror in which the individual reflects his own image" (33); in such a mirror the "self" and the "reflection" coincide. But this definition of autobiography overlooks what might be the most interesting aspect of the autobiographical: the measure to which "self" and "self-image" might not coincide, can never coincide in language—not because certain forms of self-writing are not self-conscious enough but because they have no investment in creating a cohesive self over time. Indeed, they seem to exploit difference and change over sameness and identity: their writing follows the "seam" of the conscious/unconscious where boundaries between internal and external overlap. Such writing puts into question the whole notion of "genre" as outlined by the exclusionary methods of Gusdorf's rather narrow definition of the autobiographical. And it is not surprising that the question of "genre" often rides on the question of gender.[2]

Psychic health is measured in the degree to which the "self" is constructed in separateness, the boundaries between "self" and "other" carefully circumscribed. From a Gusdorfian perspective, autobiography is a re-erecting of these psychic walls, the building of a linguistic fortress between the autobiographical subject and his interested readers: "The autobiography that is thus devoted exclusively to the defence and glorification of a man, a career, a political cause, or a skillful strategy . . . is limited almost entirely to the public sector of existence" (36). Gusdorf acknowledges that "the question changes utterly when the private face of existence assumes more importance" (37), but he suggests that "the writer who recalls his earliest years is thus exploring an enchanted realm that belongs to him alone" (37). In either kind of autobiography, the writing subject is the one presumed to *know* (himself), and this process of knowing is a process of differentiating himself from others.[3] The chain-link fence that circumscribes his unique contributions is language, representative of the very laws to which this writing subject has been subjected; that is, language is neither an external force nor a "tool" of expression, but the very symbolic system that both constructs and is constructed by the writing subject. As such, language is both internal and external, and the walls that defend the *moi* are never an entirely adequate defense network against the multiple forms of the *je*.

If the linguistic defense networks of male autobiographers more successfully keep at bay the discordant *je*, it may be because female autobiographers are more aware of their "otherness." Like men, we are subjected to the phallic law, but our experience of its social and political effects comes under the terms of another law—that of gender. Ragland-Sullivan comments that "the early mother is internalized as the source of one's own narcissism, prior to the acquisition of individual bound-aries, while the father's subsequent, symbolic role is that of teaching these boundaries—he is a limit-setter. As a result, the father is later both feared and emulated, since his presence has taught the infant about laws and taboos" (42). Language itself, as Lacan has shown, is a defense against unconscious knowledge (179). But it is not an altogether suc-cessful defense network, punctuated as it is by messages from the unconscious, messages that attempt to defeat this "fencing-off" mecha-nism; indeed, there is no clearly defined barrier between the conscious and the unconscious. Fenced in by language, the speaking subject is primordially divided.[4]

This division is apparent as well in writing, and especially in autobio-graphical writing. Denial of the division on the part of some theoreti-cians of autobiography, however, is itself a symptom of autobiographical writing—a repeated but untranslated, unconscious message. This mes-sage is directed at the culture from the position of the Other, by those who occupy positions of internal exclusion within the culture—that is, by women, blacks, Jews, homosexuals, and others who exist on the margins of society. A frequent spokesperson for those who have been denied full rights within the society on the grounds of gender, Virginia Woolf also questioned the limits of genre, with particular regard to autobiography. In 1919, at age thirty-seven, she was particularly con-cerned with these issues, thinking to what use she might put her diary and at what point in her life she would begin writing her memoirs. She begins by suggesting that "this diary does not count as writing, since I have just re-read my year's diary and am much struck by the rapid haphazard gallop at which it swings along, sometimes indeed jerking almost intolerably over the cobbles" (20 January 1919). But the next sentence justifies this fast-paced method as preserving that which "if I stopped and took thought . . . would never be written at all," that which "sweeps up accidentally several stray matters which I would exclude if I hesitated, but which are the diamonds of the dustheap." Thinking of her future self at age fifty, Woolf conjures up on the diary page an image of herself, wearing reading glasses, poring over the pages of the past in preparation for the writing of her memoirs. Many years later, when Woolf was fifty-eight, she placed her memoir writing even further in the future, commenting in her diary: "I may as well make a note I say to myself: thinking sometimes who's going to read all this scribble? I think one day I may brew a tiny ingot out of it—in my memoirs" (19 February 1940). The "brewing" method would seem to be reductive—to eliminate the dross and save the gold.

Woolf did not live to write her memoirs, and the bulk of the autobiographical Virginia Woolf exists in her diary and letters, forms whose generic boundaries she extended and reconstructed. The diary, for instance, was constantly reexamined as a cultural artifact, as a living presence, as a necessary exercise for her fatigued mind, as a secret place (she found it impossible to write in it, for instance, if anyone else were in the room). She used the diary to pose theoretical and practical questions of *writing*, a place where the very definitions of writing might be reexamined:

> There looms ahead of me the shadow of some kind of form which a diary might attain to. I might in the course of time learn what it is that one can make of this *loose, drifting material of life*; finding another use for it than the use I put it to, so much more consciously and scrupulously, in fiction. What sort of diary should I like mine to be? Something loose knit and yet not slovenly, *so elastic that it will embrace anything, solemn, slight or beautiful that comes into my mind.* I should like it *to resemble some deep old desk, or capacious hold-all*, in which one flings a mass of odds and ends without looking them through. I should like to come back, after a year or two, and *find that the collection had sorted itself and refined itself and coalesced*, as such deposits so mysteriously do, into a

mould, transparent enough to reflect the light of our life, and yet steady, tranquil compounds with the aloofness of a work of art. The main requisite, I think on re-reading my old volumes, *is not to play the part of censor*, but to write as the mood comes or of anything whatever; since I was curious to find how I went for things put in haphazard, and found the significance to lie *where I never saw it at the time*. (20 April 1919; emphasis added)

Setting aside momentarily the question of what Woolf might have done with the materials she later rediscovered in the "hold-all" of the diary, we can readily see that her efforts at defining the diary's form in the broadest terms possible ("so elastic that it will embrace anything, solemn, slight or beautiful that comes into my mind") and assigning the sorting, refining, and coalescing of such deposits into "a mould, transparent enough to reflect the light of our life," radically redefine the whole autobiographical project. Woolf does not conceive of such an undertaking in terms that Augustine, Rousseau, Montaigne, Proust, or Sir Leslie Stephen would recognize. She removes herself—that is, herself conceived as a censor—from this enterprise, discredits the notion of "self-consciousness" (indeed, she argues for the importance of the thoughtless, the loose, the unrestrained, the *unconscious*), and refrains from all efforts to shape, sort, or subordinate this material to her will. She rather systematically cuts out from under herself the props that hold up her authority as an *author*, turning authority back to the matter that constitutes her "subject"—and that subject is not necessarily the "self" of traditional autobiography. Woolf gives power to conscious artifice through fiction, a creation that also bears a relation to the "loose, drifting material of life." But for the purposes of memoir writing, she wishes to conceive of a different form and purpose—a conception that is infinitely deferred, as her own death puts an end to the project. That such a project would have followed the unconscious, would have followed the seam of writing itself, is undeniable, as the sections from *Moments of Being* discussed in the second part of this essay demonstrate.

It took me a year's groping to discover what I call my tunnelling process, by which I tell the past by installments as I have need of it. This is my prime discovery so far; and the fact that I've been so long finding it proves, I think, how false Percy Lubbock's doctrine is—that you can do this sort of thing consciously. (*Diary*, 15 October 1923)

Later she comments, "as far as I know, as a writer I am only now writing out my mind" (20 March 1926), in a turn of phrase that suggests multiple relations between "mind" and "writing." In 1933, she notes "how tremendously important unconsciousness is when one writes" (29 October 1933). Such commentaries on the workings of the mind ally themselves with others that address questions of narrative method and artistic systems. On 25 September 1929, she writes in the diary: "Yesterday morning I made another start on *The Moths* [later retitled *The Waves*] . . . and several problems cry out at once to be solved. Who thinks it? And am I outside the thinker? One wants some device which is not a trick." And on 2 October 1932, in an entirely different context, she writes in irritation at reading D. H. Lawrence's published letters of what she calls his "preaching" and "systematizing": "His ruler coming down and measuring them. Why all this criticism of other people? Why not some system that includes the good? What a discovery that would be—a system that did not shut out." The relation of the conscious to the unconscious, of the mind to writing, of the inside to the outside of political and narrative systems, indicate not only a problematizing of social and literary conventions—a questioning of the Symbolic law— but also the need to reconceptualize form itself.

In other words, where does one place the "I" of the autobiographical account? Where does the Subject locate itself? In definitions of autobiography that stress self-disclosure and narrative account, that posit a self called to witness (as an authority) to "his" own being, that propose a double referent for the first-person narrative (the present "I" and the past "I"), or that conceive of autobiography as "recapitulation and recall" (Olney 252), the Subject is made an Object of investigation (the first-person actually masks the third-person) and is further divided between the present moment of the narration and the past on which the narration is focused. These gaps in the temporal and spatial dimensions of the text itself are often successfully hidden from reader and writer, so that the fabric of the narrative appears seamless, spun of whole cloth. The effect is magical—the self appears organic, the present the sum total of the past, the past an accurate predictor of the future. This conception of the autobiographical rests on a firm belief in the *conscious* control of artist over subject matter; this view of the life history is grounded in authority. It is perhaps not surprising that those who cling to such a definition are those whose assignment under the Symbolic law is to *represent* authority, to represent the phallic power that drives inexorably toward unity, identity, sameness. And it is not surprising that those who question such authority are those who are expected to submit to it, those who line up on the other side of the sexual divide—that is, women.[5] The self that would reside at the center of the text is decentered—and often is absent altogether—in women's autobiographical texts. The very requirements of the genre are put into question by the limits of gender—which is to say, because these two terms are etymologically linked, genre itself raises questions about gender.[6]

Fissures of Female Discontinuity

> Alas, my brothers,
> Helen did not walk
> upon the ramparts,
> she whom you cursed
> was but the phantom and the shadow thrown
> of a reflection
> —H.D., *Helen in Egypt*

How do the fissures of female discontinuity display themselves, and what are their identifying features? On what authority can we ascribe certain forms of discontinuity to the female rather than to the male, assigning them as functions of gender rather than of social class, race, or sexual preference? One might remark that such issues are not raised—either directly or indirectly—by those texts that form the tradition of autobiographical writings in Western culture. The confessions of an Augustine or a Rousseau, the *Autobiography of Thomas Jefferson*, or the *Education of Henry Adams* do not admit internal cracks and disjunctures, rifts and ruptures. The whole thrust of such works is to seal up and cover over gaps in memory, dislocations in time and space, insecurities, hesitations, and blind spots. The consciousness behind the narrative "I" develops over time, encompassing more and more of the external landscape and becoming increasingly aware of the implications of action and events, but this consciousness—and the "I" it supports—remains stable. The dissection of self-analysis premises the cohesion of a restructured self. Any hint of the disparate, the disassociated, is overlooked or enfolded into a narrative of synthesis. This "model" of autobiography, a product of the metaphysic that has structured Western thinking since Plato, repeated itself with unsurprising frequency until the early twentieth century—until the advent of what we now term

Modernism put into question the organic, unifying principles of artistic creation that had reasserted themselves with such force in the nineteenth century.

The influence of Freud's discovery of the unconscious cannot be discounted in the unsettling of the "I" that had heretofore stood at the center of narrative discourse. (In accounting for this "unsettling" of self-unity, one must also consider the political and social effects of World War I, the advent of industrial mechanization, the loss of belief in God, the fall of colonial empires, and the changing status of women and minorities, all of which altered the cultural landscape against which literature was produced in the early years of the twentieth century. We live today in a world that has been constructed out of these changes; nearly all the changes that discomposed the complacent world of 1910 have been culturally assimilated, except perhaps the full force of Freud's discoveries. Predictably, its effects are most tenaciously resisted precisely where they are most evident: in language—in speech and writing.) The instability of this subject is nowhere more apparent than in women's writing of this period, in texts by Djuna Barnes, Isak Dinesen, H.D., Mina Loy, Anaïs Nin, Jean Rhys, Gertrude Stein, and Virginia Woolf, writing that puts into question the most essential component of the autobiographical—the relation between "self" and "consciousness." The simultaneous exploration of the autobiographical and probing of self-consciousness in works by each of these writers suggests not that they knew their Freud better than T. S. Eliot, James Joyce, Ezra Pound, or W. B. Yeats, but that as women they felt the effects of the psychic reality Freud described more fully than did men. Gender became a determining issue at the point at which culture (broadly defined in both its psychic and social terms) met aesthetic principles.

As I have argued elsewhere, female Modernism challenged the white, male, heterosexual ethic underlying the Modernist aesthetic of "impersonality" (e.g., the transformation of the textual "I" from the personal to the cultural).[7] It is this white, male, heterosexual ethic that post-structuralist critics have exposed behind the facade of a supposedly apolitical artistic practice.[8] Post-structuralism has taught us to read the politics of every element in narrative strategy: representation; tone; perspective; figures of speech; even the shift between first-, second-, and third-person pronouns. In identifying the "fissures of female discontinuity" in a text, for example, we also point toward a relation between the psychic and the political, the personal and the social, in the linguistic fabric.[9]

Although Virginia Woolf did not publish her memoirs, she did leave behind fragments of a memoir collected under the title *Moments of Being*. These five pieces ("Reminiscences," "A Sketch of the Past," and three readings done for the Memoir Club—"22 Hyde Park Gate," "Old Bloomsbury," and "Am I a Snob?") retrace the same material: that portion of her young adulthood between the deaths of her mother in 1895 and her father in 1904. In addition, much of this material is incorporated into two of her novels, *To the Lighthouse* and *The Years*. While the "content" of the fictions and the reminiscences is strikingly similar, the variations in perspective, through a shift of pronouns both between texts and within texts, signal discontinuities. In the memoirs in particular, these discontinuities are striking. They suggest that the entire project is poised over an abyss of selflessness, or, to put it differently, that the entire project is posed on the question of self and its relation to language and storytelling strategies.

She begins with "the first memory" of "red and purple flowers on a black ground—my mother's dress." The flowers, seen close up (she is on her mother's lap), are assumed to be anemones; the conveyance is either a train or an omnibus; the light suggests that it is evening and "we were coming back to London" (*Moments of Being* 64). As soon as this scene is suggested, however, it reverses itself, giving life to a second scene:

> But it is more convenient *artistically* to suppose that we were going to St. Ives, for that will lead to my other memory, which also seems to be my first memory, and in fact it is the most important of all my memories. If life has a base it stands upon, if it is a bowl that one fills and fills and fills—then my bowl without a doubt stands upon this memory. (64; emphasis added)

This second memory diverges both in time and place from the first. Comprised of sound rather than sight, it translates the former memory into a different medium:

> It is of lying half asleep, half awake, in bed in the nursery at St. Ives. It is of hearing the waves breaking, one, two, one, two, and sending a splash of water over the beach; and then breaking, one, two, one, two, behind a yellow blind. It is of hearing the blind draw its little acorn across the floor as the wind blew the blind out. It is of lying and hearing this splash and seeing this light, and feeling, it is almost impossible that I should be here; of feeling the purest ecstasy I can conceive. (64–65)

We know that the unconscious is comprised of just such "memories"—of images and sounds—and that later identity reflects these first sensory experiences.[10] Virginia Woolf's writing is characterized by the recurrence of such experiences; indeed, *The Waves* reflects the images and repeats the rhythms of precisely these two moments: "The sun sharpened the walls of the house, made a blue fingerprint of shadow under the leaf by the bedroom window. The blind stirred slightly, but all within was dim and unsubstantial" (*The Waves* 8). As a writer, Woolf knew how to make such experiences work toward aesthetic coherence; as critics, we know how to read such textual effects, working sound against image to make the metonymic metaphoric. But what is most striking from the "Sketch" itself is not the self-reinforcing aspect of the two memories, but the disparity between them: juxtaposed to each other within the same paragraph, they mark not only different psychic moments, but difference itself. Later in the text Woolf herself comments on this discovery of difference, but not before she has discussed artistic considerations, the place of the self in memoir writing, and the peculiarities of her social education.

The "first memory"—which is not a memory at all, strictly speaking—is displaced by an "other memory, which also seems to be my first memory." This displacement is effected for "artistic convenience," a change that reverses the narrative direction—toward St. Ives rather than toward London. But this change enforces another: although the first memory is conditioned by the light (which seems to be evening), the second memory can be reached by reversing not only the direction of the train but by inverting evening and morning: if they are leaving London for St. Ives, then the scene is lit by morning rather than evening light. Although the second memory is not dependent on light—as its "focus" is sound—the "yellow blind" of the room suggests visibility. The time of day in this second memory is unclear from an initial reading (it could be either morning or evening), and the confusion is cleared up only later, when Woolf apparently realizes the "connection" between the two scenes. Both are occasioned by displacement, and they shadow forth a doubling and displacement of "self."

Having remarked on the "pure ecstasy" that the second memory conveys, Woolf stops the narrative to comment on autobiography itself:

> I could spend hours trying to write that [the scene of the second memory] as it should be written, in order to give the feeling which is even at this moment very strong in me. But I should fail (unless I

had some wonderful luck); I dare say I should only succeed in having the luck if I had begun by describing Virginia herself. (65)

The writer's "luck" becomes dependent on conventional literary forms —here the requirement that the autobiographical begin with a description of the central character. Woolf sets aside the evidence that her method, adopted at random, "without stopping to choose my way, in the sure and certain knowledge that it will find itself" (64), has already provided crucial elements not of the *self* but of the elements out of which the unconscious is constructed. She has tapped the unconscious, and the effect has been to split the "subject" that her autobiography struggles to delineate. She has stumbled against "one of the memoir writer's difficulties—one of the reasons why, though I read so many, so many are failures. They leave out the person to whom things happened" (65). At this juncture, "Adeline Virginia Stephen, the second daughter of Leslie and Julia Prinsip Stephen, born on the 25th January 1882" is inserted into the text. But this historical Virginia Stephen is of little help to Virginia Woolf the memoirist, as neither knows how history and lineage "made them," or—more important—"what part of this" history "made me feel what I felt in the nursery at St. Ives." Woolf confesses to not knowing "how far I differ from other people." A crucial factor in this "not knowing" has been her social and educational conditioning: "Owing partly to the fact that I was never at school, never competed in any way with children of my own age, I have never been able to compare my gifts and defects with other people's" (65). Elsewhere—in her diaries and letters, in *A Room of One's Own*, in *Three Guineas*— Virginia Woolf wrote at length, with passion and anger, against the strictures of her Victorian upbringing, against its isolation, against the intellectual and emotional hardships of its expectations for women. Of whatever else this social setting deprived her, its cruelest denial was a community in which she could learn and against which she could measure herself.

Two sentences in this paragraph from "A Sketch of the Past" are linked, and they lead to an explanation for the second memory. The first sentence is the one on which the paragraph is premised ("They [memoirs] leave out the person to whom things happened"); the second is the realization that because of the circumstances of her upbringing Woolf does not know "how far I differ from other people." That is, she has been absent in her own memoir—thus committing the sin of so many memoirs—because she cannot measure her own *difference* from others. And it is precisely this difference, this individuality, on which the traditional memoir premises itself. This problem of difference suggests to Woolf "another memoir writer's difficulty." Unlike others, she has no standard of comparison, and it is this lack that leads to a rationale for the kinds of reminiscences she has already delineated:

> But of course there was one external reason for the intensity of this first impression: the impression of the waves and the acorn on the blind; the feeling, as I describe it sometimes to myself of lying in a grape and seeing through a film of semi-transparent yellow—it was due partly to the many months we spent in London. The *change of nursery was a great change*. And there was the long train journey; and the excitement. I remember the dark; the lights; the stir of the going up to bed. (65; emphasis added)[11]

The memory of the waves at St. Ives is specifically marked here as "this first impression," perhaps blotting out, or at least circumventing, that prior "first memory" of the flowers on the "black ground" of the mother's dress. The explanation for the feeling that results from this impression uses elements from both memories: although the impression of the waves and the acorn on the blind reside in hearing ("It is of hearing the blind draw its little acorn across the floor as the wind blew the blind out"), Woolf's description relies on sight ("the feeling . . . of lying in a grape and seeing through a film of semi-transparent yellow"). The two impressions belong to different sensory orders, and their coincidence (one explained in terms of the other) is the result of "a great change"—a registering of difference between the London and St. Ives nurseries. It is significant that this registration occurs in a section of the text in which individual difference is denied and made the excuse for the failure of memoir writing: "I do not know how far I differ from other people." The "I" in this sentence is absent precisely to the extent that it is doubled ("I . . . I"): selfhood registered in difference from others is demonstrated on *social* grounds to be nonexistent; coexistent selfhood across time and space is shown to be nonexistent even under the auspices of memory. These impressions displace hierarchies (first, second), refuse synthesis, and resist distinctions between external and internal, conscious and unconscious.

In these fragments from what would have become her memoirs, Woolf attempts to come to terms with the notion of "memoir" itself. She examines carefully the two presumed essential ingredients ("personal history and narrative"), posing difficult theoretical questions through her own autobiographical practice. Despite the claim that the "subject of the memoir" must be central to it—must provide not only the "I" but the "eye" of its telling—she finds it impossible to place herself in that position. Indeed, she finds it nearly impossible to name herself; "Adeline Virginia Stephen" was never a name she was known by, and in the late 1930s, when she began constructing her reminiscences, her name—the one by which she was called and by which she called herself, the name that provided the signature to her texts, including this text—was something different. The central figure of the early years of her development was her mother, the woman who—until after the writing of *To the Lighthouse*—"obsessed" Virginia Woolf:

> I could hear her voice, see her, imagine what she would do or say as I went about my day's doings. She was one of the invisible presences who after all play so important a part in every life. This influence, by which I mean the consciousness of other groups impinging upon ourselves; public opinion; what other people say and think; all those magnets which attract us this way to be like that; or repel us the other and make us different from that; has never been analyzed in any of those Lives which I so much enjoy reading, or very superficially. (80)

Such "invisible presences" keep "the subject of this memoir" in place, according to Woolf. And it is the question of place—of space—that absorbs the autobiographical writer's attention as much as the proverbial issue of time. The mother, who occupied "the very centre of that great Cathedral space which was childhood" (81), becomes an "invisible presence" in Woolf's later life. Indeed, it is her removal from temporal and spatial existence that provides the central trauma of Woolf's narrative, an absence over which scar tissue knots this narrative and refuses to let the story unwind itself over the years. Like Gertrude Stein's obsession with the year 1907 (the year Alice B. Toklas entered her life, changing its contours and directions), Virginia Woolf's continual return to the morning of her mother's death, the morning she awoke to news of this loss and was led to her mother's bedroom to kiss her goodbye, constitutes a symptom of the writing, or a scab that is picked until it bleeds and forms again. Significantly, this scene is repeated twice in the memoir fragments, is reconstructed in *The Years*, and marks the moment of temporal absence ("Time Passes") in *To the Lighthouse*. For Virginia, Julia Stephen was "the creator of that crowded merry world which spun so gaily in the centre of my childhood. . . . She was the centre; it was herself. This was proved on May 5, 1895. For after that day there was nothing left of it" (84).

The centrality of the mother to this lost world of childhood, the nearness of her presence, prevents Woolf from describing her "in the present" of the past. All that becomes available are "those descriptions and anecdotes which after she was dead imposed themselves upon my view of her" (83). That is, the action of memory has been translated through narrative (description and anecdote), leaving a hole where once there was a center: "Of course she was central. I suspect the word 'central' gets closest to the general feeling I had of living so completely in her atmosphere that one never got far enough away from her to see her as a person" (83). A first memory of this mother centers on the flowers on the black ground of her dress: "I . . . saw the flowers she was wearing very close" (64). The point is not that Woolf's mother became an "invisible presence" after her death, but that she was always an invisible presence—too central, too close, to be observed: "If we cannot analyse these invisible presences, we know very little of the subject of the memoir; and again how futile life-writing becomes. I see myself as a fish in a stream; deflected; held in place; but cannot describe the stream" (80).

Thus the workings of memory, crucial to the recollection implicit in life writing, are found to be suspect. They slip beyond the borders of the conscious world; they are traversed and transgressed by the unconscious. Every exercise in memory recall that Woolf tries in these autobiographical efforts demonstrates the futility and failure of life writing. What is directly gazed upon in the memory remains absent; what is "revealed" comes by side glances and hints, in the effects of sound, light, smell, touch. Returning to the peculiar power of the "two strong memories" that initiate "A Sketch of the Past," Woolf comments, "I am hardly aware of myself, but only of the sensation. I am only the container of the feeling of ecstasy, of the feeling of rapture" (67). She wonders whether "things we have felt with great intensity have an existence independent of our minds" and whether "some device will be invented by which we can tap them" (67). She believes that "strong emotion must leave its trace" (67). Finding a way to tap these resources, to rediscover these traces, becomes both the overriding desire in her memoir writing and the cause of its failure. She is forced to discount memories: "As an account of my life they are misleading, because the things one does not remember are as important; perhaps they are more important" (69). Woolf attempts to explain away the intellectual difficulties posed by the problem of remembering and not remembering by dividing life into "moments of being" and "moments of non-being." She constructs a tapestry in which there is "hidden a pattern" that connects both the being and nonbeing of everyday life. She tries to find a means by which to include in the "life" that which is excluded in life writing: everything that forms the background of perception and action.

Woolf's effort leads to the construction of a series of metaphors by which to image the relation of present to past, of perception to action, of writing to living. She first builds a platform, a base on which to stand in recollecting the past, and decides to "include the present—at least enough of the present to serve as platform to stand upon. It would be interesting to make the two people, I now, I then, come out in contrast" (75). There is no intention of reconciling these two people seen from the platform of the present ("I now, I then"). Woolf's project is nothing like the one James Olney describes for Richard Wright in *Black Boy*: "This double-reference 'I' delivers up a twofold *bios*—here and how, there and then, both the perpetual present and the historic past—and it is the tenuous yet tensile thread of memory that joins the two 'I's, that holds together the two *bioi*, and that successfully redeems the time of (and for) Richard Wright" (248).

Redemption and the action of recollection (in the sense of "gathering again") by which it claims to be achieved are shown by Woolf to be the deadly temptations of the autobiographical. On 25 October 1920 she had admitted to her diary the happiness that writing gave her: "and with it all how happy I am—if it weren't for my feeling that it's a strip of pavement over an abyss." Her fictional narratives (all of which could be termed "autobiographical" to some degree) were the strip of pavement over the abyss of self. While these fictions were in some sense a pretense against the primordial split subject (and were created "out of" that split), the memoir posed the question of selfhood directly; it forced Virginia Woolf to look into the abyss—something she could not do. Using a metaphor that explores surface and depth, the "experience" of present and past, along narrative movement, Woolf writes: "The past only comes back when the present runs so smoothly that it is like the sliding surface of a deep river. Then one sees through the surface to the depth" (98). This "sliding surface" is not available to conscious thought and practice; indeed, it demands an *unconsciousness* of the present. The present cannot call attention to itself (the "pavement" or "platform" of the present must be invisible). That is, "to feel the present sliding over the depths of the past, peace is necessary. The present must be smooth, habitual." Later in the same paragraph, Woolf reverses this process in an effort to restore a "sense of the present": "I write this partly in order to recover my sense of the present by getting the past to shadow this broken surface" (98).

Woolf concludes her contemplation of the autobiographical act and its relation to writing, memory, and self-consciousness by returning to its initial impetus—what she calls "scene-making":

> But, whatever the reason may be, I find that scene-making is my natural way of marking the past. Always a sense of scene has arranged itself: representative; enduring. This confirms me in my instinctive notion: (it will not bear arguing about; it is irrational) the sensation that we are sealed vessels afloat on what it is convenient to call reality; and at some moments, the sealing matter cracks; in floods reality; that is, these scenes—for why do they survive undamaged year after year unless they are made of something comparatively permanent? (122)

It is the very admission of "irrationality" that interests here. Woolf views the past not as a "subject matter"—a content as such—but rather as a method, a scene making. Such scenes arrange themselves (much as the matter in the "hold all" composed itself) in moments when the "sealing matter" of identity and selfhood cracks. Unable to argue logically the ontology of autobiography by means of self-consciousness, Woolf moves toward an "instinctive notion" that the "sealed vessel" of selfhood is an artificial construct, that it "cracks" and floods, allowing access to that which in conscious moments is considered wholly separate and different from self—"what it is convenient to call reality."

But Woolf's notion of reality would share little with T. S. Eliot's. Hers is not a shock of recognition in the mirror but rather a linguistic space (a "scene") that conceals—and tries to seal itself against—the gap (the "crack") of the unconscious. Language, which operates according to a principle of division and separation, is the medium by which and through which the "self" is constructed. "Writing the self" is therefore a process of simultaneous sealing and splitting that can only trace fissures of discontinuity. This process may take place through "the individual's special, peculiar psychic configuration," but it is never an act of "consciousness, pure and simple"; it always refers to "objects outside itself, to . . . events, and to . . . other lives"; it always participates in "the shifting, changing unrealities of mundane life"; it is never "atemporal" (Olney 239). There is no grid whose horizontal axis represents a "thrust from the present into the past" and whose vertical axis constitutes a "thrust from consciousness down into the unconscious" (Olney 239). Instead, this scene forms itself as a kind of writing:

> so it seemed to me
> that I had watched
> as a careful craftsman,
>
> the pattern shape,
> Achilles' history,
> that I had seen him like the very scenes
>
> on his famous shield,
> outlined with the graver's gold;
> true, I had met him, the New Mortal,
>
> baffled and lost,
> but I was a phantom Helen
> and he was Achilles' ghost.
>
> (*Helen in Egypt*, 262–63)

Notes

1. Olney's "Some Versions of Memory" examines the *bios* at the center of this word without attention to the terms that enclose it—auto/graphy. In particular, this essay fails to mention that without *graphé* autobiography would not exist—that is, it is known only through the writing.

2. Gusdorf's essay, "Conditions and Limits of Autobiography," opens with the declaration: "Autobiography is a solidly established literary genre" (28). James Olney's later essay in the same volume suggests "the impossibility of making any prescriptive definition for autobiography or placing any generic limitations on it at all" (237). Indeed, whether autobiography can be circumscribed within generic definitions is an important issue in autobiography studies. To date, however, there has been no rigorous investigation of the question of genre in relation to autobiography.

It is important to note that for Gusdorf autobiography is a genre that belongs to men, whose public lives it traces. Women are denied entrance to this writing for reasons examined in Susan Friedman's essay in this volume.

3. The "subject presumed to know" is a Lacanian construction belonging not, as one might expect, to the conscious realm of thinking (as "the one consciously in control") but to the unconscious. This subject is "supposed" precisely because the speaking (or writing) subject senses a lack in itself,

and supposes, in Ellie Ragland-Sullivan's terms, that "'something' somewhere knows more than he or she. That 'something' furnishes the speaker with the authority for a given opinion" (172). The sense of an internal division, the claim of an authority from "elsewhere" (in the Other residing in the unconscious), problematizes the assigning of authority in the speaking/writing situation. Both meanings of "suppose" are at work here: to believe, especially on uncertain or tentative grounds; to expect or require, to presume.

4. This division cannot be "healed"; identity itself rests in this division, the effects of the working of the unconscious. Ragland-Sullivan comments: "Humans have an unconscious because they speak; animals have no unconscious because they do not speak. Since Lacan views repression and verbal symbolization as concurrent processes, which both mark the end of the mirror stage and create a secondary unconscious, we can look for answers to the self/ontology riddle in the transformational processes that mark repression" (173). For a particularly cogent reading of the effects of this division in women's writing, see Buck.

5. Not only women are included in this group, but all humans who—for whatever reasons—are not seen to represent authority. Psychosexual identity often does not coincide with biological sexuality, and thus male homosexuals fall into this grouping (and female homosexuals resist its effects), as do all others considered powerless and marginal—blacks, Jews, the economically deprived, and so on.

6. For an exhaustive analysis of the relation of *genre* and gender, see Jacques Derrida, "La Loi du Genre/The Law of Genre," which traces the etymological transferences of the two terms, and my essay, "From Letters to Literature," which traces the effects of this law on one literary *genre*.

7. See Benstock, "Beyond the Reaches of Feminist Criticism" and *Women of the Left Bank*; DeKoven, *A Different Language*; DuPlessis, *Writing Beyond the Ending*; Friedman, "Modernism of the Scattered Remnant" and *Psyche Reborn*; Friedman and DuPlessis, "'I Had Two Loves Separate'"; Gubar, "Blessings in Disguise" and "Sapphistries"; Kolodny, "Some Notes on Defining a 'Feminist Literary Criticism'"; Marcus, "Laughing at Leviticus" and "Liberty, Sorority, Misogyny"; and Stimpson, "Gertrice/Altrude."

8. Special reference needs to be made to the work of Roland Barthes, Hélène Cixous, Jacques Derrida, Jacques Lacan, Michel Foucault, and Julia Kristeva. Interestingly, each of these people is excluded in one way or another from the dominant national discourse (French, white, male heterosexual); each sees himself or herself as (or is seen as being) an "outsider." This outsidership—which takes various forms and exerts varying effects over the "subjects" that these writers choose to discuss and the ways in which they discuss them—has been overlooked entirely by those critics who claim that collectively these people constitute a hegemonic power.

9. Lacan's reading of Freud teaches us that the social constructs the personal:

"In 'The Agency of the Letter' (1957) Lacan says that there is no original or instinctual unconscious. Everything in the unconscious gets there from the outside world via symbolization and its effects" (Ragland-Sullivan 99). This discovery by Freud and its patient explication by Lacan have been systematically disregarded by most American interpreters of this work, especially by American feminists who ground their objections to Lacan's reading on the presumption that it separates the unconscious and the social or that it gives the unconscious the power (through the phallic signifier) to construct the external environment.

10. The unconscious is composed of these initial perceptions. Because of its physical helplessness and dependency, the child spends much of its early months listening and looking, taking in the environment around itself. Although it cannot use language, it assimilates sounds and rhythms. Ellie Ragland-Sullivan writes: "earliest perception is inseparable from the effects of the outside world, both linguistic and visual. . . . Since the primordial subject of unconsciousness is formed by identification with its first images and sensory experiences, it will thereafter reflect the essence of these images and objects in identity" (18).

11. The first summer that the Stephen family spent at St. Ives was 1882, the summer following Virginia's birth on January 25. She would have been six or seven months old that summer, and it is possible that the memories she "recalls" here are not memories at all but initial impressions of her environment—impressions that preceded use of language.

Works Cited

Benstock, Shari. "Beyond the Reaches of Feminist Criticism: A Letter from Paris." *Tulsa Studies in Women's Literature* 3 (1984): 5–27. Rpt. in *Feminist Issues in Literary Scholarship*. Ed. Shari Benstock. Bloomington: Indiana University Press, 1987. 7–29.

———. "From Letters to Literature: *La Carte Postale* in the Epistolary *Genre*." *Genre* 18 (Fall 1985): 257–95.

———. *Women of the Left Bank: Paris, 1900–1940*. Austin: University of Texas Press, 1986.

Broe, Mary Lynn, ed. *Silence and Power: Djuna Barnes, A Revaluation*. Carbondale: Southern Illinois University Press, forthcoming.

Brown, Cheryl L., and Karen Olson, eds. *Feminist Criticism: Essays on Theory, Poetry and Prose*. Metuchen: Scarecrow, 1978.

Buck, Claire. "Freud and H.D.—Bisexuality and a Feminine Discourse." *m/f* 8 (1983): 53–66.

DeKoven, Marianne. *A Different Language: Gertrude Stein's Experimental Writing*. Madison: University of Wisconsin Press, 1983.

Derrida, Jacques. "*La Loi du Genre*/The Law of Genre." Trans. Avital Ronnell. *Glyph* 7 (1980): 202–32.

Doolittle, Hilda [H.D.]. *Helen in Egypt*. New York: New Directions, 1961.

DuPlessis, Rachel Blau. *Writing beyond the Ending: Narrative Strategies of Twentieth-Century Women Writers*. Bloomington: Indiana University Press, 1984.

Friedman, Susan Stanford. "Modernism of the 'Scattered Remnant': Race and Politics in H.D.'s Development." In *Feminist Issues in Literary Scholarship*. Ed. Shari Benstock. Bloomington: Indiana University Press, 1986. 208–31.

———. *Psyche Reborn: The Emergence of H.D.* Bloomington: Indiana University Press, 1981.

Friedman, Susan Stanford, and Rachel Blau DuPlessis. "'I Had Two Loves Separate': The Sexualities of H.D.'s *Her*." *Montemora* 8 (1981): 7–30.

Gubar, Susan. "Blessings in Disguise: Cross-Dressing as Re-Dressing for Female Modernists." *Massachusetts Review* 22 (1981): 477–508.

———. "Sapphistries." *Signs* 10 (1984): 43–62.

Gunn, Janet Varner. *Autobiography: Toward a Poetics of Experience*. Philadelphia: University of Pennsylvania Press, 1982.

Gusdorf, Georges. "Conditions and Limits of Autobiography." In Olney, *Autobiography* 28–48.

Heilbrun, Carolyn G., and Margaret R. Higgonet, eds. *The Representation of Women in Fiction*. Baltimore: Johns Hopkins University Press, 1983.

Kolodny, Annette. "Some Notes on Defining a 'Feminist Literary Criticism.'" In Brown and Olson, 37–58.

Marcus, Jane. "Laughing at Leviticus: *Nightwood* as Woman's Circus Epic." In Broe.

———. "Liberty, Sorority, Misogyny." In Heilbrun and Higgonet, 60–97.

Olney, James, ed. *Autobiography: Essays Theoretical and Critical*. Princeton: Princeton University Press, 1980.

———. "Some Versions of Memory/Some Versions of *Bios*: The Ontology of Autobiography." In Olney, *Autobiography* 236–67.

Perry, Ruth, and Martine Watson Brownley. *Mothering the Mind*. New York: Holmes and Meier, 1984.

Ragland-Sullivan, Ellie. *Jacques Lacan and the Philosophy of Psychoanalysis*. Urbana: University of Illinois Press, 1986.

Stimpson, Catharine R. "Gertrice/Altrude: Stein, Toklas, and the Paradox of the Happy Marriage." In Perry and Brownley, 123–29.

Woolf, Virginia. *The Diary of Virginia Woolf*. Ed. Anne Olivier Bell. 5 vols. New York: Harcourt Brace Jovanovich, 1977–84.

———. *Moments of Being*. Ed. Jeanne Schulkind. New York: Harcourt Brace Jovanovich, 1976.

———. *The Waves*. New York: Harcourt Brace Jovanovich, 1959.

Women's Autobiographical Selves
Theory and Practice

Susan Stanford Friedman

In his seminal essay, "Conditions and Limits of Autobiography" (1956), Georges Gusdorf writes that "autobiography is not possible in a cultural landscape where consciousness of self does not, properly speaking, exist" (30). The cultural precondition for autobiography, Gusdorf argues, is a pervasive concept of individualism, a "conscious awareness of the singularity of each individual life," a self-consciousness that is "the late product of a specific civilization," by which he means the post-Renaissance Western societies (29). Gusdorf is often identified as the dean of autobiographical studies, particularly for his cogent articulation of the theoretical foundations of a formerly marginalized genre of writing. His contributions are undeniable, especially his assertion that autobiographical selves are constructed through the process of writing and therefore cannot reproduce exactly the selves who lived.[1]

However, the individualistic concept of the autobiographical self that pervades Gusdorf's work raises serious theoretical problems for critics who recognize that the self, self-creation, and self-consciousness are profoundly different for women, minorities, and many non-Western peoples. The model of separate and unique selfhood that is highlighted in his work and shared by many other critics establishes a critical bias that leads to the (mis)reading and marginalization of autobiographical texts by women and minorities in the processes of canon formation. The fundamental inapplicability of individualistic models of the self to women and minorities is twofold. First, the emphasis on individualism does not take into account the importance of a culturally imposed group identity for women and minorities. Second, the emphasis on separateness ignores the differences in socialization in the construction of male and female gender identity. From both an ideological and psychological perspective, in other words, individualistic paradigms of the self ignore the role of collective and relational identities in the individuation process of women and minorities. The concepts of female selfhood in the work of feminist theorists Sheila Rowbotham and Nancy Chodorow, in contrast, are grounded in a recognition of the historically generated differences between men and women. Application of their theories of women's selfhood to women's autobiographical texts—particularly those by women who also belong to racial, ethnic, sexual, and religious minorities—illuminates the unfolding narratives of women's life writing and thereby revises the prevailing canons of autobiography.

Gusdorf's concept of autobiography is premised on a model of the self that he identifies as endemically Western and individualistic. The "metaphysical conditions" for the development of autobiography are ripe in a society that fosters "the curiosity of the individual about himself, the wonder he feels about the mystery of his own destiny" (31). Gusdorf associates this curiosity with the Copernican revolution—an odd connection, as the impact of Copernican astronomy was to diminish man's centrality in the cosmos, not to enhance it. After the Copernican revolution, "henceforth, man knows himself a responsible agent: gatherer of men, of lands, of power, maker of kingdoms or of empires, inventor of laws or of wisdom. He alone adds consciousness to nature, leaving there the sign of his presence" (31). Gusdorf thus associates "presence" and self-consciousness with the rise of the European empires and the related phenomenon of the Industrial Revolution, with its constitution of highly polarized public and private spheres. Autobiography is the literary consequence of the rise of individualism as an ideology, according to Gusdorf. As a genre, it also represents the expression of individual authority in the realm of language. The "sign" to which Gusdorf refers is, literally and literarily, the "mark" or "imprint" of man's power: his linguistic, psychological, and institutional presence in the world of letters, people, and things.

Gusdorf contrasts the culture in which autobiography can develop with cultures where autobiography does not exist at all or exists only as a cultural "transplant" from Western societies. Autobiography does not develop endemically in cultures where "the individual does not oppose himself to all others; [where] he does not feel himself to exist outside of others, and still less against others, but very much *with* others in an interdependent existence that asserts its rhythms everywhere in the community . . . [where] lives are so thoroughly entangled that each of them has its center everywhere and its circumference nowhere. The important unit is thus never the isolated being" (29–30). For Gusdorf, the consciousness of self upon which autobiography is premised is the sense of "isolated being," a belief in the self as a discrete, finite "unit" of society. Man must be an island unto himself. Then, and only then, is autobiography possible.[2]

Gusdorf's emphasis on the individual as an "isolated being" is not idiosyncratic. Similarly individualistic paradigms pervade other critical approaches to autobiography as diverse as historical, generic, post-structuralist, and psychoanalytic. According to James Olney, for example, the autobiographer is "surrounded and isolated by his own consciousness, an awareness grown out of a unique heredity and unique experience. . . . Separate selfhood is the very motive of creation" (*Metaphors* 22–23). Although Olney argues that the autobiographer creates a self in the very act of seeking it, he nonetheless invokes Plato in positing the self as a "teleological unity" whose metaphors of circularity represent "the isolate uniqueness" of the individual (20–22). An autobiography projects "a single, radical and radial energy originating in the subject center, an aggressive, creative expression of the self, a defense of individual integrity in the face of an otherwise multiple, confusing, swarming, and inimical universe" (15).[3]

Although psychoanalytic critics would disagree with Olney's Neoplatonic concept of the teleological self, they share with his approach an ultimate presumption of the self as distinct from all others. In contrast to the theories of Olney and Gusdorf, psychoanalysis focuses on the development of the self as it forms through intense interaction with others, particularly the mother and father. Consequently, psychoanalytic critics of autobiography often focus their analysis on the way in which self-creation in the text explores or recapitulates the writer's past interplay with his or her parents. Nonetheless, psychoanalytic models of the autobiographical self remain fundamentally individualistic because the healthy ego is defined in terms of its ability to separate itself from others.

According to psychoanalytic theory, psychological development moves from identification to separation. The child's ego develops as it comes to realize its difference first from the mother and then from the external world in general. Sigmund Freud wrote that "an infant at the breast does not as yet distinguish his ego from the external world as the source of the sensations flowing in upon him" (*Civilization* 13–14). But this lack of "boundary" between itself and the external world yields eventually to the "reality principle"—that is, the child gradually learns to "separate off an external world from itself," to see itself as distinct from all others (14–15).[4] In Jacques Lacan's theory, the child's separation of himself from his mother is followed by the mirror stage and a narcissistic identification first with his own image and then with others like him. The child knows himself as a separate entity by seeing his whole shape in the mirror and identifying that false image with a sense of a distinct and coherent identity. As the Oedipal phase supplants the early narcissistic sense of self, that child continues the process of self-construction through the acquisition of symbolic systems, preeminently language itself. To Lacan, the self constructed through language is also false, like the image in the mirror. This theory of the ego's inherent falseness represents a departure from Freud. But like Freud, Lacan's concept of ego formation is based on the assumption that the ego results from a process that moves away from fusion and toward separation.

These theories of ego formation often lead psychoanalytic critics of autobiography to decode the narrative as the ego's movement away from early fusion with the mother and toward the establishment of sharp boundaries between the self and others. In "Autobiography and Psycho-Analysis," for example, Bruce Mazlish states that autobiography is a "consciously shaped *literary production*" similar to the interpretive process of psychoanalysis. In both analysis and autobiography, "the self is seen as a developing entity, changing by definable stages" (36, 28). Influenced by a Lacanian model, Jeffrey Mehlman sees the narcissistic and Oedipal stages of development inscribed into the narratives of autobiography. The failures of Narcissus and Oedipus prefigure the impossible task of the autobiographer to reach a "real self." All autobiography is "necessarily fictive"; it creates a self whose very coherence is the sign of its falseness and alienation—just as the child's image in the mirror is false (*A Structural Study of Autobiography* 35–39). A number of other critics like Willis Buck, Gerald Kennedy, and Gregory Ulmer further apply to autobiography Lacanian and structuralist concepts of the self as a fictive entity constituted in images or words that cannot refer back to the "real" world because of the inherently nonreferential nature of all signs.[5] This focus on the autobiographical self's nonreferentiality nonetheless presumes, along with Gusdorf and Olney, that this false entity created in the text is distinct, separate from all others.

Although Gusdorf, Olney, Mehlman, and many others have greatly advanced our understanding of autobiography, their related individualistic paradigms for the self have obscured the presence and significance of women's autobiography in literary tradition. In fact, Gusdorf's description of the culture in which autobiography is *impossible* serves as a far better theoretical point of departure, one that re-places the works of women at the center of the autobiographical canon. His description of a culture *without* the necessary preconditions for autobiography is uncannily akin to the marginalized cultures of women. A slight alteration of his statement will serve the purposes of reversal: Autobiography is possible when "the individual does not feel *herself* to exist outside of others, and still less against others, but very much *with* others in an interdependent existence that asserts its rhythms everywhere in the community . . . [where] lives are so thoroughly entangled that each of them has its center everywhere and its circumference nowhere. The important unit is thus never the isolated being." The very sense of *identification, interdependence,* and *community* that Gusdorf dismisses from autobiographical selves are key elements in the development of a woman's identity, according to theorists like Rowbotham and Chodorow. Their models of women's selfhood highlight the unconscious masculine bias in Gusdorf's and other individualistic paradigms.

In *Woman's Consciousness, Man's World,* Rowbotham examines the role of cultural representation and material conditions in the formation of "woman's consciousness" of self. Building on *The Second Sex,* Rowbotham explores the significance for woman's sense of self of Simone de Beauvoir's assertion that woman is not born, but made. A woman cannot, Rowbotham argues, experience herself as an entirely unique entity because she is always aware of how she is being defined *as woman,* that is, as a member of a group whose identity has been defined by the dominant male culture. Like Lacan, Rowbotham uses the metaphor of mirrors to describe the development of woman's consciousness. But her mirror is the reflecting surface of cultural representation into which a woman stares to form an identity: "The prevailing social order stands as a great and resplendent hall of mirrors. It owns and occupies the world as it is and the world as it is seen and heard" (27). That mirror does not reflect back a unique, individual identity to each living woman; it projects an image of WOMAN, a category that is supposed to define the living woman's identity.

The cultural hall of mirrors—the repositories of representation—does not reflect back a unique individual when a man stands before its mirrors either. The cultural categories MAN, WHITE, CHRISTIAN, and HETEROSEXUAL in Western societies, for example, are as significant for a man of the dominant group as they are for a woman at the margins of culture. Isolate individualism is an illusion. It is also the privilege of power. A white man has the luxury of forgetting his skin color and sex. He can think of himself as an "individual." Women and minorities, reminded at every turn in the great cultural hall of mirrors of their sex or color, have no such luxury. Quoting Georg Simmel, Lynn Sukenick emphasizes the significance of group identity for women's consciousness of self:

> If we express the historic relation between the sexes crudely in terms of master and slave, it is part of the master's privileges not to have to think continuously of the fact that he is the master, while the position of the slave carries with it the constant reminder of his being a slave. It cannot be overlooked that the woman forgets far less often the fact of being a woman than the man of being a man. (28)

The emphasis on individualism as the necessary precondition for autobiography is thus a reflection of privilege, one that excludes from the canons of autobiography those writers who have been denied by history the illusion of individualism.

Women's sense of collective identity, however, is not only negative. It can also be a source of strength and transformation. As Rowbotham argues, cultural representations of woman lead not only to women's alienation, but also to the potential for a "new consciousness" of self (26–46). Not recognizing themselves in the reflections of cultural representation, women develop a dual consciousness—the self as culturally defined and the self as different from cultural prescription:

> But always we were split in two, straddling silence, not sure where we would begin to find ourselves or one another. From this division, our material dislocation, came the experience of one part of ourselves as strange, foreign and cut off from the other which we encountered as tongue-tied paralysis about our own identity. We were never all together in one place, were always in transit, immigrants into alien territory. . . . The manner in which we knew ourselves was at variance with ourselves as an historical being-woman. (31)

This description of women's double consciousness directly parallels W. E. B. Du Bois's identification of dual consciousness for blacks living in a dominant white culture.[6] In *The Souls of Black Folk*, Du Bois wrote:

"The Negro . . . is gifted with second-sight in this American world,—a world which yields him no true self-consciousness, but only lets him see himself through the revelation of the other world. It is a peculiar sensation, this double consciousness, this sense of always looking at one's self through the eyes of others, of measuring one's soul by the tape of a world that looks on in amused contempt and pity. One ever feels his twoness" (30). Du Bois's and Rowbotham's metaphors of reflection, invisibility, and silence are useful for understanding the process of alienation in the identities of any group existing at the margins of culture: women in a man's world; blacks in a white world; Jews in a Christian world; lesbians and gays in a heterosexual world; the have-nots in a world of haves.

Like Du Bois, Rowbotham says women can move beyond alienation through a collective solidarity with other women—that is, a recognition that women *as a group* can develop an alternative way of seeing themselves by constructing a group identity based on their historical experience:

> In order to create an alternative an oppressed group must at once shatter the self-reflecting world which encircles it and, at the same time, project its own image onto history. In order to discover its own identity as distinct from that of the oppressor it has to become visible to itself. All revolutionary movements create their own ways of seeing. But this is a result of great labour. People who are without names, who do not know themselves, who have no culture, experience a kind of paralysis of consciousness. The first step is to connect and learn to trust one another. . . . Solidarity has to be a collective consciousness which at once comes through individual self-consciousness and transforms it. (27, 29)

In taking the power of words, of representation, into their own hands, women project onto history an identity that is not purely individualistic. Nor is it purely collective. Instead, this new identity merges the shared and the unique. In autobiography, specifically, the self created in a woman's text is often not a "teleological entity," an "isolate being" utterly separate from all others, as Gusdorf and Olney define the autobiographical self. Nor is the self a false image of alienation, an empty play of words on the page disconnected from the realm of referentiality, as a Lacanian and post-structuralist critic of autobiography might say. Instead, the self constructed in women's autobiographical writing is often based in, but not limited to, a group consciousness—an awareness of the meaning of the cultural category WOMAN for the patterns of women's individual destiny. Alienation is not the result of creating a self in language, as it is for Lacanian and Barthesian critics of autobiography. Instead, alienation from the historically imposed image of the self is what motivates the writing, the creation of an alternate self in the autobiographical act. Writing the self shatters the cultural hall of mirrors and breaks the silence imposed by male speech.

Whereas Rowbotham focuses on ideology and institutions, Chodorow examines the psychology of gender socialization within the family. Although her emphasis is different from Rowbotham's, Chodorow's approach also suggests that the concept of isolate selfhood is inapplicable to women. Using and revising psychoanalytical objects-relations theory from a feminist perspective, she argues that "growing girls come to define themselves as continuous with others; their experience of self contains more flexible or permeable ego boundaries. Boys come to define themselves as more separate and distinct, with a greater sense of rigid ego boundaries and differentiation. The basic feminine sense of self is connected to the world, the basic masculine sense of self is separate" (169). "Girls," she writes, "come to experience themselves as less differentiated than boys, as more continuous with and related to the external object-world and as differently oriented to their inner object-world as well" (167). By "object," Chodorow does not mean "things," but rather people. Women's "object-world" remains "a more complex relational constellation than men's. . . . Masculine personality, then, comes to be defined more in terms of denial of relation and connection (and denial of femininity), whereas feminine personality comes to include a fundamental definition of self in relationship" (169). Chodorow's theory of differential gender identity highlights the unconscious equation of masculine selfhood with human selfhood in the concept of isolate identity proposed by writers like Gusdorf and Olney. Basing an examination of women's autobiography on the relational model of female selfhood in Chodorow's work, we can anticipate finding in women's texts a consciousness of self in which "the individual does not oppose herself to all others," nor "feel herself to exist outside of others," "but very much *with* others in an interdependent existence."[7]

What leads to the different sense of self in men and women, Chodorow suggests, is the importance of mother-child relationships. Following a general psychoanalytic approach, Chodorow regards the family structure, in which the mother or one woman is the primary caretaker of the child, as a universal phenomenon, although she departs from conventional theory in insisting that universal mothering is culturally, not biologically, determined (3–5, 11–39). Chodorow's premise obscures important cultural variations in the caretaking of children, but her description of mother-child relationships is nonetheless useful for the study of women's autobiography. The mother is the child's first love "object," according to the psychoanalytic theories Chodorow uses. During the Oedipal phase, the boy learns to repress that love, identify with his father, and separate himself from his mother: "Mothers experience their sons as a male opposite. Boys are more likely to have been pushed out of the preoedipal relationship, and to have had to curtail their primary love and sense of empathetic tie with their mother. A boy has engaged, and been required to engage, in a more emphatic individuation and a more defensive firming of experienced ego boundaries" (166–67). Girls, on the other hand, retain that primary attachment to their mothers even as they pass into the Oedipal phase, according to Chodorow: "Mothers tend to experience their daughters as more like, and continuous with themselves. Correspondingly, girls tend to remain part of the dyadic primary mother-child relationship itself. This means that a girl continues to experience herself as involved in issues of merging and separation, and in an attachment characterized by primary identification and the fusion of identification and object choice" (166). The mother-daughter relationship remains central to the ongoing process of female individuation, according to Chodorow. This is particularly true of lesbian women, for whom, she argues, the love of women is an extension of their love for their mothers. "Lesbian relationships," Chodorow writes, "do tend to recreate mother-daughter emotions and connections" (200).[8]

Rowbotham's conceptualization of collective alienation, consciousness, and formation of new identities through reclamation of language and image provides a richly suggestive framework for approaching the individual life stories in autobiographies by women and minorities. So does Chodorow's model of female individuation, with its emphasis on women's relational sense of self and the ongoing influence of the mother-daughter relationship. Although no critics of autobiographies by women and minorities have explicitly used the theoretical formulations of Rowbotham or Chodorow, some have been working along parallel lines. Often themselves at the margins of criticism because of the texts they discuss, a few of these critics have noted the role that group consciousness—both alienated and potentially transformative—sometimes plays in the construction of personal histories. In "In Search of the Black Female Self," Regina Blackburn argues that black women autobiographers use the genre to redefine "the black female self in black terms from a black perspective" (147). Blackburn adapts Stephen Butterfield's discussion of black consciousness in *Black Autobiography in America* for her interpretation of how black women integrate their racial and sexual identities into their individual life stories. As Butterfield writes:

> The "self" of black autobiography . . . is not an individual with a private career, but a soldier in a long, historic march toward Canaan. The self is conceived as a member of an oppressed social group, with ties and responsibilities to the other members. It is a conscious political identity, drawing sustenance from the past experience of the group. . . . The autobiographical form is one of the ways that black Americans have asserted their right to live and grow. It is a bid for freedom, a beak of hope cracking the shell of slavery and exploitation. (2–3)

Similarly, Bernice Johnson Reagon identifies black women's autobiographical writing as "cultural autobiography" because the story of a black woman's selfhood is inseparable from her sense of community. She writes: "We are, at the base of our identities, nationalists. We are people builders, carriers of cultural traditions, key to the formation and continuance of culture" (81).[9]

Mary Mason's pathbreaking introduction to *Journeys: Autobiographical Writings by Women* does not use Chodorow's developmental model of female selfhood, but Mason argues in a related vein that women's sense of self exists within a context of a deep awareness of others. "Women do not present the 'self' on a dramatic scale where a battle of opposing forces is played out" (xiv), she argues, in opposition to the models of autobiography based in the example of Saint Augustine's *Confessions*. "Nor do women," she continues, "use a Rousseauean version of the confession," in which "characters and events exist only to become part of the landscape of the hero's self-discovery" (xiv). Instead, women's autobiographical writings often include "the real presence and recognition of another consciousness. . . . While de Beauvoir argues that men have cast women into the role of 'the other' existing only in relation to the male identity, women, as revealed in our selections, seem to recognize the full autonomy of the 'other' (in this case the male) without destroying their own sense of self" (xiv). Mason's theory that many women's autobiographies create the female self by exploring her relation with a fully rendered Other is consistent with Chodorow's description of the "more complex relational constellation" of women's emotional lives.[10]

Building on the work of critics like Blackburn, Butterfield, and Mason, I want to explore the usefulness of Rowbotham's ideological focus on collective consciousness and Chodorow's psychoanalytical focus on relational gender identity for a psycho-political reading of women's autobiographical writings. The complementary models Rowbotham and Chodorow propose for women's selfhood are not equally relevant for all autobiographies, but they provide illuminating perspectives on both thematic and formalistic elements in a range of women's autobiographical writing. Although women often do not situate the self in Rowbotham's overtly political context, their awareness of group identity as it intersects with individual identity is pervasive. Instead of seeing themselves as solely unique, women often explore their sense of shared identity with other women, an aspect of identity that exists in tension with a sense of their own uniqueness. Although few women autobiographers express a fully psychoanalytic model of the self's development, Chodorow's concept of women's fluid ego boundaries and the importance of mother-daughter relationships is useful in understanding the unfolding self in women's writing.

Anaïs Nin began her diary as a child overwhelmed by her sense of abandonment when her artist-father left the family. From its beginnings, her diary functioned as a safe word-shop for self-creation, a place where she could attempt to integrate the multiplicity of selves she lived out into a meaningful whole. Certainly the selections Nin published as the eight volumes of the *Diary* testify to her sense of her own uniqueness. But uniqueness for Nin bears little relation to the concept of individualism as isolate being. Instead, Nin explores and defines her identity through relationship. When a male friend advises her "to become more egotistic . . . to live for myself, write for myself, work for myself," she responds: "But I feel alive only when I am living for or with others! And I'll be a great artist in spite of that. . . . It's right for a woman to be, above all, human. I am a woman first of all" (*Diary 1* 223). Much of the *Diary* circles around this central conflict of how to be an artist and a woman when men repeatedly tell her they are mutually exclusive kinds of being. To integrate the two, Nin uses her diary to explore the connections between herself as an artist, the category WOMAN, and other women. She observes at one point: "And what I have to say is really distinct from the artist and art. *It is the woman who has to speak.*

And it is not only the woman Anaïs who has to speak, but I who have to speak for many women. As I discover myself, I feel I am merely one of many, a symbol" (*Diary 1* 289).[11]

Nin's sense of herself as simultaneously singular and collective, particular and symbolic, does not fit into Gusdorf's concept of isolate individualism. But it does make sense within Rowbotham's analysis of women's collective consciousness. Metaphors of mirrors, silence, and speech pervade Nin's *Diary*, just as they do Rowbotham's theoretical text. The illusory and costumed selves reflected back in the literal and figurative mirrors that surround her are analogous to the alienating *imagos* Lacan describes. But Nin, like Rowbotham, is aware that these fragmentary selves reflect the meanings of woman's nature constructed by man's fantasy and desire. The *Diary* records Nin's attempt to create a whole identity in a culture that defines WOMAN in terms of her fragmented roles as mother, daughter, wife, and sister.[12]

Nin's constant search for wholeness, however, is not a quest for a sharply defined identity, outside all others. She reports that Henry Miller complained, "I feel no limit in you," and "an absence of boundary" is "perverse" (*Diary 1* 201). She thinks, in turn: "How can I accept a limited definable self when I feel, in me, all possibilities? [Dr.] Allendy may have said: 'This is the core,' but I never feel the four walls around the substance of the self, the core. I feel only space. . . . What interests me is not the core but the potentialities of this core to multiply and expand infinitely. The diffusion of the core, its suppleness and elasticity" (*Diary 1* 200–201). Nin's formulation of a fluid self anticipates Chodorow's concept of women's "more flexible or permeable ego boundaries," as does her insistence on finding an identity through empathy and relation rather than detachment and separation. The various men in the *Diary* who are disturbed by Nin's fluid, relational self (even as they benefit from it) operate from an individualistic concept of the ego which is at odds with feminine socialization.

Chodorow's theory of feminine selfhood is not prescriptive, but rather attempts to describe women's psychological development in a patriarchal society in which mothers (or women) perform the nurturing roles. While Chodorow stresses simply the differences in male and female gender identity, Nin embodies the dangers of fluidity and relationship for women in patriarchy—the destructiveness of autonomy denied. The feminine capacity for empathy and identification can lead into a kind of selfless abnegation, a self-less-ness epitomized by Nin's gift of her only typewriter to Henry Miller. To justify this act of self-negation and other, less tangible "gifts" to the male artists and analysts who feed hungrily from her empathy, Nin appeals to her identity as WOMAN. Even if she fails herself as an artist, she writes at one point, she will have been "the mother and muse and servant and inspiration" to the artist (*Diary 1* 223). In the second volume of the *Diary*, Nin prescriptively defines this mothering of the male artist as the basis for all women's creativity:

> The woman was born mother, wife, sister. She was born to represent union, communion, communication, she was born to give birth to life and not to insanity. . . . Woman was born to *be* the connecting link between man and his human self. . . . Woman has this life-role, but the woman artist has to fuse creation and life in her own way, or in her own womb if you prefer. . . . I do not delude myself as man does, that I create in proud isolation. I say we are bound, interdependent. . . . Woman's role in creation should be parallel to her role in life. (*Diary 2* 234–35)

Nin's conflation of creativity and the relational feminine self leads her into troubling cycles of giving, breakdown, and recovery, each stage of which feeds into her writing. The self she records and constructs in the *Diary* is comprehensible only within a paradigm of the self that incorporates the significance of collective consciousness and gender difference for women's individuation.

Whereas Nin tends to celebrate the very qualities of femininity that entrap her, Charlotte Perkins Gilman explores the meaning of feminine selfhood from a self-consciously feminist perspective in *The Yellow Wallpaper*, an autobiographical tale of horror in the nursery. Collective selfhood and "permeable ego boundaries" are encoded in the novella's brilliant metaphors of woman's condition in late-nineteenth-century, upper-middle-class society. Anticipating Rowbotham's theory of woman's consciousness, alienation and a liberation of sorts from a culture that confines woman's selfhood to her role as wife and mother form the basis of the narrative.

Gilman's persona is a new mother who secretly writes in her journal against her doctor-husband's express orders. Gilman charts the unnamed woman's descent into a madness that liberates her from her husband's control by detailing her growing identification with a "woman" trapped behind the yellow bars of the wallpaper's design. The more mad the new mother becomes, the more truly she sees. The woman behind the wallpaper who shakes the bars to get out is a projection of her own sense of entrapment in the roles of wife and mother. At the climax of the novella, her "ego boundaries" literally disappear in an identification with the other woman, who symbolically becomes all women freed from the hideous patterns of society. "As soon as it was moonlight and that poor thing began to crawl and shake the pattern," she writes, "I got up and ran to help her. I pulled and she shook, I shook and she pulled, and before morning we had peeled off yards of that paper" (59). At daylight, she looks out of the window and, instead of seeing only one woman crawling in the garden, "there are so many of those creeping women and they creep so fast. I wonder if they all come out of that wallpaper as I did?" (60). The end of *The Yellow Wallpaper* is simultaneously a terrifying defeat and a triumphant victory. By stripping off the wallpaper, the woman "frees" all the "women" trapped behind cultural bars and then regresses to an infant-self whose creeping over the body of her husband is a sign both of madness and of new beginnings.

Gilman's parable of female selfhood, based on her own breakdown after the birth of her daughter and written in the form of a woman's secret diary, is incomprehensible within a Gusdorfian framework. Neither the tale nor its metaphoric encoding make any sense within a paradigm of the individualistic self in which "man knows himself . . . the gatherer of men, of lands, of power," to quote Gusdorf. As the victim of just such a man—her paternalistic husband who, in the story, is the "inventor of laws or of wisdom"—Gilman's woman creates a self out of her identification with other women. Read psycho-politically, the metaphor of the wallpaper encodes this shared identity—both the alienation and the enraged desire for freedom, each disguised under the "safe" mask of madness.

While Gilman explored the meaning of group identity based on gender, a number of other writers examine individuation for women who belong to racial or religious minorities. They exist, as Blackburn argues, in a situation of "double jeopardy"—defined not only by the category WOMAN, but also by the category BLACK, JEW, or whatever other group the dominant culture has isolated from the mainstream. A shared identity with other Jews overwhelms any conventional sense of the individual in Isabella Leitner's *Fragments of Isabella: A Memoir of Auschwitz.* Indeed the obliteration of the individual subsumed into the category JEW forms the underlying narrative of horror in this memoir. Rowbotham's concept of the historically imposed group identity transformed by solidarity with others of that group illuminates the autobiography. Isabella begins her series of "fragments" with a memory of her birthday on 28 May 1944—the day of her deportation to the camps, the day the Nazis attempt to reduce her identity to that of the despised and helpless Jew. Isabella's recollections focus on her rebellious survival, which she credits to the way she and her three sisters functioned as one, held together by the memory of their dying mother's drive to keep them alive (28–29). Alone in the camps, Isabella would have died, not having the will to withstand "selection":

> If you are sisterless, you do not have the pressure, the absolute responsibility to end the day alive. How many times did that responsibility keep us alive? I cannot tell. I can only say that many times when I was caught in a selection, I knew I had to get back to my sisters, even when I was too tired to fight my way back. . . . Does staying alive not only for yourself, but also because someone else expects you to, double the life force? Perhaps. Perhaps. (44–45)

Not as an isolate individual, but as a woman whose identity is inseparable from her Jewishness and her sisters, Isabella fulfills her mother's wish. She survives and ultimately escapes during a forced march when three of the sisters suddenly act as one mind and body to take advantage of a momentary lapse in the guards' attention. The unresolved pain of her reflections centers on the fact that one sister stayed separate; she did not flee from the marching line when "one sister followed the other" (78). Adjustment to freedom in America comes slowly. When her aunt hands her a mirror, she sees no face at all, only the smoke of the crematoria: "All I can see is smoke . . . smoke circling madly on the mirror" (100). Like Rowbotham's hall of mirrors, Isabella's "mirror" reflects back to her the cultural obliteration of her identity. Recovery, self re-creation, comes literally in the reproduction of mothering. In becoming a mother, she becomes her mother and re-births herself. Leitner ends her series of fragments with Isabella's recollection of the birth of each son. Each pregnancy brings back the life-giving bond with her mother: "It is all crazy, Mama. Life is ebbing away in the mad pictures of my mind. Life is being nourished in my arms. Help me, Mama. Help me to see only life. Don't let me see the madman anymore." The image of her mother's face, no false *imago*, replaces the smoke from the crematoria.

A related concept of communal identity and sisterhood underlies the innovative characterization in Ntozake Shange's choreopoem *for colored girls who have considered suicide / when the rainbow is enuf*. Each actress in the play is designated by one of the seven colors of the rainbow—Lady in Red, Lady in Orange, and so forth. Each lady, however, plays a number of roles, thus visually forcing the audience to envision a "character" as a multiplicity of selves making up the experience of black womanhood. The Lady in Red, for example, crosses the categories of class and sexuality that conventionally divide black women from each other. She is variously a professional black woman ending an affair (13–14); a sequined "passion flower" who is every man's lover and "the wrath / of women in windows / . . . / camoflagin despair & / stretch marks" (32–34); and Crystal, the battered woman who is forced to watch Beau Willie, a Vietnam vet, drop their children out the window (58–63). All together, the ladies of color represent a family of women, united like the colors in the rainbow, though differently shaded as the children in Afro-American families so often are.[13]

For colored girls is by no means autobiography in the narrow sense. But the choreopoem belongs within the tradition of women's autobiographical writings by its identification of a collective selfhood for black women, a group identity which is a source of both alienation and transformation. The play opens with the Lady in Brown lyrically calling on the women to tell the story of black womanhood, as if all black women live out the same narrative in spite of surface differences:

> somebody/anybody
> sing a black girl's song
> bring her out
> to know herself
>
> . . . . . .
>
> she's been dead so long
> closed in silence so long
>
> . . . . . .
>
> sing her sighs
> sing the song of her possibilities
> sing a righteous gospel
> the makin of a melody
> let her be born
> let her be born
> & handled warmly.
>
> (2–3)

Deeply divided, even distrustful, during most of the play as they tell their different stories, the Ladies come together by the end, in a circle that symbolizes their re-union, to "sing a righteous gospel": "i found god in myself / & i loved her / i loved her fiercely" (67). The "i" of their song is not the "isolate being" of individualistic paradigms for autobiography, but the collective identity and solidarity defined by Rowbotham, Blackburn, and Reagon.[14]

Whereas group identity in the texts of Leitner and Shange defines the parameters of both oppression and liberation, Paule Marshall's autobiographical *Brown Girl, Brownstones* explores the conflict between the desire for individual identity and the realities of a historically imposed group identity. In this autobiographical *kunstlerroman*, Selina must develop her individual identity as an artist within the contexts of both racial and gender categories. The immediate battleground for her development as a Caribbean-American woman is Selina's relationship with her powerful mother, Silla, a personal bond whose complexity is illuminated by Chodorow's model. Silla, whose way with words casts a net over all who come into her path, introduces her daughter to the meanings of communal identity. "She could never think of the mother alone," Selina reflects early in the novel. "It was always the mother and the others, for they were alike—those watchful, wrathful women whose eyes seared and searched and laid bare, whose tongues lashed the world in unremitting distrust" (10–11). This powerful, symbolic being of the Bajan women threatens Selina's growth in her battles against her mother. They frighten her by poking at the emerging breasts on her adolescent body. Their collective will to succeed by "buying house"— especially the ruthless drive of her mother—breaks across the warmth of her relationship with her dreamy, artistic, sensual, but ineffectual father. Selina's alienation from this collectivity climaxes first in the scene where she denounces her mother as "Hitler," and finally in her plan to cheat the Bajan Association to which her mother belongs.

But when, near the end of the novel, Selina herself faces the ugly dismissal of racism after her triumphant dance, she learns to turn the mother's collective power into a source of strength. After a white woman belittles Selina's achievement in dance, Selina rushes outside and peers at her black face in a store window:

She peered shyly at her reflection—the way a child looks at himself in the mirror. And, in a sense, it was a discovery for her also. She was seeing, clearly for the first time, the image which the [white] woman—and the ones like the woman—saw when they looked at her. . . . Her dark face must be confused in their minds with what they feared most: with the night, symbol of their ancient fears, which seethed with sin and harbored violence. . . . Like the night, she was to be feared, spurned, purified—and always reminded of her darkness. (290–91)

In contrast to the *imago* in the Lacanian mirror stage, the false self in the window is not Selina's creation, but rather the cultural meaning of black womanhood that she has internalized and must destroy. Anticipating Rowbotham, Selina tries to shatter the alienating image in the cultural mirror: "With a choked cry of disgust, her arm slashed out, her fist smashed that mouth, those eyes; her flat hand tried to blot it out. She struck the reflection until the entire glass wall trembled—and still it remained, gazing at her with her own enraged and tearful aspect" (291). She is not successful in smashing that image of selfhood until she can learn to respect the Bajan community she despised. When she realizes that her mother and the Bajan Association created a powerful island in a sea of racism, then she is ready to shatter the cultural reflections of herself that had nearly shattered her. In other words, the illusion that she was a single individual who could make her way alone in the white world nearly destroyed Selina. The lesson of the mirror is the lesson of collective identity, in both its alienating and transformative aspects.

Although Selina does not, finally, follow her mother's materialist path, identification with her mother's power is what gives her the strength to strike out on her own. As the novel ends, Selina reverses the direction of her mother's immigration. She sets off for the island, "a frail sound in that utter silence" (310), both separate from and together with the Bajan community. But this act of individual assertion expresses her fundamental bond with her mother. "Everyone used to call me Deighton's Selina," she explains to Silla, "but they were wrong. Because you see I'm truly your child. Remember how you used to talk about how you left home and came here alone as a girl of eighteen and was your own woman? I used to love hearing that. And that's what I want. I want it!" (307). Silla's power becomes an inner resource for Selina at the moment when the daughter recognizes the unbroken identification between herself and her mother—precisely that quality Chodorow identifies as characteristic of mother-daughter relationships.

While Marshall's *kunstlerroman* records the tension between communal identity and the search for autonomy, other writers such as Maxine

Hong Kingston, Paula Gunn Allen, and E. M. Broner explore the conflict between gender and ethnic identity. In their autobiographical writings, women's self-creation results from the individual's negotiation between contradictory collectivities. In *Her Mothers*, for example, Broner examines her double alienation as a Jew within a dominant Christian tradition and as a woman within a patriarchal religious and cultural heritage. The identity created in the course of the mother's search for her matrilineal heritage is one that reaches back into the forgotten collective past of both Jewish women and all writing women. It also reaches forward through the speaker's effort to pass that transformed identity on to her daughter. Allen's autobiographical *The Woman Who Owned the Shadows*, about a woman writer who is part Indian, shares with Broner the double examination of gender and ethnic identities but differs in that the Indian traditions suppressed by white culture are profoundly woman-identified. Healing self-creation for Ephanie involves relearning what Indian men and women have been forced to forget—the powerful creative force of Spider Woman, the matrix of creation, and the honored position of the homosexual in traditional tribal culture. Identification of her own "spinning" of words with the Spider Woman of her forgotten heritage heals the alienation she experiences as an Indian, a woman, and a lesbian. Although the women in both *kunstlerromane* are distinct individuals, their identities are built out of the intersection of collective heritage and unique life stories. For both, the continuing bond with mythic mothers and daughters is essential for self-creation.

Solely individualistic paradigms of the self completely obscure the narrative core of such autobiographies. Rowbotham's concept of group consciousness, in contrast, makes comprehensible an autobiography such as Maxine Hong Kingston's *The Woman Warrior*, in which the negotiation between conflicting group identities is particularly paralyzing, then ultimately liberating. Kingston's persona, prophetically nicknamed Ink, stands before many distorting mirrors. As a second-generation American girl, she is aware of the pressure to become "American feminine"—that is, sweet, pretty, datable, but also good in school. As a Chinese-American, she knows that many Americans regard her as a silent Chinese doll, or worse, as "chink" and "gook" (63). As the daughter of a Chinese peasant family, she learns from her Chinese heritage that "girls are maggots in the rice," that "feeding girls is feeding cowbirds," that "when you raise girls, you're raising children for strangers" (51, 54). The proverbs are words of torture that mock her efforts to excel in school, to become a writer. Caught in the cross fire between American and Chinese feminine identities, the young girl turns to her driven and powerful mother, whose life story and "talk-story" project a double message about the cultural meaning of being female. On the one hand, Brave Orchid "said I would grow up a wife and slave," but on the other hand, she also taught "the song of the warrior woman, Fa Mu Lan," the legendary Chinese Joan of Arc figure who saved her country (24). In the chapter "White Tigers," Ink imagines herself in the role of Fa Mu Lan, who trained from girlhood to become a hero for her people. Before she sets off for battle, her parents carve words of revenge on her back, "oaths and names" that she must carry to war on behalf of her ancestral heritage (41).

This mythical Fa Mu Lan, whose individual identity is inseparable from a familial and communal one, becomes the model of selfhood for Ink: "The swordswoman and I are not so dissimilar. May my people understand the resemblance soon so that I can return to them. What we have in common are the words at our backs. . . . And I have so many words—'chink' words and 'gook' words too—that they do not fit on my skin" (62–63). As a writer, she embodies the swordswoman. With words, she must defeat the enemies of her people. With words, she must also find acceptance for herself as a woman among her people. With words, she will sing songs of "wandering" and "sadness and anger" that even the "barbarians" and "foreign ghosts" can understand (242–43). As a child whose double was the little Chinese girl who never spoke, Kingston's hero finds an identity by breaking the silences imposed by culture and reclaiming the power of words that are both communal and individual.

Like Selina, Kingston's hero successfully survives the conflict between community and individuality by recognizing her identification with the mother who had aroused so much ambivalence. In retelling her mother's story, Kingston parallels the mythical warrior woman with Brave Orchid's own heroism in the real world. "My mother may have been afraid," she recalls, "but she would be a dragoness ('my totem, your totem'). She could make herself not weak" (79). Imitating her mother, the young girl makes herself into a dragon, "not weak." "I am really a Dragon, as she is a Dragon," she thinks at one moment of reconciliation between mother and daughter (127). Like her mother, she "talks story," and to introduce the autobiography's final parable, Kingston says: "The beginning is hers, the ending, mine" (240). As Chodorow might predict, the boundaries between mother and daughter are fluid.

Consistent with Chodorow's theory of women's development, the mother-daughter bond is even more strikingly apparent in lesbian autobiographical writing. In *Zami: A New Spelling of My Name*, Audre Lorde records the difficulty of charting an individual path in an environment that imposes its representations of blacks, women, and lesbians on her younger self. "It was hard enough to be Black," she writes, "to be Black and female, to be Black, female, and gay. To be Black, female, gay, and out of the closet . . . was considered by many Black lesbians to be simply suicidal" (224). Although she was delighted in high school to discover that she "was different from my white classmates, not because I was Black, but because I was me," she comes to realize that she cannot survive as an individual: "Self-preservation warned some of us that we could not afford to settle for one easy definition, one narrow individuation" (82, 227).

As Rowbotham suggests, the historically imposed distortions of identity create a solidarity based in consciousness of group identity. For Lorde, the group that provides the necessary support is made up of women, who are extensions of her matrilineage. The autobiography is a narrative of coming to power—the roots and flowering of desire and language. This story of how she grew into "a new spelling of my name" is encircled by a prologue and epilogue which credit that growth to her love for women—first, her mother and, later, the other women to whom she was bound. Lorde's lyrical celebration of her matrilineage and lesbianism embodies Chodorow's theory of women's permeable ego boundaries. "I have felt," she begins in the prologue, "the age-old triangle of mother father and child with the 'I' at its eternal core, elongate and flatten out into the elegantly strong triad of grandmother mother daughter, with the 'I' moving back and forth flowing in either or both directions as needed" (7). After naming some of the women "who helped give me substance" in the epilogue, she writes: "Their names, selves, faces feed me like corn before labor. I live each of them as a piece of me. . . . There [in Carriacou] it is said that the desire to lie with other women is a drive from the mother's blood" (225–56).

The fluidity of the "I" in Lorde's *Zami* has been explored by other lesbian writers as well. Gertrude Stein's well-known antipathy for the whole concept of identity is rooted in the principles of modernist art, but it may also reflect a lesbian rejection of the self as an isolate being, a discrete unit.[15] *The Autobiography of Alice B. Toklas*, written by Stein, can be simultaneously regarded as a hoax (since the book focuses on Stein, not Toklas); as an ultimate act of arrogance (since Stein played the role of masculine genius to Toklas's domesticity, at least publicly); as a sign of a "self in hiding," to echo Patricia Spacks's phrase for women's auto-biographical selves (since Stein masks her voice behind that of a fictional Toklas); and as a testament to a fluid identity that Stein shared with her lover. As autobiographer, Stein pretends to let Toklas do the speaking, a strategy that conceals Stein's consciousness behind the mask of the Other. Anticipating Mason's theory of the "double focus" in women's autobiography, Stein tells her story through the voice of her lover.

The permeable ego boundaries underlying Stein's narrative strategy are the direct subject of H.D.'s autobiographical roman à clef, *HER-mione*, written in 1927 not long before Stein's "autobiography." As H.D.'s novel opens, Hermione has just flunked out of college and faces a crisis of identity. As she falls in love with the disreputable poet George Lowndes (Ezra Pound), the crisis deepens because she realizes that as his wife she will become his muse, his poem, never the poet. After falling in love with a woman, Fayne Rabb (Frances Gregg), Hermione begins to disengage from George. Where George made her feel "smudged out," her relationship with Fayne leads to a sense of identity (73). H.D. plays with Hermione's nickname, "Her," to indicate the self-discovery that results from a lesbian fusion of selves: "I know her. I know her. Her. I am Her. She is Her. Knowing her, I know Her. She is some amplification of myself like amoeba giving birth, by breaking off, to amoeba. I am a sort of mother, a sort of sister to Her" (158).[16] Instead of telling Hermione that "you are a poem, though your poem's naught," as George does, Fayne says, "Your writing is the thin flute holding you to eternity" (211, 161). Hermione thinks of herself as Narcissa, a woman who has fallen in love with herself in the other. Revising Freud's theory of narcissism, H.D. did not regard Her's narcissism as a regression, but instead as the beginning point of self-love and self-creation, both essential for the budding artist in Hermione.[17]

Women's autobiography comes alive as a literary tradition of self-creation when we approach its texts from a psycho-political perspective based in the lives of women. Historically, women as a group have never been the "gatherer of men, of lands, of power, maker of kingdoms or of empires," to echo Gusdorf once again. Instead, they have been the gathered, the colonized, the ruled. Seldom the "inventor of laws and of wisdom," they have been born into those inventions—all the more so if their race, religion, class, or sexual preferences also marginalized them. Nonetheless, this historical oppression has not destroyed women's consciousness of self. As Rowbotham says, woman have shattered the distorting identities imposed by culture and left "the sign" of their "presence" in their autobiographical writings. Their signs, however, remain marginal or even untranslatable when they are placed in a context in which individuation is defined as the separation of the self from all others. Individualistic paradigms do not take into account the central role collective consciousness of self plays in the lives of women and minorities. They do not recognize the significance of interpersonal relationships and community in women's self-definition, nor do they explain the ongoing identification of the daughter with her mother. Rowbotham's historical and Chodorow's psychoanalytic models, on the other hand, offer a basis for exploring the self as women have constituted it in their writings. To echo and reverse Gusdorf once more, this autobiographical self often does not oppose herself to all others, does not feel herself to exist outside of others, and still less against others, but very much *with* others in an interdependent existence that asserts its rhythms everywhere in the community.

Notes

For their criticism and bibliographic help, I am indebted to Nellie McKay, Elizabeth Hirsh, Marilyn Young, and Steven Feierman. A version of this essay was presented at the Modern Language Association meeting in December 1984.

1. See also Pascal for an important early statement on autobiographical self-construction.

2. Gusdorf's "pre-conditions for autobiography" do not take into account the phenomenon of non-Western autobiographies. Many of these predate contact with the West, and others are connected to indigenous traditions that should not be dismissed as "transplanted." For Asian and African autobiographies, for example, see Muraski, Bowring, Shen, Honig, Curtin, Wright, and Cunnison. Gusdorf also does not recognize the importance of early Christian spiritual autobiographies for the later secular genre. See, for example, Augustine and Pomerleau. His dating particularly ignores the early autobiographical writings of women. See, for example, Hildegard's *Vita* (1160s); Margery Kempe's *The Book of Margery Kempe* (early 1400s); Sor Juana's *La Respuesta* (1691); Gluckel's *The Memoirs of Gluckel of Hameln* (1689–1719); Alice Thornton's *The Autobiography of Mrs. Alice Thornton* (late seventeenth century); Kempe's *Book* is the first extant autobiography in English.

3. Many other valuable studies of autobiography also assume an individualistic model of the self. See for example Bruss, Buck, Gunn, Jay, Lejeune,

Mazlish, Pascal, Spengemann, and Weintraub. These excellent studies draw their examples from an overwhelmingly white, male canon. Stone is an important exception. Although he emphasizes the "linkage of individualism, democratic pluralism, and autobiography," his valuable study of American "cultural narratives" extensively incorporates the work of women and minorities (9). In stressing the impact of cultural history and heritage on autobiography, he has moved away from a concept of the self as a purely isolate entity.

4. See also Neumann (5–195) for a Jungian version of Freud's emphasis on separation in the individuation process.

5. See also Mazlish, Mehlman.

6. According to Paul Lauter, Rowbotham is familiar with Du Bois's concept of double consciousness (conversation with Lauter).

7. Stone also refers to Chodorow's concept of women's relational identity in his chapter on women's autobiographies, but only to dismiss it, not to use it. He argues that such relational definitions are ideological, the kind of "social myth" which must be abandoned if we are to understand women's texts. See also Gilligan and Peck for discussion of the impact of relational models of female selfhood for understanding women's experience. Gilligan's application of Chodorow's model to gender differences in ethical development should prove especially useful for understanding autobiography, since life stories so often involve ethical crises.

8. For discussion of the pre-Oedipal period and lesbianism, see Freud, "Femininity," and Friedman and DuPlessis. For a lesbian critique of this pre-Oedipal model for adult lesbian relationships, see the papers from the panel entitled "Mothering Theory in Lesbian Writing," Division of Gay Studies, Modern Language Association meeting, December 1986.

9. See also Taylor.

10. See also Mason, "The Other Voice," and Billson and Smith. For important applications of Chodorow's concept of women's relational identity to women's fiction and poetry, see Gardiner and Ostriker.

11. See Stone's different analysis of this passage (209–25).

12. See, for example, Nin, *Diary 1* 47, 91, 103, 105, 270, 286, 293, 351.

13. I am indebted to Nellie McKay for explaining that the rainbow is a common metaphor in Afro-American culture for the phenomenon of children in the same family being different shades of color.

14. For another influential communal "I," see Woolf's *A Room of One's Own*, in which she replaces the conventional authoritative "I" of the essay genre with the communal "I" based in the four Marys of the ballad "Mary Hamilton."

15. See, for example, Breslin; also Stein, *Everybody's Autobiography*.

16. See Friedman and DuPlessis. Having read widely in the psychoanalytic literature, H.D. may have developed the amoeba image for lesbianism in response to Freud's use of the metaphor. He wrote: "The condition in which the ego retains the libido is called by us "narcissism. . . . Thus in our view the

individual advances from narcissism to object-love. But we do not believe that the *whole* of the libido ever passes over from the ego to objects. . . . The ego is a great reservoir from which the libido that is destined for objects flows out and into which it flows back from those objects. . . . For complete health, it is essential that the libido should not lose this full mobility. An illustration of this state of things we may think of as an amoeba, whose viscous substance puts out pseudopodia, elongations into which the substance of the body extends but which can be retracted at any time so that the form of the protoplasmic mass is restored" ("A Difficulty" 139).

17. See Freud, "On Narcissism," and Friedman and DuPlessis. Although H.D.'s image of an ideal lesbian love is consistent with Chodorow's concept of fluid ego boundaries, the family analogue that H.D. emphasizes is the union of twin sisters rather than the mother-daughter relationship. In fact, the mother in the novel is primarily a negative figure of social convention who has allowed her own identity to be subsumed in her family. Chodorow's model of the fluid mother-daughter boundaries needs to be expanded to incorporate mother-daughter conflict, particularly the problems daughters often face in attempting some measure of separation from their mothers. Such an extended model would be particularly useful in discussing texts such as *Brown Girl, Brownstones* and *A Woman Warrior*, in which the daughters must simultaneously identify with and separate from their powerful, even invasive mothers.

Works Cited

Allen, Paula Gunn. *The Woman Who Owned the Shadows*. San Francisco: Spinsters Ink, 1984.

Augustine, Saint. *Confessions*. Trans. Albert C. Outler. Philadelphia: Westminster Press, 1955.

Billson, Marcus K., and Sidonie A. Smith. "Lillian Hellman and the Strategy of the 'Other.'" In Jelinek, 163–79.

Bowring, Richard. "The Female Hand in Heian Japan: A First Reading." In Stanton, 55–62.

Broner, E. M. *Her Mothers*. Berkeley: Berkeley Medallion, 1975.

Blackburn, Regina. "In Search of the Black Female Self: African-American Women's Autobiographies and Ethnicity." In Jelinek, 133–48.

Breslin, James E. "Gertrude Stein and the Problems of Autobiography." In Jelinek, 149–62.

Bruss, Elizabeth W. *Autobiographical Acts: The Changing Situation of a Literary Genre*. Baltimore: Johns Hopkins University Press, 1976.

Buck, William R., Jr. "Reading Autobiography." *Genre* 13 (Winter 1980): 477–98.

Butterfield, Stephen. *Black Autobiography in America*. Amherst: University of Massachusetts Press, 1974.

Chodorow, Nancy. *Psychoanalysis and the Sociology of Gender*. Berkeley: University of California Press, 1978.

Cunnison, Ian. "History and Genealogies in a Conquest State." *American Anthropologist* 59 (1957): 20–31.

_____. "Perpetual Kinship: A Political Institution of the Lulapula Peoples." *Rhodes-Livingston Journal* 20 (1956): 28–48.

Curtin, Philip, ed. *Africa Remembered: Narratives by West Africans from the Era of the Slave Trade*. Madison: University of Wisconsin Press, 1967.

Du Bois, W. E. B. *The Souls of Black Folk*. 1903. Rpt. in *Black Voices: An Anthology of Afro-American Literature*. Ed. Abraham Chapman. New York: New American Library, 1968.

Fleishman, Avrom. *Figures of Autobiography: The Language of Self-Writing in Victorian and Modern England*. Berkeley: University of California Press, 1983.

Freud, Sigmund. *Civilization and Its Discontents*. 1930. Trans. James Strachey. New York: Norton, 1961.

_____. "A Difficulty in the Path of Psychoanalysis." 1917. In *Standard Edition of Sigmund Freud*. Ed. James Strachey. London: Hogarth Press, 1955. 17:137–44.

_____. "Femininity." 1933. In *New Introductory Lectures*. Trans. James Strachey. New York: Norton, 1965. 112–35.

_____. "On Narcissism." 1914. In *General Psychological Theory: Papers on Metapsychology*. Ed. Philip Rieff. New York: Collier, 1963.

Friedman, Susan Stanford. "Theories of Autobiography and Fictions of the Self in H.D.'s Canon." In *Self-Representations: Autobiographical Writings of the Nineteenth and Twentieth Centuries*. Ed. Thomas R. Smith. Forthcoming.

Friedman, Susan Stanford, and Rachel Blau DuPlessis. "'I Had Two Loves Separate': The Sexualities of H.D.'s *Her*." *Montemora* 8 (1981): 7–30.

Gardiner, Judith Kegan. "On Female Identity and Writing by Women." *Critical Inquiry* 8 (Winter 1981): 347–61.

Gilligan, Carol. *In a Different Voice: Psychological Theory and Women's Development*. Cambridge: Harvard University Press, 1982.

Gilman, Charlotte Perkins. *The Yellow Wallpaper*. 1892. Old Westbury: Feminist Press, 1973.

Gluckel. *The Memoirs of Gluckel of Hameln*. Trans. Marvin Lowenthal. New York: Schocken, 1977.

Goulianos, Joan, ed. *By a Woman Writt: Literature from Six Centuries by and about Women*. Baltimore: Penguin, 1973.

Gunn, Janet Varner. *Autobiography: Toward a Poetics of Experience*. Philadelphia: University of Pennsylvania Press, 1982.

Gusdorf, Georges. "Conditions and Limits of Autobiography." 1956. Trans. James Olney. In Olney, *Autobiography* 28–48.

H.D. [Hilda Doolittle]. *HERmione*. New York: New Directions, 1981.

Hildegard of Bingen. *Vita*. Excerpted in *Women Writers of the Middle Ages: A Critical Study of Texts from Perpetua (d. 203) to Marguerite Porete (d. 1310)*. Ed. Peter Dronke. Cambridge: Cambridge University Press, 1984. 144–201, 231–64.

Honig, Emily. "Private Issues, Public Discourse: The Life and Times of Yu Luojin." *Pacific Affairs* 57 (Summer 1984): 252–64.

Jelinek, Estelle C., ed. *Women's Autobiography: Essays in Criticism*. Bloomington: Indiana University Press, 1980.

Jay, Paul. *Being in the Text: Self-Representation from Wordsworth to Roland Barthes*. Ithaca: Cornell University Press, 1984.

Juana Ines de la Cruz, Sor. *La Respuesta*. 1691. In *A Woman of Genius: An Intellectual Autobiography of Sor Juana Ines de la Cruz*. Trans. Margaret Sayers Peden. Salisbury: Lime Rock Press, 1982.

Kempe, Margery. *The Book of Margery Kempe*. In Goulianos, 3–20.

Kennedy, Gerald. "Roland Barthes, Autobiography, and the End of Writing." *Georgia Review* 35 (Summer 1981): 381–400.

Kingston, Maxine Hong. *The Woman Warrior: Memoirs of a Girlhood among Ghosts*. New York: Vintage, 1977.

Lacan, Jacques. *Ecrits: A Selection*. Trans. Alan Sheridan. New York: Norton, 1977.

Leitner, Isabella. *Fragments of Isabella: A Memoir of Auschwitz*. New York: Dell, 1978.

Lejeune, Philippe. "Autobiography in the Third Person." *New Literary History* 9 (1977): 27–50.

Lorde, Audre. *Zami: A New Spelling of My Name*. Trumansburg: Crossing Press, 1982.

Marshall, Paule. *Brown Girl, Brownstones*. 1959. Old Westbury: Feminist Press, 1981.

Mason, Mary G. "The Other Voice: Autobiographies of Women Writers." In Olney, *Autobiography* 207–35.

Mason, Mary G., and Carol Hurd Greed, eds. *Journeys: Autobiographical Writings by Women*. Boston: G. K. Hall, 1979.

Mazlish, Bruce. "Autobiography and Psychoanalysis: Between Truth and Self-Deception." *Encounter* 35 (October 1970): 28–37.

Mehlman, Jeffrey. *A Structural Study of Autobiography: Proust, Leiris, Sartre, Lévi-Strauss*. Ithaca: Cornell University Press, 1974.

Muraski, Shikibu. *The Tale of Genji*. Trans. Arthur Waley. New York: Modern Library, 1960.

Neumann, Erich. *The Origins and History of Consciousness*. Trans. R. F. C. Hull. Princeton: Princeton University Press, 1954.

Nin, Anaïs. *The Diary: Volume One, 1931–1934*. Ed. Gunther Stuhlmann. New York: Harcourt Brace Jovanovich, 1966.

———. *The Diary: Volume Two, 1934–1939*. Ed. Gunther Stuhlmann. New York: Harcourt Brace Jovanovich, 1967.

Olney, James, ed. *Autobiography: Essays Theoretical and Critical*. Princeton: Princeton University Press, 1980.

———. *Metaphors of Self: The Meaning of Autobiography*. Princeton: Princeton University Press, 1972.

Ostriker, Alicia. "'If I be you': Self-Other Identification in Women's Poetry." Paper delivered at the Modern Language Association meeting, December 1984.

Pascal, Roy. *Design and Truth in Autobiography*. London: Routledge and Kegan Paul, 1960.

Peck, Teresa. "Attachment and Separation Mold Women's Experience." *Women's Studies Research Center Newsletter* 5 (Winter 1984): 5.

Pomerleau, Cynthia S. "The Emergence of Women's Autobiography in England." In Jelinek, 21–38.

Reagon, Bernice Johnson. "My Black Mothers and Sisters or On Beginning a Cultural Autobiography." *Feminist Studies* 8 (Spring 1982): 81–95.

Rowbotham, Sheila. *Woman's Consciousness, Man's World*. London: Penguin, 1973.

Shange, Ntozake. *For colored girls who have considered suicide / when the rainbow is enuf: a choreopoem*. New York: Bantam, 1977.

Shen Fu. *Six Chapters in a Floating Life: The Autobiography of a Chinese Artist*. Trans. by Shirley M. Black. New York: Oxford University Press, 1960.

Spacks, Patricia Meyer. "Selves in Hiding." In Jelinek, 112–32.

Spengemann, William. *The Forms of Autobiography: Episodes in the History of a Literary Genre*. New Haven: Yale University Press, 1980.

Stanton, Domna C., ed. *The Female Autograph*. New York: Literary Forum, 1985.

Stein, Gertrude. *The Autobiography of Alice B. Toklas*. New York: Vintage, 1960.

———. *Everybody's Autobiography*. 1937. New York: Cooper Square, 1971.

Stone, Alfred E. *Autobiographical Occasions and Original Acts: Versions of American Identity from Henry Adams to Nate Shaw*. Philadelphia: University of Pennsylvania Press, 1982.

Sukenick, Lynn. "On Women and Fiction." In *The Authority of Experience: Essays in Feminist Criticism*. Ed. Arlyn Diamond and Lee R. Edwards. Amherst: University of Massachusetts Press, 1977. 28–44.

Taylor, Gordon O. "Voices from the Veil: Black American Autobiography." *Georgia Review* 35 (Summer 1981): 341–61.

Thornton, Alice. "The Autobiography of Alice Thornton." Excerpted in Goulianos, 31–53.

Ulmer, Gregory L. "The Discourse of the Imaginary." *Diacritics* 10 (March 1980): 61–75.

Weintraub, Karl J. "Autobiography and Historical Consciousness." *Critical Inquiry* 1 (June 1975): 821–48.

Woolf, Virginia. *A Room of One's Own*. 1929. New York: Harcourt Brace World, 1957.

Wright, Marcia. *Women in Peril*. Lusaka: University of Zambia, 1984.

––––––. "Women in Peril: A Commentary on the Life Stories of Captives in 19th Century East-Central Africa." *African Social Research* 20 (December 1975): 800–819.

My Statue, My Self
Autobiographical Writings of Afro-American Women

Elizabeth Fox-Genovese

Zora Neale Hurston, in her troubling autobiography *Dust Tracks on a Road*, unmistakably identifies the problematic relation between her private self and her self-representation: "I did not know then, as I know now, that people are prone to build a statue of the kind of person that it pleases them to be." Few people, she adds, "want to be forced to ask themselves, 'What if there is no me like my statue?' The thing to do is to grab the broom of anger and drive off the beast of fear" (34).

Hurston's statue has recently been rescued from the attics of marginal memory and received its deserved place in the museum of cultural history. But its rescuers have authenticated it in the name of values that Hurston herself might have found puzzling and perhaps would not even have entirely approved. While she might have been delighted to be acknowledged, finally, as the centerpiece of an Afro-American female literary tradition, she might also have been secretly disappointed to be acknowledged as only that. More than anything, she might have been surprised to see her multiple—and intentionally duplicitous—self-re-presentations accepted as a progenitor of the new Afro-American female self. She might even have laughed before drawing herself up to look mean and impressive. For the rescue of Hurston's statue has been effected, at least in part, at the expense of the anger and the fear and of their consequences for the ways in which she chose publicly to represent her very private self.

The authentication of Hurston's statue cannot be divorced from the authentication of the Afro-American female literary tradition as a whole.

In the search for mothers' gardens, it is both central and pivotal.[1] For Hurston, as often as not, speaks in the language of everyday use. But what are we to make of her when she does not? What, especially, do we make of the autobiography in which she does not? Hurston continually challenges us to rethink our preconceptions, to forswear our fantasies. Attentively read, she reminds that more often than not the autobiographies of Afro-American women have been written from within the cage. Frequently they sing with the voice of freedom, but always they betray the confinement from which that freedom is wrested. Linda Brent, crouched in her grandmother's attic, knows more freedom than she knew as the prey of Dr. Flint's assaults, but the freedom of her soul cannot relieve the confinement of her body. The self, in other words, develops in opposition to, rather than as an articulation of, condition. Yet the condition remains as that against which the self is forged. And the condition, as much as the representations of self, constitutes an inescapable aspect of the Afro-American female literary tradition, especially of Afro-American women's autobiographies.

Hurston's statue, like that of her foremothers and successors, was fashioned of disparate materials. Uneasily poised between the discourses through which any writer represents the self and the conditions of gender, class, and race through which any personal experience is articulated, the statue embodies elements of both. But the combining of elements transforms them. Hurston does not simply "tell it like it is," does not write directly out of experience. The discourses through which she works—and presumably expects to be read—shape her presentation of experience even as her specific experience shapes the ways in which she locates herself in discourses.

Hurston, in fact, never explicitly describes her own statue, although internal evidence suggests that she, like other female autobiographers (notably Simone de Beauvoir), had set her sights on an ideal beyond the horizon of everyday life, beyond the boundaries of her immediate community, beyond the confines of her gender.[2] For Hurston, the statue figures as the ideal for the self or, in psychoanalytic language, the ego ideal. The challenge of the autobiography, then, is to relate the ideal self to the self of everyday life—the contingent self. In Hurston's case, the statue might be said to consist primarily in a freedom from the contingent self that would permit her access as an equal to the republic of letters, the ideal interpretive community. Yet her picture of her contingent self emphasizes all the attributes that would bar her from membership in that community: her gender, her race, her identification with place. It also presents her progress towards her statue as, in large part, a succession of dependencies. Like the fool of Shakespearian drama, she fawns and flatters, reserving to herself the right to speak difficult truths that her demeanor and role appear to belie. Like the trickster of Afro-American folk culture, she speaks with a double tongue. Like the exile, she re-creates her own previous life as a function of her nostalgia. How, in the midst of this deliberate evasiveness that borders on willful duplicity, are we to locate the core of her self-representation? And how are we to locate it in relation to black women's tradition of autobiography?

A literary tradition, even an autobiographical tradition, constitutes something more than a running, unmediated account of the experience of a particular group. The coherence of such a tradition consists as much in unfolding strategies of representation as in experience itself. Some would even argue that the coherence of a tradition is only to be sought in the strategies of representation; the self is a function of discourse—a textual construct—not of experience at all. Others, including many black feminist critics, would emphasize black women's writing as personal testimony to oppression, thus emphasizing experience at the expense of text. Neither extreme will do. The coherence of black women's autobiographical discourse does incontrovertibly derive from black women's experience, although less from experience in the narrow empirical sense than from condition—the condition or interlocking structures of gender, class, and race. But it derives even more from the tension between condition and discourse, from the changing ways in which black women writers have attempted to represent a personal experience of condition through available discourses and in interaction with imagined readers.

Autobiographies of black women, each of which is necessarily personal and unique, constitute a running commentary on the collective experience of black women in the United States. They are inescapably grounded in the experience of slavery and the literary tradition of the slave narratives. Their common denominator, which establishes their integrity as a subgenre, derives not from the general categories of race or sex, but from the historical experience of being black and female in a specific society at a specific moment and over succeeding generations.[3] Black women's autobiographies resist reduction to either political or critical pieties and resist even more firmly reduction to mindless empiricism. In short, they command an attention to theory and method that respects their distinctiveness as a discourse and their relation to other discourses.

In what sense can black women's autobiographies be read as constituting a distinct discourse? Why should they not be lumped with those of black men or those of white women? Politics justifies the differentiation, but its introduction disputes what some would see as the self-referential nature of the autobiographical text. To categorize autobiographies according to the race and gender of those who write them is to acknowledge some relation, however problematical, between the text and its author and, more, between the text and its author's experience. And to acknowledge this relation is to dispute prevailing theories of the multiple deaths of the subject, the self, and the author. Much contemporary theory has found the relations between politics—understood broadly as collective human experience—and the text problematic. These autobiographies defy any apolitical reading of texts, even—perhaps especially—when they seem to invite it.

To accept the ruling pieties about double oppression will not do. Simple addition does not amount to a new theoretical category. Sex assigns black women to the same category as white women; race assigns them to the same category as black men. Both feminist and black-nationalist critics consider their particular claims prior and decisive. Neither group shows much interest in class relations in particular or social relations in general. In all fairness, sex and race more readily lend themselves to symbolization than does class, and thus they also more readily lend themselves to representation, fabulation, and myth. Sex and race more obviously define what we intuitively perceive ourselves to be: male or female, white or black. But even these basic self-perceptions are socially learned and result from acts of (re)cognition. The question thus remains: Why do we find it so much more acceptable to perceive ourselves as members of a sex or a race than as members of a gender or, even more, of a class?[4]

Americans, as a people, do not like fences. Yet as a people we have spent most of our history in raising them. Our open lands lie carved, parceled, and constructed. Our landscape features barriers. Gender and class transform sex and race into barriers, transform the forms of their exclusion into positive social values. To argue for the centrality of gender and class to any analysis of women's self-representation is not to deny the overpowering force of the racism and sexism that stalk women's experience. It is, rather, to argue that if we focus exclusively on sexism and racism we remain mired in the myths we are trying to dissipate.

In theory, it is possible to write about black women's autobiographies as so many discrete cases of the genre "autobiography." Like other autobiographers, black women construct prose portraits of themselves as histories of their lives or of the salient aspects of their lives. The special relation between the autobiographer and the final text outshines all other considerations, especially referential considerations, and reduces specific aspects of the individual history to accidents. There is no theoretical distinction to be made between Jean-Jacques Rousseau's *Confessions* and Zora Neale Hurston's *Dust Tracks*.[5]

Feminist critics, like critics of Afro-American and Third World literatures, are beginning to refuse the implied blackmail of Western, white, male criticism. The death of the subject and of the author may accurately reflect the perceived crisis of Western culture and the bottomless anxieties of its most privileged subjects—the white male authors who had presumed to define it. Those subjects and those authors may, as it were, be dying, but it remains to be demonstrated that their deaths constitute the collective or generic death of subject and author. There remain plenty of subjects and authors who, never having had much opportunity to write in their own names or the names of their kind, much less in the name of the culture as a whole, are eager to seize the abandoned podium. The white male cultural elite has not in fact abandoned the podium; it has merely insisted that the podium cannot be claimed in the name of any particular personal experience. And it has been busily trying to convince the world that intellectual excellence requires depersonalization and abstraction. The virtuosity, born of centuries of privilege, with which these ghosts of authors make their case demands that others, who have something else to say, meet the ghosts' standards of pyrotechnics.[6]

Rejection of the prevailing pyrotechnics does not guarantee their replacement by something better. The theoretical challenge lies in bringing sophisticated skills to the service of a politically informed reading of texts. To read well, to read fully, is inescapably to read politically, but to foreground the politics, as if these could somehow be distinguished from the reading itself, is to render the reading suspect. Political and social considerations inform any reading, for all readers are political and social beings. To deny the applicability of political or social considerations is to take a political position. The reading of black women's autobiographies forcefully exposes the extent to which the tools of criticism are shaped by the politics that guide them. Wole

Soyinka insists upon the bourgeois character of "culture"—its origins, its finality, and its instruments—but he also insists that the dismissal of all "culture" on the grounds of bourgeois contamination ends in "the destruction of all discourse" (55).

Black women's autobiography, as a category, requires justification, and justification requires classification and the delineation of principles and practices of reading.[7] The classification of black women's autobiography forces careful consideration of extratextual conditions. Some current critical tendencies reject the relevance of the extratextual and insist, in a manner reminiscent of the once New Criticism, on evaluating the text on its aesthetic merits, free of such extraneous influences as the experience of the author. These days, evaluating the autobiographical text on its merits is further seen to expose as romanticism and humanism any concern with the self as in some way prior to the text. These views embody a sharp and understandable reaction against the more sentimental manifestations of bourgeois individualism, but they hardly provide adequate critical standards for the classification of black women's autobiography as a distinct subgenre.

To take the text on its merits legitimates Mattie Griffith's *Autobiography of a Slave Girl* as the autobiography of an Afro-American slave—which it was not. As Robert Stepto has tellingly argued, authentication of the author as author of his or her own text ranked as an important concern for the authors of slave narratives. Stepto proposes a categorization of slave narratives according to the relation between plot or narrative and legitimation in the text as a whole.[8] Although Stepto does not discuss the earliest known prose writings by Afro-American women, both Harriet Jacobs's *Incidents in the Life of a Slave Girl* and Harriet Wilson's *Our Nig* contain legitimating documentation that different readers may perceive as more or less integral parts of the texts. But both Harriet Jacobs, who wrote under a pseudonym, and Harriet Wilson, who did not, felt impelled if not obliged to provide verification of their being both themselves and worthy women. These tactical maneuvers to authenticate the black woman's authorship oblige modern readers to respect these authors' concern for the relation between their texts and their experience. They do not oblige us to take any of the history offered in the texts at face value. Rather, we should be prepared merely to accept the text as bearing some (possibly distorted) relation to reality.

The principles of classification must begin with history. Barbara Christian insists upon the significance of periodization for understanding the development of black women's fiction during the twentieth century. Gwendolyn Brooks, who organized her own autobiography around the historical sea change of the emergence of a new form of black consciousness in the 1960s, forcefully emphasizes the relation between history and consciousness. "There is indeed," she wrote in 1972 in *Report from Part One*, "a new black today. He is different from any the world has known. . . . And he is understood by no white." And, she adds: "I have hopes for myself."[9] For Christian, Brooks, and other critics of and participants in black women's culture, the relevant history concerns the coming to consciousness of Afro-Americans during the second half of the twentieth century, and perhaps the growth of American women's consciousness during the same period. The black movement and the feminist movement, with all their internal currents and tensions, have presided over the recent developments in Afro-American women's political and self-consciousness. Both have contributed to the growing emphasis on varieties of Pan-Africanism, including Pan-African feminism, and the repudiation of slavery as a significant contributor to contemporary black consciousness. In this general respect, race is taken to transcend class in the forging of Afro-American identities. Notwithstanding these long, tempestuous, and unresolvable debates, a specific case can be made for the autobiographies of black women.

Nikki Giovanni has, with special force, made the case for the relation of black women's autobiographies to changing political conditions. She attacks the assumption "that the self is not part of the body politic," insisting, "there's no separation" (Tate 62). Giovanni believes that literature, to be worthy of its claims, must reflect and seek to change reality. And the reality black people have known has left much to be desired: "It's very difficult to gauge what we have done as a people when we have been systematically subjected to the whims of other people" (Tate 63). According to Giovanni, this collective subjection to the whims of others has resulted in the alienation of black Americans from other Americans. For as black Americans "living in a foreign nation we are, as the wandering Jew, both myth and reality." Giovanni believes that black Americans will always be "strangers. But our alienation is our greatest strength" (Tate 70). She does not believe that the alienation, or the collective history that produced it, makes black experience or writing incomprehensible to others. "I have not created a totally unique, incomprehensible feat. I can understand Milton and T. S. Eliot, so the critic can understand me. That's the critic's job" (Tate 64).

Personal experience must be understood in social context. Its representation is susceptible to the critic's reading, regardless of whether he or she shares the personal experience. Giovanni rejects the claim that black writing should be the exclusive preserve of black critics—that it is qualitatively different from white writing, immune to any common principles of analysis, and thus severed from any common discourse. There is no argument about the ways in which the common discourse has treated black writing, especially the writing of black women: shamefully, outrageously, contemptuously, and silently. The argument concerns who can read black texts and the principles of the reading. For, as Soyinka said, if the denial of bourgeois culture ends in the destruction of discourse, the refusal of critical distance ends in the acceptance of an exceptionalism that portends extreme political danger. Giovanni explicitly and implicitly makes the main points: the identity of the self remains hostage to the history of the collectivity; the representation of the self in prose or verse invites the critical scrutiny of the culture. Both points undercut the myth of the unique individual and force a fresh look at the autobiographies of black women.

Selwyn R. Cudjoe, writing of Maya Angelou, has insisted that Afro-American autobiography "as a form tends to be bereft of any *excessive subjectivism* and *mindless* egotism." Rather, Afro-American autobiographies present the experience of the individual "as reflecting a much more *im-personal* condition, the autobiographical subject emerging as an almost random member of the group, selected to tell his/her tale." Accordingly, he views Afro-American autobiography as "a *public* rather than a *private* gesture, *me-ism* gives way to *our-ism* and superficial concerns about *individual subject* usually give way to the *collective subjection* of the group" (9). Cudjoe contends that these characteristics establish black autobiography as objective and realistic. In so arguing, he is extending significantly the tradition of the slave narratives that sought to provide living, firsthand accounts of the evils of "that demon slavery" for a northern audience.[10]

The genre of black autobiography contains an important strand that could be subsumed under the general rubric of "report from the war zone." Brooks uses "report" in her title, *Report From Part One*. Giovanni's *Gemini* features a rather staccato, journalistic style. Both depict the author's "self" indirectly, obliquely, through reports of actions more than through discussions of states of mind. The responsibility to report on experience even more clearly shapes such autobiographies as those of Ida B. Wells and Era Bell Thompson. In their representations of a specific life, the autobiographical writings of many black women, like those of many black men, do bear witness to a collective experience—to black powers of survival and creativity as well as to white oppression. Much of the autobiographical writing of black women eschews the confessional mode—the examinations of personal motives, the searchings of the soul—that white women autobiographers so frequently adopt. Black women's autobiographies seem torn between exhibitionism and secrecy, between self-display and self-concealment. The same is true of all autobiographies, but the proportions differ from text to text, perhaps from group to group of autobiographers. And the emotions and events displayed or concealed also differ.

All autobiographers confront the problem of readers, the audience to whom their self-representation is addressed. Black female autobiographers confront the problem in especially acute form—or so their texts suggest.[11] Harriet Jacobs and Harriet Wilson seem to have assumed that most of their readers would be white abolitionists or potential abolitionists. Both, especially Harriet Jacobs, also seem to have addressed themselves especially to white, middle-class women. Neither Jacobs nor Wilson identified with those likely readers, but both sought to interest them. And in both cases, the professed reason for seeking that interest was to instruct white women in the special horrors of slavery for women and the ways in which the tentacles of slavery reached into the interstices of northern society. Both texts reveal that their authors harbored deep bitterness toward northern society in general and northern white women in particular, even though they frequently expressed it indirectly. And that bitterness inescapably spills over into their imagined relations to their readers, into the ways in which they present themselves and their histories.

There is little evidence that black women autobiographers assumed that any significant number of other black women would read their work. To the extent that they have, until very recently, written for other black women, they seem to have written for younger women, for daughters, for those who would come after. Black women's autobiographies abound with evidence of or references to the love that black female autobiographers felt for and felt from their female elders: mothers, aunts, grandmothers. For the most part, those female elders are represented as rural in identification and origin, if not always in current location; immersed in folk communities; deeply religious; and the privileged custodians of the values and, especially, of the highest standards of their people. They are not necessarily literate, and those who are literate are unlikely to spend money on any books except the Bible.

From Harriet Jacobs and Harriet Wilson onward, black female autobiographers wrote to be read by those who might influence the course of public events, might pay money for their books, or might authenticate them as authors. Neither Jacobs nor Wilson wrote primarily, much less exclusively, for members of the slave community. How could they have? Subsequent black women autobiographers, many of whom have been writers or professional women, have also tended to write as much for white readers, or for black male intellectuals, as for other black women. Their focus has been changing recently with the explosion of Afro-American women's fiction in the work of Toni Morrison, Alice Walker, Ntozake Shange, Gloria Naylor, and many others.[12] But regardless of the present circumstances, it is difficult to find evidence for the emergence of a distinctive Afro-American domestic literary tradition or women's culture during the nineteenth and even the first half of the twentieth century.

Afro-American women have written of themselves as persons and as women under special conditions of colonization. In this respect, their writings cry out for comparison with those of white women. Prevailing opinion insists upon the special tradition of white American women's writing during the nineteenth and early twentieth centuries. Despite frequently sharp differences among feminist critics, there remains a general consensus that white women wrote themselves out of their domestic tradition in both senses of the phrase: they wrote from the experience, and they wrote to subvert the constraints it imposed upon them. It is not fashionable to insist upon the colonization of the imagination of white women writers, but it, too, has existed. For white women did suffer exclusion from the dominant cultural traditions and frequently from the educations and careers that provided the institutional foundations for equal participation in those traditions. That is a different problem, but it deserves mention as a way of locating the experience of black women in relation to the complexities of American culture as a system. It has been possible for feminist critics to pass briefly over white women's relation to the "high culture" of their period, in part, because of the general agreement about women's identification with literary domesticity. White women largely accepted the limitations of their sphere, sometimes turning the limitations to their advantage, and wrote either as representatives of its values, or for its other members, or both. However one assesses the value of their efforts and of their contributions (neglected, silenced) to American culture, it remains beyond dispute that they self-consciously wrote as women, as the representatives of a gender.[13]

For white American women, the self comes wrapped in gender, or rather, gender constitutes the invisible, seamless wrapping of the self. Such is the point of gender in a stable society. For in stable societies gender, in the sense of society's prescriptions for how to grow up as a man or as a woman, is inculcated in tandem with and indissolubly bound to the child's growing sense of "who I am." To be an "I" at all, to be a self, is to belong to a gender. Any society contains individuals who, for whatever reason, find their gender identification problematic. During the nineteenth and twentieth centuries, many American women began to question the attributes of or limitations on their gender. But, at least until World War II, most white American women apparently accepted their society's view of gender as in some deep way related to the persons they perceived themselves to be. For gender, understood as the social construction of sexuality, mediates between sexual identity and social identity—it binds the former to the latter and roots the latter in the former.

Under unstable social conditions, it is possible for gender, as a normative model of being male or female, to come unstuck from sexuality. Once the gaps between sexuality and gender begin to appear, men and women can begin to question whether gender flows naturally from sexuality, whether social demands on the individual are biologically determined. Gender identities derive from a system of gender relations. How to be a woman is defined in relation to how to be a man and the reverse. Neither masculinity nor femininity exists as an absolute.

In a society and culture like that of the United States, a dominant gender system or model of gender relations wrestles with various subsystems or alternate systems. But from at least the beginnings of the nineteenth century and the consolidation of the special American version of the ideology of separate spheres, the dominant model of gender relations has exercised hegemony, in part because of its importance as an alternative to class relations as a system of social classification, and in part because of its invitation to different groups of immigrants who brought with them one or another version of separate male and female spheres and a commitment to one or another form of male dominance. The hegemony of that gender system has influenced the ways in which most American women have written about themselves and their lives, and it especially has influenced their sense of their readers.

The experience and writings of Afro-American women have departed significantly from this model. For the experience of Afro-American women has left them simultaneously alienated from and bound to the dominant models in ways that sharply differentiate their experience from that of white women. There is no reason to believe that Afro-American women experienced gender as the seamless wrapping of their selves. Slavery bequeathed to Afro-American women a double view of gender relations that fully exposed the artificial or problematic aspects of gender identification. Slavery stripped black men of the social attributes of manhood in general and fatherhood in particular. As a result, black women had no satisfactory social definition of themselves as women. This social "unmanning" of the men, with its negative consequences for the women, should not be confused with the personal emasculation upon which some historians have erroneously insisted.[14] Sojourner Truth captured the contradictions in her address "Ar'n't I a Woman?" In effect Truth was insisting on her own femaleness and then querying the relation between her experience of being female and the white, middle-class experience of being a woman. She may not have put it quite that way, and she may not fully have elaborated the depths of the pain and the contradictions, but she exposed the main aspect of the problem: black slave women had suffered the pain of childbirth and the sorrow of losing children and had labored like men. Were they or were they not women?[15]

Truth's query has been widely recognized as a challenge to the possible self-satisfaction of middle-class men and women with respect to black slave women, who were not normally helped over puddles or wrapped in protective coverings. It has been recognized less widely as a challenge to assumptions about the nature of the links between femaleness and self-perception or identity in Afro-American women. Truth effectively chided white men and women for their racism—for not welcoming black women into the sisterhood of womanhood. But there is more to the story.

Truth counterposed "I"—the self—and "woman" in her hostile challenge to her white audience. Black female autobiographers have done the same, although not always with such open defiance. The tension at the heart of black women's autobiography derives in large part from the chasm between an autobiographer's intuitive sense of herself and her attitude toward her probable readers. Imagined readers shape the ways in which an autobiographer constructs the narrative of her life. Harriet Jacobs, in *Incidents in the Life of a Slave Girl*, left no doubt about the audience for whom she thought she was writing: "O, you happy free women, contrast *your* New Year's day with that of the poor bond-woman!" (14).

Jacobs wrote, at least in part, to introduce the world to the special horrors of slavery for women. To achieve her goal, she sought to touch the hearts of northern white women and, accordingly, wrote as far as possible in their idiom. She so doggedly followed the model of sentimental domestic fiction that for a long time it was assumed that her editor, Lydia Maria Child, had written the book. Jacobs's surviving correspondence proves that she, not Child, wrote her own story, as she claimed in its subtitle: "written by herself."[16] And Jacobs's text differs significantly in tone and content from other examples of domestic fiction. In particular, her withering indictment of slavery portrays the institution as a violation of womanhood. Time and again she not merely asserts but demonstrates that if slavery is bad for men, it is worse for women. Thinking that she understands the northern, middle-class female audience, she specifically relates the horrors of slavery for women to assaults upon female chastity and conjugal domesticity.

Linda Brent, Jacobs's self in the narrative, grows up in the shadow of her master's determination to possess her sexually. She claims to fend off his advances as an affront to her chastity. Ultimately, her determination to avoid him leads her, after her master has prohibited her sale and marriage to the free black man she loves, to accept another white man as a lover and to bear him two children. One important strand of her story concerns the ways in which she atones for this "fall" and, especially, regains the respect and love of her own daughter. In some sense Jacobs attempts to present her resistance to her master as a defense of her virtue, even though that defense leads her into a loss of "virtue" by another route. Jacobs does not fully resolve the contradictions in her behavior and principles at this level of discourse, however hard she tries. Ultimately, she throws herself on the pity—and guilt—of her readers, as she threw herself on the pity of her daughter. But Jacobs's text also invites another reading or, to put it differently, conceals another text.

Jacobs begins her narrative: "I was born a slave; but I never knew it till six years of happy childhood had passed away" (3). The claim not to have recognized one's condition—of race or of enslavement—until six or seven years of age is common among Afro-American authors.[17] For Jacobs, that opening sentence underscores the difference between condition and consciousness and thereby distances the self from the condition. But Jacobs never suggests that the condition does not, in some measure, influence the self. She insists that her father "had more of the feelings of a freeman than is common among slaves," thereby implicitly acknowledging the difference between slavery and freedom in the development of an independent self. In the same passage she reveals how heavily slavery could weigh upon the slave's sense of manhood. On one occasion Jacobs's father and mistress both happened to call her brother at the same moment. The boy, after a moment's hesitation, went to the mistress. The father sharply reproved him: "You are *my* child . . . and when I call you, you should come immediately, if you have to pass through fire and water" (7). The father's desire to command the primary obedience of his own child flows from his feelings of being a free man and contradicts the harshest realities of slavery. Slavery stripped men of fatherhood. Even a free father could not unambiguously call his child by a slave wife his own, for the child, following the condition of the mother, remained a slave. Jacobs is, surely not by accident, depicting a spirit of manliness and an instinctive grasp of the virtues of freedom in her father as the introduction to her own story of resistance.

Jacobs's narrative embodies every conceivable element of fantasy and ambiguity. Her father and mother were mulattoes who lived in a model of conjugal domesticity. Her maternal grandmother was the daughter of a South Carolina planter who apparently has inherited the lowcountry, slaveholding elite's own sense of honor—more than could be said for her owners. Jacobs, in other words, endows herself with a pedigree of physical, mental, and moral comeliness. She is not like the other slaves among whom she lives. She has the capacity to rise above her condition. Her sense of herself in relation to the other slaves leaves something to be desired for an opponent of slavery; worse, it reflects either her assimilation of "white" values or her determination to play to the prejudices of her audience. Jacobs offers a confused picture of the relation between the identity and behavior of Afro-Americans, including herself, and the effects of slavery. If slavery is evil, it has evil consequences. If those evil consequences include a breaking of the spirit of the enslaved, then how can slaves be credited with character and will? The questions circle on and on, admitting of no easy answers. Clearly they plague Jacobs.

These difficult questions do not seriously cloud Jacobs's sense of self. They do affect her sense of how best to present that self to others, her sense of the relation between her self and her gender, and her sense of the relation between self and social condition. The awareness of white readers deeply influences the ways in which she depicts life under slavery. But under, or woven through, the discourse for the readers runs a discourse for herself. For Jacobs herself, the primary issue between her and her master was not one of virtue, chastity, sexuality, or any of the rest. It was the conflict of two wills. Having described her master's foul intentions toward her, she adds that he had told her "I was made for his use, made to obey his command in *every* thing; that I was nothing but a slave, whose will must and should surrender to his." (16). The words make her "puny" arm feel stronger than it ever had: "The war of my life had begun; and though one of God's most powerless creatures, I resolved never to be conquered. Alas, for me!" (17). The "alas for me" should not be read as regret about her determination or as any acknowledgement that such willful feelings might be inappropriate for a woman, but as a confirmation that everything that follows stems directly from her determination not to be conquered.

Jacobs's narrative of her successful flight from slavery can be read as a journey or progress from her initial state of innocence; through the mires of her struggle against her social condition; to a prolonged period of ritual, or mythic, concealment; on to the flight itself; and finally to the state of knowledge that accompanies her ultimate acquisition of freedom. The myth or metaphor of the journey to selfhood is as old as culture, although it has carried a special resonance for Western Christian, notably Protestant, culture. Jacobs, in some respects like Harriet Wilson, registers the end of the journey as a somewhat bleak dawn on a troubled landscape. Here is no pot of gold at the end of the rainbow. The accrued self-knowledge consists above all in the recognition that there is no resting place for the fugitive. The struggle for the dignity of the self persists. Insults and injuries abound in freedom as under slavery, albeit in different forms. Life remains a war. But the focused struggle of wills with the master has given way to a more generalized struggle to affirm the self in a hostile, or indifferent, environment.

Significantly, Harriet Wilson, whose narrative unfolds entirely in freedom, portrays the primary enemy as a woman rather than a man. To explore the respective cultural roles of men and women as heads of households in slave and free society would take us far afield. But the difference should be noted, not least because Wilson's enemy represents the world of female domesticity and, inescapably, underscores the possible adversarial relation between the Afro-American female autobiographer and her readers.[18] Wilson's narrative remains even more problematical as autobiography than Jacobs's, for it is cast as a fiction—and it remains, overall, far more disturbing. I can only note in passing that its structure commands close attention, especially Wilson's purpose in beginning with the story of her white mother, Mag Smith, who, as the only alternative to starvation, married a black man who loves her.

Taken together, Jacobs's and Wilson's narratives establish some important characteristics of black women's autobiographical writing. Both use the metaphor of the journey. Both betray mixed emotions toward their probable and intended (white, female) readers. Both embrace some of the rhetoric and conventions of literary domesticity even as they challenge the reigning pieties of its discourse. Both subvert the promised candor toward those readers.

The problem of readers, of those for whom one writes, persists in the autobiographical writing of black women, although it assumes a variety of forms. Writing in the late 1960s, Maya Angelou noted in an apparent aside in the first volume of her own autobiography: "If you ask a negro where he's been, he'll tell you where he's going" (86). Her observation should be appreciated in the context of Zora Neale Hurston's calling storytelling "lying"—and then offering the world her own demonstrably inaccurate autobiography.[19]

Hurston's autobiography poignantly captures the dilemmas that seemed to confront black women writers—or intellectuals—of her generation. Dust Tracks on a Road inimitably combines all the best and worst of Hurston's intellect and imagination. Critics and scholars have demonstrated that it does not pass muster as a factual account of her life, beginning with its inaccurate recording of her date of birth. Theoretically, that mere inaccuracy should not matter to modern critics of the text-in-itself: take the text on its merits and to hell with the facts. But Hurston's deceptions in Dust Tracks may exceed mere facts. She embellishes the text with a series of observations on contemporary politics and race relations that have seriously disturbed some of her most devoted would-be admirers. Finally, although Hurston wrote much more in the idiom of Afro-American culture, even of folk culture, than Jacobs or Wilson, her text does not inspire confidence in the "authenticity" of her self-revelation. In most respects, Dust Tracks constitutes a marvel of self-concealment. Hurston, like the storytellers on the porch whom she celebrated in Mules and Men, delighted in "lying."

As the single most important link between the different phases in black women's autobiographies, Hurston's autobiography commands at least a preliminary assessment.[20] Hurston should be understood as a woman who was, regarding her self-representation, concerned primarily with a "self" unconstrained by gender in particular and condition in general. Her life made her an expert on anger and fear. Determined to become a respected person, to become someone, she wrestled—not always gracefully or successfully—with the expectations of those around her. In mediating between the world of Eatonville from which she came and the worlds of Baltimore, Washington, and New York to which she moved, she functioned as a translator. In fact, Hurston used her acquired skills as an anthropologist to describe the world of her childhood. Her uncommon gift for language brought that world to life in her pages, but her obsession with self-concealment led her to veil the nature of her identification with her origins. Hurston's narrator is her statue—the amused observer she wished to become.

Hurston's autobiography singularly lacks any convincing picture of her own feelings. Her little essay on "love," which purports to convey her adult feelings toward men, reads like the amused and balanced memories of a perfectly successful individual. Men are presented as having loved her even more than she loved them. Love is portrayed as having invariably treated her well. She gives no hint of bitter disappointment, longing, or crippling loss. Maybe she suffered none, although extratextual sources invite skepticism. But the passage itself looks more like a screen than a window. There is nothing in *Dust Tracks* to suggest that Hurston trusted her readers. She never precisely identifies them, although she cultivates an arresting mixture of the urbane intellectual and the *enfant terrible*. Presumably she expected to be read by New York intellectuals, black and white. And, presumably, she was not about to trust them with her private self.

Hurston provides clues about where she wants to go, what kind of statue she wants to build. She resoundingly repudiates any possible connection between slavery and her own life or self-representation. Slavery, however unfortunate, belongs to a past that has left no relevant legacy: "I have no personal memory of those times, and no responsibility for them" (282). Above all, she fears the debilitating effects of bitterness; to be bitter is to become dependent, crippled, humiliated. She appears to have forgotten her own earlier evocation of the "broom of anger," appears not to want to explore the place of righteous anger in her responses. The purpose of the broom of anger was to sweep away fear, and she is no longer acknowledging fear. By collapsing anger into bitterness and repudiating bitterness as, in some way, an unclean emotion, she is denying the need for anger. Facing the white reader, she prefers to deny the relevance of previous oppression to her sense of herself. Just as clearly as Jacobs, she expects "you" (her reader) to be white: "So I give you all my right hand of fellowship and love. . . . In my eyesight, you lose nothing by not looking just like me. . . . Let us all be kissing-friends" (286).

Hurston also refuses to attribute any significance to race. Having been bombarded with the problem of race for years, she saw the light when she "realized that I did not have to consider any racial group as a whole. God made them duck by duck and that was the only way I could see them" (235). She learned that the color of the skin provided no measure of the person inside, even though she acerbically points out that blacks, like whites, rank blacks according to the degree of lightness of their skin. She then reminds her readers that she is of mixed race. Finally, with deep ambiguity, she asserts: "I maintain that I have been a Negro three times—a Negro baby, a Negro girl and a Negro woman." Yet she knows not what "the Negro in America is like" (237). The Negro does not exist. Independent of its political problems—and Hurston's politics were nothing if not complex—this statement creates considerable doubt about her identification as a woman. If the Negro does not exist, and the only times that she has been a Negro included the times at which she was a girl and a woman, then what? The reader is left to complete the syllogism.

Dust Tracks constitutes only one panel in the triptych of Hurston's autobiography. The second can be found in her extraordinary novel, *Their Eyes Were Watching God*, and the third in her collections of black folklore, notably *Mules and Men*. Hurston's collections of folklore provide a way for her to appropriate the collective history of the community to which she belongs. *Their Eyes Were Watching God*, which is widely recognized as an autobiographical novel, offers her most sustained attempt to provide some representation of her own emotional life. Here, evoking the novel as an indispensable counterpoint to *Dust Tracks*, I would emphasize one theme. In the book's most famous passage, the protagonist Janie's grandmother says: "Honey, de white man is de ruler of everything as fur as Ah been able tuh find out." There may be some place "way off in de ocean" in which the black man rules, "but we don't know nothin' but what we see." The white man throws down his load and forces the black man to pick it up. "He pick it up because he have to, but he don't tote it. He hand it to his womenfolks. De nigger woman is de mule uh de world so fur as Ah can see" (29). Janie's grandmother has been praying that things will be different with her. Hurston portrays the answer to that prayer as Janie's relations with Teacake—a mutual delight in shared sexuality.

The world that Hurston depicts in *Their Eyes Were Watching God* closely resembles Maya Angelou's Stamps, Arkansas. Hurston does not emphasize the oppressive weight of the neighboring white community as much as Angelou does, but she does not shy away from its influence on the possible conditions of black lives, even in an entirely black community. And her plot mercilessly reveals the burdens that a legacy of slavery and racism impose on black people. In particular she subtly, almost deceptively, offers hints of her real feelings about what it means to be a black woman. She reveals the extent to which the black community—or black men—have embraced the gender conventions of white bourgeois society. Black men seek to transfer their burdens to black women by forcing those women into domestic corsets. A woman like Janie resists. She retains her commitment to equality and partnership with the man she loves. Above all, she retains a commitment to the possible joy of love and sexuality. But even at her moment of greatest success, the legacy of the social features of black manhood leads Teacake into a terrible battle. At the novel's close, which is also its beginning, she is returning home to other black women—alone and childless. Mules. Are they metaphors or reality? Mules abound in Hurston's work. Is she inviting us to understand black women like herself as being of mixed ancestry and incapable of reproduction? Is she inviting us—as she seems to be—to recognize both the richness and the dead-endedness of black women's own traditions? To attempt a clear answer would seem to be premature, but the elements of the puzzle should not be denied.

Throughout *Dust Tracks*, Hurston provides numerous clues that her primary identification, her primary sense of herself, transcends gender. Most dramatically, in a passage reminiscent of other tales of mythic births on mythically stormy nights, she relates that at her birth her mother was unprepared and without assistance.[21] Fate intervened by sending "a white man of many acres and things" to "granny" for her mother—to fill in for the missing midwife, Aunt Judy. It is a tale of wonderful reversals: Zora was brought into the world by a man rather than a woman, by a white rather than a black. The chapter in which she relates her birth concludes with a passage about her mother's alarm that at an early age Zora manifested a clear tendency to keep on walking toward the horizon. The mother explained this behavior by blaming "a woman who was an enemy of hers" for sprinkling "'travel dust' around the doorstep the day I was born." Zora wonders at her mother's acceptance of such an explanation. "I don't know why it never occurred to her to connect my tendency with my father, who didn't have a thing on his mind but this town and the next one." She might have taken a hint from his wanderlust. "Some children are just bound to take after their fathers in spite of women's prayers" (32).

Hurston vacillates among sympathy, scorn, and amused tolerance in her discussion of the women of the black community from which she springs. She movingly depicts her grief and guilt at her own inability to carry out her dying mother's instructions due to the opposition of the other members of the black community. And she clearly links her own departure from the world of her childhood with her mother's death. She shows flashes of tenderness. But her identification with other black women remains shaky. She refuses the double role of victim and warrior that Jacobs constructs for herself. For Hurston to admit the conditions or causes of her possible victimization is to belittle herself. But her goals for herself—her statue—remain shaped by that refusal: she aspires, in some way, to transcend the constraints of group identification. By insisting on being a self independent of history, race, and gender, she comes close to insisting on being a self independent of body.

Hurston wrote under the influence of the Harlem Renaissance and the increasingly successful attempts of Afro-American men to establish a model of cultural respectability, and she wrote under the shadow of emerging professional successes for some middle-class white women. That is, she sought to carve a compelling statue for herself at a particular historical moment. Much like Harriet Jacobs, she pictured herself at war with the world in her attempt to defend her integrity. Much like Harriet Jacobs, she refused the limitations of gender and cultivated what she took to be the language of her readers only to subvert—or manipulate—their values. But where Jacobs warred with slavery, Hurston warred with a dominant bourgeois culture in which she sought acceptance as an equal. No less than Jacobs, Hurston warred with the legacy of slavery for black women. But changing times had made it difficult for her to name that war. And, unable or unwilling to name it, she spun web upon web of deception so that her statue of herself would appear to be standing in clouds.

Those who came after—especially Angelou, Giovanni, and Brooks—would find new names for the war and a new acceptance of their own black female bodies. But they would also benefit from the slow emergence of black women readers. And even they would remain at odds with the gender identifications of white society. The gap between black women and the dominant model of womanhood continues to add richness and mystery to black women's writing. The account of origins remains, at least in part, a map of "where I'm bound." The account of the black woman's self cannot be divorced from the history of that self or the history of the people among whom it took shape. It also cannot be divorced from the language through which it is represented, or from the readers of other classes and races who not only lay claim to it but who have helped to shape it. To write the account of one's self is to inscribe it in a culture that for each of us is only partially our own. For black women autobiographers, the gap between the self and the language in which it is inscribed looms especially large and remains fraught with struggle.

Above all, black women's autobiographies suggest a tension in black women's relations to various dominant discourses. Jacobs and Wilson both self-consciously sought to work within bourgeois women's domestic discourse, even as they subverted its deepest premises about the relation between the female self and gender. Their concern for discursive respectability persisted in the works of many black women from Reconstruction to the 1920s and flowered in the works of Jessie Fauset and Nella Larsen. This concern should be understood in the context of black people's struggle for respect within the confines of dominant American bourgeois conventions, even if the female embodiments of the tradition invariably, if covertly, challenged its stereotypical views of gender relations and gender identity. Hurston makes explicit two contradictory and submerged elements of that tradition: first, and most visibly, she restores funkiness and folk roots to black women's discourse; second, and no less important, she dares to articulate black women's craving for independent recognition in the republic of letters. Recent critics have reminded us that Harriet Beecher Stowe and Susan Warner deserve considerably more respect than the dominant (male) tradition chose to accord them.[22] But Hurston also had her eyes on the pinnacles of the prestigious tradition of Western letters, on Shakespeare and his canonized successors. Even her representation of black women's private selves was informed with this ambition. Her difficulty in clearly depicting her own statue resulted at least in part from the deadlock between her commitment to her roots as a black woman in a black community and her commitment to transcending all social and gender roots in her craft. In her fictional and anthropological writings, she could distance herself as artist—as translator—from the immediacy of her material. When she came to depict herself, the strategy faltered. How could she bear to lay bare that private self for which the canon allowed no position of respect? Nevertheless, the best clue to the essence of that private self lies in the troubling autobiography, which, more than all the other writings, reveals the struggles that wracked the self, even if it does not directly testify to them—does not, as it were, confess.

Few have written more movingly or with greater anger of the toll extracted by cultural colonization than Franz Fanon. Fanon, in particular, walked the narrow boundary between recording the dreadful impact of specific instances of colonization and raising the concept of colonization to the status of a metaphor for the dependent status of all subgroups in a dominant culture. The autobiographies of Afro-American women similarly delineate a specific history of colonization and offer a compelling metaphor for the human spirit's dependency on the communities and forms of expression to which it belongs. Black women like Jacobs and Wilson insisted on their right to an independent self under conditions in which they could counterpoise the self to enslavement. Since emancipation, black women have been torn between their independent relation to the dominant culture and their people's relation to it. In complex ways, their self-perceptions retain a characteristically uneasy relation to the wrappings of gender. Is the black woman writer first a self, a solitary statue? Or is she first a woman—and if so, in relation to whom? No dilemma could more clearly expose the condition of any self as hostage to society, politics, and language.

Notes

1. See Walker, *In Search of Our Mothers' Gardens*. On new directions in black feminist criticism, see Smith; McDowell.

2. See Miller.

3. Black women's "autobiographies," as used here, includes some autobiographical fiction as well as formal autobiographies, both streams of which have sources in a rich oral Afro-American culture.

4. I am using *gender* to mean the social construction of sexuality.

5. For my own views on autobiography as a genre, see Fox-Genovese, *Autobiography of Du Pont de Nemours*, 38–51. Among the many other recent works on autobiography, see Olney, *Autobiography*; Weintraub; Lejeune; Gunn; Stone; and—for a review of recent critical trends—Lang, "Autobiography in the Aftermath of Romanticism."

6. The quintessential statement of the position remains Michel Foucault, "Qu'est-ce un auteur?" For a feminist defense of deconstruction in terms of the Third World, see Spivak, "'Draupadi,'" but for a defense of the claims of gender and race, see her "Politics of Interpretation."

7. On the general problem of black women's autobiography, see Blackburn.

8. See Stepto. This article was apparently reprinted in the Davis collection from Stepto's *From Behind the Veil: A Study of Afro-American Narrative* (Urbana: University of Illinois Press, 1979).

9. Brooks's autobiography should be read in conjunction with her autobiographical novel, *Maud Martha.* See also Washington; Christian, *Black Literature and Literary Theory* and *Black Feminist Criticism.*

10. The phrase "demon slavery" is from Harriet Wilson, *Our Nig.*

11. See Tompkins, *Reader-Response Criticism*; Flynn and Schweickart, *Gender and Reading.*

12. See Christian, *Black Women Novelists*, for a preliminary periodization. For a sharp assessment of the relation between one black novelist and her readers, see Harris.

13. The work on white women's writing, in sharp contrast to that on black women's writing, has grown extensive. Among many, see Baym, Kelley, and Kolodny.

14. See Elkins, in particular. Elkins has not significantly revised his position in the two subsequent editions of *Slavery.* See, for instance, Lane. For alternate views on the effect of slavery on Afro-American men, see Harding and Genovese.

15. For a recent overview of women's position under slavery, see White.

16. See Yellin, "Texts and Contexts" and "Written by Herself." Henceforth, Yellin's edition of *Incidents* will be the standard, but it did not appear in time for me to use it in this essay. For Jacobs's account of her experience and authorship, see her correspondence in the Post family papers, University of Rochester Library. Dorothy Sterling has reprinted some of Jacobs's letters in her excellent anthology, *We Are Your Sisters.* On the general tradition of the slave narrative, see, among many, Starling; Sekora and Turner; Olney, "'I Was Born'"; Baker; and Davis, "The Slave Narrative." As a rule, treatments of slave narratives take little or no account of any female perception, in part because so few women either escaped or wrote narratives.

17. See, among many, Hurston's *Their Eyes Were Watching God*: "Ah was wid dem white chillun so much till Ah didn't know Ah wuzn't white till Ah was round six years old" (21).

18. See Gates's introduction to *Our Nig.* He offers a preliminary exploration of the role of white women in the novel but does not discuss the problem of Wilson's attitude toward her readers. For a fuller discussion of the differences between women's roles in northern and southern households, see Fox-Genovese, *Within the Plantation Household.*

19. On the facts of Hurston's life and the variants of the text, see Hemmenway's introduction to *Dust Tracks*; see also his comprehensive study of her life and work, *Zora Neale Hurston.* For a composite picture of Hurston culled from her own writings, see Walker, *I Love Myself When I Am Laughing.* See also

Walker's essay on Hurston in *In Search of Our Mothers' Gardens*; Johnson, "Metaphor, Metonymy, and Voice"; Hurston, *Tell My Horse*.

20. On the successive phases of Afro-American women's writing, see Mc-Caskill. The generation of Afro-American women writers that preceded Hurston, including Frances Ellen Watkins Harper, Amanda Smith, Julia Foote, Elizabeth Keckley, and Bethany Veney, focused on racial uplift and on proving the respectability of Afro-American womanhood.

21. Black women writers' use of African and Western myths deserves more attention than it has yet received. Angelou, for example, in *Gather Together in My Name*, reworks the Persephone myth for her own purposes. Jacobs, in the account of her period of concealment and flight, draws on African mythology. Gates's concept of the "signifying monkey" opens the discussion but does not pay special attention to the blending of cultures in Afro-American women's imaginations (see his "The 'Blackness of Blackness'" and *The Signifying Monkey*). For a sensitive discussion of Afro-American culture, see Levine.

22. See Tompkins; and Ann Douglas's introduction to Stowe.

Works Cited

Angelou, Maya. *I Know Why the Caged Bird Sings*. New York: Random House, 1969.

———. *Gather Together in My Name*. New York: Random House, 1974.

Baker, Houston A., Jr. "Autobiographical Acts and the Voice of the Southern Slave." In Davis, 242–61.

Baym, Nina. *Woman's Fiction: A Guide to Novels by and about Women in America, 1820–1870*. Ithaca: Cornell University Press, 1978.

Blackburn, Regina. "In Search of the Black Female Self: African-American Women's Autobiographies and Ethnicity." In Jelinek, 133–48.

Brooks, Gwendolyn. *Maud Martha*. Boston: Atlantic Monthly Press, 1953.

———. *Report from Part One*. Detroit: Broadside Press, 1972.

Christian, Barbara. *Black Feminist Criticism: Perspectives on Black Women Writers*. New York: Pergamon Press, 1985.

———. *Black Women Novelists: The Development of a Tradition, 1892–1976*. Westport: Greenwood Press, 1980.

———. *Perspectives on Black Women Writers*. New York: Pergamon Press, 1985.

Cudjoe, Selwyn R. "Maya Angelou and the Autobiographical Statement." In Evans, 6–24.

Davis, Charles T. "The Slave Narrative: First Major Art Form in an Emerging Black Tradition." In Davis and Gates, 83–119.

———. *Black Is the Color of the Cosmos: Essays on Afro-American Literature and Culture, 1942–1981.* Ed. Henry Louis Gates. New York: Garland Publishing, 1982.

Davis, Charles T., and Henry Louis Gates, eds. *The Slave's Narrative.* New York: Oxford University Press, 1985.

Elkins, Stanley. *Slavery: A Problem in American Institutional and Intellectual Life.* Chicago: University of Chicago Press, 1959.

Evans, Mari. *Black Women Writers (1950–1980).* Garden City: Anchor Books, 1984.

Flynn, Elizabeth A., and Patrocinio P. Schweickart. *Gender and Reading: Essays on Readers, Texts, and Contexts.* Baltimore: Johns Hopkins University Press, 1986.

Foucault, Michel. "Qu'est-ce un auteur?" *Bulletin de la Société Française de Philosophie* 63.3 (1969): 75–104.

Fox-Genovese, Elizabeth. *Within the Plantation Household: Black and White Women of the Old South.* Chapel Hill: University of North Carolina Press, 1988.

————, ed. and trans. *The Autobiography of Du Pont de Nemours.* Wilmington: Scholarly Resources Press, 1984.

Gates, Henry Louis, Jr. "The 'Blackness of Blackness': A Critique of the Sign and the Signifying Monkey." *Critical Inquiry* 9.4 (1983): 685–724.

————, ed. *Black Literature and Literary Theory.* New York: Methuen, 1984.

Genovese, Eugene D. *Roll, Jordan, Roll: The World the Slaves Made.* New York: Pantheon, 1974.

Gilbert, Olive, comp. *Narrative of Sojourner Truth: A Bondswoman of Olden Time.* 1878. New York: Arno Press, 1968.

Giovanni, Nikki. *Gemini: An Extended Autobiographical Statement on My First Twenty-Five Years of Being a Black Poet.* Indianapolis: Bobbs-Merrill, 1971.

Griffiths, Mattie. *Autobiography of a Female Slave.* 1857. Miami: Mnemosyne, 1969.

Gunn, Janet Varner. *Autobiography: Toward a Poetics of Experience.* Philadelphia: University of Pennsylvania Press, 1982.

Harding, Vincent. *There Is a River: The Black Struggle for Freedom in America.* New York: Harcourt Brace Jovanovich, 1981.

Harris, Trudier. "On *The Color Purple,* Stereotypes, and Silence." *Black American Literature Forum* 18.4 (1984): 155–61.

Hemenway, Robert. *Zora Neale Hurston: A Literary Biography.* Urbana: University of Illinois Press, 1977.

Hurston, Zora Neale. *Dust Tracks on a Road: An Autobiography.* 1942. Ed. Robert Hemmenway. 2d ed. Urbana: University of Illinois Press, 1984.

————. *Mules and Men.* 1935. New York: Harper and Row, 1970.

————. *Tell My Horse.* 1938. Berkeley: Turtle Island, 1981.

————. *Their Eyes Were Watching God.* 1937. Urbana: University of Illinois Press, 1978.

Jacobs, Harriet [Linda Brent]. *Incidents in the Life of a Slave Girl, Written by Herself*. Ed. Lydia Maria Child. 1861. New ed. Walter Teller. New York: Harcourt Brace Jovanovich, 1973.

———. *Incidents in the Life of a Slave Girl, Written by Herself*. Ed. Jean Fagan Yellin. Cambridge: Harvard University Press, 1987.

Jelinek, Estelle, ed. *Women's Autobiography: Essays in Criticism*. Bloomington: Indiana University Press, 1980.

Johnson, Barbara. "Metaphor, Metonymy and Voice in *Their Eyes Were Watching God*." In Gates, *Black Literature* 205–20.

Kelley, Mary. *Private Woman, Public Stage: Literary Domesticity in Nineteenth-Century America*. New York: Oxford University Press, 1984.

Kolodny, Annette. *The Land Before Her: Fantasy and Experience of the American Frontiers, 1630–1860*. Chapel Hill: University of North Carolina Press, 1984.

Lane, Ann J., ed. *The Debate over Slavery: Stanley Elkins and His Critics*. Urbana: University of Illinois Press, 1971.

Lang, Candace. "Autobiography in the Aftermath of Romanticism." *Diacritics* 12 (Winter 1982): 2–16.

Lejeune, Philippe. *Le pacte autobiographique*. Paris: Editions du Seuil, 1975.

Levine, Lawrence W. *Black Culture and Black Consciousness: Afro-American Folk Thought from Slavery to Freedom*. New York: Oxford University Press, 1977.

McCaskill, Barbara. "Eternity for Telling: Topological Traditions in Afro-American Women's Literature." Ph.D. diss., Emory University, 1988.

McConnell-Ginet, Sally, Ruth Borker, and Nelly Furman, eds. *Women and Language in Literature and Society*. New York: Praeger, 1980.

McDowell, Deborah E. "New Directions for Black Feminist Criticism." In Showalter, 186–99.

Miller, Nancy K. "Women's Autobiography in France: For a Dialectics of Identification." In McConnell-Ginet et al., 258–73.

Olney, James. *Autobiography: Essays Theoretical and Critical*. Princeton: Princeton University Press, 1980.

———. "'I Was Born': Slave Narratives, Their Status as Autobiography and as Literature." In Davis and Gates, 148–75.

Sekora, John, and Darwin T. Turner, eds. *The Art of Slave Narrative*. Macomb: Northern Illinois University Press, 1982.

Showalter, Elaine, ed. *Feminist Criticism: Essays on Women, Literature, Theory*. New York: Pantheon, 1985.

Smith, Barbara. "Toward a Black Feminist Criticism." In Showalter, 168–85.

Soyinka, Wole. "The Critic and Society: Barthes, Leftocracy and Other Mythologies." In Gates, *Black Literature* 27–58.

Spivak, Gayatri Chakravorty. "'Drapaudi' by Mahasveta Devi." *Critical Inquiry* 8.2 (1981): 381–402.

———. "The Politics of Interpretation." *Critical Inquiry* 9.1 (1982): 259–78.

Starling, Marion Wilson. *The Slave Narrative: Its Place in History.* Boston: G. K. Hall, 1981.

Stepto, Robert Burns. "I Rose and Found My Voice: Narration, Authentication, and Authorial Control in Four Slave Narratives." In Davis and Gates, 225–41.

Sterling, Dorothy, ed. *We Are Your Sisters: Black Women in the Nineteenth Century.* New York: Norton, 1984.

Stone, Albert E. *Autobiographical Occasions and Original Acts.* Philadelphia: University of Pennsylvania Press, 1982.

Stowe, Harriet Beecher. *Uncle Tom's Cabin or, Life among the Lowly.* 1852. New York: Penguin, 1981.

Tate, Claudia, ed. *Black Women Writers at Work.* New York: Continuum, 1983.

Thompson, Era Bell. *American Daughter.* Rev. ed. Chicago: University of Chicago Press, 1967.

Tompkins, Jane P., ed. *Reader-Response Criticism: From Formalism to Post-Structuralism.* Baltimore: Johns Hopkins University Press, 1980.

———. *Sensational Designs: The Cultural Work of American Fiction 1790–1860.* New York: Oxford University Press, 1985.

Walker, Alice. *In Search of Our Mothers' Gardens: Womanist Prose.* New York: Harcourt Brace Jovanovich, 1983.

———. "Looking for Zora." In Walker, *In Search of Our Mothers' Gardens.*

———. "Zora Neale Hurston: A Cautionary Tale and a Partisan Review." In Walker, *In Search of Our Mothers' Gardens.*

———, ed. *I Love Myself When I Am Laughing . . . and Then Again When I Am Looking Mean and Impressive: A Zora Neale Hurston Reader.* Old Westbury: Feminist Press, 1979.

Washington, Mary Helen. "'Taming All That Anger Down': Rage and Silence in Gwendolyn Brooks' *Maud Martha.*" In Gates, *Black Literature* 249–62.

Weintraub, Karl H. *The Value of the Individual: Self and Circumstance in Autobiography.* Chicago: University of Chicago Press, 1978.

Wells, Ida B. *The Autobiography of Ida B. Wells.* Ed. Alfred M. Duster. Chicago: University of Chicago Press, 1970.

White, Deborah G. *Ar'n't I a Woman: Female Slaves in the Plantation South.* New York: Norton, 1985.

Wilson, Harriet E. *Our Nig: Or, Stretches from the Life of a Free Black, in a Two-Story White House, North. Showing That Slavery's Shadows Fall Even There. By "Our Nig."* Ed. Henry Louis Gates. New York: Vintage, 1983.

Yellin, Jean Fagan. "Texts and Contexts of Harriet Jacobs' *Incidents in the Life of a Slave Girl: Written by Herself.*" In Davis and Gates, 262–82.

———. "Written By Herself: *Harriet Jacobs' Slave Narrative.*" *American Literature* 53.3 (1981): 479–86.

Simone de Beauvoir
Aging and Its Discontents

Kathleen Woodward

"Young" and "old" now appear to me to be the greatest opposites of which human life is capable, and an understanding between the representatives of each is impossible.
—Sigmund Freud, letter to Ernest Jones, 3 May 1928

Like *The Second Sex*, Simone de Beauvoir's *The Coming of Age* is an original and prodigious contribution to critiques of the oppression of one social group by another in the twentieth-century industrial West. Importantly for our purposes, both books arose out of Beauvoir's desire to write from the base of her own experience, which led her, unerringly, to two of the most pressing social issues of our time: the subjection of women and the devaluation of the elderly. Yet while *The Second Sex* is still read today, *The Coming of Age*, which went out of print several years ago, has been virtually ignored by intellectuals and academics in the United States—even by those who are interested in the work of Beauvoir. This lacuna I have long found puzzling. More generally, among the categories of social division in a given culture and historical period (we may include race, gender, class, and age) only *age* has remained invisible, not subject to analysis. Yet for women it is especially important to think carefully about what it means to grow old in Western culture, because it is then that we are necessarily subject to—at the minimum— a double marginality. Aging—how we define ourselves as women as our social roles, our bodies, and our subjectivities change over time—is one of the great autobiographical themes, and one which has not received sufficient attention.

The encyclopedic *La Vieillesse* (the title under which the book was published in France in 1970) explores the roots of the dismaying treatment of the elderly in the West with a breadth of investigation that is stunning. Beauvoir's research extends to ethology, anthropology, biology, psychology, and psychoanalysis, as well as to the literary and artistic record. Significantly, in refusing to sentimentalize old age, she calls received opinion into question, concluding (among other things): that tribal cultures and the ancient civilizations of Greece and Rome did not sanctify old age per se, but rather granted status to the elderly on the basis of their power; that the elderly are without value in capitalist societies because they do not contribute significantly to the business of production; and that today's evaluation of the elderly is yet another symptom of the decay of Western civilization as a whole. An omnibus volume of research (much of which was conducted at the Bibliothèque Nationale in Paris), *The Coming of Age* is a manifesto for social action. Its tone is passionate, not balanced. But Beauvoir's salutary polemical purpose would not seem to fully account for her hostile and bitterly dark portrait of old age.

Thus *The Coming of Age*, notwithstanding the undeniable importance of its contribution to the study of aging and the politics of the elderly, must be read critically and, given the concerns of this book, in the context of her other writing as well. I read her representation of old age, in great part, as a symptom of personal concerns and obsessions, as a *figure* on which she has both projected her subjectivity and displaced her anxieties. For as we will see, her personal concern with aging manifested itself long before she began systematic research on the subject at the age of sixty. Beauvoir perceived herself as aging—as an old woman, in fact—long before anyone (except, of course, a child) could possibly have considered her old. This is all the more noteworthy because one of her major points in *The Coming of Age* is that we are made aware of our old age only by the gaze of the other, by seeing ourselves reflected in the eyes of others or by seeing ourselves in the mirror as though through the eyes of a stranger. She theorizes that the shock of recognition of our own old age comes to us from outside ourselves. But in her other work, she speaks of aging and old age as a depressive state of mind that periodically invades the imagination just as old age will ultimately take up residence in the body.

Many of us use old age as a metaphor for a temporary lack of enthusiasm or interest in life—"I must be getting old," we will say—but Beauvoir is unusually literal when she uses this commonplace expression. In her second volume of memoirs—entitled, ironically enough, *The Prime of Life* and published in 1960, when she was fifty-two—she writes about her late twenties, the years before she had published the first of her twenty-odd books: "I was getting old. Neither my general health nor my facial appearance bore witness to the fact, but from time to time I felt everything was going gray and colorless around me and began to lament the decrepitude of my senses" (168). Just as Freud was obsessed with certain ages at which he felt he was destined to die, Beauvoir experienced crisis points to which she referred as moments of aging. Typically she emerged from these crises by plunging into one of her projects, by writing. Referring in *The Prime of Life* to her depression in her late twenties, she observes, "I would not have had the feeling of aging and marking time if I had gone out into the world instead of isolating myself within my own private routine" (174). Of the novel she began, *She Came to Stay*, she says that it "embodied my future, and I moved toward this goal with effortless speed; I no longer thought of myself as old at all" (274).

The Prime of Life concludes on Beauvoir's terror of death, a preoccupation dating from early childhood. The origin of that terror was an existential insight: it occurred in the realm of thought rather than by way of *la force des choses*—the experience of the death of people close to her. Death later became associated in her mind with old age, and the relationship between the two helps explain the intensity of Beauvoir's fear of aging. Given the economy of her psychic life, it seems no accident that her third volume of memoirs, *La Force des Choses*, published when she was fifty-five, closed on the despairing note of old age. Indeed, the entire book is a chronicle of the crises of aging that she experienced between the ages of thirty-five and forty-five. She tells us that when she was thirty-six she calmly accepted the fact that she was old—although we cannot believe her: "I was old . . . a fact I noted without the slightest bitterness" (11). But at forty-two she ended her affair with Nelson Algren, and her fears of old age, now linked in her mind with disease, surface again: "I had become an object of horror in my own eyes. Why? Why? Why must I wake up every morning filled with rage and pain, infected to the very marrow of my bones with a disease I could neither accept nor exorcise?" (584).

I will not dwell on the many signs of Beauvoir's preoccupation with aging that permeate her memoirs, the middle two volumes in particular. But before turning to specific aspects of her characterization of old age in *The Coming of Age*, I do want to note that her concern with aging also pervades her fiction. The most striking example is her novel, *All Men Are Mortal*, published in France in 1946 when she was thirty-eight. A peculiar blend of fantasy and the novel of ideas, this book is Beauvoir's version of the myth of Prometheus, who was chained to a rock for disobeying the gods and was subjected to nightly mutilation. The moral of Beauvoir's version of the tale is not that death is a good (we would not expect this from her) but rather that interminable age is an excruciating punishment because one is repeatedly subjected to the pain of losing an important part of oneself, losses for which there is no restitution. In her best-known novel, *The Mandarins*, the theme of old age is also important: the thirty-nine-year-old psychoanalyst Anna Dubreuilh sinks into a deep depression, believing that old age, and thus death in life, is lying in wait for her and that, like everyone else, she will soon cross that black line separating middle age from old age—at forty! And in two of Beauvoir's later books of fiction—the novel *Les Belles images* (1956) and the collection of three short stories entitled *The Woman Destroyed* (published in France in 1967 under the title *La Femme rompue*)—the psychological horror of aging for women in their forties, fifties, and early sixties is the dominant theme.

Throughout Beauvoir's life as a writer, old age served her as a metaphor for disease, depression, and death. When she undertook the study of old age as a literal condition, it remained charged with the intensity with which she had earlier invested it. To be sure, there is a truth here: the category "old age" is rooted in the personal imagination as well as the physical world of the body and the social order. But in *The Coming of Age*, Beauvoir makes the mistake of unconsciously merging the metaphorical and the literal. (Unlike Susan Sontag, whose *Illness as Metaphor* shows how harmful it is to use such words as "cancer" to describe conditions other than the clinical disease, Beauvoir, I think, would have been incapable of writing a book on old age as metaphor.) While I do not deny the tragic view to which she subscribes, for me the real questions are what lies behind her obsession and how does it bias her view of old age? In the following pages I focus on three aspects of old age in *The Coming of Age*—physical deterioration, memory loss, and the loss of others—in the context of her work, especially her memoirs. My purpose is not to accuse Beauvoir of contradictions between what might be called the theory of *The Coming of Age* and her experience as presented to us in her more overtly autobiographical writing. Rather, it is to show that these disparities, or continuities, can help us understand how the theoretical and the autobiographical, in the extended sense of the term, are always and inevitably intertwined.

The Aging Body

A recurring theme in *The Coming of Age* is the mutilation of the body by old age, a disfiguration that Beauvoir theorizes is repugnant both to others and to oneself because aging is an unambiguous sign of our mortality.[1] Although she qualifies this assertion by cautioning that she is referring to the decrepitude of *advanced* age only, in fact the overwhelming weight of her book—pages upon pages of testimony of well-known cultural figures who voice their disgust at their aging bodies—suggests that Beauvoir is abnormally sensitive to the physical changes that accompany old age, even before it has advanced very far. This seems strange in a book whose mission is to rescue old age from contempt, and it is all the stranger because I do not think we can attribute her view to undue personal vanity; throughout her life Beauvoir did not seem to have even a conventional concern with her personal appearance (on the contrary, in her memoirs she presents herself as a woman unconcerned with her appearance, to the point of carelessness). Nor were her childhood and youth characterized by profound and negative experiences with the elderly. But if we turn to the first volume of her memoirs and to *The Second Sex*, we find a surprising source for her attitude toward the aging body.

The opening pages of *Memoirs of a Dutiful Daughter*, published in France in 1958, are among the most captivating in all of her memoirs. Her sensibility as a child (or so she tells us as an adult) was Keatsian—but with a gaiety untouched by melancholy. She was enchanted by sweets and dazzled by the sensuality of feminine fabrics, by laces, taffetas, silks. She was also subject to tantrums that would shake her entire body and to physical revulsions. Certain tastes and consistencies revolted her, and the details she provides are fascinating. She remembers, for example, that whenever her aunt served pumpkin pie she "would rush from the table in tears" (67). Nor would she eat cheese. She further reports that "the insipidity of milk puddings, porridge, and mashes of bread and butter made me burst into tears, the oiliness of fat meat and the clammy mysteries of shellfish revolted me; my repugnance was so deeply rooted that in the end they gave up trying to force me to eat those disgusting things" (6). The lack of firmness and solidity, that is, the indeterminate identity of a substance—is it solid or liquid?—was offensive to her.[2] Such substances she found inane, innocuous, banal, lacking in originality or character, insipid. Her reference to the "clammy mysteries of shellfish" is telling. That something was hidden inside, the internal workings concealed, destroyed her composure, as did outer dampness and unusual coolness, which repelled her sense of touch.

Her extreme reactions lead us to ask what is involved in the attraction—or power—of what one finds horrible. Is it not possible that the feeling of horror is structured by a norm, which may very well be hidden to us? This would explain why we are simultaneously attracted to the horrible and repelled by it, and thus it would help us understand Beauvoir's obsession with the aging body as repellent. Her obsession conceals a norm: for her the ideal body—that is the "normal" body—is young and active. By contrast, the body of a person of advanced age, a decrepit body, is marked by imminent dissolution, by a lack of firmness, by frailty, by decay, and hence by a lack of identity.

But Beauvoir's obsession is not limited to her disgust with an aged body. Its roots are deeper, its territory wider than that. Throughout *Memoirs of a Dutiful Daughter* the word "repulsion" resounds, and most of her associations are to changes in the human body *in general*. As an adolescent the very word "development," which she associated with menstruation, repelled her, as did menstruation itself. She detested the thought that her breasts would swell (she would not even use the word "breasts," substituting the more clinical "chest"). She admits forthrightly (her candor occasionally comes close to a sense of humor about herself and is one of her most engaging qualities) that as an adolescent sexuality frightened her and that as a young adult she found physical desire "repulsive," "a shameful disease" (*Prime*, 6). Indeed, in four volumes of memoirs noteworthy for their frankness, we find next to nothing about her sexual life with Sartre or Algren or with Lanzmann, the only man with whom she ever shared living quarters. In short, it would seem that changes in the body in general arouse in her a deep-seated dislike of what is, for her, a sign of transformation as well as the thing itself. This view is confirmed in *The Second Sex*.

Although I agree with Beauvoir's major arguments about the oppression of women in Western culture, I find her attitude toward the reproductive nature or function of women quite odd, even bizarre. In *The Second Sex*, she writes at great length about menstruation as humiliating and painful, about pregnancy as an invasion by an alien being, and about childbirth as dangerous as well as painful. She asserts that this is the condition of women and concludes that, relative to the bodies of men, the bodies of women are characterized by weakness, instability, lack of control, and fragility. According to Beauvoir, woman's body is a burden, and only after menopause is a woman truly herself. Only then are a woman and her body one, as they were when she was a young child—when her body was firm and active and had not undergone any of the changes associated either with maturation or aging. Just as Beauvoir associates old age with death (she relates men's horror of decrepitude in women "logically" to their own fear of death), so too she links woman's capacity to give birth with death: "the function of gestation," she believes, "still inspires a spontaneous feeling of revulsion" in men (*Second Sex*, 165). Nauseated as a child by the soft substances of cheese and pumpkin pie, Beauvoir was also repelled by any transformation in the female body toward softness and the unfirm (dangerously close in her mind to infirmity, to sickness).

The root of her disgust of the decrepit body is not so much a theoretical position as an aversion to bodily transformation, a loathing which may have had its origin in her early childhood. Just as some children are shy from birth and we cannot say why they are (that is, we cannot explain their temperament on the basis of their environment, their social context, or their place in history), Beauvoir seems to have been temperamentally repelled by changes in the body. This aversion then surfaces in her theoretical position—whether on women or on the elderly—in another guise. She generalizes without justification: "Men and women all feel the shame of their flesh; in its pure, inactive presence, its unjustified immanence, the flesh exists, under the gaze of the other, in its absurd contingence" (*Second Sex*, 425). Concealed within the language and theory of existentialism is her prudery (self-confessed in *The Prime of Life*) and distaste for the human body in any state which is not the *ideal* state. We may now wonder less at the source of an anecdote told in passing early in *Memoirs of a Dutiful Daughter*. There Beauvoir tells of the good times she and her younger sister had during summer vacations in the country, and she pauses just long enough to recall: "We despised mature *ceps* whose flesh was beginning to go soft and produce greenish whiskers. We only gathered young ones with nicely curved stalks and caps covered with a fine nigger-brown or bluish nap" (79).

Memory, Reminiscence, Knowledge

In *The Coming of Age* Beauvoir flatly rejects any fruitful role memory might play in the lives of the elderly. Given her existential posture, of course, she sees identity (it is her word) as created by actions: one is defined by what she calls one's projects or activities. Thus, she argues that women can achieve selfhood only through production, not reproduction, and that anything having to do with a woman's biological self has nothing to do with the authentic creation of her self. As she writes in *The Second Sex*, "giving birth and suckling are not *activities*, they are natural *functions*; no project is involved" (71). I will not pause here to consider her position; I will only observe that in *The Second Sex* Beauvoir valorizes male labor as it has been traditionally defined in the West and is contemptuous of what we have traditionally called women's work. But what is important for our present purpose is her dismissal of a certain kind of psychological work which may be associated with a biological stage in life—for, like motherhood, old age is a distinct stage in the biological life of a person. Beauvoir does not ignore this point. Indeed, she makes much of the physical suffering which is likely to accompany old age. But just as she refuses to lend any cultural dignity or meaning to childbearing, so she denies that memory may play a critical role in one's psychological life when one approaches death.

Beauvoir thus necessarily sees old age as a tragedy, a view in great part prescribed by the dictates of her inflexible existentialism. In *The Second Sex*, she asserts bluntly that "there is no justification for present existence other than its expansion into an indefinitely open future," explaining that "every time transcendence falls back into immanence, stagnation, there is a degradation of existence into the '*en-soi.*' . . . It is an absolute evil" (xxxiii). In *The Coming of Age*, she continues this line of reasoning. The tragedy is that the elderly can only escape stagnation by undertaking projects, but those very projects require "an indefinitely open future," and a future is precisely what the elderly will not have. Therefore they are doomed. The tragedy of old age has an ontological dimension that can never be avoided or escaped, because the very definition—or meaning—of old age is that one is at the end of one's life span and does not possess a future. Predictably, Beauvoir counsels the elderly to pursue projects and activities, but she is not sanguine about the outcome. Although she recounts with admiration the activities of many productive people in their old age (among them Georges Clemenceau, Victor Hugo, Lou Andreas-Salomé, and Francisco Goya), the accounts are gloomy. As we learn from her memoirs, so is her view of her own experience. Over and over she repeats that the body of her work is essentially formed. To write another book would be merely additive; it would not appreciably change that body of work—her measure of her identity—in any way. The past she refers to as a weight, a burden that grows heavier as one grows older, a prison.

In Beauvoir's view, memory by its very nature is the antithesis of the future-oriented project and thus is an ignoble means of escape from the present. She is contemptuous of the elderly who look back, and she offers stereotyped pictures of tedious old men and women who tell the same stories over and over. Although she has an intuitive grasp of the psychological impetus for the turn of the aged mind toward the past, she rejects *la vie intérieure*. Her interest is in social oppression, not psychic repression, in liberation, not happiness. Certainly her view of memory is linked to her existential philosophical posture, but, again, I think she devalues memory for more personal reasons as well, reasons that have to do with the *texture* of her own mind rather than the *logic* of a philosophy.

In *The Coming of Age* Beauvoir asks to what degree the elderly can recover the past. This is a strange question to pose, peculiar because it supposes a scientific, objective, qualitative criterion for measuring the success of memory. The way in which Beauvoir defines the problem—and the very fact that she defines it as a *problem*—is telling. Viewed as a process of information retrieval, it is a project bound by definition to fail. For Beauvoir, the appropriate or valuable form of memory is not *personal* memory, but rather *social* memory, described as "an intellectual operation that reconstructs and localizes past facts, basing itself upon physiological data, images and a certain knowledge, and making use of logical categories. This is the only one that allows us to some degree, to tell ourselves our own history" (539). In order to tell a life story well, she continues, certain conditions must be met, the most important of which is that "this history must have been recorded," that is, it must have already been written (539).

Memory, to Beauvoir, is not a matter of considering one's relationship to the past—to work, mates, children, parents, community—in terms of affect. She converts the psychological task of memory, of recovering one's personal past, into the project of what we would call today social history, of taking oneself as a document of the times. Memory is defined as a form of archival research. It is clinical and pictorial in nature, and the results can never be perfectly pure, flawlessly eidetic. The further we stand from an event in our past, she argues, the less likely we are to perceive it with clarity. Beauvoir has no theory of perspective, no sense of needing time and space to see clearly, no belief in a wisdom achieved over time. Thus the elderly are doubly damned: they lack a future and they lack an unobstructed vision of the past.

Memory for Beauvoir is thus basically limited to the retrieval of the factual record and linked to the presentation of a public self, if often under the guise of a private self. I call this *archival memory*. Here I want to distinguish between two other forms of memory, both of which are, in my judgment, crucial to autobiographical practice: *reminiscence*, which I associate with remembrance and the private self; and *knowledge*, in the sense of *savoir*, which I associate with the achieved understanding of one's psychic past (and present) in the psychoanalytic mode. I want further to suggest that Beauvoir's belief that memory (in the sense of archival memory) dims over time is one of the reasons why she was able to write memoirs only (they are a combination of archival memory and reminiscence), and not autobiography (with, we will see, one important exception).

Here I go against the grain of some recent work in women's autobiography as well as against what we might call postmodern or post-structuralist definitions of autobiography, which have expanded to include virtually every form of writing. In her introduction to *Women's Autobiography: Essays in Criticism*, Estelle Jelinek, noting that male autobiography is more connected to a public world than is female autobiography (this, of course, is not the case for Beauvoir, who wrote her memoirs, she tells us, in order to show how she came to be a writer), makes the interesting observation that we have long erred in assuming that the autobiographical mode is necessarily an introspective and intimate one, characterized by a self-conscious and sustained effort to make sense of the narrative (I would add, the *narratives*) of one's life. Instead female "life stories"—the term she uses to cover the vast span of different forms—are more often discontinuous and fragmentary, written in a straightforward, objective manner, yet nonetheless emphasizing the personal rather than the public. I reserve Jelinek's characterization of the female life story for the *memoir*. For *autobiography* I still insist on the dimension of the interpretive, on a hermeneutics of the texts narrating a life; I agree with Karl Weintraub that autobiography derives its "value from rendering significant portions of the past as *interpreted past*" (827), where the past so interpreted gives knowledge (*savoir*) in the psychoanalytic sense. At the same time I want to insist—and this has been my implicit assumption and strategy all along—that the memoir as well as more explicitly theoretical works contains autobiographical materials or, as Marcus Billson and Sidonie Smith put it, that "the memorialist's vision of the outer world is as much a projection and refraction of the self as the autobiographer's" (163). In the psychoanalytic sense, then, I would add that in Beauvoir's writing, the theoretical works (*The Coming of Age*, *The Second Sex*), the four memoirs of her own life, and the memoir of Sartre present the *acting out*, while autobiography (as we find it in *A Very Easy Death*) presents, and represents, the *working through*. I believe that autobiography has a *plot*, in Peter Brooks's sense of the term, but just what kind of plot remains to be seen.

As Beauvoir reveals in the introduction to *Force of Circumstance* (*La Force des Choses*), she felt compelled to record events and feelings in the present because she was convinced that in her old age, "serene or sour, the influence of decrepitude would keep me from grasping my subject: that moment when, hard upon a still vibrant past, the decline sets in" (v). Throughout her memoirs, what at first appears to be an interpretive impulse to autobiography turns into the wish to paint an accurate portrait of herself at an earlier age. At times Beauvoir believed that an earlier self had disappeared entirely. Whereas in *The Prime of Life*, for example, she refers to one of her earliest childhood memories (it had come back to her with particular force when she was in her thirties), in *Force of Circumstance*, which appeared only two years later, she can no longer grasp the child she once was. Poignantly she tells us: "*The little girl whose future has become my past no longer exists. There are times when I want to believe that I still carry her inside me. . . . She has disappeared without leaving even a tiny skeleton to remind me that she did once exist*" (371–72).

We should not be surprised by such a statement. Beauvoir's memoirs suggest that her relationship to her past is not a particularly personal one. Indeed, one of the reasons her memoirs fail as autobiography is that she chronicles the past in a monotone—the names of the people and movies she saw in a given year, the details of her various trips abroad, a catalog of recent political events in France. Only rarely does she *evoke* her past. For the most part, she plods through it. Her pace is the result, in part, of her practice as a writer of memoirs. She kept voluminous diaries, and in preparing to write her memoirs (her method is not meditative but bibliographical) she spent days, she tells us, in the

Bibliothèque Nationale reading old newspapers and journals, immersing herself in the public period of her memoir, refreshing her memory of the historical record. As she confesses, in a fascinating passage from *Force of Circumstance*, her secret dream was not to discover the pattern of her past but to possess the complete record of every detail of her life: "*I have always had the secret fantasy that my life was being recorded, down to the tiniest detail, on some tape recorder, and that the day would come when I should play back the whole of my past*" (371).

"So many memories are failures," Virginia Woolf once remarked, "because they leave out the person to whom things happened" (65). Beauvoir's memoirs disappoint us because they are too connected with the outside world and do not seem motivated by a need to discover her own past. Although she does describe her feelings about her friends and her thoughts about old age—presumably intimate topics—the descriptions read as if she is not present in her own past. She admitted as much in a documentary movie: "I don't have," she said, "very warm, lively memories of what happened to me in the past" (Dayan and Ribowska 92). We may judge her memoirs by the standard Walter Benjamin set for the storyteller and find them lacking. Benjamin claimed that "not only a man's knowledge or wisdom, but above all his real life—and this is the stuff that stories are made of—first assume transmissible form at the moment of his death" ("The Storyteller" 94). In her memoirs, Beauvoir's life never assumed this "transmissible form." And unfortunately, in *The Coming of Age*, she concludes that images of the past are impoverished and colorless for everyone, and that they only become more so as one grows older. (Here again we see the danger of projecting onto old age in general the attitudes, beliefs, and texture of mind that may be idiosyncratic to us as individuals.)

Beauvoir's memoirs reveal a person for whom coming to terms with a personal past is simple, not an important concern; they present us with a portrait of a well-adjusted and confident woman who—at least at the time that she wrote them—did not need to do the kind of psychic work that Robert Butler theorizes is especially important in old age (486–96);the author harbors almost no discernible nostalgia for the past and seems to have no pressing need to ingratiate herself with herself. What, then, compelled her to write her memoirs? They seem to function as a diary, as a collection of events that will help her recall the past, should she ever want to or need to. But my guess is that she wrote them for another reason as well. We should remember that Beauvoir's great ambition was to be a writer. Yet throughout her life as a writer she continually questioned what she should write about and what form her writing should take. The form of the memoir provided her with inexhaustible, ready-made material. It may well have satisfied her need to write *something*, *anything* to fill page after page as she sat in cafés, in her hotel room, in her studio. The memoir also allowed her, or so she thought, to avoid something she despised in an artist: repetition. Of course, it is ironic that the very person who inveighed against the return to the past which occupies many elderly people should herself have written four volumes of memoirs.

Of the many contradictions between Beauvoir's theoretical positions and her experience as represented in her writing, I will point to two only. The first is by far the most important because it involves *A Very Easy Death*, the only book of Beauvoir's which, to my mind, attains the status of a small masterpiece in the autobiographical mode. Of all Beauvoir's books, this narrative, occasioned by her elderly mother's painful death from intestinal cancer, is the most accomplished in terms of style, structure, voice, and subtlety of observation. It is also the most reflective in its remembrances, with its chapters alternating between the anguished present in the hospital and the past of childhood, with Beauvoir the daughter coming to understand her mother and thus *to be present with her mother* in a way that we are given to understand had never happened before. The space of the book encompasses a moment of *savoir*. For the book is as much about Beauvoir as it is about her mother. In its pages Beauvoir discovers (or should we say, creates?) a meaning to her mother's death and a pattern to her life—to both of their lives. This book has the ring of deep affective truth, the truth which, as Elizabeth Bruss wrote in *Autobiographical Acts*, must always characterize the intent of the writer of autobiography.

In one magical passage Beauvoir, who all her life had resisted identification with her mother, embraces it. The woman who had *reasoned*, logically, that her mother, now in her seventies, was after all of an age to die was quite unprepared for the storm of emotions that overtook her as she kept watch over her dying mother in the hospital. The watching transformed her. "I had put Maman's mouth on my own face and in spite of myself, I copied its movements," she wrote. "Her whole person, her whole being was concentrated there, and compassion wrung my heart" (37–38). It is an uncanny moment: the daughter taking on the suffering body of the mother, incorporating the mother in what we may conclude was an unconscious act of reparation in the Kleinian sense. For Beauvoir tells us that she was not consciously aware of her gesture—

it was Sartre who, watching Beauvoir, recognized the body of the mother in the daughter. It is Beauvoir the writer who incorporates that moment in self-conscious reflection. Perhaps even more important, Beauvoir, who in a later conversation with Alice Schwartzer revealed that she had always understood herself to have played the role of a son to her mother, here assumes the role of the daughter. It is as if, for a moment, the daughter becomes the mother and the mother, the daughter. If the most excruciating test to which a woman can be put is the loss of her child, then Beauvoir suffers here as if from the death of the child she never had. It is only in *A Very Easy Death* that Beauvoir reinserts herself into the fabric of the family, her only family, since she did not desire to make one for herself. It is important that she dedicates the book to her only sibling, her sister.

A Very Easy Death is the only book in which Beauvoir permits the past to have an effect on the present, in which she allows a reciprocity between the past and the present in the psychoanalytic sense.[3] When Beauvoir refers to her mother's death in her memoir, *All Said and Done*, she reduces it to a colorless, unambiguous event that serves to illustrate the threats of today's medical technology. In both *The Coming of Age* and *All Said and Done*, she does not recall that her need to write about her mother was a need to reestablish a bond between them—precisely in the mode of psychic work which she would deny to the elderly.

My second example of the contradictions between Beauvoir's theory and her writing practices is found in *All Said and Done*. In this book, published only two years after *The Coming of Age*, in which she rejected reminiscence, Beauvoir on the contrary admits to the pleasures of reminiscence, just as she mentions for the first time the gratification she derives from dreams precisely because "they have no dimension in the future" (107). In her early sixties at the time of writing *All Said and Done*, she tells us her concern is "recovering my life—reviving forgotten memories, re-reading, re-seeing, rounding off incomplete pieces of knowledge, filling gaps, clarifying obscurities, gathering scattered elements together. Just as though there had to be a study on the moment when my experience was to be summed up, and as though it mattered that this summing-up should be done" (48). She speaks warmly of the Left Bank of Paris as a place rich in memories and observes that she has always taken pleasure in talking over old times with her sister, Sartre, and her friends. Whereas before she vehemently denied any link between identity and reminiscence, now she embraces such a link, and her concern with reminiscence sounds very much like Butler's notion of the life review. Yet Beauvoir does not seem to be aware of a change in her thinking. In this matter, her thought lacks dialectical insight. After the first few chapters of *All Said and Done*, incipient autobiography breaks down into the half-life and soon thereafter the quarter-life of the march of events. What seems to have begun as a life review in Butler's sense devolves into a chronicle, a recitation of events, a diary.

I think Beauvoir's inability to see this contradiction, to take into account the lie her experience gave to her theory over time, is related to her sense of the human life span as ideally unchanging. She never considered, seriously or even indifferently, notions of psychological stages in human development such as those proposed by Erik Erikson. Yet throughout her life she was fascinated with the relationship of identity to time. Her intuitions were precocious. In *Memoirs of a Dutiful Daughter* she tells us that at age three or so, gazing at her mother's empty armchair, she understood that time would wrench her from the secure world of her mother's body, her presence, and she thought to herself: "'I won't be able to sit on her knee any more if I go on growing up.' Suddenly the future existed; it would turn me into another being, someone who would still be, and yet no longer seem myself" (7). This mystery of human identity, the shadowy relation we adults bear to our childhood, captivated her. One fairy tale in particular enchanted her— the story of Charlotte, whose body shrinks to miniature proportions and then swells to gigantic dimensions. As a little girl, Beauvoir imagined herself to be Charlotte and commented with palpable relief: "I came out of the adventure *safe and sound* after having been reduced to a foetus and then blown up to matronly dimensions" (8; emphasis mine). Almost obsessively she associates the miniature and the *gigantesque* with changes in the body, with a condition to be feared and avoided—with, in short, pregnancy and motherhood. Surely it is not insignificant that neither as an adolescent nor as an adult did she see motherhood as part of her future.

As a woman in late middle age, the author of *The Coming of Age* advised the elderly to remain involved in the activities of their middle years. She was committed to this philosophy, but I would again observe that she was projecting onto old age in general a quality unique to her— the way she had led her own adult life up to age sixty. Despite Beauvoir's transformation from a rather solitary university student into a public figure, her life is remarkable for its *lack* of change. As she is fond of noting, she lived her entire life in the same "village," a small section on the Left Bank of Paris. Until his death in 1980 Jean-Paul Sartre was her constant companion. Throughout her adult years she pursued the same occupation—writing—and had many friends to whom she remained attached for years. Her life was never punctuated by the birth and growth of children. It was, in other words, distinguished by remarkable continuity. Her own experience must have reinforced her philosophical conviction that the ideal life span is one that is not marred by intrusive change, whether biological change (puberty, motherhood, old age) or an abandonment of the goals defined for oneself in the early years of adulthood.

Mourning and Melancholia, Desire and Anxiety

I have argued that Beauvoir's dark portrait of old age is due in part to her personal revulsion for changes in the human body and to her particular temperament, which does not value certain forms of memory. I also think that her grim view of old age may have sprung from the working out of one of her personal obsessions—that of death and the concomitant fear of loss which she believed advancing years would inevitably bring. In *The Coming of Age*, Beauvoir details the various forms melancholia may take in old age. But more important for our present purposes is her observation that the death wish is a strong urge present in all of us, not just in those who suffer from the chronic and increasingly painful condition of dispossession in old age.

I have already mentioned that a preoccupation with death saturates Beauvoir's work and life. This preoccupation has been amply discussed by Elaine Marks and others, and there is no need to trace that theme here.[4] Instead I should like to suggest that at the root of her fears about old age—fears expressed through her obsessively catastrophic view in *The Coming of Age*—is not so much panic at the prospect of her own death but rather her dread of losing Sartre to death.

Here I turn to the psychoanalyst Gregory Rochlin's theory of the loss complex. Although Freud's speculations on the relationship between mourning and melancholia are seminal, he devoted only a few pages to the problem, and I have long wished for a more extended treatment of it. Rochlin's wise, book-length *Griefs and Discontents: The Forces of Change* fills this gap with a general theory that has a developmental basis: Rochlin concludes that our relationship to loss changes over the course of the life span. He argues that our lives are marked by an ongoing, continuous cycle of loss and restitution, which he calls the loss complex. Although the foundation of his theory is Freud's distinction between mourning and melancholia, Rochlin's contribution to an understanding of these two psychological states pivots on Freud's earlier insight that we never willingly give anything up. "Really we never can relinquish anything," Freud declared in an essay published almost a decade before his 1917 essay on mourning and melancholia; "we only exchange one thing for something else. When we appear to give something up, all we really do is to adopt a substitute" ("Relation of the Poet to Day-Dreaming" 46). The work of mourning is completed only when all libido has been withdrawn *and* attached to a new object, a substitute for the lost object—a loss which can never be tolerated and which is but one in a series of losses, of substitutions, in an infinite regression. The work of mourning, then, is to restore what has been lost, to bring us back to our previous condition.

Rochlin casts Freud's distinction between the psychological states of mourning and melancholy onto another plane, differentiating between the cycle of *loss and restitution*, which I would call the normal process of mourning, and the cycle of *loss and impoverishment*, which indeed may not be a cycle at all but instead a dead end, the cessation of restitution, the pathological state of melancholia understood clinically as depression. According to Rochlin, the stage of life known as old age is almost invariably marked by impoverishment. It is characterized by a series of severe losses for which we cannot reasonably expect to find substitutes.

Rochlin believes that throughout our lives we work, consciously and unconsciously, to shore up our defenses against future losses. His clinical research has led him to conclude that old age is a special phase of development whose psychological work is triggered by the combination of the loss of physical function (degenerative processes) and the loss of loved objects. "Paradoxically," he judges, "the intensified defenses of this period are more attached to the *fantasies* of loss than to the reality of losses" (xix; emphasis mine). In its simplest form, the loss complex is an expression of the dread of abandonment. In old age as well as throughout the life span, the work of the loss complex is thus in great part *prospective*, a technique of mastering deprivation in anticipation of a final loss. It is anticipatory grief.

Beauvoir associates old age in general with melancholia, a terrible solitude and loss, and, specifically, with the death of Sartre, which for her would be catastrophic. Unlike Proust, who was obsessed with the recovery of the past, she was obsessed with the tragedy that she believed the future would inevitably bring. This concern hovered between fear and hysteria and sprang, I think, from the all-important role which a close mate played throughout her life. At the precocious age of three, Beauvoir reports in *Dutiful Daughter*, she "had forebodings of all the separations, the refusals, the desertions to come, and of the long succession of my various deaths" (7). This intimation of loss was repeated over and over again, rehearsed in her fiction and her memoirs, played out in her critical writing. Throughout her life, the death of the self—her self—is linked indissolubly to the loss of others, to abandonment, to aging, to solitude, to death. Beauvoir explains in *Dutiful Daughter* that at an early age—when she was only about six—she understood that "a partner was absolutely essential to me if I was to bring my imaginary stories to life" (43). She was speaking of her relationship with her younger sister Poupette, the only member of her family to whom she was really close.

Beauvoir's feelings of panic at the thought of the loss of a loved one seem to have been reinforced by World War I. Although she had never experienced the loss of someone important to her, she fantasized what such a loss would mean: "I used to choke with dread whenever I thought of mortal death which separates forever those who love one another" (64). Until Beauvoir met Zaza at school, Poupette was her only "partner," her only close friend. In her relationship to Zaza, we see Beauvoir playing out in fantasy the cycle of loss and impoverishment followed by the cycle of loss and the attempt at restitution. She imagines the absence of Zaza. In *Dutiful Daughter* she tells us how one day she walked into school and, staring with stupefaction at Zaza's empty seat, thought to herself, "'What if she were never to sit there again, what if she were to die, then what would happen to me?'" This experience is for her a "blinding revelation" (95), the realization that a future loss will have apocalyptic force for her. But this realization, generated by the imagination, will also blind her to a more balanced view of life processes. It is her blind spot. I am not suggesting that hers are idle imaginings or petty forebodings—indeed Zaza did die at a very early age—but rather that they were particularly intense and functioned blindly as well as presciently in the economy of her imagination. The very strength and force of this insight concealed as much as it revealed.

Although the two had drifted somewhat apart, Zaza's death devastated Beauvoir. It was through her relationship with Zaza that she had come to value the pleasures of a daily, intimate companionship and intellectual exchange with another person. Their friendship would be, for the rest of her life, the model of a meaningful relationship with another person—a relationship with an equal partner, not with a parent or a child. It is not surprising that Beauvoir concludes the first volume of her memoirs with the death of Zaza, whom she tried again and again to resurrect in the imagination, in the world of her writing; that resurrection would be, for her, a form of restitution for the loss.

As an adult Beauvoir was convinced that harm could come to her from Sartre only if he were to die before she did. His imperfect health frightened her. She dismissed the prospect of sharing old age with him as an impossible fantasy. It was, as she put it in *Force of Circumstance*, a "refuge" from reality, an absurd, "far-off, well-behaved dream" (135). Her association of the terror of old age with the death of Sartre is seen even more clearly later in *Force of Circumstance*, when she recounts what the experience of Sartre's dreadful illness in 1954 meant to her. Seeing him in the hospital in Brazil, she suddenly realized that "he was carrying his own death within him," that death was no longer, for her, "a metaphysical scandal, it was a quality of our arteries" (306). Later when he falls ill in Paris—exhausted, confusing his words, mumbling presciently and aphasically about his trouble with the "thickets of the heart"—his death is more than an intimate presence to her: now it possesses her. She writes: "This subjection, this possession, had a name . . . old age" (453). As she had written earlier in *The Prime of Life*, "my greatest wish was to die with the one I loved" (477). Beauvoir had an intuition amounting to conviction that Sartre would die before she did and that the loss would be intolerable. Her fiction enacts that dread of abandonment. One of the major themes of her short fiction is the loss of a mate due to dependency. Her fictional preoccupation with abandonment is so emphatic that we can read it as a symptom of her obsession with the loss of Sartre.

I am arguing that much of Beauvoir's writing took place under the sign of anxiety, not desire. In *Beyond the Pleasure Principle*, Freud distinguishes between fright, fear, and anxiety. Whereas both fear and fright are associated with the present (for fear there must be a definite object of which one is afraid, and fright is the state of encountering a danger unprepared), anxiety is associated with the future. Anxiety is a state of expecting a danger and preparing oneself for it, although the danger may be unknown to oneself, that is, not consciously known.

In a fundamental sense, of course, as Freud and Lacan have taught us, all narrative has to do with loss in the past. But it is wrong, I think, to read all narrative under the sign of desire—that ubiquitous word—for the originary lost object. André Green, in his essay "The Double and Its Absent," writes without hesitation that "the work of writing presupposes a wound and a loss, a work of mourning, of which the text is the transformation into a fictitious positivity" (283). The emphasis is on past loss. But the wound itself may be "fictitious," or yet to come. In *Reading for the Plot*, Peter Brooks, like Green, reaches certain conclusions about narrative based on his reading of Freud, and in particular on his reading of *Beyond the Pleasure Principle*. In Brooks's view, narrative essentially has to do with the recovery of the past (with this I, of course, agree), but with *desire* as its motive force. He makes an excellent distinction, I think, between repetition as the assertion of mastery (the *fort-da*) and repetition as a "process of *binding* toward the creation of an energetic constant-state situation which will permit the emergence of mastery and the possibility of postponement" (101). The thematic and figural repetition of old age throughout Beauvoir's writing works precisely, it seems to me, to permit both mastery and postponement. It is as though she creates the symbolic world in which she fears to live so as to acquaint herself with, and thus inure herself to, future loss. But her model is not desire; it is, rather, anxiety. We may speculate that the narrative of desire is a traditional male model, and the narrative of anxiety a female model. Freud has written that the most important event in a man's life is the death of his father, a death that frees a space for the enactment of desire. But, as I have already proposed, for a woman—a mother—is not that event the death of her child, a loss that is always projected in the future, a possible loss encircled with anxiety? And did not Sartre represent in Beauvoir's life father, husband, and child?

Restitution may be accomplished in actuality or in fantasy, consciously or unconsciously, by the process of symbolization or by the process of substitution. Beauvoir saw her book *The Coming of Age* as a means of alerting Western society to the perils of old age. She believed that the book might result in efforts to alleviate the disgraceful treatment of the elderly by society as a whole. By writing that book—an act unconsciously informed by fear of her personal loss of Sartre—she also may have accomplished, in the world of words, a kind of restitution.

An Epilogue: Not All Said and Done

In *Force of Circumstance*, Beauvoir muses that her severe anxiety attacks "were a last revolt before resigning myself to age and the end that follows it" (128). She opens the epilogue to this volume of her memoirs with a paean to her life with Sartre: "There has been one undoubted success in my life: my relationship with Sartre. In more than thirty years, we have only once gone to sleep at night disunited" (643). She concludes the volume with an emotionally charged evaluation of what aging has meant to her. Her epilogue is indeed a sign or symptom of an anxiety attack.

She writes of aging as a mutilation, as the most "irreparable" thing that has happened to her since the end of World War II. She laments that the world has contracted for her. She chafes against the fact that her experience of human suffering and injustice in the world has led to a lessening of her horror at human misery. The result of having made choices in living her life is that she has been limited by those choices, and she is saddened by this. Her imagery is of calcification, hardening, imprisonment. Aging is "petrification" (655), a "pox" (656). And she detests the physical signs of it. "I loathe my appearance now: the eyebrows slipping down toward the eyes, the bags underneath, the excessive fullness of the cheeks, and that air of sadness around the mouth that wrinkles always bring" (656). She speaks of her strengths having "dimmed" (656), of the coming "deteriorations" (657), of plea-sures having "paled" (657), of the loss of all desire, all sexuality. In this sense her very body is absent to her, dead—"it's strange not to be a body any more" (657)—at the same time as it is ominously present as a prison. "I try not to think: in ten years, in a year. Memories grow thin, myths crack and peep, projects rot in the bud" (657). These words, melancholic and near-hysterical at once—we read also of the "furious gallop to the tomb" (657)—were written, we must not forget, when Beauvoir was only in her mid-fifties.

But by the time she wrote *All Said and Done*, the fourth volume of her memoirs, when she was sixty-three, a sea change had taken place. Her crises ceased. The woman who had always been contemptuous of a philosophic calm, who had always raged and hammered against old age and death, now speaks of her peace with death and of the heroic quality of Freud's resignation in his last years. With the publication of *All Said and Done*, the woman who had always defined herself as a writer virtually gave up writing—it now seemed pointless to her—and turned to active political work. Beauvoir tells us that it was in her early fifties that her aging had become apparent to her. Now, in her early sixties, she found she had reached an unanticipated plateau. She writes: "The first thing that strikes me when I look back at the ten years that have passed since I finished *Force of Circumstance* is that I do not feel that I have aged" (38). She admits that her long-held fears about old age have in great part been proven wrong. Although she sees her life as a chronicle of losses, she realizes anew that it is also characterized by the continual creation of new friendships.

In *All Said and Done*, Beauvoir implicitly acknowledges two stages of old age. The first has come as a surprise to her: it is characterized by health and by changes in attitude which she had not foreseen. This is what gerontologists in the United States now refer to as the period of the "young old." The second stage is that period of tragic decline and ill health which she had believed characterized old age as a whole; this is more or less what gerontologists now call the period of the "old old," seventy-five and over. Having entered old age and discovered that it did not accord with her bleak and grim expectations, she defers her original view of old age as a period of decrepitude until later.

Later, as it turns out, will indeed come much later. In mourning for Sartre, Beauvoir turned again to writing, chronicling the last ten years of his life in *Adieux: A Farewell to Sartre*. She did survive his loss—so well that she could astonish me with her words of 1982 in which she passes, we might say, from the world of men (that is, Sartre) to the world of women, telling Alice Schwartzer that she believed that, whereas love affairs between men and women often do not last, by contrast great friendships between women often endure. She asserts in complete confidence, in the same conversation with Schwartzer, that "up to my death, I will never be alone" (Schwartzer 21; translation mine).

But I want to insist again, in closing, that it was not only the reality of Beauvoir's experience of old age that led her to these conclusions. A lifetime of the projection of loss and anxiety in writing may well have constituted significant psychological work. Although that work took the form of melancholia (Julia Kristeva has theorized that all writing is melancholic), it may also have served the purpose of mourning in advance of actual loss—mourning that helped her overcome the actual loss of Sartre and that prepared her for other losses to come in her own old age.

Notes

1. For a more extended discussion of Beauvoir's view of the aging body, see Woodward, "Instant Repulsion."

2. Julia Kristeva recounts, in *The Powers of Horror*, a personal story similar to those of Beauvoir: she tells us that as a child she was revolted by the layer of cream—the skin—which rises to the surface of milk.

3. I comment further on *A Very Easy Death* in "Frailty and the Meanings of Literature." For recent work on aging from literary and psychoanalytic perspectives, see Woodward and Schwartz, *Memory and Desire;* the volume contains essays by Carolyn Asp, Herbert Blau, Leslie A. Fiedler, Diana Hume George, Norman N. Holland, William Kerrigan, Mary Lydon, John Muller, Ellie Ragland-Sullivan, and Gabriele Schwab.

4. See especially Marks, *Simone de Beauvoir*. Marks takes Beauvoir to task for her preoccupation with how the deaths of others will (or did) affect her, to the exclusion of a more appropriate empathy with the person who is dying. Marks sees Beauvoir as focusing selfishly on her own feelings and the consequences for her of the suffering of others rather than on their pain. In my judgment, this view is too hard on Beauvoir and does not acknowledge that Beauvoir's attention to the process of her own bereavement is refreshingly candid and frank, an admission of the implacable force of our own ego above all else.

Works Cited

Beauvoir, Simone de. *Adieux: A Farewell to Sartre*. Trans. Patrick O'Brian. Harmondsworth, Eng.: Penguin, 1984.

———. *All Said and Done*. Trans. Patrick O'Brian. New York: Warner, 1975.

———. *The Coming of Age*. Trans. Patrick O'Brian. New York: Warner, 1972.

———. *Force of Circumstance*. Trans. Richard Howard. New York: Putnam, 1964.

———. *Memoirs of a Dutiful Daughter*. Trans. James Kirkup. New York: Harper Colophon, 1974.

———. *The Prime of Life*. Trans. Peter Green. New York: Harper, 1976.

———. *The Second Sex*. Trans. H. M. Parshley. New York: Vintage, 1974.

———. *A Very Easy Death*. Trans. Patrick O'Brian. New York: Warner, 1966.

Benjamin, Walter. *Illuminations*. Ed. Hannah Arendt. Trans. Harry Zohn. New York: Harcourt, 1968.

———. "The Storyteller." 1936. In Benjamin, *Illuminations* 83–109.

Billson, Marcus K., and Sidonie A. Smith. "Lillian Hellman and the Strategy of the 'Other.'" In Jelinek, 163–79.

Brooks, Peter. *Reading for the Plot: Design and Intention in Narrative*. New York: Knopf, 1984.

Bruss, Elizabeth. *Autobiographical Acts: The Changing Situation of a Literary Genre*. Baltimore: Johns Hopkins University Press, 1976.

Butler, Robert N. "The Life Review: An Interpretation of Reminiscence in the Aged." 1963. In Neugarten, 486–96.

Dayan, Josée, and Malka Ribowska. *Simone de Beauvoir*. Paris: Gallimard, 1978.

Freud, Sigmund. *Beyond the Pleasure Principle*. Ed. James Strachey. London: Hogarth Press, 1955.

_____. *On Creativity and the Unconscious: Papers on the Psychology of Art, Literature, Love, Religion*. Ed. Benjamin Nelson. New York: Harper, 1958.

_____. "The Relation of the Poet to Day-Dreaming." 1916. Trans. I. F. Grant Duff. In Freud, *On Creativity* 44–54.

Green, André. "The Double and Its Absent." In *Psychoanalysis, Creativity, and Literature: A French-American Inquiry*. Ed. Alan Roland. New York: Columbia University Press, 1978. 271–92.

Jelinek, Estelle C., ed. *Women's Autobiography: Essays in Criticism*. Bloomington: Indiana University Press, 1980.

Kristeva, Julia. "The Discourse of Love and Metaphor." Lecture given at Center for Twentieth Century Studies, University of Wisconsin. Milwaukee, 2 November 1982.

_____. *The Powers of Horror*. Trans. Leon S. Roudiez. New York: Columbia University Press, 1982.

Marks, Elaine. *Simone de Beauvoir: Encounters with Death*. New Brunswick: Rutgers University Press, 1973.

Neugarten, Bernice L. *Middle Age and Aging*. Chicago: University of Chicago Press, 1968.

Rochlin, Gregory. *Griefs and Discontents: The Forces of Change*. Boston: Little, Brown, 1965.

Schwartzer, Alice. *Simone de Beauvoir Aujourd'hui: Entretiens*. Paris: Mercure de France, 1984.

Spicker, Stuart F., and Stanley R. Ingman, eds. *Vitalizing Long-Term Care: The Teaching Nursing Home and Other Perspectives*. New York: Springer, 1984.

Weintraub, Karl. "Autobiography and Historical Consciousness." *Critical Inquiry* 1:4 (June 1975): 821–48.

Woodward, Kathleen. "Frailty and the Meanings of Literature." In Spicker and Ingman, 128–37.

_____. "Instant Repulsion: Decrepitude, the Mirror Stage, and the Literary Imagination." *Kenyon Review* 5 (1983): 43–66.

Woodward, Kathleen, and Murray M. Schwartz, eds. *Memory and Desire: Aging—Literature—Psychoanalysis*. Bloomington: Indiana University Press, 1986.

Woolf, Virginia. "A Sketch of the Past." In *Moments of Being*. Ed. Jeanne Schulkind. New York: Harcourt Brace Jovanovich, 1976.

CHAPTER FIVE

Invincible Mediocrity
The Private Selves of Public Women

Jane Marcus

Re/Signing the Self

The primary signatures of the white, privileged, turn-of-the-century women under discussion here were the marks they made in the public world, often as the first women of achievement in their fields. To write, they resigned from public discourse into private discourse. Their autobiographies represent a re/signing of their names in women's history. Enacting a deliberate resignation from the public world and patriarchal history, which had already erased or was expected to erase their names and their works, they re/signed their private lives into domestic discourse. The trajectory of these moves is the opposite of the one feminist historians have chosen to study, the move from private to public. Some were more resigned than others about anticipated erasure, but each woman chose a re/signing of self in the private collective world of women readers as a bid for immortality. Signing themselves into seeming insignificance in the apron pocket of history, they anticipated the present project of women's history to study the signature of the self. What seems significant is not the female struggle to enter male public discourse, which feminist scholars have documented, but the recognition of the inability of that discourse to include their voices in its history, the necessity of the return to the personal.

Ironically, the moment of our recovery of the "re/signed" from their historical abjection coincides with a postmodern critical practice (in which all autobiographical acts are fictions) that questions any account of truth or self that claims a stable reference to reality. Feminist critics may face this dilemma in several ways while trying to avoid de-facement or effacement of the lives of their subjects. A pragmatic "gynocritical" approach could restore historical specificity and take pleasure in the return of the repressed narratives of women, as much of the present paper does. A strong ethical imperative exists for such a practice.

We may deconstruct these texts according to contemporary theories of women's language and subjectivity. Yet it goes against the grain to accept the claim that all authors are dead in regard to unread texts. Is it possible to negotiate between a study of authentic female experience of selfhood in the text and what Luce Irigaray calls the "elsewhereness" of women speaking and writing in patriarchal culture? The first position reproduces the abjection of the author's choice of private over public discourse. The second position erases historically specific resignation from writing as re/signing.

Also troublesome is the sense that the study of female subjectivity in narratives of self reduces author and text to the object. Our voices assign the writers to categories and design the trajectory of their return to the realm of the read. Our compositions, to paraphrase Gertrude Stein, are their explanations. We retell their tales so that they are the told and not the tellers. Our criticism leaves telltale marks on their texts. One solution is to look at the ways they theorized self and writing as well as the ways they wrote them. To destabilize my own position of knowing I use an essay by Virginia Woolf which theorizes life writing from a perspective contemporary to the writers.

The essay is flawed by Woolf's inability to reject the canon altogether, by her (uncomfortable) reliance on traditional aesthetic categories of major and minor. She asserts her own tastes as a reader without rejecting patriarchal notions of universal greatness. Autobiography as a genre is justified as being the ground against which great figures operate. Although Woolf does not destroy the canon, she does destabilize it, offering the readers' tastes as a parallel value system. She un-signs authority so that it may be re/signed by contemporary theory.[1]

When Woolf defined herself as a critic she also destabilized the critic's role from an authoritarian act of the one who stands in for the reader to a common practice of one who stands with and among other readers. The word "common," which had come to mean coarse or vulgar, is restored to its democratic origins in her notion of the common reader. Woolf's use of the word "mediocrity" in her description of obscure autobiographers is also re/signed to mean "centered in the middle of the body." And her naming of the "middlebrow" reader works out a similar construction.

Woolf sees autobiography as a *rehearsal* for other art forms; writing the self is practice for writing the world. Reading autobiography is a rehearsal for reading the world. The writer is a reader. Any teacher of women and minorities knows how radically effective this practice is for re/signing the self into history. Woolf claims, like Paul de Man, that the site of autobiography is in the reading process itself. Centered in the commonality of collective reading experience, the writer makes a self. The reader participates in this process, re/signing herself from the author's signature.

The Resurrecting Reader

In a brilliant and forgotten essay called "The Lives of the Obscure" (1925), Virginia Woolf, in her usual sly and subtle manner as a critic, proposed a theory of autobiography as the genre of the oppressed. From a postmodern perspective, Woolf's inability to reject the canon altogether, as well as her outmoded reliance on aesthetic categories, marks the position of the beginning of a feminist critique of patriarchal categories. Her struggle is painful. What a debt of gratitude we owe the obscure who wrote autobiographies, as well as the biographers of the obscure, she wrote:

> for persisting in spite of their *invincible mediocrity*, in writing their memoirs; for providing precisely that background, atmosphere and standing of common earth which nourish people of greater importance and prevent them from shrivelling to dry sticks or congealing to splendid pinnacles of inaccessible ice. For imagine a literature composed entirely of good books. . . . Starvation would soon ensue. No one would read at all. . . . The great literatures of Greece and Rome, so much admired, but so seldom read, prove how difficult it is for good books to survive unless they are liberally supported by bad ones. The isolation is too great. There is nothing handy and personal to pull oneself up by. There are no gradations of merit, but we are faced directly by the sublime and precipitous—by Aeschylus, Sophocles, Lucretius, Plato, Virgil, Aristotle. There is no W. E. Norris, no Creevey; no Indiscretions of a Countess, no Mrs. Pilkington. (381–82; emphasis mine)

Woolf's persona here, as in all her essays, is never the writer, but the reader, and not the individual reader, but a member of the community of readers stretched out through history as actual collaborators in the making of culture, and without whom writers could not exist. Woolf's antagonistic stance toward European individualism—and particularly its deeply rooted romantic notions about individual genius, especially in its artists—is a position we share, although we no longer view "people of greater importance" as "better than" obscure autobiographers. The argument, clearly explicated in *A Room of One's Own* (written shortly after "The Lives of the Obscure"), that "masterpieces are not single and solitary births" (68–69), but the product of centuries of writing and experience, defines Shakespeare as a product of his age; later, in "A Sketch of the Past," Woolf makes her point again: "There is no Shakespeare. . . . There is no Beethoven. . . . Certainly and emphatically there is no god. We are the words; we are the music; we are the thing itself" (72).

Theories of autobiography, from Georges Gusdorf to Roland Barthes to James Olney, persist in maintaining the idea of individual genius. However much post-structuralism points out the fictionality of the self and the nonreferentiality of language, the selves and the texts under discussion turn out to be an unspoken canon of white male autobiographers, often including Augustine and Rousseau. Even Marxism and deconstruction in current practice would choose to explicate the works of Aristotle or Aeschylus rather than W. E. Norris or Mrs. Pilkington. Before dismissing Woolf as an unsophisticated historicist looking for "truth value" when we all agree that the works she is reading are only fictions after all, let us look more closely at her essay, which re/signs the word "mediocrity" to its original positive meaning associated with the middle of the body in the same way as she rescued the word "common" from negativity in her idea of "the common reader," without anticipating that her socialist recovery of these two words would be read in the future as elitist.

She has drawn here a landscape of culture. You may say it is a dated one, that you recognize the figures of readers as cows dotted all over this naive primitive painting of reading as eating, or walking, or mountain climbing on a hill with *Indiscretions of a Countess* at the bottom and Plato at the top. Yes, you may say, she appears to be democratic, with all her attacks on ranking and canons of literature in *A Room of One's Own*, but in this essay the Greeks are "sublime," and autobiography is obviously at the bottom of a literary scale of value. But note in this geography of reading that readers are really on the map, in equality with writers as makers of culture. Note how neatly "invincible" vanquishes "mediocrity," how "good" books "shrivel" and "congeal" without the liberal support of "bad" ones. The effect of the passage is to call into question the categories of good and bad and to privilege the memoirs of the obscure because they are *read*. Obscurity, as readers of *A Room of One's Own* and *Three Guineas* know, is the great virtue of all women and lower-class men in whose alliance she places her hopes for the end of war, imperialism, and patriarchy. Because memoir is the form chosen by the obscure, its "standing of common earth" suggests material reality in these texts rather than abstractions. She suggests that the canon of great books by great men is dead, that the patriarchy, by keeping its heroes in a "sublime and precipitous" position—that is, away from common readers—kills its own culture. The subculture of obscurity is characterized by its vitality:

> But such trivial ephemeral books do not merely break the ascent and encourage us to mightier efforts. They are the dressingrooms, the workshops, the wings, the sculleries, the bubbling cauldrons, where life seethes and steams and is forever on the boil. By sousing ourselves in memoirs we keep our minds supple, and so when at last we tackle the finished product—Hamlet for example—we bring to the understanding of him fertile minds imbued with ideas, at once *creative and receptive*. So we can never approach Ajax and Electra; and in consequence they are never taken into the depths of our beings, but remain always a little craggy, a little indissoluble, an inch or two beyond our grasp. For literature did undoubtedly once lie down with life, and all her progeny, being the result of that misalliance, are more or less impure. To understand them we must live. And then, since we are seeking excuses, who can say where life ends and literature begins? And then who can guide us? And then how delicious to ramble and explore! (381–82)

Autobiography is important because it stretches the reader's mind. The reader remains at the center of Woolf's discourse. The relationship between life, autobiography, and the reader is a sexual one, and the metaphors of wings and sculleries imply that the actual play or dinner is removed from the excitement of its material production, that autobiography is less a fiction than "higher forms of literature." Autobiography is liquid literature as opposed to solid drama. Woolf can read *Hamlet* creatively and receptively because she has read Elizabethan memoirs. But the Greeks remain abstract because she has never read the life stories of ordinary people in that age. Contemporary criticism would say that autobiography is no closer to "life" than other genres. But common sense tells us that Woolf is right. If we are measuring the "impurity" of genres, the memoir has indeed more "life" than more deliberately artificial forms. Woolf was after a sense of what the daily life of kitchenmaids was like, or what it felt like to live the obscure life, and "literature" seldom bothered to tell her. She confesses that she reads memoirs with missionary zeal, speaking directly to feminist critics of the last decade:

> One likes romantically to feel oneself a deliverer advancing with lights across the waste of years to the rescue of some stranded ghost—a Mrs. Pilkington, a Rev. Henry Elman, a Miss Ann Gilbert—who has been waiting, appealing, forgotten in the growing gloom. Possibly they hear one coming. They shuffle; they preen; they bridle. Old secrets well up to their lips. The divine relief of communication will soon again be theirs. The dust shifts and Mrs. Gilbert—but the contact with life is instantly salutary.

The obscure feminist, black, Chicana, or lesbian critic looking for her people, left out of literature and history, shining lights in out-of-the-way libraries and second-hand bookshops, does feel like a missionary. As we have rescued our own stranded ghosts, read them, reprinted them, and urged others to read them, we have played the life-giving role Woolf assigns to readers here. What is that role? Her Dantesque portrait of a literary limbo containing all the lost souls of women and other obscure autobiographers throughout history endows their readers, their discoverers, with powers of resurrection. Such readers are gods, providing "the divine relief of communication" to dead souls. I confess to similar delusions, and am sure that many colleagues agree. The contact is not only salutary for the ghost but for the resurrector. Miss Gilbert becomes Mrs. in the process. Or perhaps she has only aged. The idea of the reader as Messiah certainly gives one pause.

Those particular "stranded ghosts" whom I have rescued for discussion here—though not, of course, single-handedly—were not obscure in their own day. That is why they raise interesting questions for a theory of women's autobiography. They were famous women, in the public eye. They left their signatures on public discourse. But they anticipated obscurity because of their gender, and they wrote their memoirs as a hedge against certain deflation of their reputations. They were not writers but made themselves into writers in a bid for eternity. Their memoirs were all very successful when they were published but are now out of print, shuffling about in the dusty limbo of unread books that Woolf describes.

There are two factors that interest me in the study of these works. First, I would argue that the very *mediocrity* (in Woolf's re/signing of the meaning of the word) of the genre in the tradition of patriarchal canons assisted in the survival of the form for use by women and other "obscure" people. Unlike epic poetry, the drama, or the novel, the memoir made no grand claims to high artistic achievement. Consequently women could write in this genre without threatening male hegemony or offering claims to competition. Because autobiography was a "lesser" form, requiring from its author keen observation rather than divine creativity, men were less likely to criticize women for engaging in a harmless activity that required only talent, not genius. The eighteenth and nineteenth centuries in France, Germany, and England saw a proliferation of memoirs by women of letters, their observations of politics and people providing a rich source for historians. Since they did not pretend to *be* social historians, they could be encouraged, and a professional or serious historian could raid this enormous wealth of detailed observation for an anecdote or for a portrait of a minister of state. The genius of Madame de Staël could be modestly cloaked by these obscure and "mediocre" forms.

Second, the intended audience for women's memoirs was other women, and thus they described a circle in which the obscure read the obscure; serious men could dip into the circle of women's memoirs for amusement. The intimacy of women's conversation could be maintained in a literary form, retaining sincerity and a certain naive realism in relation to more self-conscious and artificial forms of writing. The woman diarist or memoir writer could be seen as recording culture, neither creating nor analyzing it. Thus women close to great men wrote their lives, and sometimes a subtext of their own lives provided variety in the lives and letters of such men, as Annie Thackeray emerged in her introductions to her father's works or as Proust's maid lives herself in her memoir of him. The wives, daughters, sisters, and mistresses of these men revealed themselves as they kept alive the legends of their masters.

Spiritual autobiography is also an acceptable script for a woman's life in Western Christian culture, and this form has flourished from Margery Kempe to Saint Teresa. It even expands to include the Jewish Holocaust narrative of Anne Frank's diary and its successors. For the female life as a religious experience is as neatly framed by a Nazi oven as it is by a convent cell. The prostitute is as popular as the nun, and lives of the mistresses of kings and presidents never lack an audience.[2] Virginia Woolf refers to the *Memoirs of Hariette Wilson* so often that it is clear she regarded them as important works of art. Actresses' memoirs also promise scandalous tidbits to the reader as well as hints on how to succeed in the same business. The moral uplift in Lauren Bacall's autobiography, its strong assertion of family loyalty, is satisfying to bourgeois readers who see the melodrama of their own domestic lives writ large and glamorous. All of these women had some relation to great men—or to god, the ultimate great man. What about women of great personal achievement?

I propose to explore the memoirs of women of genius in their own right, to study the construction of the self in a series of late Victorian and Edwardian autobiographies by women who achieved greatness in their day. It is too simple to say they were forgotten *because* they were important individually, not in relation to great men. Some of them were clever enough to construct their autobiographies as if they were important only in relation to great men—surely because the history of autobiography made clear that these were the kind of works that did survive. None of these women considered themselves to be primarily writers, yet each produced one or several works of genius in the genre of autobiography, diary, or memoir.

Elizabeth Robins (1862–1952), the Ibsen actress and suffragette, transformed the moribund London stage in the 1890s and theatricalized the suffrage movement. She was an American who lived in England for most of her life, yet none of the countries or movements whose interests she served have yet done her justice.[3] Dame Ethel Smyth (1858–1944), the English composer who studied in Leipzig with Johannes Brahms, wrote a Mass, a symphony, several operas including *The Wreckers*, song cycles, and other musical pieces, was unlucky in being caught in the enmity between England and Germany, which led several times to the cancellation of performances of her works. The genius of her memoirs was recognized in her own day, and she produced several volumes after the initial success of her two-volume *Impressions That Remained*.[4] Sophie Kovalevsky (1850–1891), the Russian mathematician, was finally awarded a doctorate after she solved two very important problems proposed by her mentor, Karl Theodore Weierstrass. Since women were not allowed to teach in Russia, she taught at the University of Stockholm. Her memoir, *A Russian Childhood*, is a remarkable piece of work.[5]

Jane Ellen Harrison (1851–1928), the classical anthropologist, is included here because Virginia Woolf urged her to write *Reminiscences of a Student's Life*, which Woolf published at the Hogarth Press in 1925; Woolf somehow anticipated the future neglect of those brilliant volumes, from *Prolegomena to the Study of Greek Religion* to *Themis*, in favor of Sir James Frazer or Claude Lévi-Strauss. Marie Bashkirtseff (1860–1884), the Russian painter who studied in Paris and exhibited at the Salon, died young and left behind a celebrated journal, which was published by her mother. The journal was reprinted several times, drawing much attention to Bashkirtseff's scandalously "unfeminine" ego. But it has not been celebrated or reprinted by contemporary feminist scholarship precisely because her supposed vanity and selfishness challenge our romantic notions about virtue in women of the past.[6] Whenever I wish to make generalizations or propose a theory of women's autobiography based on writing through the Other, or in community with other women *as* the Other in a patriarchal world, I am faced with the stark egotism of Marie Bashkirtseff: "I am my own heroine"; "I love myself." Victorian reformer W. T. Stead, who went to prison in order to expose the evils of "white slavery" in London, was shocked to the depths of his chivalrous Puritan soul by Bashkirtseff's journal. It was in response to Stead's review that George Bernard Shaw claimed that women artists were members of the "third or Bashkirtseff sex," an idea that he used over and over again in his theater criticism of the nineties and in his own creation of "new women" characters on the stage.

To theorize over this limbo of women's autobiographies, one is forced to recognize that only two common threads unite the writers: they anticipate the coming of the resurrecting reader and speak directly to her; and they write consciously in the female tradition of European memoir, letting the stress fall more heavily on the life than the work. Each woman's troubled emotional life in relation to her own femaleness and to the social constructions of femininity—in unrequited love, failed marriages, and lesbian relationships—earned her membership in Shaw's "third or Bashkirtseff sex." The work always takes second place to the life. Ethel Smyth, bursting with anecdotes and detailed descriptions of Brahms and his circle, fails to tell us what it felt like to compose music. Bashkirtseff bares her jealous soul for all to see and reveals her petty and grand ambitions. She details the drives to the country to paint one of her pictures, her frenzy to finish before the apple blossoms fall, the disaster that she averts after putting too much oil in her paint, thus turning the blossoms yellow on her canvas. We see her emotions from the inside; we enter her teacher's atelier, but we do not see the inside of that celebrated mind. Jane Harrison lets us know immediately that as a true Yorkshirewoman she abhors showing off and publicity. It is up to the reader to read her books and essays and to judge her genius and originality. She did not claim her place as the founder of the interdisciplinary field of classical anthropology and archaeology and, although James Frazer and Claude Lévi-Strauss acknowledged her in ample footnotes, their followers claimed the men as the founding fathers. Elizabeth Robins is so reticent about her own role in translating, producing, and acting Ibsen in England that theater historians persist in attributing to Shaw the accomplishments of a young American actress of genius. Sometimes I suspect that her supposed modesty comes from an ego powerful enough to turn the theatrical world on its head and trembling in suppression beneath her praise of men of genius. Kovalevsky believes wholeheartedly in the power of her native Russian soil to produce genius but not to nourish it. She writes consciously as an intellectual historian of the soul, speaking to the generations of women of scientific genius she hopes will come after her.

The Third or Bashkirtseff Sex

In two illuminating and wide-ranging essays, "Women's Autobiographical Selves: Theory and Practice" (included in this collection) and "Theories of Autobiography and Fictions of the Self in H.D.'s Canon," Susan Stanford Friedman establishes a solid and workable feminist theory of autobiography, a theory that is useful not only for the explication of women's texts, but also those of blacks, lesbians, and other outsiders to mainstream patriarchal culture.[7] Friedman uses the historical and psychological feminist theories of Sheila Rowbotham and Nancy Chodorow to argue that Gusdorf's emphasis on the individuality of autobiographical selves constructed in the writing process does not apply to culturally imposed group or gender identities in the case of women and minorities. She argues that women, for both social and psychological reasons, are less separated from others and experience themselves as bonded to and in community with others. Friedman argues that women's double consciousness, like that of Jews or blacks or homosexuals, results in autobiographical forms that are not only individualistic, but also collective.

Bernice Johnson Reagon argues that black women's life stories are really cultural histories, self-consciously carrying on from slave narratives.[8] And Mary Mason has described women's autobiographies as diverging from the male focus on the individual self, in that there is so often a fully rendered Other in these texts. Mason's theory is particularly applicable to Elizabeth Robins's autobiographies, as revealed in their very titles: *Ibsen and the Actress; Theater and Friendship*, a narrative based on Henry James's letters to her; *Both Sides of the Curtain*, a book that resolutely stays on one side (and was, incidentally, given its title by Virginia Woolf, who was as tireless in getting other people to write their memoirs as she was in *not* writing her own); *Raymond and I*, the story of her trip to Alaska to find her lost brother; and, anonymously, *Ancilla's Share*, a study of the aftermath of the feminist movement in England that analyzes woman's role as "Other," "handmaiden of the lord," or *ancilla*.

Although feminists will find the journal of Marie Bashkirtseff the most disturbing of the texts under discussion here, male theorists of autobiography—Georges Gusdorf, Roy Pascal, or James Olney, for example—would, I am certain (if they read women's autobiographies), immediately classify it as a "great" book. They would, of course, be echoing an earlier male audience that championed the genius of the journal, from W. K. Gladstone to Maurice Barrès. Its very self-consciousness, an awareness of the creation of the self through writing and the fiction of that creation, and the anguish of its confessional tone, which links it to Augustine and Rousseau, makes the *journal* a classic in the male tradition. Bashkirtseff's powerful belief in her own individuality and uniqueness, her struggle for self-expression in every possible form—singing, painting, writing her journal, even her dress and the decoration of her rooms—is an extreme form of the romantic ideology of individualism. It is also the one work which fits Paul de Man's "defacement" in that it proleptically figures her death and her presence with the reader after death in face and form as well as in writing. Sophie Kovalevsky's *A Russian Childhood*, on the other hand, writes the self as a cultural history of a people, and thus her work fits into Bernice Reagon's analysis of black women's autobiographies. The stubborn recalcitrance of a Jane Harrison or an Elizabeth Robins, in refusing to present the self while continually creating the Other, reveals a deep anxiety about exposing female selfhood as egotism when Victorian ideals of women's selflessness were deeply ingrained in their consciousness. Consequently, Patricia Meyer Spacks's analysis is pertinent here, as well as Mason's. But in the case of Ethel Smyth's prolific and illustrious memoirs, we are faced with the lack of an adequate theory to explain them.

Friedman's definition of women's autobiographies as partially unique and partially steeped in community will take us part of the way toward an explanation.[9]

In 1917, while Ethel Smyth was in Paris doing volunteer war work, she became deaf, and she wrote in a 1923 preface to a Knopf reprint of *Impressions That Remained* that she despaired of ever hearing music again, let alone composing. While seeing her aurist, she also visited her friend, the young Count Joachim Clary, who had become crippled and blind; she entertained him with stories of her youth. He and her friend Madame "Toche" Bulteau, who had "written a remarkable book called *L'Âme des Anglais*," urged Smyth to write her memoirs. She claimed in her books that she hoped "many readers would say to themselves: 'I am not an artist, nor, so far as I am aware, have I ever attempted to hit any difficult mark; yet this woman's experiences are curiously like my own.'" She appears to have believed that the artist is the *type* of all humanity, that in writing her own life, she was writing the life of Woman.

From hints in her letters and from Christopher St. John's biography, it appears that Smyth's depression came not only from deafness but from an unhappy love affair, presumably with the one woman whose portrait does not appear in her memoirs. The method of life writing is also distinctive. It deliberately exposes the reader to the raw materials which aid the writer rather than creating a distance from them. Smyth wrote using her own diaries and letters to friends and family as her raw materials, but she also liberally used their letters to her, and often little packets of these letters are tacked on to the ends of chapters, allowing readers to see the patchwork of the life-writing process and thereby encouraging the reader to write from a similar store of letters from friends and family. Clearly, the identity crisis for a composer who was losing her hearing was solved by writing. If "I write; therefore I am" helped Smyth regain her strength, "they write to me; therefore I am" increased her powers even more. What began as therapy continued as a necessity. Even when she recovered her hearing (she did not become totally deaf until the 1930s), she believed that the more she lived and recreated that life in memoirs, the more power her music had to express life. If one uses a Barthesian or Lacanian model, one may see that the writing of music, putting down notes on a page to represent the sounds of instruments, is a very powerful form of symbolic inscription. Smyth's tremendous success at the game of *écriture* came from her ability to re/sign the drive to create music into storytelling and to write the Kristevan "semiotic" in her memoirs.

Mathematics is another highly symbolic form of inscription, and Sophie Kovalevsky believed that her writing came from the same source as her mathematics:

> You are surprised at my working simultaneously in literature and in mathematics. Many people who never had occasion to learn what mathematics is confuse it with arithmetic and consider it a dry and arid science. In actual fact it is the science which demands the utmost imagination. One of the foremost mathematicians of our century says very justly that it is impossible to be a mathematician without also being a poet in spirit. It goes without saying that to understand the truth of this statement one must repudiate the old prejudice by which poets are supposed to fabricate what does not exist, and that imagination is the same thing as "making things up." It seems to me that the poet must see what others do not see, must see more deeply than other people. And the mathematician must do the same. (35)

In what way were the female identities of Ethel Smyth and Sophie Kovalevsky affected by the ability to create in those highly regarded and jealously guarded male symbolic preserves of music and mathematics? Both women were fluent speakers and writers of many languages, and mathematics and music are also "languages." Did Smyth and Kovalevsky construct a self in those languages as well as in memoirs? In what ways is making up the self in memoir like or unlike making up a theorem or composing a Mass? For that matter, how does the creation of characters other than the self in collaboration with a playwright affect an actress such as Elizabeth Robins when she becomes an autobiographer? Jane Harrison spent her whole career trying to create from pots, vases, and artifacts the religious life of the preclassical Greeks—that is, life *before* the texts of the classics. How did this work affect her own imagination of herself? One senses in Marie Bashkirtseff's habit of keeping a diary from an early age that she needed to separate herself from her Russian relatives, that the act of writing prevented her from being engulfed and swallowed up by her mother and aunts. Perhaps she was free to capture the expressivity, as she called it, of her subjects in painting because she had created herself in her diary.

"Great men" feel a social obligation to contribute their autobiographies to the history of patriarchy. Women of extraordinary achievement in late Victorian and Edwardian Europe were not in positions equal to men. They were often the first of their sex to break the barriers of fields that had hitherto belonged solely to men. Often one feels there is a problematic split between the subjects' wish to write in the tradition of German or French aristocratic or intellectual women observers of their culture and the desire to imitate the male mode of the maker of culture. One solution was to remove the self from the center of preoccupation, as Ethel Smyth creates circle after circle of overlapping communities of female friendship. Her self is defined in relationship. She creates not Ethel Smyth, the English composer, but Ethel, the friend of so and so. She loves herself because she is beloved, and the reader willingly enters the circle of loving friendship. The more she tells anecdotes about her foolishness or rashness and creates her own eccentric character on the page, the less she reveals of her own inner weakness, pain, or suffering. As public figures of great intellectual or artistic achievement, the women discussed here used their autobiographies to show that they were also women, creatures for whom relationship and community were very important. Their achievements were brilliant, but they show themselves in the *mediocrity* of their lives as women who are connected to community by the ordinariness and materiality of their womanhood.

We may also ask ourselves what the relation is between the *form* of women's autobiographical writing and female identity. Martin Sommerfield's classification of diary as the lyric of self, memoir as epic, and autobiography as drama is pertinent to this question. Ethel Smyth's memoirs—an enormous production, on the huge scale of nineteenth-century opera—are grand in scope and theme. Marie Bashkirtseff's diary is as intense and poignant in its sense of impending death, its cries of delight and sadness, as lyrics by Keats. The autobiographical forms chosen by Sophie Kovalevsky, Elizabeth Robins, and Jane Harrison are structured as drama, and characters act their parts on the stage of the text.

But, as Roy Pascal points out, class is also a determining factor in the choice of form. It is difficult to determine whether class or gender played a more determining role in Ethel Smyth's choice of the grand manner in memoir. As a general's daughter with upper-class connections through her French mother, she sees her life as a series of battlefields; her victories and defeats are duly recorded. She admires the clever strategies of her enemies and gives detailed descriptions of her onslaughts against the prejudices of famous conductors and composers in order to get her works heard and played. But along with this picture of life as a military campaign against the combined forces of the international patriarchal musical establishment, with Smyth as Joan of Arc, the memoir contains another text of an ongoing historical conversation between women about their own lives. This radical discourse is what holds the reader's fascinated attention, for here is a woman-centered universe, where all love and passion is generated by women for women. It is the essence of civilization. Without embarrassment or shame, Dame Ethel records passion after passion for other women, unrolling on a huge canvas the great lesbian romances of her life on a grand and noble scale. She paints herself as a genius of loving friendship and boasts of never losing a friend. All the characters take on the classic beauty and power of Greek statues. No justification is necessary. This is how life is lived by those who have "great" souls and "great" hearts. Women loving one another is what makes the world go round and creates all human social life. It is a breath-taking accomplishment. She tells the story of her tragic love for Lisl von Herzogenberg, the wife of her composition teacher in Leipzig, as if it were the story of Romeo and Juliet or Heloise and Abelard, and, not only does she get away with it, but the reader is convinced that it is indeed one of the great historical love stories of all time. When she tells her readers in the preface that although they may not be composers they will find their own lives in these pages, Smyth means that women have always had primary relationships with each other, but few since Sappho have dared to write them down.

Both class and gender determine the form of Kovalevsky's autobiography. As a radical member of the generation of Russian nihilist aristocratic intelligentsia, she is recording before it disappears altogether (a prospect she looks forward to as a woman and a socialist) the life of the ruling class of Tsarist Russia. The tone is a bittersweet mixture of nostalgia and political dismay. As a "European" and a scientist, Kovalevsky sees Russia as savage and cruel. As a woman and a Russian, she recreates the scenes of family life and intellectual awakening that created her own consciousness and drove her away. There is a real tension in the writing that casts a spell on the reader. For to write old Russia, to recreate her childhood, is an antirevolutionary act. She is creating what she wishes to destroy, breathing life into a system that politically she believes should die.

Writing her Russian memoir in Stockholm, with no prospect of ever having a professorship in Russia, having tried to no avail to get a position in France, where her lover (also named Kovalevsky, but no relation to her husband, who had killed himself) was living, mourning for the loss of her beloved sister, who died young before fulfilling her promise as a writer, Kovalevsky wrote for and about her sister, as if she could only resurrect her own ghost in the process of bringing Aniuta back to life. In fact, the chapter from *A Russian Childhood* that is best known—and is often compared to Tolstoy and Turgenev—is the story of Dostoevsky's courtship of her sister. Sophie had become a celebrity as the first important woman mathematician. As a young bride in England, she had met George Eliot several times and had been introduced by her to Herbert Spencer as "a living refutation" of his theories. But to Sophie it was her sister Aniuta—six years older, beautiful, brilliant, and determined—who was the genius. Aniuta had dared to write and to publish, to arrange the paper marriages that got them out of Russia to study, and her radical dedication was one of the major forces in the Paris Commune of 1870. She edited the commune's newspaper and formulated many of its policies regarding women, health, and education. After her death, Sophie wrote: "There is no one left for whom I can be that bashful, diffident, clinging little Sonya" (33).

Kovalevsky's memoir is by genre dramatic for several other reasons. She wrote it in Sweden, surrounded by feminist friends who urged her to write. During her six-year stay in Russia without the opportunity to do mathematics, she had written theater criticism. As Aniuta's agonizingly slow and painful illness progressed, Sophie collaborated with the feminist writer Anne-Charlotte Mittag-Leffler, sister of the mathematician who had gotten her an academic appointment. Together they wrote a pair of plays, "How It Was" and "How It Might Have Been," under the title *The Struggle for Happiness*. The Ibsen/Strindberg battle in drama over the nature of woman was in full swing. In fact, Strindberg had attacked Kovalevsky's appointment in a newspaper article, saying that "a female professor of mathematics is a pernicious and unpleasant phenomenon—even, one might say, a monstrosity" (Kovalevsky 27). The fear of being thought a "monster" is faced by all women who break the barriers in male-dominated fields. In the chapter called "Earliest Memories," Sophie records her horror of physical deformity and the recurring nightmare of being shadowed by a three-legged man. In *Oedipus* the riddle of the sphinx defines the three-legged man as an old man with a cane, and certainly there were many important older men in Kovalevsky's life: the uncle who taught her mathematics as a child; Weierstrass, the great mathematician with whom she studied; one might even include her teenage passion for her sister's suitor, Dostoevsky. The three-legged man might also express her fear of male sexuality. Certainly Kovalevsky was not happy with her "paper" husband and appears to have consummated this marriage many years later, reluctantly and out of guilt. The second Kovalevsky also made her very unhappy and refused to marry her unless she gave up mathematics. It was on her return from a stormy visit to him in France over the Christmas holidays in 1891 that she caught pneumonia and died at age forty-one. She had begun the memoir to entertain him, and she said that he always filled her with the desire to write.

The memoir was first published as a novel, *The Rajevski Sisters*, in Swedish, and it was a great success. A year later, it came out in Russian in its original, first-person form. During this very creative period in the late 1880s in Stockholm, Kovalevsky also solved an important mathematical problem, for which she won the Prix Bordin from the French Academy of Sciences. But when she wrote in collaboration with Anne-Charlotte Mittag-Leffler, she worked out the incidents and psychology of the characters while her friend wrote the lines in Swedish. Sophie embroidered furiously while Charlotte wrote. In 1890 Kovalevsky wrote her novel, *A Nihilist Girl*. The circle of women around her seems to have encouraged her creativity, as in her youth in Berlin; while her "paper" husband was studying elsewhere, she lived with her dearest friend, Julia Lermontova, and solved the problems that Weierstrass had worked on for years. (He eventually got her a degree from Göttingen on the strength of this work, which was presented *in absentia*.)

Sophie was interested in her own psychology and that of women in general. She considered herself "nervous" and high-strung and tried to analyze whether there was any real basis for her powerful feeling of being unloved. She discussed childhood depressions that often awoke as twilight approached: a feeling of terror brought on by "the sensation of *oncoming* darkness" (57), or a similar fear that occurred at the sight of "big, unfinished houses with naked brick walls and empty spaces instead of windows." She could not bear the sight of broken dolls and was brought almost to convulsions when Aniuta teased her with "a wax doll with a broken black eye dangling out of its head."[10] This insecurity contributed to her fear of failure if she accepted the teaching post at Stockholm. After Kovalevsky's death, Lermontova wrote: "Like all the prejudices we must struggle against, the prejudice against the ability of women to do intellectual work exists not only in those around us, but also in ourselves" (Kovalevsky 44). Sophie also wrote two essays on the treatment of female hysteria, one on Dr. Louis's psychiatric sessions with women patients at La Charité in Paris, and another highly critical of Charcot's treatment of hysterical women by hypnosis. Charcot's practice is now famous because of Freud's attendance at these same lectures, and feminist theorists have begun to study his approach (34). Kovalevsky was greatly depressed by the treatment of women as if they were deaf and unfeeling animals (Kennedy 274). Left unfinished at her death was a novel, *Vae Victis*, which Beatrice Stillman describes as an "anti-apotheosis of spring, depicting it not in conventional poetic terms but as a crude sensual force which awakens desire and seems to offer a mass of promises but fulfills none of them" (Kovalevsky 34).

The drama of *A Russian Childhood* is effective because it evokes sisterhood. While Kovalevsky tells her own story, that story is set against the vivid and contrasting successes of Aniuta as a writer, a beauty, and a radical. Aniuta rejects Dostoevsky because "he needs a different kind of wife from me. His wife will have to dedicate herself to him utterly, utterly, to give her whole life to him, to think about nothing but him. And I can't do that, I want to live myself!" (40). Sophie tells us that her own feeling was the wish to sacrifice herself to a great love. In fact, Aniuta's marriage to the French communist, Jaclar, was as demanding as the life she had rejected earlier, and Sophie never seems to have found a mate who could both love her and let her work.

The other drama of the memoir is created from the lives of women servants and serfs and their crimes and punishments, vividly described from the child's point of view. As Sophie's "I" emerges in relation to her sister and her beloved Nanny, she witnesses, remembers, and writes down a simultaneous extinguishing or thwarting of developing self in the women servants around her. But the text draws no moral; like the writings of Turgenev, it describes and the reader judges. Reading Kovalevsky's portrait of her hated, narrow-minded English governess, one suspects that Sophie began to write in her late thirties because she had been forbidden to write poetry as a child: "She mercilessly hunted down all my poetic efforts. If, to my misfortune, she spied a scrap of paper with my doggerel scrawled on it, she would instantly pin it to my shoulder. And then, in the presence of my brother and sister, she would declaim the hapless piece out loud—twisting and distorting it cruelly" (102). There is a vivid portrait of the servants' joy on a mushrooming expedition to the forest, and the terrifying story of an aunt who had been so cruel to her serfs that she was strangled under a featherbed by a whole household of servants led by her personal maid, even though they knew they would all go to Siberia as punishment.

There is only one mention of mathematics in the memoir, and it is a curious one. When the Kryukovsky family moved to Palibino, there was not enough wallpaper for the whole house, and one of the nursery rooms was papered with Sophie's father's university lecture notes on differential and integral calculus. She was fascinated by the "strange unintelligible formulas" and stood for hours as a child trying to figure them out and to understand the sequence. Later, when she studied with a professor, he was amazed at the speed with which she understood concepts of limit and derivatives, "exactly as if you knew them in advance" (123). It is possible that Sophie's way of differentiating herself from Aniuta was to work in the symbolic language of mathematics, or even that in doing mathematics she reproduced the writing on the wall, and thereby the feeling of security she had in the nursery with her nanny.

In a later autobiographical sketch, written for a Russian newspaper in 1890, Sophie again told the story of the writing on the wall, attributing her interest in mathematics to her uncle's "mysterious" talk about "squaring the circle" and "the asymptote, the straight line which the curve approaches without ever quite meeting it." She described the yellow sheets on the nursery wall as "hieroglyphics" she was determined to puzzle out. The only reason her father allowed her to go to Petersburg to study was because Professor Tyrtov had left a copy of his book on physics at Palibino and on a later visit she told him how much she had liked it. Unschooled in trigonometry, she had made up her own system, using chords instead of sines. Tyrtov compared her to Pascal and insisted that she be given training. In the newspaper sketch as well as the memoir, Kovalevsky writes as a celebrated public woman, deliberately revealing her weaknesses and unhappiness to encourage women readers to follow in her footsteps, as she also had spent much effort to help young women get out of Russia to study and had helped to start a school for women in Petersburg. She makes only one confession in these memoirs: that she wasted six years in Russia not doing mathematics, trying instead to be a wife to Kovalevsky and a mother to their children, and that they had lost everything in capitalist adventures in real estate (220). She uses the phrase "confess my sins" only in relation to this social and political activity, not her personal life, and she praises Sweden for its democratic systems and free university.

A Russian Childhood dramatizes class conflicts between landowners and serfs and sets the upper-class female self against the lives of women servants and serfs. Even Kovalevsky's first memory of identity is of being asked her name at church and being unable to reply. Her nurse's friend says she can remember her father's name, Kryukovsky, because there is a kryuk, or hook, on the gate of their house. Her opening lines reinforce my thesis in this essay that there is a special relationship between the female writer and her reader in women's autobiographies, reproducing a natural, intimate conversation between women that is simultaneously personal and social and is conceived as the basis of civilization. Kovalevsky's own memories are like the "hieroglyphics" on the nursery wall, a problem to puzzle out. First she must find the sequence:

> I would like to know whether there is anyone who can pinpoint the precise instant of existence when a clear awareness of his or her own "I" emerged for the first time: the earliest glimmer of conscious life. I cannot do it at all. When I start sorting through my first memories and classifying them, the same thing happens to me every time: these memories always seem to slide apart before my eyes. Here it is, it seems—I've found it, the first impression that left a distinct memory trace. But no sooner do I focus my thoughts on it for a while than other impressions from an even earlier time immediately appear and take form. And the most troublesome thing about it is that I myself am utterly unable to determine which of these impressions I actually remember from experience and which of them I only heard about later in my childhood. . . . And what is worse—I can never manage to call up a single one of these primal memories in all its purity without unwittingly mixing something alien with it during the actual process of remembering. (47–48)

Kovalevsky asks for the reader's response. She lays out the problem of truth in memory as clearly as possible, setting her own writing not as the individual, antisocial act that the critics describe as the essence of male autobiography, but as part of the collective desire to explore the psychological processes of the human mind. We are invited to participate in the process of mutual resurrection of our pasts, to follow her example and to contribute an analysis of our own struggles with memory and truth. "I would like to know," as opposed to "let me tell you," suggests continuing inquiry, question and response, and this is the shape of women's autobiographical discourse. The writer asks the reader to write her self.

Collaboration as Co-Creation

In comparison with *A Russian Childhood*, the diary of Marie Bashkirtseff, Kovalevsky's compatriot, seems primitively individualistic and formed on the male model of outdoing everyone in anguish and suffering. But Bashkirtseff was very young when it was written, and perhaps if we had the scraps of paper that the stern English governess, Miss Margaret Smith, pinned to the shoulders of the teenage Sophie Kovalevsky and mocked, they would ring with the same adolescent megalomania and self-pity. Perhaps these are the qualities that have made Bashkirtseff's journal so admired by men: the anxieties of self-infatuation and the naked drive to outshine her competitors and become famous are so "unwomanly" because they are so antisocial. Whereas Kovalevsky's method is an enactment of her radical social beliefs, in which writing one's life is part of the social history, Bashkirtseff had no vocabulary of community. When her painting took a third rather than a second in the Paris Salon, she believed it was because she was a Russian, not because she was a woman. The relationship between reader and writer established immediately by Marie Bashkirtseff is intense and demanding. She is the victim and we are her saviors. By reading her we make her live and fulfill her desires, and in a curious way we are asked to be her sexual partners. She has never been loved, she cries, and one rushes to assure her that she is loved. Here Woolf's claim that as readers we like to see ourselves romantically as deliverers is powerfully evoked, and all chivalrous readers—most male, but, I suspect, some female—are inspired by this text to see themselves charging to her rescue on white horses:

> This poor journal, the confidant of all my strivings toward the light, all these outbursts, which would be regarded as the outbursts of imprisoned genius if my aspirations were to be finally crowned by success, but which will be regarded as the vain ravings of a commonplace creature if I am destined to languish forever in obscurity. To marry and have children? Any washerwoman can do that. What then do I desire? Ah, you know well what I desire—I desire fame. It is not this journal that will give it to me, however. This journal will be published only after my death for I show myself too *nakedly* in it to wish it to be read during my lifetime. (*Journal*, 1876: 90)

Bashkirtseff knows very well that she consciously creates herself in the diary:

> I must repeat to myself again that no advice in the world—nothing but personal experience—could ever have kept me from doing anything I wished to do. That is because the woman who writes

these words and the woman she is writing about are two different persons. What do all these sufferings matter to *me*? I write them down; I analyze them; I transcribe my daily life, but to *me*, to *me myself*, all that is completely indifferent. It is my pride, my self-love, my interests, my complexion, my eyes, that suffer, that weep, that rejoice; but *I*, I take part in it all only to observe, to narrate, to write about and reason coldly concerning all these trifles, like Gulliver among the Lilliputians. (*Journal*, 1877: 149)

Bashkirtseff demands pity: "Can you not fancy you already see me feeble, emaciated, pale, dying, dead? It is not atrocious that this should be so? But, dying young, I shall at least inspire everyone with pity. I am myself touched with compassion when I think of my fate" (*Journal*, 1881: 273). At the time these words were written, Bashkirtseff was suffering from tuberculosis and was growing deaf; she had already lost her voice and given up her ambition to sing in favor of painting. Bashkirtseff's translator says she has "all the cynicism of a Machiavelli and the naiveté of an ardent and enthusiastic girl." Despite winning a medal at the Salon, Marie's fame as a painter quickly receded as the fame of Impressionists increased. "The Meeting," a large realistic painting of Paris street urchins, was found abandoned in the attic of the Newberry Library in Chicago in 1973. When I ask feminist art historians why Bashkirtseff is not included in their books, they cite the vanity of the diary as a reason. In a preface written in 1884, just before her death, Bashkirtseff asserts the power of her diary as "a human document" that would interest Zola, Goncourt, or Maupassant. The expressive realism or naturalism of her writing is as much of the period as her paintings and those of her beloved Bastien Lepage—now thoroughly overshadowed by Impressionism. Marie herself looks down on the "childishness" of Manet and all those who paint "pretty subjects," and yet the diary bursts with details of her concern over her appearance: dresses, hats, flowers, decorations for her room, even the white leather cases for the very diary in which she writes. She jumps from philosophizing to boasting that she owns seven hundred books. In the preface she worries that publishing the diary might destroy its value and proclaims her *sincerity*:

If this book is not the *exact*, the *absolute*, the *strict* truth, it has no *raison d'être*. Not only do I always write what I think, but I have not even dreamed, for a single instant, of disguising anything that was to my disadvantage, or that might make me appear ridiculous.

Besides, I think myself too admirable for censure. You may be very certain, then, charitable readers, that I exhibited myself in the pages *just as I am*. (*Journal* ix)

She grudgingly reveals her birth date (11 November 1860): "Only to write it down is frightful. But then I console myself by thinking that I shall be no age at all when you read this journal" (*Journal* x). She prepares the journal for publication, fearing that her family might destroy it on her death:

and soon nothing would be left of me—nothing—nothing—nothing! This is the thought that has always terrified me. To live, to have so much ambition, to suffer, to weep, to struggle, and in the end to be forgotten;—as if I had never existed. . . . The record of a woman's life, written down day by day, without any attempt at concealment, as if no one in the world were ever to read it, yet with the purpose of being read, is always interesting. I am certain that I shall be found sympathetic, and I write down everything, everything, everything. (*Journal* xiv)

At age sixteen (although the dates may have been changed later to make her appear younger than she was), Bashkirtseff wrote:

What ever I may become in the future, I bequeath my journal to the world. I offer you here what no one has ever yet seen. All the memoirs, the journals, the letters, which are given to the public are only inventions glossed over, and intended to deceive the world; I have neither any political action to gloss over, nor any unworthy action to conceal. No one troubles himself whether I am in love or not, whether I laugh. (*Journal* 55)

Bashkirtseff's journal enjoyed several years of fame and then it—and she—disappeared from history. But in 1911 it was still popular enough to inspire an anonymous parody: *Super Soul: The Memoirs of Marie Mushenough*. Bashkirtseff's myth was taken up by Maurice Barrès as "the representation of the eternal force which calls forth heroes in each generation" and by "Our Lady Who is Never Satisfied," a right-wing idealization of certain forms of womanhood that also used the figure of Joan of Arc, who was not canonized until the 1920s. It is unfortunate that we do not have a reliable text of the diary as Bashkirtseff wrote it. According to her friend Bojidar Karageorgevitch, the enormous manuscript was cut by her mother and by Theuriet, a friend of Bastien Lepage who wished to stress Marie's relationship with the painter. Karageorge-vitch deplores the changing of the dates to make her appear as "a sentimental freak only twelve years of age" and complains that "legend has seized hold of Maria Bashkirtseff and daily defaces more and more her real character." The omissions in the diary are also important:

> Marie was one of the first apostles of feminism. She aided in the publication of the *Citoyenne*, a feminist newspaper which preceded the *Fronde* . . . for which she wrote art criticism. . . . For a while she was devoted, body and soul, to feminism. She used to be present at the meetings in the Petrelle Hall, and scolded me as if I were the lowest of creatures, because my interest in these questions was not sufficiently lively. . . . "You are a wretch," she said, "you have no right to refuse to be interested in a question which is going to change the face of the earth." (Karageorgevitch 648)

Despite these problems with the text, Bashkirtseff's journal remains the great lyric outpouring of the striving woman artist.[11] Its "de-facement," in Paul de Man's terms, is successful.

In comparison to the flood of feeling that overwhelms the reader of Bashkirtseff, Elizabeth Robins's memoirs, including *Ibsen and the Actress*, and Jane Harrison's *Reminiscences of a Student's Life* are restrained and modest. They are so brief, compared to the major achievements of these women's lives, that one asks whether there is indeed any common thread running through women's autobiographies. The answer, I believe, lies in the relation of the writer to her reader. If we agree that the writer resurrects herself through memory, then the reader also resurrects the writer through reading her. This *collaboration* is a reproduction of women's culture as conversation. It does not occur in the male model of individualistic autobiography, where the reader is not expected to take such an active role. Both Harrison and Robins expect the reader to know their accomplishments in detail and to have judged them important before reading the memoir, as if in conversation with women friends certain things do not need to be said. The reader collaborates actively by providing all the missing information. Thus Robins and Harrison are more demanding of the reader as co-maker of the memoir than is Bashkirtseff, who tells all. Beneath the surface modesty of Robins and Harrison is the sure conviction of each that she is already a heroine for her reader. The memoirs of both were written in response to requests from Virginia Woolf at the Hogarth Press, the champion of "the Common Reader" who often proclaimed: "Of all literature . . . I love autobiography most" (*Letters* 5, no. 2687). In a sense, they could argue that their memoirs were not self-generated but were written in response to the reader's demand.

Collaboration is, in fact, the *subject* of Robins's *Ibsen and the Actress*, which argues that a drama does not live unless it is acted and gives to the actress and actor the same important collaborative role as Virginia Woolf gives to the reader of books. Does Robins really expect of her reader the same enormous dedication and passion that she herself gave to translating, producing, and acting Ibsen's plays in London in the nineties? Yes, I think so. Just as she argues that Ibsen's words on the page would never have lived unless they had become flesh in the persons of actors, so she sketches out her character and her own little drama of how two young American women were able to accomplish a major event in theater history; she expects the reader to fill in all the details, to develop from the barest sketch the full dramatic history of that period, thirty-five years earlier: "Without the help of the stage the world would not have had an Ibsen to celebrate; and without Ibsen the world would not have had the stage as it became after his plays were acted" (*Ibsen and the Actress* 8). She begins by establishing the world of women in the theater, and she praises Janet Achurch, the first English Nora, and Charrington's production of *A Doll's House* in 1899 as "less like a play than like a *personal meeting* with people and issues that seized us and held us, and wouldn't let us go" (11). In a conversational tone, she lets us know that she has played more than three hundred roles in repertory in the United States, and her criticism of the English actor-manager system is voiced as a series of jokes about Beerbohm Tree and other dominant figures. Like the gradual revelations of the best drama, it slowly dawns on the reader of Robins's memoir that the repertory system and national theater which we consider a great English tradition was actually begun by a young American woman.

Robins goes on to describe her famous roles as the first English Hedda Gabler, then as Hilda. She argues that critics still don't understand Hedda, who is "a bundle of unused opportunities," a person whose nervous system generates more force than the engine of her opportunity can use up, and she defends Hedda's suicide as displaying a certain form of courage. She praises Marion Lea and the other actresses in the early productions for caring more about the play than their individual parts and for creating a *collective* of actors, audience, and readers around these experimental productions, which replaced the patriarchal, individualistic, male-dominated West End theater. She describes critic William Archer (not Shaw) as the "bridge" between Ibsen and the actress and regales us with Henry James's criticism of her costume as Hilda. This role in *The Master Builder* gave her "release, such a conviction of having the audience with me, and at the same time such freedom from the yoke of the audience" (47). But her main point is: "More than anybody who ever wrote for the stage, Ibsen could, and usually did, collaborate with his actors. . . . It was as if he knew that only so could he get his effects—that is, by standing aside and watching his spell work not only through the actors, but *by* the actor as fellow-creator" (53). She ends by quoting Maeterlinck on collaboration as the highest form of art. By imitating the collaboration of playwright and actress in her memoir, she gives the reader an active role in making history. The woman autobiographer gives her reader a speaking part. Robins was taking the same risk for which she admired Ibsen. So far, however, her women readers and critics have had little luck in re/signing British theater history in its female American script.

Jane Ellen Harrison's brief and modest *Reminiscences of a Student's Life* is equally risky and sketchy. The intrepid student of anthropology or of women's history knows the big green volumes of *Prolegomena to the Study of Greek Religions*, *Themis*, and *Epilogomena*. By assuming the guise of student even in old age, Harrison can continue the role of eccentric and *enfant terrible* and play down the immense erudition and scholarship of her work. But "student" stands in her title as the Yorkshire-woman's silent rebuke of the patriarchal establishment of the study of classics at Cambridge—she was never awarded the professorship she so abundantly earned.

The brevity of Harrison's text enforces her statement that in Yorkshire silence about self is strongly valued. She tells the story of her father's loss of patience with her talkative stepmother, a harsh evangelical who had been their housekeeper before her mother's death. Her father did not insult his wife. He merely brought down from the attic a portrait of his first wife, who was highly regarded for her silence, and hung it in a prominent place in the dining room. Harrison tells this story to restrain herself, for she had made her living as a lively and dynamic lecturer: "I regret those lecturing years. I was voluble and had instant success, but it was mentally demoralizing and very exhausting. . . . I was almost fatally fluent" (63). The absences in the text must be filled in by the reader, much as the reader of *A Room of One's Own* fills in the name of the heroine of that text, "the great J—— H——," whose presence is so strongly evoked by absence, just after her death.

Such spirits or ghosts—here "bogeys" of past "matriarchal" religion standing behind Greek classical writings—and their rituals were the origin of Greek drama, Harrison argued in the groundbreaking works that founded the interdisciplinary field of classical anthropology and archaeology. To the Cambridge classicists, glued to their books and reading Greek society from texts, Harrison was an iconoclast who insisted on studying cultural artifacts, going to digs, unraveling the meanings of figures on vases, arguing that Medusa's head was symbolic and not a picture of a monster. Her pioneering work on what structuralists now call *sign* and *signified* is yet to be acknowledged. Like the phantom figures whose origins she traces from the Greek plays back into the unwritten past, she is a ghost in her own memoir as she is a ghost in Woolf's essay. How much she must have enjoyed telling her readers that she *is* Aunt Glegg in George Eliot's novel *The Mill on the Floss* and, radical that she was, insisting on her profound conservatism.

Jane Harrison was perceived by angry classicists, those strict formalists of her day who worshiped the text, as antitextual. Her major works were written in the vivid, colloquial style of women's conversation, punctuated with jokes and asides as well as the personal thrill of intellectual discovery. She saw no reason why scholarship should be dull. Her memoir is similarly antitextual, as if in avoiding dates and refusing to take herself seriously as the subject of archaeological inquiry, she is leaving the task of bringing her ghost to life for some equally adventurous biographer, and she ends with thanks for spending her old age in the companionship of Hope Mirrlees, as a "ghostly daughter." Harrison's method is to unite past and present. She is in Paris pursuing her studies of Russian bear stories and their relation to ancient bear cults, and so she says that her first memory is of the word Moscow, the name of her dog, and of Russian toys and food and a sled that her father and uncle brought back from their travels. After defining herself as Aunt Glegg, "rigidly, irrationally conservative, fibrous with prejudice" and attacking "pretentiousness," she describes her meetings with the famous—who were mostly women, including her heroine, George Eliot. But each past moment is countered by a present moment. She has just read *Ulysses* and finds it both "a drain of obscenities" and a work of genius that tries to "make conscious the subconscious." This juxtaposition of memory and present concern is also typical of Ethel Smyth's later memoirs. It is the characteristic of natural conversation rather than established literary form that gives women autobiographers their nonlinear model from life instead of art. In a story that marks her rejection of formalism for the study of material culture in relation to texts, Harrison tells how Francis Darwin reproved her for writing an article on "Mystica vannus Iacchi," defined as a fan, without ever having seen one. He found this "fan" in France, where it had been used since ancient times for winnowing, and he had a farmer demonstrate its use to her. "I had been reared in a school that thought it was far more important to parse a word than to understand it" (58), she wrote. This discovery marked a turning point in her career.

There is some nostalgia in *Reminiscences.* Harrison knows her work will be forgotten and praises her colleague, James Frazer, for his cleverness in titling his book *The Golden Bough*, while apologizing for her own "clumsy and pedantic titles." In the end she returns to Russia and tells her dream of being in "a dreaming wood . : . with huge bears softly dancing." She is trying to teach them a square dance but they continue their own dance: "It was for me to learn, not to teach" (78). Harrison declares that she would devote herself to language if she could live her life over again. She ends with an attack on marriage and the patriarchal family, praising community life and wishing she had been able to live in a convent, in a community of learned women. Her concept of "themis"—the spirit of community life in which individual lives were shaped in preclassical Greece, informed by the ritual of the life and death of the Year-Spirit—was the subject of her work and part of her philosophy of life.

The idea of themis as a structure of communal ritual that shapes the individual life to that of the community might be seen as the spirit of women's autobiographical discourse. The structure that insists on the reader's response and sets the writer in conversation with her own community is "common" and "mediocre" culture. Despite what men do in parliaments and on battlefields, it is the women writing their autobiographies, invincible in their "mediocrity," who make civilization.[12] They re/sign themselves to their readers, who in the reading process are taught to move from reading a self to writing a self.

Notes

I am indebted to the Research Institute of the University of Texas for travel and research grants that facilitated the writing of this essay, and also to the kind hospitality of the University of Strasbourg, France, where it was written in May and June 1985. Because I have been thinking about women's autobiographies for more than a decade, I am indebted as always to Northwestern University

Library, where much of the original research was done; to Cathy Henderson of the Humanities Research Center at the University of Texas; and to my husband, Michael Marcus, who first introduced me to the work of Sophie Kovalevsky.

1. For a critique of Woolf's use of "major and minor," see Mudge.

2. In the enchantingly female novel, *The Enchanted April* (1922), by Elizabeth Russell, the author of *Elizabeth, Her German Garden*, there is a wonderful pseudonymous Hampstead writer who makes his living writing the autobiographies of mistresses of great men from their memoirs in the British Museum. The poor of the parish are supported by the money he makes on these books because his wife refuses to live on the wages of sin.

3. My 1973 dissertation from Northwestern University is a biography of Elizabeth Robins. For more biographical information, see Marcus, "Art and Anger," and my introduction to Robins's suffrage novel, *The Convert.*

4. Feminist musicologist Elizabeth Wood is writing a biography of Ethel Smyth; see also her essay "Music into Words." I am editing Smyth's letters to Virginia Woolf. Christopher St. John's biography of Dame Ethel presents many problems, and it appears that St. John destroyed many original letters and diaries after using (or not using) them. Smyth's musical manuscripts are in the British Library, and there is an interesting collection of her papers at the University of Michigan, Ann Arbor. The two-volume *Impressions That Remained* (London: Longman's Green, 1919) was reprinted by Knopf in 1946. In 1981 Da Capo reprinted it in an expensive edition with an introduction by Roland Crichton; they also reprinted an edition of the splendid *Mass in D* with an introduction by Jane Bernstein. In 1987 Viking published an edition of selections from the volumes of memoirs. After the success of *Impressions*, Dame Ethel wrote *Streaks of Life* (1921), well known for its portrait of the Empress Eugénie; *A Three-Legged Tour in Greece* (1927); *A Final Burning of Boats* (1928); *Female Pipings in Eden* (1933); *Beecham and Pharaoh* (1935); *As Time Went On* (1936); and *What Happened Next* (1940).

5. Sophie Kovalevsky's memoir, *A Russian Childhood*, is published in an edition with an introduction by Beatrice Stillman and an analysis of Kovalevsky's mathematics by P. Y. Kochina. Kovalevsky also wrote a series of parallel dramas, *The Struggle for Happiness*, in collaboration with Swedish feminist Anne-Charlotte Mittag-Leffler; part of a novel, *Vae Victis*; and a novel called *A Nihilist Girl*; as well as other essays that have not been translated into English. There are two recent biographies of Kovalevsky. The first, by journalist Don H. Kennedy, was written for his Russian wife, using her translations of primary materials, to oppose the Soviet view of Kovalevsky as a heroine of science and a revolutionary. He stresses "the highly gifted families that not only shaped her development but supplied the genes of her inheritance" (ix), and he shapes her life into a romantic tragedy fascinating for the reader. Ann Hibner Koblitz, in *A Convergence of Lives*, ignores Kovalevsky's life and sees her writing as a minor

part of her life as a scientist. Koblitz wants to remove the personal from Kovalevsky's life, concentrating only on her mathematics.

6. The edition of Marie Bashkirtseff's *Journal* quoted here is the 1919 revised version translated by Mary J. Serrano (published by Dutton in 1928). The journal appeared first in 1889–90 and was translated from the French into many languages. The text is totally unreliable. Additional parts of the journal were published later. There is an introduction by Bashkirtseff herself dated May 1884, just before her death. In the course of keeping the diary, Marie rewrote some parts and speaks in an older voice of the follies of her youth. It also seems possible that her mother may have cut passages that did not agree with her version of the Bashkirtseff myth.

7. In "Theories of Autobiography," Friedman writes: "A woman's life story is unique, but it also reflects her interaction with the cultural meanings of Woman, and the Otherness to which patriarchy has confined her and with the aspects of identity she shares with other women. Learning to read a woman's autobiography, therefore, necessitates a re-vision of the concept of selfhood to incorporate the significance of collective identities of the individual."

8. Kovalevsky's experience of being a Russian in European society might well be analyzed in Reagon's terms, in which one's own autobiography is a part of the history of one's people.

9. See also Schenck and Brodzki; Stanton.

10. For a discussion of dolls in women's writing, see Marcus, "Laughing at Leviticus." This essay also discusses the gender bias of Freud's essay on the uncanny. Kovalevsky's fears might well be analyzed in these terms.

11. See Bashkirtseff, *The New Journal*, and Vincent Cronin's treatment in *The Romantic Way*. Cronin thinks she should have been spanked. Gladstone's review of the diary (in *The Nineteenth Century*) calls it "a book without parallel." There is an interesting account of Marie's lavish funeral and her monument at Passy in *The Critic* (5 July 1890): 7. There is a long essay by Helen Zimmern in *Blackwood* 146 (1889): 300–320, and "Two Views of Marie Bashkirtseff" in *Century* 40 (1980): 28–32, one of which criticizes her "lack of maidenliness" in "her treatment of her own soul and body," which the writer attributes to her savage Russian blood spoiled in the hot-house atmosphere of Nice and Paris; the other of which complains that naturalism has caused Bashkirtseff to give details of her feelings that properly should have been put into fictional form.

12. Among recent examples of women's autobiographical writing that deserve close analysis is Angelica Garnett's *Deceived by Kindness*, which challenges the prevailing view of Bloomsbury as sexually free. Garnett was, as Louise DeSalvo argues in her review (*Women's Review of Books*), adored, petted, infantilized, and denied a decent education. She did not know that Clive Bell was not her father until she had grown up, and she was a sex object for both her

mother, Vanessa Bell, and her aunt, Virginia Woolf, as DeSalvo argues. Her brother, Quentin Bell, dismisses the autobiography as unreliable in the 1985 issue of the *Bulletin of the Charleston Trust*.

Equally stunning in the confessional mode is poet Valentine Ackland's *For Sylvia: An Honest Account*, which reveals her secret alcoholism to her lover of almost forty years, Sylvia Townsend Warner, as well as details of her childhood, her early sexual experiences, and her unconsummated marriage. See also *Elsa Lanchester, Herself*, which shapes its author's life around the question of how a daughter can rebel against radical parents. The central focus of the book is not her marriage to Charles Laughton. Rather, it is her mother, Biddy, one of the first generation of educated women in England, who became the heroine of leftists and feminists in the 1890s when she set up housekeeping with a working man, Shamus Sullivan, and was committed to an insane asylum by her father and brothers on the grounds that "over-education" drove her to such a rash act. Lanchester reveals little about herself personally but a great deal about the history of her times, from the socialist and feminist activities of her childhood to her cabaret work in the Cave of Harmony and the 1917 Club. The details of her life fascinate the reader: the cabaret act she did with a friend in the 1920s, in which they played two charwomen soaking their feet and talking over the day's news; or another act that she called "Krafft-Ebing Case #74B Zurich," in which she played a nun named Blankebin who spends her life looking for the foreskin left from Christ's circumcision. Virginia Woolf's cook, Nelly Boxall, who occupies such a disturbing space in Woolf's diaries and letters, was apparently a welcome addition to the Lanchester/Laughton London household.

Students of women's diaries should look at Nancy Reich's *Clara Schumann* as a powerful example of the father-daughter story or as a version of Coppola/ Olympia, a daddy's doll story, in *Tales of Hoffmann*. The child prodigy pianist and composer did not speak at all until she was five. Until Clara married Robert Shumann and was rejected by her father, the father kept her diary, writing in *her* voice, recording *her* successes. Afterward she kept a "marriage diary," in which she and Robert wrote what they were unable to say to each other.

Works Cited

Ackland, Valentine. *For Sylvia: An Honest Account*. London: Chatto and Windus, 1985.

Ascher, Carol, Louise DeSalvo, and Sara Ruddick, eds. *Between Women*. Boston: Beacon Press, 1984.

Bashkirtseff, Marie. *Journal*. Trans. Mary J. Serrano. New York: Dutton, 1928.

———. *The New Journal of Marie Bashkirtseff*. Trans. Mary J. Safford. New York: Dodd and Mead, 1912.

Broe, Mary Lynn, ed. *Silence and Power: Djuna Barnes, a Revaluation*. Carbondale: University of Southern Illinois Press, forthcoming.

Cronin, Vincent. *The Romantic Way*. Boston: Houghton Mifflin, 1966.

DeSalvo, Louise A. Review of Garnett, *Deceived by Kindness*. *Women's Review of Books* 11 (1985): 11.

Frieden, Sandra. *Autobiography, Self into Form: German Language Autobiographical Writings of the 1970s*. New York: Peter Lang, 1983.

Friedman, Susan Stanford. "Theories of Autobiography and Fictions of the Self in H.D.'s Canon." In Smith.

Garnett, Angelica. *Deceived by Kindness*. New York: Harcourt Brace Jovanovich, 1985.

Gusdorf, Georges. "Conditions and Limits of Autobiography." In Olney, 24–48.

Harrison, Jane Ellen. *Prologomena to the Study of Greek Religions*. 1908. London: Merlin Press, 1962.

———. *Themis*. 1912. London: Merlin Press, 1962.

———. *Epilogomena*. 1921. London: Merlin Press, 1961.

———. *Reminiscences of a Student's Life*. London: Hogarth Press, 1925.

Irigaray, Luce. *Speculum of the Other Woman*. Trans. Gillian C. Gill. Ithaca: Cornell University Press, 1985.

Karageorgevitch, Bojidar. "Marie Bashkirtseff." *Fortnightly Review* 6 (1903): 647-53.

Kennedy, Don H. *The Little Sparrow*. Athens: Ohio University Press, 1983.

Kovalevsky, Sophie. *A Russian Childhood*. Ed. Beatrice Stillman. New York: Springer-Verlag, 1978.

Koblitz, Ann Hibner. *A Convergence of Lives*. Boston: Birkhauser, 1983.

Lanchester, Elsa. *Elsa Lanchester, Herself*. New York: St. Martin's, 1983.

Marcus, Jane. "Art and Anger." *Feminist Studies* 4 (1978): 68–98.

———. "Laughing at Leviticus: *Nightwood* as Women's Circus Epic." In Broe.

Mason, Mary G. "The Other Voice: Autobiographies of Women Writers." In Olney.

Mason, Mary G., and Carol Hurd Green, eds. *Journeys: Autobiographical Writings by Women*. Boston: G. K. Hall, 1979.

Mudge, Bradford K. "Burning Down the House: Sara Coleridge, Virginia Woolf, and the Politics of Literary Revision." *Tulsa Studies in Women's Literature* 5.2 (Fall 1986): 229–50.

Olney, James, ed. *Autobiography: Essays Theoretical and Critical*. Princeton: Princeton University Press, 1980.

Pascal, Roy. *Design and Truth in Autobiography*. Cambridge: Harvard University Press, 1960.

Reagon, Bernice Johnson. "My Black Mothers and Sisters or On Beginning Cultural Autobiography." *Feminist Studies* 8 (1982): 81–95.

Reich, Nancy. *Clara Schumann*. Ithaca: Cornell University Press, 1985.

Robins, Elizabeth. *Ancilla's Share: An Indictment of Sex Antagonism*. London: Hutchinson, 1924.

―――. *Both Sides of the Curtain*. London: Heinemann, 1940.

―――. *The Convert*. Intro. by Jane Marcus. New York: Feminist Press, 1980.

―――. *Ibsen and the Actress*. Hogarth Essays, 2d ser., no. 15, London: Hogarth Press, 1928.

―――. *Raymond and I*. London: Hogarth Press, 1956.

―――. *Theatre and Friendship*. Life and Letters Series. London: Jonathan Cape, 1932.

Russell, Elizabeth. *Elizabeth, Her German Garden*. 1897. London: Macmillan, 1946.

Schenck, Celeste M., and Bella Brodzki, eds. *Life/Lines: Theoretical Essays on Women's Autobiography*. Ithaca: Cornell University Press, 1988.

Smith, Thomas, ed. *Self-Representations: Nineteenth and Twentieth Century Autobiography*. Forthcoming.

Smyth, Ethel. *Impressions That Remained*. 1919. Rpt. New York: Da Capo, 1981.

Sommerfield, Martin. "Die dichterische Autobiographie seit Goethe." Cited in Frieden.

Stanton, Domna C., ed. *The Female Autograph*. New York: Literary Forum, 1985.

Wood, Elizabeth. "Music into Words." In Ascher et al., 71–84.

Woolf, Virginia. *The Letters of Virginia Woolf*. Ed. Nigel Nicolson and Joanne Trautmann. 6 Vols. New York: Harcourt Brace Jovanovich, 1977–82.

―――. "The Lives of the Obscure." *Dial* (May 1925): 381–82.

―――. *A Room of One's Own*. New York: Harcourt Brace Jovanovich, 1928.

―――. "A Sketch of the Past." In *Moments of Being*. Ed. Jeanne Schulkind. London: Hogarth Press, 1976.

Eighteenth-Century Women's Autobiographical Commonplaces

Felicity A. Nussbaum

We have got a sort of literary Curiosity amongst us; the foul Copy of Pope's Homer, with all his old Intended Verses, Sketches, emendations & c. strange that a Man shd keep such Things!—stranger still that a Woman should write such a Book as this; put down every Occurrence of her Life, every Emotion of her Heart, & call it a *Thraliana* forsooth—but then I mean to destroy it.
    —Hester Thrale, *Thraliana*

Women writers have been seeking their own spaces, metaphorical rooms of their own, for centuries. Among those who have described such a gynocentric space is American feminist Elaine Showalter, who defines it as a female wilderness or wild zone: "Spatially it stands for an area which is literally no-man's-land, a place forbidden to men. . . . Experientially it stands for the aspects of the female life-style which are outside of and unlike those of men" (262). As Showalter sees it, the problem in speaking and writing such a space is that women, denied the "full resources of language," have been suppressed and silenced; the insufficiency is not in language but in its repression. But American feminists such as Showalter and others have been loathe to people this "woman's land" with the traditional woman who, somehow closer to nature, can only represent the opposite of what is valued in the dominant male culture. French feminists such as Luce Irigaray, Monique Wittig, Annie LeClerc, Julia Kristeva, and Hélène Cixous also seek female spaces. Revolutionary and utopian, their space is unspeakable and mysterious, yet penetrable. Cixous, for example, describes it as a

Dark Continent that "is neither dark nor unexplorable" (255). This territory that will dislocate and explode male discourse is "without" male discourse, a place that issues forth from the body of women's difference—from breast, vagina, and womb. While American feminists have been criticized for the value they assign to female experience, French feminists have been accused of creating new prisons for women in their bodies. But what these diverse critics seem to agree upon is that women's spaces are largely unspoken, unwritten, and unrepresented ones that have not yet been fully articulated or explained.

Most recently Alice Jardine has attempted to negotiate a theoretical common place between American and French feminists. The conflict between these feminists, as she describes it, derives from the emphasis on the graphic or the corporeal, the *written* body or the written *body*: "To refuse 'woman' or the 'feminine' as cultural and libidinal constructions . . . is, ironically, to return to metaphysical—anatomical—definitions of sexual identity"; but its contrary reduces woman to the symbolic ("a semiosis of woman") and again erases woman, marginalizes her, and requires her absence. Jardine thus positions herself between the American feminists' attempt to recover women's real selves and experience, and the French feminists' apparent recognition that there is no unmediated access to female lives (*Gynesis* 39). She coins the term *gynesis* to signify "the space 'outside of' the conscious subject [that] has always connoted the feminine in the history of western thought."[1]

But thinking about women's spaces—the spoken and unspoken commonplaces that they share—must be grounded, I think, in particular and local instances of history if we are to avoid the generalizations that contribute to an oppression based on gender. Materialist feminists provide some help here in questioning the significance of the author's gender, the relevance of experience to its representation in text, and whether a given work can be said to possess an inherent ideology of "sexism" or "feminism." Focusing on these issues makes it possible to historicize the concepts of woman, feminism, and female experience. That is, "woman" can be read as a historically and culturally produced category situated within material conditions that vary at historical moments and in regional locations. Within these parameters, we may then identify certain regimes of truth, of discourse, and of subjectivity available to women. For example, eighteenth-century women, as a gendered category, had little access to philosophical discourse, to equal wages, or to equality under the law—all of which distinguished their lived experience, in differing degrees, from some classes of eighteenth-century men or from twentieth-century women of privilege. Yet I think we can, without totalizing, isolate aspects of women's experience as constructed by law, medicine, and education that, in a particular historical period, mark this representation of experience as peculiar to one gender. It is my argument that this experience, as variously depicted in autobiographical texts, both participates in and contests existing categories of woman. Thus, women's commonplaces—the places where meanings about gender meet and struggle for dominance—are not universal categories but may serve various and contradictory ideological purposes in the writing of gendered subjectivity.[2]

It is in these spaces between the cultural constructions of the female and the articulation of individual selves and their lived experience, between cultural assignments of gender and the individual's translation of them into text, that a discussion of women's autobiographical writing can be helpful. In this essay I will explore the ways women's self-writing in eighteenth-century England ventriloquates male ideologies of gender while it allows alternative discourses of "experience" to erupt at the margins of meanings. Women's autobiographical writing, especially the private writing of diary and journal, is one location of these contradictions that both produce and reflect historicized concepts of self and gender while sometimes threatening to disrupt or transform them.

My arguments rely on a number of assumptions that I will mention only briefly here: that paradigms of spiritual autobiography on the one hand and the realist novel on the other have dominated our readings of eighteenth-century autobiographical texts; that the relationship between lived experience and its representation in text is vexed and complicated, the real never completely accessible; that cultural constructions of self and gender intermingle with the individual subject's interest and engagement in taking up the particular discourses available at given historical moments; and that ideologies of the Cartesian self as rational, whole, autonomous, and volitional are constructs rather than eternal verities.[3] Most crucial in formulating these ideas are post-Lacanian and post-Althusserian theorists who have questioned the universality and essentialism of human nature and have substituted a human subject constituted by history, language, and culture. This reformulated "self," then, is a product of specific discourse and social process. Individuals construct themselves as subjects through language, but individual subjects—rather than being the source of their own self-generated and self-expressive meaning—adopt positions available within the language at a given moment.[4] This disruption of the traditional self redefines the individual as a position, a *locus* where discourses intersect, and subjectivity as a social construct that is constantly being reorganized. The intersections between social relations and individual subjects perpetually shift and change to produce an inconsistent and contradictory subject. As Mieke Bal has written on subjectivity: "The discourses [that language] produces are (located in) common places, be it institutions, groups or, sometimes, and by accident, individuals. Those common places are the places where meanings meet" (341). Thus, to be an eighteenth-century woman speaking and writing is to appropriate cultural positions that may essentialize woman within the language of domination—to make woman seem whole and understand able. Recognizing this allows us to rethink gendered identity and subjectivity and their representation in the narratives of experience. Eighteenth-century woman's autobiography, then, may be regarded as a matrix where gender and identity meet, a common place where individual women's subject positions converge to produce a representation of something we call "the female self."

No history of women's autobiographical writing in the period has yet been published, and the usual attitude in the many historical and critical studies of self-reflexive writing is to ignore it or treat it as inferior to the male corpus. Karl Weintraub's *The Value of the Individual*, a monumental study of the modern self, considers only Richard Baxter, John Bunyan, Benjamin Franklin, and Jean-Jacques Rousseau as Restoration and eighteenth-century examples; William Spengemann's historical and generic study, *The Forms of Autobiography*, also treats Bunyan, Franklin, and Rousseau and ignores women's forms; John Morris's *Versions of the Self* defines a male canon that includes Roger North, Edward Gibbon, James Boswell, George Fox, John Wesley, and William Cowper, but no female selves.

Though Paul Delany's *British Autobiography in the Seventeenth Century*, Wayne Shumaker's *English Autobiography*, and Donald Stauffer's *The Art of Biography in Eighteenth-Century England* admit women into the canon, only Patricia Meyer Spacks, in a series of articles and books, has probed women's life writing in detail. Discussing Laetitia Pilkington, Charlotte Charke, Lady Mary Wortley Montagu, Hester Thrale, and Fanny Burney, Spacks argues thematically that women share a public self-representation of weakness and passivity, and that women autobiographers possess a "dichotomy between public passivity and private energy." Society,

Spacks concludes, "makes women dwell in a state of internal conflict with necessarily intricate psychic consequences" (*Imagining a Self* 89). Finding that the "self" is less a thing than an attitude, a way of reading experience, Spacks recognizes a double positioning of women between public and private, between their own expectations and those of others, and she implies a difference in women's consciousness as well as content. Though Spacks does not develop these concepts theoretically, she takes women's writing seriously and begins to reformulate the traditionally male canon.

Mapping the territory of Restoration and eighteenth-century female autobiographical subjectivity more fully might include, then, the seventeenth-century gentlewomen; the spiritual autobiographers, including Quaker, Baptist, and Methodist journalists; the apologists (usually called scandalous memoirists), beginning in the 1740s and extending to the early nineteenth century; the noteworthy diarists and letter writers such as Lady Mary Wortley Montagu, Hester Thrale, and Fanny Burney; and numerous unpublished diaries and letters throughout the century. In each of these categories, as women become the subjects and objects of their own scrutiny, they take up stances in the ideologies of gender. The seventeenth-century gentlewomen, for example, intimated through their choice of content that their husbands' lives superseded theirs in importance; they defined self by relationship. The religious women generally adopted the mode of discourse established by their (male) religious leaders—Fox, Bunyan, Wesley—or found their voices usurped by husbands or fathers who formed their biographies into the expected shape.[5] They inscribed themselves, or were inscribed, in the familiar patterns of awakening, conversion, and ministry, their "selves" shaped in imitation of Christ and his (male) disciples. These women learned what sorts of lives to lead and to tell principally from hearing and reading men's lives, from the cultural practices that confined their subjectivity, and from the religious doctrines that forced closure on their ideas about identity and selfhood.

Other women imitated ancient forms or invented new modes of representing experience in order to tell their gendered "selves." The apologists revived the ancient (male) form of public self-defense in the agora, but their content was a uniquely female situation—the fall from chastity that transformed all other experience. Charlotte Charke, Laetitia Pilkington, Anne Sheldon, Elizabeth Gooch, George Anne Bellamy, Margaret Leeson, and others have in common that their self-writing takes its genesis in an accusation.[6] Each text vindicates the apologist from blame at the same time that, in contradiction, it attempts to escape the moral and social system which requires explanation.

When we regard these disparate modes of self-writing through the ideological filter of gender, we can begin to decipher the historical and cultural categories that surface. These categories are *commonplaces* in the multiple senses of the word—the places where meanings gather and collide as well as the set topics that women speak and write. A "commonplace" book is at once the location of the ordinary and the extraordinary. It is a place to record memorable and unusual sayings or events, but in another context it is something that is familiar, habitual, and conventional. Critics have ferreted out a number of commonplace themes of women's writing in attempting to define women's difference—our physical bodies, life cycles, relationships to others, love, independence, power, passivity, madness. These studies, important in the evolution of feminist theory, assert the authority of women's experience and imagination to claim a particular *content* in women's lives. Such approaches seek a female voice and argue that when we write about ourselves and our experience, the language we use derives from our own subjectivity—what is often called "expressing ourselves." As language emerges and evolves—in the historical moment of women taking up the public pen—individual girls and women describe themselves and their experience to speak and write a gendered subjectivity. But that subjectivity is, to a large extent, conditioned by the discourses encoded in language, especially the way discourse is gendered.

From our present perspective, then, it seems important to take closer account of the ways in which that difference is produced and how it reinscribes the heterosexual gender system to confine women to the familiar second sphere. We can begin by accounting for certain kinds of gendered subjectivity, historicizing the female subject, and acknowledging the ways in which different individuals take up various discursive positions in order to grapple with the historical and material world of women—the intersections of class, race, and culture—rather than to insist that women's writing inherently differs from men's.

For example, one of the commonplaces of feminist criticism is the frequent claim that diaries and journals are an intrinsically female form, and that women's experience particularly lends itself to the diffuse for its expression. Among these critics are Lynn Bloom and Orlee Holder, who argue that "women's autobiographies tend to be much less clearly organized, much less synthetic" (213), and Suzanne Juhasz, who contends that Kate Millett's style develops from "the concept of dailiness as a structuring principle for women's lives" (222). Estelle Jelinek seems to agree in suggesting that "irregularity rather than orderliness informs the self-portraits by women" (17). Women's autobiographies, she claims, are fragmented, interrupted, formless, and even when basically linear are anecdotal and disruptive. Such reasoning, however, fails to account, on the one hand, for the large number of diaries and journals written by men and, on the other hand, for many women's autobiographies (such as conversion narratives, for example) that display narrative closure—a beginning, middle, and end, with an epiphanal moment of crisis that reveals the full and transcendent self.

Before testing these ideas about women's diaries in the specific social formation of the eighteenth century, I want to sketch briefly some of the conditions that encouraged the formation of a large body of private self-reflexive writing in the period before the Enlightenment. Diaries and journals, written by both men and women, proliferated in the late seventeenth century with the expansion of literacy. Among the many factors that contributed to fashioning a self as the source and center of meaning were the Protestant Nonconformist sects, which encouraged the formation of "self" as a unique individual who consciously reflects on her/his differentness from others.[7] Diaries and journals emerged especially from the Dissenting groups of Quakers, Methodists, and Baptists, who urged conversion narratives on their members. In the seventeenth century, the Puritan oral conversion narrative was similarly submitted to an authoritative auditor, the consensual body of the church congregation. Those stories that deviated excessively from the accepted patterns for spiritual conversion experience were judged to be illegitimate representations by that body of believers.[8]

Quaker journals were frequently published before 1725, but most other journals were private documents written when spiritual and divine authority was transferred to the secular and personal realm, and when that *person*, the modern human being, was freed from emulating a divine identity but could not yet turn to the human sciences for an explanation of self.[9] Writing about the "self" reinforces the concept of an independent and hardworking individual who "lives" in the present moment, but the Nonconformist and newly literate classes writing in their diaries may also privately contest the hegemonic institutions of the Church of England, the state, and, in the case of women, the patriarchy. Their loose narrative forms may well issue from the individual subject's dilemma in asking who grants her/his autonomy and authority. In short, the crisis of transition from spiritual to secular understandings yielded an increased number of introspective diaries and journals as first-person narrators attempted to fit representations of their lives into authoritative paradigms.

Writing and re-writing, reading and re-reading autobiographical texts such as diaries or commonplace books in eighteenth-century England, then, may have been a way for both sexes to attempt to escape dominant formulations of individuality. In the private writing of diary and journal, whole, coherent, and consistent selves did not have to be molded from the incoherence of a daily experience. If gendered subjectivity did not fit into established paradigms, it did not have to be contracted and condensed into recognized genres in order to attract subscribers and patrons, or to satisfy other authorities. In writing to themselves, eighteenth-century women, in particular, could create a private place in which to speak the unthought, unsaid, and undervalued. In writing private daily records, they could speak as subjects who reflected and produced their multiple positions in text and in culture as they read, reread, and revised their gendered textual formulations.

In part, of course, the language for these multiple and serial subjectivities derives from the dominant male culture and its constructions of the figure of woman. Eighteenth-century women who represented their subjectivity in text, even private texts, were inevitably caught in mimicking male definitions of themselves. Their self-fashionings were bound up in cultural definitions of gender—those assumed, prescribed, and embedded in their consciousness, as well as their subversive thoughts and acts in contradiction to those definitions. Eighteenth-century women were labeled lustful, vain, and inconstant; yet they were also judged capable of "overcoming" the "natural" tendencies of their sex to display the "manly Soul" of Swift's Stella or to become "a softer man" like Pope's Martha Blount in "Epistle to a Lady."[10] Pope defines woman's identity as a complex of contrarieties: "Nothing so true as what you once let fall, / 'Most Women have no Characters at all.'" The negation at once implies its opposites and denies them. The "Epistle" insists on sexual difference, crucial for the maintenance of heterosexual relationships, while it also refuses women the essential identity that sexual difference requires. The effect of the satire is both to generalize and to negate woman's identity—to deny her a space of selfhood, even in the portraits the narrator describes. The "Epistle" places eighteenth-century women in the irreconcilable position of being urged to construct themselves as idealized wholes while being positioned in the narratives of knowledge as frail, delicate, and irritable—"a contradiction still." Eighteenth-century women's actions and behaviors, then, are taken to reflect an interior core that cannot be overcome and cannot meet the male measure. In other words, the historically specific perception of female behavior is defined as an easily recognizable instance of the universal essence.

Eighteenth-century writing women certainly positioned themselves all along the spectrum from antifeminist to feminist, from the discourse of inferiority to the assertion of equality. Some women of the period speak as harshly as men about the female sex. Although Lady Chudleigh argues that she wishes to improve the understanding of her sex, she expresses a common sentiment in her concern for women's lack of reason:

> I heartily wish my Sex wou'd keep a stricter Guard over their Passions, and amidst all the various Occurrences of Life, consult neither their Ease, the Gratification of their Humour, nor the Satisfaction of others, when 'tis in Opposition to their Reason; . . . that all who see 'em may have just cause to conclude, from the Regularity of their Actions, the Calmness of their Tempers, and the Serenity of their Looks . . . that they are infinitely better pleas'd with the secret Plaudits of their own Consciences, than they would be with the flattering Acclamations of a deceitful inconstant World; but such an Evenness, such a Tranquility of Mind, is not attainable without much Study, and the closest Application of Thought; it must be the work of Time, and the Effect of a daily Practice. (Preface)

Chudleigh, like other feminists of the period, recognizes that women's inferiority is based on custom rather than an essential female nature, and she urges women to engage in private self-regulation in order to convey a consistent public character. Eighteenth-century women defend their own sex; they also become, at times, antifeminist satirists. Similarly, it is common for women to position themselves simultaneously in opposing attitudes toward self and gender in their autobiographical writings, in an attempt to find a coherent subject position, to declare a consistent "I."[11] They may assume a position that implies moral or spiritual superiority; they may speak their own denigration and collude in their subjugation; or they may attempt to disrupt the ideology of gender by disguising themselves as males. Some eighteenth-century women's diaries, memoirs, and autobiographies, particularly spiritual autobiographies, incorporate that ideology and reproduce it, while others challenge it with alternative discourses. Such gendered positions may be assumed by either sex.[12]

Faced with the absence of the female "self" from theological and philosophical formulations of identity in the period, and told they had no characters at all, eighteenth-century women were still encouraged to make themselves into coherent identities. Urged to have "character"—a public phenomenon—yet increasingly relegated to the private sphere, some eighteenth-century women used diaries to construct a private space that questions the gendered positions available for women (and men) and as a place to contest the closure of "self" and text. Women writers insert the possibility of making themselves their own object and, in doing so, subvert and contest modes of conceiving "self" in the paradigms made available for them. Though even secret writing cannot escape its intersections with social relations, private writing in eighteenth-century England was often an attempt to find words without masters, to speak "outside" familiar discourses. In imitating the incoherence of interiority before it is offered for public scrutiny, these unfinished modes describe historical truth or human chronology without forcing or requiring its coercion into a known truth or preconceived structure, into tropes or heroic models of a life well lived.[13] The contradictions that eighteenth-century woman may experience in attempting to shape her self-representation may leak through the fissures of existent models and assumptions to speak discontinuity and produce revision and resistance. In short, these serial texts confirm the conventions for "woman," while they also may allow alternative configurations of identity to emerge at the periphery of the available range of meanings. Specific women, at particular historical moments, have used the serial, repetitious, and discontinuous emergent genre of the private diary to speak the plurality of their gendered positions and to bear witness to the insufficiency of those positions to render their "experience" as eighteenth-century writing women.

I want to turn now to a brief consideration of one instance of the contradictions that emerge within a woman's private diary writing. By the latter half of the eighteenth century, a private subject who engaged in constant self-scrutiny through his or her life was a commonplace. James Boswell, Fanny Burney, and Hester Thrale wrote multiple serial volumes accounting for their activities and desires. Fully absorbing the doctrine of secular self-regulation, Boswell wrote that he wanted to live no more than he could record, to which Thrale countered, "'tis a good way, but Life is scarce long enough to talk, & to write, and to live to rejoyce in what one has written" (*Thraliana* 257). For Hester Thrale, private—even secret—writing became an end in itself as she described her various positionings as wife, mother, intellectual, writer, trades-woman, election campaigner, and hostess and confidante to Samuel Johnson. Unlike Boswell, who writes of the male social institutions of clubs and coffeehouses, Thrale records the world of children, home, and relationships. She is remarkable for having taken her work as a bearer and educator of her children and as the cultural protector of "family" so seriously that she makes regular written representation of it.

Keeping voluminous private journals and notes all her life, Hester Thrale wrote and re-wrote the subjectivity that she apparently consid-ered too diffuse and multifarious to confine to one version. In her various journals and through her many relationships, she represented her own identity as defying categorization and simplification. In addi-tion to compiling books of Johnson's sayings, she simultaneously re-corded the remarks of famous contemporaries; she collected two books of her precocious first-born Queeney's achievements—the "blue Cover Book" and the "little red Book"—as well as a "Family Book" of her children's births, deaths, illnesses, and achievements. Further, she kept a "New Common-Place Book," various small diaries, and later, as Mrs. Piozzi, she prepared a five-volume literary autobiography for her adopted son, John Salusbury.[14] From 1776 until 1809 she regularly made entries in *Thraliana*, a diary of anecdotes, personal history, and noteworthy stories. These various notebooks afforded a safe, secret place to accumulate the commonplaces of her life, a record of her subjectivity and the thoughts and events that gave "meaning" to her existence. Not one of Mrs. Thrale's notebooks and diaries is an auto-biography with a beginning, middle, and end. All lack a crisis which, in retrospect, is described as the moment when one's real "self" begins or the critical moment when the meaning of experience unfolds. The diary, by its structure of daily entry and repetition, in its encouraging re-reading of the previous day and its revision in succeeding entries, makes the eliding of contradictions seem possible. Thus, the diary is a particularly apt ideological grid for a subject held in perpetual conflict with itself yet believing itself to be free and whole. Without forging a unified, rational, and autonomous self from her various autobiographi-cal texts, Hester Thrale articulates the conflicts and attempts to situate herself in a position of regulating her experience through writing it.

Adopting the language of difference in her private journals, Thrale takes care to make strong gender distinctions between the minds and characters of men and women. For example, she writes that women uphold morality and virtue and should display good humor, conversational power, useful and ornamental knowledge, and a pleasant mien, whereas men are distinguished by religion, morality, scholarship, and general knowledge. In addition, she believes that women have a special talent for business because of their sexual power over men: "Women have a manifest Advantage over Men in the doing Business; every thing smooths down before them, & to be a Female is commonly sufficient to be successful" (*Thraliana* 313). She mocks the ignorance of girls who are purportedly educated in geography, criticism, and verse, but who lack practical skills and are "unable to cut out a Shirt or Shift, or do one earthly thing of Use: and all for the sake of the *Sciences*" (259).

In addition to the conventional expectations of women that Hester Thrale rehearses with conviction, where does the language for her multiple subjectivities come from? The female tradition of private writing, the verbatim transcription of wise sayings from Johnson and other "great men," and the burgeoning series of medical and educational works directed at mothers make up some of the diverse and discrepant discourses that Thrale adopts to define her own experience. In part Thrale takes her self-reflecting language from a newly emergent literary and intellectual tradition of women's keeping private documents, such as Swift's Stella or Sterne's Eliza, women whose fame came from their association with a major literary figure. Thrale writes, "I do not think my bons Mots like Stella's the best among those of my Friends, but I think Stella's very paltry ones; and much wonder at the moderate degree of Excellence with which Dr. Swift was contented to make a Bustel with my Namesake Miss *Hester* Johnson" (*Thraliana* 156). In fact, she notes, "Hester is a Word signifying *Secret* we all know," and, she concludes, it is a silly name (800). But she also recognizes and records the perils of women's intellectual display, through Johnson's report: "He used to mention Harry Fielding's behaviour to her [Sarah] as a melancholy instance of narrowness; while She only read English Books, and made English Verses it seems, he fondled her Fancy, & encourag'd her Genius, but as soon [as] he perceived She once read Virgil, Farewell to Fondness, the Author's Jealousy was become stronger than the Brother's Affections" (79). Thrale's journals are a "person" to whom something precious is trusted—a repository, in the obscure sense of the word as "confidante." Though she confides to Sophia Streatfeild that she keeps

Thraliana, she allows that only God will read it. She attempts to protect the *Thraliana* from prying eyes and hopes to keep its existence a secret (323, 460). Similarly, her "Family Book," providing a private place away from the enormous demands on her, becomes a place to relieve an overburdened consciousness: "I have nobody to tell my Uneasinesses to, no Mother, no Female Friend—no nothing: so I must eat up my own Heart & be quiet" (198).

At other times Hester Thrale recognizes the contradictory idea that her brand of diary keeping has no tradition and is an unprecedented oddity: "Stranger still that a Woman should write such a Book as this; put down every Occurrence of her Life, every Emotion of her Heart, & call it a *Thraliana* forsooth—but then I mean to destroy it" (which, of course, she did not do) (464). Occasionally she dismisses what she writes as mere trash, nonsense, or trifles—a view she cannot reconcile with her devotion to the task: "But when the last [volume] comes as near to ending as this now does—my fingers will shake lest I should be near ending as well as my Book. My heart tells me that he [Henry Thrale, her husband] said something when he presented me with the Volumes, as if—I don't know as if: but this I know, that fifteen Years have elapsed since I first made the *Thraliana* my Confident, my solitary Comfort, and Depositary of every Thought as it arose" (799). She characterizes the volumes as "so madly selected, so awkwardly put together" (840), the keeping of ana "a silly desire" (467). Several times she indicates that it is "a good Repository" for her "Nonsense." Yet in this secret nonsense, the *Thraliana*, Hester Thrale creates what her editor, Katharine Balderston, has called "almost, if not quite, the first English ana" (xi) in its collections of notable sayings, literary trifles, and anecdotes. Thus, in repeatedly emphasizing the human quality of the *Thraliana*, she constructs it as a unified person whom she denigrates yet values highly, someone who can contain the contradictions of a woman's lived experience.

Married in 1763, Hester Lynch Salusbury had brought an ancient family name to the wealthy but unconnected Henry Thrale, a brewer ten years her senior with a country home at Streatham. Mr. Thrale thought of her, she felt, as "a passive, tho' well born & educated Girl; who would be contented to dwell in the Borough, which other Women had refused to do" (*Thraliana* 307). Hester Thrale rapidly became an assiduous historian of the private—of one eighteenth-century nuclear family unit—and in writing seemingly aimless quotidian histories of her relatively isolated family unit, she attempts to give validity to her position as procreator, nurturer, and indefatigable worker. She establishes herself as a guardian of the domestic, a middle-class woman who values fostering the development of an individual character in each child. Positioned as "a Centre of Unity" in her parents' unhappy marriage, she, too, thought that children would cement the connection. Eager for an heir, she welcomed each of her pregnancies, the first of which began after two months of marriage. From 1764 to 1778 Thrale bore twelve children, who lived anywhere from ten hours (Penelope, born 15 September 1772) to ninety-two years (Queeney, the first born). Hester Lynch Thrale began her "Family Book," first named the "Children's Book," by recording this first daughter's birth: "Hester Maria Thrale [Queeney] born on the 17:Septr. 1764 at her Father's House, Southwark" (21). In this "Register of my Children's Powers of Mind and Body" (254), she measures her life in pregnancies, children's birthdays, illnesses, deaths, and the visits of Samuel Johnson. She had to marry well, have no friends, obey her mother, and serve her husband, for she had fully absorbed the expectations of her class and gender. In the "Family Book," Thrale frequently indicates that she fully accepts her economic function as a breeder—she is to produce an heir, preferably a male heir, and she is to educate him and keep him alive. She also wishes to keep her own estate in her family (190), and thus she indulges in long fantasies of exchanging her life for a live son: "Why if I *should* die! what does it signify? Let me *but* leave a Son, I shall die happy enough" (201).

The "Family Book," like *Thraliana*, is an extraordinary work, and its editor, Mary Hyde, wonders about its origin: "Since the undertaking was so unusual, one wonders how the idea came to Mrs. Thrale" (vii). Hyde accounts for it through Johnson's influence, Queeney's precosity, and Mrs. Thrale's predilection to keep diaries. But the language for Mrs. Thrale's thinking and writing about herself is less expressive of her "self" or of a female voice than it is a site for the contest over the privatizing of woman and the production of the desire to bear children and protect them from disease. In the mid-eighteenth century, a large body of child-rearing books directed at a newly literate and largely bourgeois female audience were published, books that for the first time named women as "managers" of their children and of the domestic space. Such texts were quite specifically aimed at defining the proper measures necessary to raise gender- and class-identified children and, in so doing, to perpetuate these categories. The books included William Cadogan's *An Essay Upon Nursing, and the Management of Children, from their Birth to Three Years of Age* (1748), T. Mantell's *Short Directions for the Management of*

Infants (1780), William Moss's *An Essay on the Management and Nursing of Children in the Earlier Periods of Infancy* (1781), and Michael Underwood's *A Treatise on the Disorders of Childhood and Management of Infants from the Birth; Adapted to Domestic Use* (1797). These works were written mostly by men (usually doctors) and addressed to women, though occasionally one was published under a female pseudonym. Women were taught in "plain words" the received wisdom about children's education and medical care. In this way, women were granted ostensible authority and responsibility for the physical care of their children, in assistance to the physicians, but without sufficient knowledge to effect change in the practice of medicine or in the way women and their offspring were regarded by the medical profession.

This explicit public ideology that women should be chiefly responsible for the health and welfare of their own children served the interests of the formation of a new individualism. It also helped maintain new work patterns in which the bourgeois family was separated from the work site, privatized, and its labor (especially the labor of women and servants) made invisible. At the same time, the hierarchy of male over female labor was enforced. Texts such as the "Family Book" and *Thraliana*, then, confirm prevailing assumptions about women as they carve out private female subjects who, in reflecting on themselves, do not recognize the ways their individual subjectivity intermingles with the structure of social relations designed to keep them in their place.

Taking up her woman's role as one who bears and educates the children and perpetuates culture, Hester Thrale documents each child's regular progress (or disturbing lack of it) in the "Family Book," teaching Queeney astronomy, geography, multiplication, and religion at age two: "She has this day repeated her Catechism quite thro', her Latin Grammar to the end of the 5 Declensions, a Fable in Phaedrus, an Epigram in Martial, the Revolutions Diameters & Distance of the Planets. . . . With regard to her Person it is accounted exquisitely pretty; her Hair is sandy, her Eyes of a very dark blue, & their Lustre particularly fine; her Complexion delicate, and her Carriage uncommonly genteel" (29–30). Thrale tells us that, while pregnant or recovering from childbirth, she constantly tutors the children and records their mutual achievement. On occasion her despair at investing energy in educating children who may soon die breaks through. She finds teaching her seventh child, Sophia Thrale, an unbearable task: "I have really listened to Babies Learning till I am half stupified—& all my pains have answered so poorly—I have no heart to battle with Sophy. . . but I will not make her

Life miserable as I suppose it will be short. . . . At Present I can not begin battling with Babies—I have already spent my whole youth at it & lost my Reward at last" (163).

Her domestic labor, although not given a wage value, has an important economic and cultural function to which she professes considerable allegiance, if occasional ambivalence and exhaustion. Hester Thrale inscribes her activities as a way of declaring their value and importance, even though she senses that while she devotes herself to the children other opportunities are passing her by. The "Family Book," and later the *Thraliana*, took on the function of helping her cope with the various splittings required of her:

> All my Friends reproach me with neglecting to write down such Things as drop from him [Johnson] almost perpetually. . . but ever since that Time I have been the Mother of Children, and little do these wise Men know or feel, that the Crying of a young Child, or the Perverseness of an elder, or the Danger however trifling of any one—will soon drive out of a female Parent's head a conversation concerning Wit, Science or Sentiment, however She may appear to be impressed with it at the moment: besides that to a *Mere de famille* doing something is more necessary & suitable than even hearing something; and if one is to listen al Even and write all Morning what one has heard; where will be the time for tutoring, caressing, or what is still more useful, for having one's Children about one: I therefore charge all my Neglect to my young ones Account, and feel myself at this moment very miserable that I have at last, after being married fourteen Years and bringing eleven Children, leisure to write a *Thraliana* forsooth:—though the second Volume *does* begin with Mr. Johnson. (*Thraliana* 158)

Clearly Mrs. Thrale finds particularly perturbing the incongruity between the duties of a mother and those of a writing woman.

The "Family Book" also carefully chronicles her medical efforts and judgments in an age when a child could quite literally have a fever in the morning and die in the afternoon. It is a place to record their sufferings in excruciating detail—Lucy's ear that seeps a perpetual infection, Ralph's smallpox, Queeney's worms. Just before Henry's death after a few hours of infection, she writes, "a universal Shriek called us all together to Harry's Bedside, where he struggled a Moment—thrusting his Finger down his Throat to excite Vomiting, & then—turning to Nurse said very distinctly—don't Scream so—I *know* I must die" (152).

In fact, when Hester Thrale fails as doctor to Henry, her sole male heir, she takes her failed identity from Pope's "Epistle to A Lady"; the line "Childless with all her Children—wants an heir" runs through her head (162). She quarrels with doctors over the proper medication. When the children, each in succession, catch measles, she tends to them herself: "I sent for no Drs. or 'Pothecaries, but kept diluting all I could with cooling Liquors varied so as to avoid Disgust" (74), but for Lucy (who dies at age four), she appeals to a stream of advisers: "[I] applied to Pinkstan who ordered the Sarsaparilla Tea & bid me do nothing else. Lucy however [was] fading away very fast, though every body in the house persisted She was well, I took her to Herbert Lawrence, who said it was the original humour repelled by Pinkstan, which was fastening on her Brain but that he would try to restore it" (83). The physical state of the children and their proper medical care consume her conversation and her attention as she attempts to locate the proper treatment and ultimately to take the responsibility for it. In fact, her disagreement with her friend Giuseppe Baretti over the treatment for Queeney's persistent worms eventually caused an altercation that was never resolved.

The contradiction between Thrale's ostensible wifely duties as nurse and her retention of a sense of a private personal dignity is made especially visible when she finds herself nursing the venereal disease that Mr. Thrale apparently acquired from his mistress: "No peace saith my God for the wicked! no quiet Gestation for me! on Sunday Night the 3d. of Sept. Mr. Thrale told me he had an Ailment, & shewed me a Testicle swelled to an immense Size" ("Family Book" 166). After Mr. Thrale proposes sending for a doctor who specializes in venereal complaints, she recognizes, to her relief, that the disease is not cancer, and she becomes grateful that it is only the pox: "I now began to understand where I was, and to perceive that my poor Father's Prophecy was verified who said If you marry that Scoundrel he will catch the Pox, [&] for your Amusement set you to make his Pultices. This is now literally made out; and I am preparing Pultices as he said, and Fomenting this elegant Ailment every Night & Morning for an Hour together on my Knees, & receiving for my Reward such Impatient Expressions as disagreable Confinement happens to dictate" (166). Mrs. Thrale was pleased that the disease was not life threatening because she feared for the economic survival of the family, but she felt contempt for a husband who had caught the clap and expected her, though pregnant, to minister cheerfully to him. "I have always sacrificed my own Choice to that of others," she writes in another context (*Thraliana* 544). Oddly, this moment of contradiction marked the beginning of her most sustained period of diary keeping since, in gratitude for her nursing, Mr. Thrale gave her the six bound volumes imprinted with *Thraliana* on the cover. The gift suggests her husband's silent collusion in enabling Hester Thrale to construct a secret anecdotal "self," for Mr. Thrale's behavior seems to authorize her production of an interiority in a private place. Providing the *Thraliana* to a woman who kept journals compulsively was a tacit acknowledgment that her private subjectivity was fundamentally at odds with the public positions demanded of her as procreator and nurturer, yet the action suppresses the threat of conflict by relegating it to the private sphere.

Though her husband provided the volumes for the journals, it was Samuel Johnson who urged Thrale to keep diaries, in part as an antidote to depression. In spite of Johnson's heavy demands on her time during his regular visits, she counted him at times as her closest friend. Johnson gave her intellectual companionship, but he also advised her to stay young and gay. Though her mother (who lived with the Thrales until her death) insisted that Thrale remain at home to nurse her babies, Johnson told her in counterpoint that she should learn the brewing trade and attend to her husband in order to please him: "You divide your Time between your Mamma & your Babies, & wonder you do not by that means become agreable to your Husband" (309). She did not, however, enter the public forum until six years later, for to take his advice, she thought, would destroy her mother.

In *Thraliana* as in "The Family Book," the patterns of subjectivity are not organized or pressured into assigning meaning to experience, and though the memories are always vivid, they remain repetitive and incomplete. Of considerable interest is Thrale's autobiographical fragment, written when, morbidly obsessed with the fantasy that she might die while giving birth to Henrietta Sophia, she determines to set down a record of herself, "a little Epitome of whence I came, who I am & c. before I go hence and am no more seen" (*Thraliana* 274). In the incomplete "character" included in the fragment, she is severely self-critical of her own studied grace, irascible temper, avariciousness, and poor poetry. But the fragment of the intended "life of my self" does not attempt narrative closure or the formulation of a fixed or finished character. Hester's memories of childhood's random incidents lack thematic unity—seeing the eclipse of the sun through smoked glasses, contracting smallpox and being pushed out to the home of a mantuamaker, being pinched and having her hair pulled by Lord North when she was fifteen, reading Milton to Lord Godolphin, learning to dance, Sukey Hill dying of consumption.

The early parts of the autobiographical fragment seem to create crisis and resolution, economic despair and recovery. But the loose narrative forms and the commonplace content Thrale adopts to represent her gendered identity are filled with narrative ruptures, for her life cannot fit easily into a publicly recognized pattern such as the fallen woman, the rebellious child, or the spiritual heroine. Neither will the compelling familial myth of separation and reunion, of independence accepted and rewarded, suit Thrale's structuring of experience. The imitations, translations, bad verse, and letters to the newspaper contained in the *Thraliana* become Hester Thrale's cryptic substitute for a typology. She uses the volumes to practice her own imitations, translations, and occasional poems and to hone her writing skills, as well as to record authoritative comments uttered in her hearing. When she ventures her own opinion, it is usually one of agreement, even when the advice is against her own best interests. What holds all these disparate fragments together is her conceptualization of the text as an auditor, a friend, and a unified subject who remains constant.

Thraliana, like the "Family Book," assembles its comments and observations side by side without assigning a relative value to each, and thus suggests that each insertion is equal to the next. Thrale inserts bits and pieces in a common place—as if all held equal power, value, and rank— to interrogate (male) ideologies that would assign differing values to the various entries. As Mária Minich Brewer has written about Annie LeClerc's works: "It is the very act of bringing subjects without common measure or value into contiguity, subjects that have their assigned place elsewhere, that challenges the narrative closures in which they are ordinarily held" (1150).[15]

In *Thraliana* Hester Thrale includes personal revelations (especially about Samuel Johnson), reports of social gatherings and visits, a series of stories on an arbitrary topic, tidbits of information about everything from her black-and-white speckled hen to determining a tree's longevity—whatever occurs or is told to her that is worth remembering. The journals are a mnemonic device as well: "I now wish I had pursued Mr Murphy's Advice of marking down all Passages from different Books which strike by their Resemblance to each other . . . for one forgets again in the hurry & Tumult of Life's Cares or Pleasures almost every thing that one does not commit to paper" (24). But Mrs. Thrale's character has no conclusion, and in the silence that might have been the rounding out of her character, she includes lengthy translations and imitations of Voltaire. Hester Thrale's subversive act is to collect anecdotes that do not have public validation. Even if some of the bits and pieces seem significant to the larger culture (such as Johnson's witty sayings), their removal to private text, where they are juxtaposed with the newly valued, daily, lived experience and its representation, holds the disarming potential to force their re-evaluation.

For Thrale, then, and perhaps for other eighteenth-century women, diaries and journals are a common place to record commonplaces, a site to represent female experience, even those judged trivial by the hegemonic, and to assign them parity with representations valued by the culture. She may use the dominant culture's mode to define herself as the prototypical bourgeois mother in "Family Book," but she assigns the role sufficient value to take pleasure in reproducing that experience in detail. And in *Thraliana*, she marks the high moments of Johnson's conversation while placing them in contiguity with the supposed trivialities of her life. If we can read eighteenth-century women's diaries and journals without assuming that all the pieces will fit into coherent female "selves," then the text need not resolve itself into a unified whole. In other words, Mrs. Thrale's construction of experience is the thing itself, not a failed version of a (male) heroic self and autobiography. Thrale's journals re-cover the lost and radically reassign "meaning" to it, a single human consciousness of writer and reader being the only assumed organizing principle.

Hester Thrale's journals confirm and contest, recuperate and sabotage, the (male) culture's signifying practices about gender and identity through the content and narrative form of her self-representations. Thrale's writings attempt to organize and elaborate on male patriarchal principles, while her position as wife and mother leads her to reproduce and perpetuate the pervasive medical and educational definitions of female difference. By insisting on her difference from men, Thrale unwittingly colludes in reinscribing her inferior status. Her diaries do not so much express the essential female voice as they reflect the heterosexual division that the culture required to reproduce itself and its prevailing notions of gender. Unable to escape her construction in ideology, Thrale instead contains it in private writing that is, nevertheless, finally insufficient to forge powerful alternative organizations to dominant values. Thus she offers us a paradigmatic instance of a woman who resisted hegemonic formulations of gendered subjectivity even as she reproduced them.

Taken as a body of narratives, women's autobiographical writing in the eighteenth century provides a spectrum of gendered identity within a range of meanings that is circumscribed by the culture in which it is embedded. Thrale's journals claim an area within which they witness to and subvert the culture's production of the female and her relegation to the private sphere. The "Family Book" and *Thraliana* unmask the relations of domination by reversing hierarchies of value; but by holding them within the private sphere Thrale sets up a cycle of self reading self, of woman reading woman, of complicity in the containment of female transgression. As such, she succeeds in reproducing a bourgeois gendered subject, a commonplace of the dominant culture. Women's autobiographies, then, are gendered sites of containment, cooptation, and resistance. We can, I think, draw new attention to the relations of domination and open ways of re-thinking eighteenth-century autobiographical writing if we resist confining Hester Lynch Salusbury Thrale Piozzi, "eighteenth-century woman," to any of her commonplaces in our attempt to find the difference of women's writing.

Notes

1. Jardine elaborates on her definition in *Gynesis* 24–26, 36–38, 69–70. For summaries of the questions addressed by women on both sides of the Atlantic, see Jones and Crowder.

2. For discussions of the complicated relationships between feminism, culture, and politics, see the Cambridge Women's Studies Group collection, *Women in Society*.

3. On the new history, see especially LaCapra and Howard.

4. An influential essay is Louis Althusser's "Ideology and Ideological State Apparatuses" in *Lenin* 127–86. On the historicity of the self, see Foucault 303–87 and, most recently, Henriques. On specific (male) concepts of identity in eighteenth-century England (though not from a postmodern perspective), Christopher Fox's essay is particularly helpful. Fox argues persuasively that even before David Hume's *Treatise* (1739–40) made the idea of the discontinuous self current, John Locke's earlier work on identity (2d ed., 1696) had been the subject of much philosophical debate.

5. Important archival work has begun retrieving women's early autobiographical writing (see, for example, Rose). Patricia Caldwell's fine study deals with women's conversion narratives, but without discussing gender implications.

6. The Greek public square provided a public arena for vindicating one's public character. For a discussion in relation to ancient (male) biography and

autobiography, see Bakhtin 130–46. For a study of the eighteenth-century female apologists, see Nussbaum, "Heteroclites."

7. Diaries and memoirs in earlier centuries, as Stephen Greenblatt (143) has pointed out, do not exhibit the repetitive, intimate self-scrutiny of later works and, I would add, they were seldom published until the nineteenth century. Karl Weintraub argues that the idea of the "self" as an individual and unique being who consciously reflects on his separateness and differentness from others, and who attaches meaning to his past experiences, is a historical phenomenon of the seventeenth and eighteenth centuries in western Europe and America.

8. Patricia Caldwell examines fifty-one oral confessions given in the congregation of the First Church of Cambridge, Massachusetts, from 1637 to 1645, to find the *topoi* that mark them as American self-representations.

9. For arguments that the concept of "man" is not constituted until the Enlightenment, see, for example, Foucault.

10. Recent studies of these works include Nussbaum, *"The Brink of All We Hate"*; also both Pollak and Brown on Pope's poetry, especially the "Epistle to A Lady" and "Rape of the Lock."

11. Catherine Belsey postulates that contemporary women are "produced and inhibited by contradictory discourses." For example, women placed between a liberal humanism that prescribes independence, on the one hand, and the misogynist definition of female inferiority, on the other, find themselves unable "to locate a single and coherent subject-position within these contradictory discourses" (65).

12. For a brief study of the complications of assigning gender to authorial signatures in eighteenth-century writings, see Nancy K. Miller's work on *The Letters of a Portuguese Nun* (1669).

13. Hayden White provides a theoretical model for treating narratives that frustrate the desire for closure. He sees annals and chronicles "as particular conceptions of historical reality, conceptions that are alternatives to, rather than failed anticipations of, the fully realized historical discourse that the modern history form is supposed to embody" (10), and he calls attention to the apparent "absence of a principle for assigning importance or significance to events" (14).

14. For descriptions of Hester Thrale's extensive autobiographical writings, see the introductory material to James Clifford's biography (and appendix C 466–67), Mary Hyde's edition of the "Family Book," and Katharine Balderston's two-volume edition of *Thraliana*. Also, Patricia Spacks provides specific details of Thrale's autobiographical writing in her later life ("Scrapbook").

15. I am indebted here to Wendy Hollway's essay on gender; Domna Stanton's provocative piece, in which she coins the term *autogynography*; and Mária Minich Brewer's arguments concerning women's writing and narrative closure.

Works Cited

Althusser, Louis. *Lenin and Philosophy and Other Essays.* New York: Monthly Review Press, 1971.

Bakhtin, Mikhail. *The Dialogic Imagination: Four Essays.* Ed. Michael Holquist. Trans. Caryl Emerson and Michael Holquist. Austin: University of Texas Press, 1981.

Bal, Mieke. "The Rhetoric of Subjectivity." *Poetics Today* 5 (1984): 337–76.

Bellamy, George Anne. *An Apology for the Life of George Anne Bellamy, Late of Covent Garden Theatre. Written by Herself. To Which Is Annexed Her Original Letter to John Calcraft. . . .* 2d ed. 6 vols. London and Dublin, 1785.

Belsey, Catherine. *Critical Practice.* New Accents Series. Gen. ed. Terence Hawkes. London: Methuen, 1980.

Bloom, Lynn Z., and Orlee Holder. "Anaïs Nin's *Diary* in Context." In Jelinek, 206–20.

Brewer, Mária Minich. "A Loosening of Tongues: From Narrative Economy to Women's Writing." *MLN* 99 (1984): 1141–61.

Brown, Laura. *Rereading Literature: Alexander Pope.* Oxford: Basil Blackwell, 1985.

Caldwell, Patricia. *The Puritan Conversion Narrative: The Beginnings of American Expression.* Cambridge: Cambridge University Press, 1983.

Cambridge Women's Studies Group. *Women in Society: Interdisciplinary Essays.* London: Virago, 1981.

Charke, Charlotte. *A Narrative of the Life of Mrs. Charlotte Charke.* London, 1755. Ed. Leonard Ashley. Gainesville, Fla.: Scholar's Facsimiles and Reprints, 1969.

Chudleigh, Lady Mary. *The Ladies Defence; or, "The Bride-Womans Counsellor" Answer'd: A Poem.* London: John Deeve, 1701.

Cixous, Hélène. "The Laugh of the Medusa." In Marks and Courtivron, 245–64.

Clifford, James L. *Hester Lynch Piozzi (Mrs. Thrale).* Oxford: Clarendon, 1941.

Crowder, Diane Griffin. "Amazons and Mothers? Monique Wittig, Hélène Cixous and Theories of Women's Writing." *Contemporary Literature* 24 (1983): 177–244.

Delany, Paul. *British Autobiography in the Seventeenth Century.* London: Routledge and Kegan Paul, 1969.

Foucault, Michel. *The Order of Things: An Archeology of the Human Sciences.* New York: Random House, 1970.

Fox, Christopher. "Locke and the Scriblerians: The Discussion of Identity in Early Eighteenth-Century England." *Eighteenth-Century Studies* 16 (1982): 1–26.

Gooch, Elizabeth. *Life of Mrs. Gooch, Written by Herself, Dedicated to the Public.* 3 vols. London: G. and G. Kearsley, 1792.

Greenblatt, Stephen. *Renaissance Self-Fashioning from More to Shakespeare*. Chicago: University of Chicago Press, 1980.

Henriques, Julian, Wendy Hollway, Cathy Urwin, Couze Venn, and Valerie Walkerdine, eds. *Changing the Subject: Psychology, Social Regulation, and Subjectivity*. London: Methuen, 1984.

Hollway, Wendy. "Gender Difference and the Production of Subjectivity." In Henriques, 227–63.

Howard, Jean E. "The New Historicism in Renaissance Studies." *English Literary Renaissance* 16 (1986): 13–43.

Jardine, Alice. "Gynesis." *Diacritics* 12 (1982): 54–65.

————. *Gynesis: Configurations of Woman and Modernity*. Ithaca: Cornell University Press, 1985.

Jelinek, Estelle C., ed. *Women's Autobiography: Essays in Criticism*. Bloomington: Indiana University Press, 1980.

Jones, Ann Rosalind. "Writing the Body: Toward an Understanding of *L'Ecriture féminine*." In Showalter, 361–77.

Juhasz, Suzanne. "Towards a Theory of Form in Feminist Autobiography: Kate Millett's *Flying* and *Sita*; Maxine Hong Kingston's *The Woman Warrior*." In Jelinek, 221–37.

LaCapra, Dominick. *Rethinking Intellectual History: Texts, Contexts, and Language*. Ithaca: Cornell University Press, 1983.

Leeson, Margaret. *Memoirs of Mrs. Margaret Leeson. Written by Herself; in Which Are Given Anecdotes, Sketches of the Lives and Bons Mots of Some of the Most Celebrated Characters in Great-Britain and Ireland, Particularly of All the Filles des Joys and Men of Pleasure and Gallantry Which Have Usually Frequented Her Citherean Temple for These Thirty Years Past. A New Edition with Considerable Additions*. 3 vols. Dublin, 1797.

Marks, Elaine, and Isabelle de Courtivron, eds. *New French Feminisms*. New York: Schocken, 1981.

Miller, Nancy K. "'I's' in Drag: The Sex of Recollection." *The Eighteenth Century: Theory and Interpretation* 22 (1981): 45–57.

Morris, John. *Versions of the Self: Studies in English Autobiography from John Bunyan to John Stuart Mill*. New York: Basic Books, 1966.

Nussbaum, Felicity. *"The Brink of All We Hate": English Satires on Women, 1660–1750*. Lexington: University Press of Kentucky, 1984.

————. "Heteroclites: The Gender of Character in the Scandalous Memoirs." In *The New Eighteenth Century: Theory/Politics/English Literature*. Ed. Felicity Nussbaum and Laura Brown. New York: Methuen, 1987. 144–67.

Pascal, Roy. *Design and Truth in Autobiography*. London: Routledge and Kegan Paul, 1960.

Pilkington, Laetitia. *Memoirs of Mrs. Laetitia Pilkington, Wife to the Rev. Matthew Pilkington, Written by Herself, Wherein Are Occasionally Interspersed All Her poems, with Anecdotes of Several Eminent Persons Living and Dead*. London, 1748–54. Rpt. Intro. Iris Barry. New York: George Routledge and Sons, 1928.

Pollak, Ellen M. "Pope and Sexual Difference: Woman as Part and Counterpart in the 'Epistle to A Lady.'" *Studies in English Literature, 1500–1900* 24 (1984): 461–81.

Pope, Alexander. "Epistle to A Lady." In *Epistles to Several Persons (Moral Essays)*. Ed. F. W. Bateson. Twickenham Edition. London: Methuen, 1950. III, ii: 46–74.

Rose, Mary Beth. "Gender, Genre, and History: Seventeenth-Century English Women and the Art of Autobiography." In *Women in the Middle Ages and the Renaissance: Literary and Historical Perspectives*. Syracuse: Syracuse University Press, 1986.

Sheldon, Ann. *Memoirs of Miss Ann Sheldon (Now Mrs. Archer). A Lady Who Figured, during Several Years, in the Highest Line of Public Life, and in Whose History Will Be Found, All the Vicissitudes, Which So Constantly Attend on Women of Her Description*. 4 vols. (in 2). London, 1787.

Showalter, Elaine. "Feminist Criticism in the Wilderness." In *The New Feminist Criticism: Essays on Women, Literature, and Theory*. Ed. Elaine Showalter. New York: Pantheon, 1985.

Shumaker, Wayne. *English Autobiography: Its Emergence, Materials, and Form*. Berkeley and Los Angeles: University of California Press, 1954.

Spacks, Patricia Meyer. *The Female Imagination*. New York: Knopf, 1972.

———. *Imagining a Self: Autobiography and Novel in Eighteenth-Century England*. Cambridge: Harvard University Press, 1976.

———. "Reflecting Women." *Yale Review* 63 (1973): 26–42.

———. "Scrapbook of a Self: Mrs. Piozzi's Later Journals." *Harvard Library Bulletin* 18 (1970): 221–47.

Spengemann, William. *The Forms of Autobiography: Episodes in the History of a Literary Genre*. New Haven: Yale University Press, 1980.

Stanton, Domna C. "Autogynography: Is the Subject Different?" In *The Female Autograph*. Ed. Domna C. Stanton. New York: Literary Forum, 1985. 5–22.

Stauffer, Donald. *The Art of Biography in Eighteenth-Century England*. Princeton: Princeton University Press, 1941.

Thrale, Hester. "The Family Book." In *The Thrales of Streatham Park*. Ed. Mary Hyde. Cambridge: Harvard University Press, 1977.

———. *Thraliana: The Diary of Mrs. Hester Lynch Thrale (Later Mrs. Piozzi)*. Ed. Katharine C. Balderston. 2d ed. 2 vols. Oxford: Clarendon, 1951.

Weintraub, Karl. *The Value of the Individual: Self and Circumstance in Autobiography*. Chicago: University of Chicago Press, 1978.

White, Hayden. "The Value of Narrativity in the Representation of Reality." *Critical Inquiry* 7 (1980): 5–27.

Autobiographical Practices

Essays in this section open the question of individual practices of autobiographical writing across three centuries. The focus is on the various forms of autobiographical writings—letters, instruction manuals, novels of education, journals, diaries, and works published as "autobiography." In particular, the effort is to examine *women's* autobiographical practices across a wide range of forms that might more generally be distinguished as autobiographical, rather than attempting to define the generic contours of those forms as such. The background against which these essays define the work of the autobiographical is that set of male models that privilege only certain forms of life writing, so that the notion of the "autobiographical" is extended, particularly as women's writings upset and invert the standard patterns of life writing. The authors pay close attention to the ways in which these writings reflect the cultural doubleness women experience under patriarchy (both in terms of women's responsibilities and in the opposite of those responsibilities—the instances of withdrawal from the world), to the rhetorical forms and generic norms that are employed in women's writings, and to the links between autobiographical writing and literary creativity, political commitment, domestic duties, and educational practices.

The space mapped by the essays in this section is the space in which the private and public notions of writing separate themselves. The feeling that autobiographical writings locate themselves generally on the side of private writing provides the authors with an opportunity to comment on the relation of gender and form, subject matter, style, and attitude in women's writings, suggesting as well that such writings serve multiple purposes for the writer—purposes that could not be served by more openly "public" forms of writing.

Patricia Meyer Spacks's essay, "Female Rhetorics," argues that in general "eighteenth-century letters by women reflect and elucidate the conflict between the desire for self-assertion and the need for self-suppression, and they demonstrate strategies of deflection." Looking closely at the writings of three women who conducted voluminous correspondences—Lady Mary Wortley Montagu, Mary Delany, and Elizabeth Carter—the essay examines the theme of "self-elucidation" in these letters, suggesting that female correspondence in this period supplied "a means of evasive self-definition" and that gender "informs their use of the epistolary form." Bound to her social situation (domestic) and her social value (unappreciated), the eighteenth-century woman tried to overcome such disabling conditions through forms of autobiographical writing that wrote about the "self" under a historical dictum for self suppression. The female self attempts definition against the models of individual selfhood implicit in men's writings to construct a quite different self that subjects its own concerns to concern for others, writing—as Spacks demonstrates—to and about others.

Mitzi Myers, in "Pedagogy as Self-Expression in Mary Wollstonecraft," examines the full range of Wollstonecraft's works to analyze the ways in which "the autobiographical impulse" to define female selfhood is deflected into forms of writing other than the strictly autobiographical: "novels of education, children's books, expository manuals of instruction and advice." Of particular interest here is Wollstonecraft's concern with pedagogy, which "reimagines [women's] culturally assigned roles in terms of increased rationality, autonomy, and responsibility." Again, women's writings focus on female selfhood and employ "covertly self-expressive forms as products of multiple pedagogic relationships" that take up questions of self-definition. Mary Wollstonecraft is exemplary of a number of eighteenth-century women whose writings "illuminate the fruitful alliances between teaching (the modeling of others) and the molding of self."

In her essay, "Representing Two Cultures: Jane Austen's Letters," Deborah Kaplan argues that Austen's letters (often overlooked in favor of reading Austen's life through her literary works) demonstrate her simultaneous participation in the gentry culture of her day and in a female subculture. These cultures are "textualized" variously through Austen's letters to family members and friends. The discussion of Austen's letters forces an examination of the relation between letters and literature, which reflects the relation between the gentry and women's cultures in which Austen lived. Here women disguise their presences in texts by performing social functions through the text (passing on information, etc.). Austen's letters, like those examined by Patricia Spacks, tell the stories of others—through gossip and anecdote—under a guise of "stylistic propriety" that masks aspects of the storyteller's identity. Because the letters are a "private" form by comparison with the public novels, they can express multiple, even contradictory views, permitting a "full representation" of the complexities of Austen's cultural life. The novels, on the other hand, "through their particular conflation of gentry and women's cultures, seek to avoid contradictions." For this reason, Kaplan argues, Austen's novels fail to persuade.

James Holt McGavran's essay, "Dorothy Wordsworth's Journals: Putting Herself Down," explores the terms of Dorothy Wordsworth's self-effacement through a substitution of the "eye" for the "I" in the journals on which her brother relied for the creation of his poetry. McGavran states that the journals are evidence of Dorothy Wordsworth's "relinquished psyche," a poetic psyche of great power, and her autobiographical writing forms provided an occasion for self-deprecation and self-transcendence—both methods of "self-avoidance." McGavran's examination of the effects of Wordsworth's "putting herself down" involves a multiple reading of Dorothy's relation to William, her relation to the culture and landscape that provided inspiration for his poetry and her journals, and the implications of a gendered vision in which the "eye" effaces the liminal "I" of a developing selfhood and in which the "eye" belongs to the female observer and the "I" to the traditional male poet whose "I" is constructed through the poetry. McGavran asks what effects this conflation of "eye" and "I"—"cross readings of nature and selves and texts"—has on Dorothy Wordsworth's "powers of seeing and knowing and writing."

Joanne Braxton's "Charlotte Forten Grimké" focuses on the diaries of a turn-of-the-century black woman poet. The author's opening gesture is a self-reflexive one: it admits her difficulties, as a black woman critic, in coming to these writings and her eventual discovery of a voice "struggling to be heard." Through careful archival scholarship, Braxton traces the development of Forten's published work and reads against that public record the means by which the public voice was forged. The essay analyzes Forten's diary "as a tool for the development of her political and artistic consciousness and as a means of self-evaluation." In the process of creating a "black and female poetic identity" against "potentially shattering encounters" with racism and sexism, the diaries serve as "a place of restoration and self-healing." In addition, the diaries document Forten's search for literary models, tracking the poet's readings and efforts to shape literary and personal identities against the dominant white culture. The "public voice" that Forten eventually discovers is, according to Braxton, the "standard English voice" that Braxton initially resisted, a voice that marked Forten as an "outsider" within certain forms of black experience and culture. Thus the voice that is discovered through the writing is one that challenges its own claims and, in complex ways, masks its internalized sense of alienation.

Nancy Walker's treatment of "Public Presence and Private Self" in the works of Emily Dickinson, Alice James, and Virginia Woolf takes up the tensions between personal and public lives by putting the autobiographical writings of these three women in counterbalance to one another. Of particular concern to Walker are the ways in which the tensions of the public and private construct the style and subject matter of the autobiographical writings. Walker records the ways in which each of these women "assert[s] an individuality by rejecting the 'normal' role of women (a rejection that results in mental and/or physical anguish)"; the use of masked identities within the private writings; and the terms by which these private writings covertly address themselves to a "public" with which the writer "has an uneasy relationship." Walker traces through these writings the "often painful evidence of . . . life . . . for relatively privileged white women in the Victorian and post-Victorian periods," with specific interest in the ways in which the writings record the efforts of Dickinson, James, and Woolf "to free themselves of the constraints of 'true womanhood' in order to participate in the life of the intellect." Walker argues that the three women negotiated the space between the private and public through writings that make claims on both localities and that explore the tensions between them. These writings demonstrate that, for women, the private and public sectors are often opposed rather than being mutually supporting or defining as they frequently are for men.

CHAPTER SEVEN

Female Rhetorics

Patricia Meyer Spacks

Personal letters, published, entice readers by fictions of self-revelation. In eighteenth-century England, much epistolary rhetoric encouraged such fictions. Letter writers—at least those whose communications have survived in print—proclaim to one another their sincerity and artlessness. "Now as I love you better than most I have ever met with in the world . . . ; so inevitably I write to you more negligently, that is more openly, and what all but such as love another will call writing worse." That comes from a letter from Alexander Pope to Jonathan Swift (28 Nov. 1729, Sherburn 3). Samuel Johnson, with his usual bracing realism, suggested that friendships involving perfect self-revelation belonged to children, or to the Golden Age, but letters between intimates continued to insist on their own candor. Many that survive sound like works written with an eye to publication: Pope, Swift, and Walpole, with their artifices of naturalness, glance toward posterity. But whether the famous letters of the eighteenth century *construct* or *reveal* a self, they encourage readers to acknowledge a personality so compelling as to constitute selfhood.

For eighteenth-century women as letter writers, the notion of direct self-revelation and self-assertion would conflict with ideas about femininity deeply inscribed in the culture. A chilling passage in *Clarissa* suggests the female obligation to self-suppression. Aunt Hervey reproaches her niece for alluding to a suitor's "unworthiness": "Not so fast, my dear. Does not this look like setting a high value on yourself?" (Richardson 1:373). The high value may—as in Clarissa's case—accurately assess worth, but no speaker has the right to claim it for herself.

Eighteenth-century letters by women reflect and elucidate the conflict between the desire for self-assertion and the need for self-suppression, and they demonstrate strategies of deflection. Lady Mary Wortley Montagu, Mary Delany, and Elizabeth Carter, my three subjects, all conducted voluminous correspondences in which they worked out ways of understanding themselves: each set of letters reveals its own dominant theme of self-elucidation. But the writers also find ways to avoid the troubling threat of egotism. Female correspondence, their letters suggest, supplies means of evasive self-definition, and the sex of women letter writers informs their use of the epistolary form.

The twentieth-century reputations of Lady Mary, Delany, and Carter confirm the women's avoidance of excessive personal claims. Most people who now recognize the name of Elizabeth Carter dimly recollect Johnson's praise of her as one who could make good puddings as well as translate Greek. Lady Mary Wortley Montagu survives in present-day consciousness because Pope attacked her. The entry for Mary Delany in the *Concise Dictionary of National Biography* begins, "Friend of Swift." All three women lived prolonged lives (Carter died at eighty-nine, Delany at eighty-eight, Lady Mary at seventy-three) of various accomplishment: among other things, Carter translated Epictetus; Delany invented the paper mosaic, a mode of representing flowers with accuracy and beauty by layered shapes of colored paper; Lady Mary introduced small-pox inoculation into England. But their modern fame, such as it is, rests largely on their associations with distinguished men.

The women's published letters exist in different states of completeness and accuracy. Lady Mary Wortley Montagu, born earliest of the three (in 1689), has been most recently edited; her letters appeared in 1966 in unexpurgated, lucidly annotated form, comprising three volumes of correspondence beginning in her twentieth year and extending to a few weeks before her death. Lady Llanover, a descendant of Mary Granville Delany's sister Ann, produced six volumes of Delany's letters, each more than six hundred pages long, in 1861. The reverential tone of her preface conveys her high regard for her subject (born in 1700), but the editor fails to explain her editorial principles; we cannot know what has been silently omitted. At least equally reverential, and irritatingly self-satisfied about his severe censorship, the Reverend Montagu Pennington, nephew of Elizabeth Carter, published four volumes of her letters in 1809, only three years after her death (she was born in 1717). "Nothing has been added to any of the Letters," he assures his readers, "but a good deal has been left out of trifling chit-chat and confidential communications"—exactly what a modern reader might most wish to see. Moreover, Pennington prints only two specific sets of letters, one containing communications between Carter and Catherine Talbot, the other composed of letters from Carter to Elizabeth Vesey. He explains that Carter burned some of her letters and ordered others returned to their senders; he chooses from those remaining apparently on the basis of their moral and theological wisdom.

The letters' originators differed from one another in circumstance and background. Elizabeth Carter never married and, during the thirty years of her correspondence with Catherine Talbot (1741–70), she lived mainly with her father at Deal, in the south of England. She had already established herself as an intellectual, mastering several foreign languages and reading in many fields, but in her letters she shows herself more concerned to display her piety than her literary gifts. In 1758 she published her translation of Epictetus, with a commentary about the relation of his philosophy to the principles of Christianity. Talbot, four years younger than Carter, always deferred to her as an intellectual superior. Mary Delany, a descendant of the aristocratic Granville family, also emphasized piety in a long series of letters beginning in her twenty-first year. She first married, at the urging of her family, a man named Pendarves, much older than she and utterly incompatible. Widowed six years later, she spent fifteen years as a cheerfully unattached woman, then made her own choice—Patrick Delany, a clergyman fifteen years her senior, with whom she lived happily. Neither marriage produced children. Lady Mary Wortley Montagu, daughter of Evelyn Pierrepont, first Marquess of Dorchester, cared about this world, not the next. After eloping with the man of her choice, against parental opposition, she embarked on a marriage so unhappy that she spent relatively little time with her husband, to whom, however, she bore a son and a daughter. The son proved utterly unsatisfactory, beginning his career as a con man during his school days; he ran away from Westminster School at the age of thirteen and tried to pass himself off as an Oxford student. The daughter married an impecunious Scottish peer, Lord Bute, who subsequently became prime minister of England. Lady Mary lived the last thirty years of her life alone in Italy, raising silkworms and poultry and writing long letters to her daughter.

The problem of egotism explicitly concerns all three of these women. When they write about their own actions, thoughts, or feelings, they worry about seeming too self-involved; often they deprecate the activities they report. Carter explains that she had read nothing except *Joseph Andrews* and Ariosto for some time, because she has been much involved "in the important affair of working a pair of ruffles and handkerchief." She has also developed a passion for dancing, but she assures her correspondent that she will soon move on to something new: "learning the Chinese language, or studying Duns Scotus and Thomas Aquinas." Then she apologizes for the paragraph she has just written: "I ought to beg your pardon for all this egotism, but after the description I have given you of my employments, you will easily imagine I am at a loss of a subject" (1 Jan. 1743, Pennington 1:24, 25). She thus articulates a female problem: if one does nothing important and feels guilty at betraying self-concern, what can one write about? Later in their correspondence, Catherine Talbot confesses: "Talkativeness and egotism are my vices" (23 Dec. 1751, 2:67). Considering letters as equivalent to conversation—an almost universal eighteenth-century equation—one might wonder how any writer of personal letters can avoid such "vices." Lady Mary apologizes when she tells Lady Pomfret something of her life in Italy and of her feelings: "I beg your pardon (dear madam) for this impertinent account of myself; you ought to forgive it, since you would not be troubled with it, if I did not depend upon it, that your friendship for me interests you in all my concerns" (11 Nov. 1740, Halsband 3:210). Self-revelation constitutes an "impertinent" act unless it is justified by profound friendship. Even writing to her beloved sister, Ann, Delany apologizes for speaking of her own illness: "Have I not said enough of myself? Yes, surely!" (30 Dec. 1758, Llanover 3:531).

In an early letter to Ann, Delany complains about another correspondent who adopts too "cramped" and obscure an epistolary style. "The beauty of writing (in my opinion)," she concludes, "consists in telling our sentiments in an easy natural way" (14 Mar. 1728–29, 1:196). Almost a quarter of a century later, she complains because Ann has shown Samuel Richardson some of Delany's letters to her. "Indeed, such careless and incorrect letters as mine are to you, should not be exposed: were they put in the best dress I could put them into, they have nothing to recommend them but the warm overflowing of a most affectionate heart, which can only give pleasure to the partial friend they are addressed to" (17 Nov. 1750, 2:617). Stressing the importance of epistolary style, these comments also differentiate appropriate styles in relation to levels of intimacy. The "easy and natural" mode desirable in letters between friends provides an appropriate "dress" for the telling of sentiments—meaning, epistolary practice suggests, the expression of views about such matters as books and current political happenings. Only between extreme intimates can feeling be allowed simply to overflow, justifying "careless and incorrect" style, but also shaping letters inappropriate for any audience but the intended recipient. From a modern perspective, even Delany's most intimate letters sound highly controlled, sharply restraining their expression of personal feeling. But she manifestly experiences more freedom in writing her sister than in other correspondences; in that context she allows herself at least the possibility of focusing on her own emotions.

The conventions of female correspondence resemble those dominating its male counterpart. Women's letters almost ritualistically apologize for their own length; they reiterate ardent professions of friendship. Pope and Swift do the same thing, but because the women often apparently have less to write about, their conventional protestations assume a larger place in their letters. In her old age, Delany would offer lessons in "propriety" to her little grandniece, pointing out that propriety amounts to thoughtfulness, a way to demonstrate concern for others. The stylized aspects her letters share with those of other women express their status as communications dominated by consciousness of *the other*. Hence the special importance of self-subordination: concern for self must not be allowed to block sensitivity to the imagined needs of the recipient. Hence the insistent recurrence, within these texts, of rituals of politeness.

The ideology of self-subordination implies, among other things, suppression of narrative about the self. Even when these letter writers experience their own emotional dramas, they frequently fail to report them directly. Lady Mary, in her premarital letters to Wortley and in her later passionate correspondence with the young Italian Algarotti, with whom she fell in love in her middle age (he, bisexual in orientation, apparently preferred Lord Hervey), expresses herself rather like a literary heroine; she calls attention to the analogy between her situation and Clarissa's in a letter written late in her life. But she elides the aftermath of her romantic predicaments, hardly hinting at her unhappiness with her husband in letters to intimates and never revealing what has happened with Algarotti, much less how she feels about it. Delany, for some years during her first widowhood, participated in a flirtation? a courtship? *some* kind of relationship with Lord Baltimore. She probably wished to marry him; certainly she expected him to propose. Like Lovelace in *Clarissa*, he finally proposed in terms that made it impossible for her immediately to accept him; then for some years he disappeared from her life. One deduces this story not from Delany's letters, which largely ignore it, but from Llanover's editorial comments. Carter received at least one proposal of marriage during the years of the Talbot correspondence; she hints at more. She tells the story of the proposal in a comic mode, and quickly. Of psychosexual drama in her life, she says nothing.

Why should a modern reader feel interested in women who avoid self-revelation and personal narrative, concern themselves obsessively with stylistic propriety, and fill their letters with courteous protestation? One may note in such phenomena evidence of familiar social attitudes toward women and of the internalization of these attitudes by the women themselves; that once said, why bother? In fact, these letters create an impression of vitality and emotional tension comparable to that generated by the fictional letters conveying the drama of such novels as *Pamela* and *Clarissa*. If real female letter writers eschew narratives focused on themselves and avoid direct outpourings of emotion, they nonetheless find ways of indirect self-dramatization, codes for revealing the self.

In her first letter to Wortley after their marriage, Lady Mary describes the family in which she is living—five children, a mother, and a father. Then she remarks, "I don't know whether you will presently find out that this seeming Impertinent Account is the tenderest expressions [*sic*] of my Love to you, but it furnishes my imagination with agreeable pictures of our future life, and I flatter my self with the hope of one day enjoying with you the same satisfactions" (22 Oct. [1722], 1:168). She thus suggests that anecdotes about other people supply metaphors for her desire. Carter's and Delany's letters as well as Lady Mary's abound in stories serving comparable functions.

The stories, however, rarely concern domestic bliss. Lady Mary's anecdotes more often dwell on the corruptions of high life with gusto and with brilliant detail. In her letters, as in Delany's, rich young men commit public suicide, footmen rape peeresses, men try successfully or futilely to obtain divorces in order to enact their lustful desires with younger women, randy middle-aged women entice young men to their beds. A particularly delicious narrative concerns an unmarried aristocratic couple, interrupted in an assignation by "a tall, musical, silly, ugly thing, . . . call'd Miss Leigh." They urge her to play the harpsichord for them; when she begins, they "decamp'd to the Bed Chamber," returning to invite her to perform another piece, only to disappear once more. Finally, at the third repetition, Miss Leigh leaves in a rage, telling everyone in town what has happened; "and poor Edgcombe met with nothing where ever he went but compliments about his third tune, which is reckon'd very handsome in a Lover past forty" (to Lady Mar [23 June 1727], 2:78–79).

At the end of this same letter (2:80), Lady Mary observes, "I send you a novell instead of a letter." She thus calls attention to the flavor of fictionality in her most compelling narratives. The stories she sketches resemble in substance the novels she and her contemporaries read. (By "novell," in 1727, Lady Mary of course meant something more like what we now call "romance.") More than a quarter century later, she reports to her daughter a scandalous-sentimental narrative which, she says, "in Richardson's hands would serve very well to furnish out 7 or 8 volumes" (8 Dec. [1754], 3:70). Like Carter and Delany, she finds the stuff of fiction in the world she knows.

Lady Mary states most directly a theme implicit in the stories all three women tell. Sounding like Mr. Bennet in *Pride and Prejudice*, she writes her sister, "I own I enjoy vast delight in the Folly of Mankind, and God be prais'd that is an inexhaustible Source of Entertainment" ([Sept. 1725], 2:56). The narrative energy of these female letters often derives from their loving rendition of mankind's—and womankind's—folly:

> What a sad story of that vile Miss T. who has run away with Mr. O., and poor Mrs. O *run mad*, and gone into the Bedlam! An intrigue was discovered last year, and hushed up, and Miss T. was more circumspect in her behavior, and it made no noise, but about a month ago she left her father's house under pretence of going to see her mother, she took her maid in the post-chaise with her, all her jewels, her best clothes, and £700, and went off to France; she was pursued but not overtaken. (Delany to Mrs. Dewes, undated, Llanover 3:452)

Delany loves such episodes; she reports many of them. Even Carter, despite her "insignificancy" ("I often secretly exult in the privileges that attend one's being suffered to go in and out of a room with as much silence, and as little ceremony as the cat" [14 Sept. 1754, 2:182]), and despite her editor's excisions, relates, for example, the tale of a rich man who shut himself up in his house, running to lock the door if he spied a human being nearby, and associating only with six "conversible" hogs (23 Jan. 1744, 1:48).

Such narratives substitute for narratives of the self—most strikingly, perhaps, in Delany's reports of her association with King George III and Queen Charlotte. Day after day, she renders in loving detail everything said and done at court and during royal visits, suppressing the fact of her own presence as much as possible, while yet emphasizing her powerful role as observer and narrator. In most of the anecdotes told by the other women, the tellers have not actually witnessed the events they report. Yet all, like Delany, assert by their narratives the traditional resources of women: to notice, to interpret, to tell.

The often scandalous stories incorporated in female correspondences help to define their reporters by the principle of differentiation—the women tell of lives led by other values and based on other assumptions than their own. They also satisfy forbidden wishes by brief vicarious excitement, reminding themselves of possibilities for the unconventional—if also, often, of the likelihood of retribution for deviation. And, of course, they enjoy the power of their knowledge and their telling, of being able to convey titillating information that their correspondent lacks. But their stories of male and female enactments of desire most forcefully convey their musings on the relative positions and possibilities accessible to men and women in their society. Their expedients for self-definition involve reflection on the same compelling subject.

The topic of women's position explicitly informs Lady Mary's project of self-definition. Characteristically her letters move from her own particular situation or that of another to meditations on the general—the social and psychological possibilities and limitations of the female. Lady Mary feels especially conscious of women's destiny of subordination; she cannot even choose an Italian tutor for herself but must accept her father's selection, since "tis allwais the Fate of Women to obey" (to Frances Hewet, [13 Feb. 1710], Halsband 1:21). Women have long been labeled frivolous, creatures of "trifling inclinations" (to Wortley, [28 Mar. 1710], 1:24); Lady Mary insists on her own difference. But she recurs frequently to the notion that Wortley cannot "esteem" her because he assumes her participation in the universal female weakness. She wishes that she could accept the fact that *all* men fail to esteem women; then she might rest content because her lover grants her wit and beauty and would not worry because he also assumes her folly and weakness ([25 Apr. 1710], 1:29). Writing to Bishop Gilbert Burnet, sending him her translation from a Latin version of Epictetus (unlike Carter, she had not mastered Greek), she comments that "Folly [is] reckon'd . . . our proper Sphere," and education is forbidden to women on the grounds that it makes them "tattling, impertinent, vain, and conceited" creatures. She will not argue, she says, for the equality of the sexes; she accepts the necessity of female submission. But she begs for the right to alleviate in herself the ignorance that allows women to be readily seduced, intellectually and morally (20 July 1710, 1:44, 45, 46).

These early statements set the tone for Lady Mary's utterances on the subject, typically marked by the same combination of announced resignation and ill-concealed resentment. Angry at Wortley, she acknowledges the wisdom of women who base their happiness on trifles because they, unlike her, yearn for what they can attain ([26 Feb. 1711], 1:83–4). Much later, to a woman friend (Barbara Calthorpe), she writes: "To say Truth, I have never had any great Esteem for the generality of the fair Sex, and my only consolation for being of the gender has been the assurance it gave me of never being marry'd to anyone amongst them." She adds, however, that she feels ashamed of her sex because of Lady Holderness's indiscreet marital plans (7 Dec. [1723], 2:33)—explicit evidence of how scandalous stories provoke thought about gender. In letters to her sister, Lady Mary poignantly recalls their early belief that marriage would solve all problems and childbearing would make one happy forever. She reflects on the world's tendency to generalize about her sex on the basis of a few women's reprehensible actions; she speaks insistently about the problem of interpretation, the way in which men understand all female responses as functions of women's sexuality. From the beginning, she has tried to separate herself from other women on the basis of her special intelligence, her unique "sincerity." Finally she accepts her participation in the female situation, advising her daughter about the education of girls, acknowledging the inevitability of disappointment, demonstrating the possibility of contentment despite the limited choices and limited resources inherent in the conditions of eighteenth-century womanhood. Even in this more resigned period of her life, however, she bursts out from time to time, as when she praises Francis Sydenham for his analysis of hysteria: "He clearly proves that your wise honourable spleen is the same disorder [as female hysteria]; but you vile usurpers do not only engross learning, power, and authority to yourselves, but will be our superiors even in constitution of mind" (to Sir James Steuart, [5 Sept. 1758], 3:171–2).

In her reflections about women, Lady Mary expresses the dilemmas of her own sense of specialness, her desire to declare her difference, and then her need at last to find what she shares with others of her kind. Mary Delany, compliant where Lady Mary was rebellious and leading a conventional rather than an ostentatiously original life, makes community her theme from the beginning—a more indirect way of thinking about women and of thinking about herself. Even her earliest letters to her sister emphasize the importance of "friendship." "I am convinced," the then Mrs. Pendarves writes her sister in 1727, after the death of her first husband,

> there is no real happiness but in a faithful friend. As Doctor Swift says to his Vanessa, it is a *"rational delight,"* it fills the mind with generous motives, and I must have a mean opinion of those that call it *romantic*: it is the most improper name for it in the world, for the foundation of a worthy friendship is truth. People may fancy themselves in love, and work up their imagination to such a pitch as to really believe themselves possessed of that passion, but I never yet heard of anybody's carrying friendship on by mere imagination. (25 Nov. 1727, Llanover 1:148)

This is her fullest and most explicit explanation of what she means by "friendship," an important ideal of her period, a noun Delany applies consistently to her relation with her sister, a term of transcendent value. Despite her disclaimer, imagination plays its part in her friendships, particularly the one with her sister. "Though so many hills and vales separate our bodies, thought (that is free and unlimited) makes up in some measure that misfortune, and though my eyes are shut, I see my dearest sister in my dreams. I talked with you all last night and was mortified when the vision fled" (30 May 1724, 1:98). The human connection between Delany and her sister, like that between her and her other female intimates, feels more solidly based than alliances with men. As a widow, after her miserable marriage at her uncle's behest, she expresses vehement distaste for marriage as an institution:

> Matrimony! I marry! Yes, there's a blessed scene before my eyes of the comforts of that state.—A sick husband, squalling brats, a cross mother-in-law, and a thousand unavoidable impertinences . . . : but stop my rage! be not too fierce. I may be dashed on the very rock I endeavour to avoid, and therefore I will say no more against a station of life which in the opinion of some people is not in our power to prevent. (19 Mar. 1727/8, 1:164–65)

She often writes of male-female union in comparably negative terms. When her beloved sister marries, Delany observes to a friend that "marriage *is serious and hazardous*" (to Lady Throckmorton, 5 Dec. 1740, 2:134). Like Lady Mary Wortley Montagu, Mary Pendarves comments on the persistence with which men interpret women to the disadvantage of her sex; she complains that men lead women astray and then blame them for their weakness. Men are not to be trusted; to trust women, on the other hand, makes the happiness of her life. She says this, one way and another, again and again.

Finally she marries happily—marries a man so dedicated to virtue, so supportive of all her endeavors, that he possesses the qualities Mrs. Delany more consistently found in women. Even during her second marriage, however, she continues to defend the notion that women should possess the choice of remaining single (see letter to Ann Dewes, 31 Mar. 1759, 3:544). Her vision of good marriage more and more approximates her notion of friendship: "we are worthy of being their [men's] companions, their friends, *their advisors*, as well as *they ours*" (to Mrs. Dewes, 14 Apr. 1759, 3:547).

As Delany ages, as friends and relatives in increasing numbers die, she realizes the moral problem implicit in commitment to human connection. Such commitment involves valuing the things of this world, whereas one's thoughts and feelings should properly direct themselves to preparing for the afterlife. On the other hand, at the age of eighty-six she writes to a friend: "Time and absence, I think, rather increase than diminish affection, when we from time to time communicate that mutual remembrance and regard which *had lasted so many years!*" (to Mrs. F. Hamilton, 24 Sept. 1786, 6:391). "Tho' I dayly feel a decay of my faculties," she tells her niece, "there is none in my affection" (to Mrs. Port, 21 Dec. 1785, 6:324). Her central preoccupation continued to dominate her letters until her death.

Delany's concern with relationships serves the same psychic purpose as Lady Mary's dwelling on the situation of her sex; both women thus confront the problem of their function in the world. In her earlier years Lady Mary occasionally published bits of poetry and prose—anonymously, sometimes employing a male persona—but she developed no real literary career. Her ne'er-do-well son made her feel a failure as a mother; her self-willed marriage hardly provided self-justification; her efforts to find romance in middle age proved disastrous. She could not hope to proclaim her worth by her accomplishments. The letters show her gradual reconciliation to a life dedicated more to *being* than to *doing*, reflecting on hers as a woman's fate. Delany, childless, kept herself constantly occupied. As the letters report, she did needlework, supervised the servants, endlessly copied other people's paintings, and created almost a thousand "paper mosaics" that were much praised by those who saw them. But she could not think of such work as supplying her life's meaning—meaning she found primarily in her human connections.

The thematic emphasis of Elizabeth Carter's letters to Catherine Talbot reflects yet another female strategy of self-presentation: constant disclaimers of the self's significance. Carter apologizes for the contents of her letters, characterizing them as "nonsense"; if she allows herself to move freely from one subject to another, she feels that she has imposed on her correspondent. The puddings Johnson praised have more problematic meaning for her: at the age of thirty, she reports an episode from her teens, when she "produced a pudding of a new invention, so overcharged with pepper and brandy that it put the whole family in a flame. The children all set up their little throats against Greek and Latin, and I found this unlucky event was like to prove my everlasting disgrace" (15 Sept. 1747, Pennington 1:218). The children's association of domestic failure with intellectual preoccupation underlines Carter's anxiety about the propriety of her own concerns. She accuses herself of inability to make good use of time. "I am perpetually amusing myself with schemes of a hundred agreeable employments, which appear mighty practicable till I come to undertake them, and then, to my great mortification, I find it impossible to apply myself a single hour to any one thing without growing stupid, and feeling all manner of distempers" (29 Oct. 1747, 1:233). She suffers from bad nerves and headaches, but also, she says, from native dullness; she eagerly desires improvement, but feels a "tormenting incapacity of attaining it" (13 July 1748, 1:275). If she makes a joke about how the author of a play should assign his hero to some such quiet person as her or her correspondent, she immediately castigates herself for vanity. And so on.

This consistent self-deprecation is neither verbal tic nor mere convention. It reflects a profound "bashfulness" infecting the writer's entire life:

Something must be said in answer to your kind exhortations for me to get rid of my awkward bashfulness, and yet what to say I know not, as it seems an incurable evil. From the very first remembrance of myself I can recollect frequent instances of this folly, when the terrors I was in about entering a room used to damp all the joy that children feel at the thoughts of going abroad. . . . Even in this place, where we are all nearly on a level, I am often as much flurried as in ever so splendid an assembly; and often have been kept from a favourite walk, where we all meet of an evening, because there was not any person of years and experience in the world there, to take me by the hand and introduce me. . . . [W]hether such untractable things as trembling nerves and fluttering spirits are to be reasoned into firmness and tranquility is by no means clear; and I much question whether the strongest arguments in the world could help me to make a graceful curtsey or enter a room with a becoming air. (23 June 1752, 2:82–3)

That passage occurs in a letter written when the author was thirty-five. A year and a half later, Carter explains the etiology of her shyness. Her friend has written about the omnipresence of female vanity; in the very nursery, Talbot says, "we are told to *hold up our heads for there is money bid for us*; and . . . , to own a mortifying truth, few girls can become of any consideration in the world, but from the proper regard paid to them by someone *of the condescending Lords of the creation*" (12 Nov. 1753, 2:146). Carter, replying, denies in herself any share of specifically female vanity—implicitly rejecting also the female role as economic commodity, seldom so starkly stated as in Talbot's letter:

Whereas the other misses of this world are told to *hold up their heads*, I was always encouraged to hang mine down; I cannot exactly trace from whence I derived some odd notions upon this subject; possibly my mother, from observing the little propriety and decorum with which affairs of gallantry are usually conducted in such kind of places as this, might be particularly careful to give my thoughts a different turn. Whatever might be the reason, I can perfectly well remember that when I was about ten years old, I looked upon having a *sweetheart* with as much horror as if it had been one of the seven deadly sins; and when I had heard that my favorite playfellow was actually guilty of it, I was so shocked at the atrocity of the thing, that if, in consequence of a most profound and wise lecture, she had not flatly denied the charge, I know not whether we had ever rompt together again. (10 Dec. 1753, 2:149–50)

Shyness is a strategy of avoidance, protecting its victim from attracting one of the condescending lords of creation. Carter's reminiscence asserts a connection between suppressed female vanity, denied self-esteem, and repressed sexuality. Carter continues metaphorically to hang her head down, to deny her own importance, to experience social difficulties, and to refuse sexual connections. Like Delany, she writes passionately of her disinclination for marriage: "If I have suffered from the troubles of others, who have more sense, more understanding, and more virtues than I might reasonably have expected to find, what might I not have suffered from a husband! Perhaps be needlessly thwarted and contradicted in every innocent enjoyment of life: involved in all his schemes right or wrong, and perhaps not allowed the liberty of even silently seeming to disapprove them!" (21 May 1751, 2:29). She sees marriage, for a woman, as a situation of "voluntary dependence" and feels grateful to her father for allowing her to refuse it (28 Apr. 1750, 1:338). Her own "insignificant," private life strikes her as infinitely preferable.

Carter's protestations of insufficiency protect a treasured realm of private possibility. Occasionally she betrays resentment about the limiting rules of female decorum—after a lovely rural evening, for example, she cannot be allowed to walk home alone. But a sense of contentment emerges beneath her self-deprecations:

> Sometimes . . . I have the grace to be ashamed, and really think I am living to no kind of purpose; at others I look round the world, and see most folks in it as foolishly busied, and take comfort. . . . At one time I think it must proceed from a voluntary dilatoriness that I do so little, at another the whole fault is thrown upon some natural defect, some unavoidable slowness of constitution. At last, tired with all these various conjectures and speculations, and not pleased nor perfectly satisfied with any of them, I make the shirts I have to make, hear the lessons I have to hear, and upon the whole, go on in the same daily track tolerably well contented. (21 Oct. 1751, 2:54)

By making no claim to the world, Carter gains the internal freedom she needs. She understands that she pays a higher price than men do for such freedom; on one occasion she comments: "Besides all my other important engagements, I have been working my eyes out in making shirts for my brother; I want mightily to reform the world in this particular, and therefore, am resolved when I come into your neighborhood, and am blessed with a family of boys, they shall all learn to make their own shirts" (25 Jan. 1747, 1:108). But such playful utopian fantasies serve only to entertain her; on the whole she rests content with a state of being in which she can escape more demanding responsibilities than shirtmaking. She feels no need to write, she insists: "If a thousand good subjects were now to fall in my way, not the least propensity should I feel to write one word about any of them. Almost the only motive of my ever taking a pen into my hand, is the hope of preserving a place in the remembrance of some few friends by whom I cannot bear the thoughts of being forgot" (13 June 1755, 2:208). She thus echoes Delany's stress on friendship—for all three women a crucial resource.

Delany's primary concern with relationship, Lady Mary's obsession with the condition of women, Carter's proclamations of her own insignificance—such preoccupations help define the writers to themselves and locate them in the context of their society. The three women, despite their differences, share central concerns: female concerns. Their letters demonstrate not only the varied possibilities of self-presentation inherent in the epistolary act but also the degree to which self-exploration and self-presentation lead women to ruminate, implicitly or explicitly, on the special conditions of their sex.

Works Cited

Halsband, Robert, ed. *The Complete Letters of Lady Mary Wortley Montagu.* 3 vols. Oxford: Clarendon, 1966.

Llanover, Lady, ed. *The Autobiography and Correspondence of Mary Granville, Mrs. Delany.* 6 vols. London: Bentley, 1861.

Pennington, Montagu, ed. *A Series of Letters between Mrs. Elizabeth Carter and Miss Catherine Talbot, from the Year 1741 to 1770.* 4 vols. London: Rivington, 1809.

Richardson, Samuel. *Clarissa, or, the History of a Young Lady.* 4 vols. London: Dent, 1932.

Sherburn, George, ed. *The Correspondence of Alexander Pope.* 5 vols. Oxford: Clarendon, 1956.

Pedagogy as Self-Expression in Mary Wollstonecraft
Exorcising the Past, Finding a Voice

Mitzi Myers

My approach to Wollstonecraft's self-revelatory writings applies more globally to other women writers as well, but my exploration is not primarily an exercise in generic definition. Although the field of auto-biography studies is still young, it already seems too late to dare a definition that encompasses the whole of a protean genre. (Indeed, if Michael Sprinker is correct, it's even too late to *write* autobiography as well.) In any case, most recent theories of what autobiographies are and how they function are skewed in favor of male models, privileging certain forms of life writing and casting different self-expressive modes beyond the generic pale. I think here of Karl J. Weintraub's investigations of "Western Man" (both words aggrandized by capitalization) and his "genuine autobiographic effort" ("Autobiography and Historical Consciousness" 821, 824), the kind of retrospective retracing of a whole life written by such predictable figures as Augustine or Franklin (*The Value of the Individual*). Weintraub and other theorists typically favor criteria such as achieved integration of being, finality of insight, and formal completeness as hallmarks of "real" autobiography. They seek overt self-expression, whether it be a public voice as in Gibbon's orderly self-portrait in terms of his profession—a man is his work—or the more inner-directed proclamations of Rousseau's private voice.

Tracers of the female autobiographical impulse notice, however, that women's life studies depart significantly from typical male patterns. Mary G. Mason argues that fewer women write autobiography undis-guised, that women discover and delineate an identity "by way of alterity." She thinks of women as "double-focus" writers; she believes that a "grounding of identity through relation to the chosen other, seems . . . to enable women to write about themselves" (231, 226, 210). Estelle C. Jelinek's research finds—for both sexes—a "discrepancy between the critical ideal of autobiography as a genre of disclosure" and the mostly nonconfessional actuality. Nevertheless, Jelinek speaks, like Mason, of "a literary tradition in which women write autobiography that is different from that by men." She cites, for example, women's tendency to write in miscellaneous or discontinuous, "process" forms, such as letters, diaries, journals; to emphasize the personal over the professional; and to understate their self-images and self-assertions, rather than idealizing or heroicizing as male autobiographers often do (*Women's Autobiography* 13, xi–xii, 15). These two quite distinct formulations of "an autobiographical tradition different from the male tradition" (6) overlap in their notion of obliquity: women's discoveries of self take a more circuitous route; their self-representations wear camouflage.[1]

Especially is this true of eighteenth-century writings, in which the autobiographical impulse is often deflected into other forms: novels of education, children's books, expository manuals of instruction and advice. In this key transitional period that witnessed, as one social historian puts it, a "substantive redefinition of the maternal role," the female persona frequently speaks through pedagogy (Bloch 113). Reimagining their culturally assigned roles in terms of increased rationality, autonomy, and responsibility, women educators manifest heartening and confident self-images as teachers, nurturers, and surrogate mothers. Through their educational orientation, which functions for them something like James Olney's concept of a guiding metaphor, women's voices are empowered toward self-creation and re-creation. Educating others, they reeducate themselves to explore new dimensions of womanly experience. By way of children's literature, for example, many late-Georgian women authors express new ideals of womanhood and fresh perspectives on women's situation in their guise of mother-teacher. Advice books, too, involve stories that women tell about their lives: an autobiographical subtext informs women's educational texts, and here again women's records "reveal . . . a self-consciousness and a need to sift through their lives for explanation and understanding . . . to clarify, to affirm, and to authenticate their self-image" (Jelinek, *Women's Autobiography* 15). To readers attuned to nuance and to historical context, such oblique forms may be even more revelatory, more demonstrative of a distinct and emphatic female voice, than autobiography proper. Moreover, educational genres necessarily treat in depth issues crucial to the period's female self-definition: the difficult relationships between nurturance and autonomy, community and independence, reason and feeling. Building on Mason's and Jelinek's suggestions, I want to consider women's autobiographic voices from a pedagogic point of view, to think about their covertly self-expressive forms as products of multiple pedagogic relationships: between one version of the self and another; between the self as student and an external mentor; between teachers and pupils (or parents and children) within texts; between the instructing persona of a work and her varied audiences (children, other women, men); and even intertextually, as when one of an author's educational works comments on or subverts another.

Mary Wollstonecraft is an ideal—but not isolated—case. She is a prime example because her work encompasses the full range of self-expressive educational forms that Georgian women write and because her career illuminates the fruitful alliance between teaching (the modeling of others) and the molding of self. Although she never wrote a formal autobiography, a distinctive persona and a vibrant personal voice characterize her entire literary production. When she mentions the *Rights of Woman* to a friend, for example, she indicatively images the book as a "likeness," a "more faithful sketch" than the portrait for which she is sitting, a book "in which I myself shall certainly appear, head and heart"—and her remark embraces the rest of her output as well (*Collected Letters* 203). I have argued elsewhere that her Scandinavian travel book—*Letters Written During a Short Residence in Sweden, Norway, and Denmark* (1796)—wants to be read as a species of autobiography; here I want to consider three early works from a similar perspective. *Thoughts on the Education of Daughters: With Reflections on Female Conduct, in the More Important Duties of Life* (1787), her first work, reaps knowledge hard won by raising sisters and keeping a girls' school, and paired works appeared almost simultaneously in 1788: Wollstonecraft's thinly veiled autobiographic record of her girlhood, *Mary, a Fiction*, a sentimental novel of self-education that rewrites the lesson of Rousseau in the female gender; and her "book for young people, which," she rightly remarks, "I think has some merit" (*Collected Letters* 166). This latter work features a surrogate mother-governess, Mrs. Mason, a woman of Olympian strength and self-possession, and her two charges, Mary, fourteen, and Caroline, twelve, and is entitled *Original Stories from Real*

Life; with Conversations Calculated to Regulate the Affections, and Form the Mind to Truth and Goodness. I also touch on Wollstonecraft's letters registering the experiences as teacher and as governess to three young ladies in a family of Irish landed wealth that fed her early educational explorations.

Each of these works is, in effect, a stock-taking response to her own traumatic history—her painful childhood, her thought-provoking stints as pedagogue, the loss of her beloved best friend, Fanny Blood. I read these three works as pointers toward Wollstonecraft's later achievement, as experiments in selfhood, and as tentative educational scenarios in which she obliquely explains, justifies, and compensates for her current sense of herself.[2] (The reader will have noticed how obsessively Wollstonecraft affixes her own signature in her characters' names, a trait also exemplified in her rewriting of C. G. Salzmann's book for youngsters, *Elements of Morality* [1791], and in the novel she left unfinished at her early death following childbirth, *The Wrongs of Woman: Or, Maria* [1798]; Wollstonecraft similarly called her first daughter "Fanny," and that name, too, echoes through her work.)

Wollstonecraft's brief and dramatic life has always loomed over her writing; critical discussion has only recently emerged from the naively autobiographical readings that go back to the reactionary critics of the 1790s.[3] They saw a "philosophical wanton" with a bad family background and a bastard daughter; her works, in their view, were nothing more than apologies for a misspent life ("Review of *Memoirs*" 246). That Wollstonecraft's difficult early years with a drunken, brutal father and a cold, weak mother profoundly influenced her career is a truism with sympathetic modern critics as well, but her works cannot be read as a simple equation of self and character. Rather, Wollstonecraft transforms personal dilemma into alternative images of female selfhood, images not idiosyncratic to herself, but endemic to her period. Abandoned child, protective parent, romantic heroine, mother-teacher, rational educator—again and again she is led to reshape and reevaluate her childhood and her character and to image models of female growth and nurturance that would issue in more fully realized capacities, a more integrated sense of self. Always reformist by way of education—the *Rights of Woman* (1792) was correctly located by its initial reviewers as an educational polemic (see Janes)—Wollstonecraft was also a lifelong examiner of her own experience. In the last of her works published while she was alive, she still struggles intensely toward self-awareness:

"What a long time it requires to know ourselves," she exclaims, "and yet almost every one has more of this knowledge than he is willing to own, even to himself" (*Letters Written* 117). (As here, her very prose style often enacts this process of perception and the movement of the contemplating mind.)

Especially was Wollstonecraft haunted by those familial years that formed the woman she was and engendered alternative versions of the woman she might be—and which also fostered the visions of educational, family, and cultural reform that are the heart of the *Rights of Woman* (Myers, "Reform or Ruin"; Brody). I have observed before that Wollstonecraft "has always an unusual gift for dramatizing or mythologizing her personal difficulties into issues of larger consequence" and that critics have taken "too limited a view of her use of personal material" ("Mary Wollstonecraft's *Letters*" 176). If her novels hover obsessively around the intellectual and emotional deprivations that scarred her childhood, and if her educational exposition has an unmistakable personal bite, Wollstonecraft's preoccupation with self also leads her beyond herself, beyond narcissism toward the enlargement attendant upon analysis that is the core of autobiography. Throughout her work she insistently recurs to the image of life as education, and her literary production fuses personal event, female self-definition, and educational format.

Wollstonecraft's career and her output imply a paradigm whose shaping assumptions go something like these: that she grapples with the problems of her life through reworking that life in a variety of educational forms; that she acquires a more forceful voice and a more coherent self as her self-revelations, through the imposition of pedagogy, acquire a larger frame of reference; that in interlocking pedagogic relations with a variety of imagined readers and teachers, she in effect teaches herself, defining her own position through confrontation with prescriptive instructors (like the conduct-book writers whom she refutes in *Rights of Woman*) and with more innovative mentors like Rousseau (whom she half-loved, imitated, and scolded); and, finally, that it is in fact the obliquity of pedagogy that encourages her firmest and most developed sense of herself and, by extension, of women's potential—the kind of educational voice heard in her mature work, one which marries reason and feeling, cultural criticism and self-expression, and which attempts to harmonize communal duties and private needs, to unify public consciousness and individual vision.

The complex pattern of pedagogic experiment and personal growth that culminated in Wollstonecraft's most mature writing emerges clearly in her three earliest instructional texts. *Thoughts*, *Mary*, and *Original Stories* demonstrate how a revelatory autobiographic voice informs her educational tracts and ostensibly fictive work; as embryonic and sometimes awkward feminist pedagogy, they illustrate with peculiar force how personal reflection evades generic boundaries as it seeks to evade conventional feminine stereotypes. Wollstonecraft, most students agree, wears two faces, the romanticist and the reformer. Now she extols feeling, asserting that love and friendship are the deepest wants of her heart; now she pledges allegiance to reason, insisting that all personal and social relationships are amenable to rational reform.

This dialectic of reason and feeling, central not only in Wollstonecraft's writings but also in Georgian female life, plays through these three texts. To argue for women as rational beings—educable, self-disciplined, self-dependent—is, in historical context, something of a radical claim (and it sounds insistently in the period's women writers, from Wollstonecraft to Edgeworth to Austen). To present women as creatures of feeling is dangerous, for that ascribed cultural heritage often limits them, but feeling can also liberate. Like her sometime teacher Rousseau, Wollstonecraft is an early romantic who recognizes the revolutionary challenge to the conventional order posed by individual perception and individual passion. But whether we trace the features of Wollstonecraft the rationalist (who predominates in the *Thoughts* and the *Stories*) or Wollstonecraft the romanticist (who tries to imagine her life into a fresh brand of heroism in *Mary*), we are looking at the educator.

Wollstonecraft turned writer by instructing a new audience about the only field she knew: teaching girls. When she returned from watching over Fanny Blood's deathbed in Portugal, she found that her school had faltered in her sisters' hands; she earned her first authorial pounds by collecting her *Thoughts*. In this collection of essays Wollstonecraft, whose education was fairly catch-as-catch-can (she has been called an autodidact), begins to display the familiarity with educational literature that develops into the structural backbone of *Rights of Woman*—a familiarity fostered by many of her later reviews as a hack journalist and exemplified in her 1789 compendium of educational extracts, *The Female Reader*, typically subtitled *For the Improvement of Young Women*. Not yet having achieved her final mix of cultural critique and self-expressivity, Wollstonecraft blends personality and philosophy un-evenly. She seems to want to be objective but cannot keep down an autobiographical undercurrent. She eventually knew firsthand all the caretaking occupations that were the only jobs available for a middle-class woman, and she found them all wanting. "You have read my sentiments relative to those unfortunate females who are left by incon-siderate parents to struggle with the world, and whose cultivation of mind renders the endeavour doubly painful—I felt what I wrote!" she later told a friend about *Education of Daughters* (*Collected Letters* 161). A hired companion was "shut out from equality and confidence," she recalls, whereas "a teacher at a school is only a kind of upper servant, who has more work than the menial ones. A governess to young ladies is equally disagreeable" (*Thoughts* 71–72).

As would the later *Rights of Woman*, Wollstonecraft's *Education of Daughters* progressively recodifies the rules of exemplary female behav-ior. Critical of current pedagogy, pessimistic about women's limited options, its voices are mixed and its structure digressive and associa-tional. Now tartly assured, now moralistic and religious, Wollstonecraft ranges from emotionally charged self-revelation to counsels of self-discipline and self-control. "I wish them to be taught to think," she urges her maternal audience of their girls (22), and the book itself exemplifies the balancing act between reason and feeling that the Geor-gian thinking woman felt called upon to perform. With its discontinu-ous essay format—it covers everything from "The Nursery" to "Dress" to "Desultory Thoughts" to "The Benefits Which Arise from Disappoint-ments" and more—and its subordination of self to the advice-manual genre, the book formally enacts the critical notion of obliquity discussed earlier. All the same, the book was a step toward a stance. Wollstone-craft's sisters floundered along as humdrum teachers all their days. Interpreting and reinterpreting the circumstances of her life in a variety of educational modes for an ever-widening audience, Wollstonecraft achieved the authoritative pedagogic voice, the defined *writing* self, that allowed her escape to a larger, freer life as an educational philosopher and cultural critic.

It was a blow, then, to leave off writing and go to the aristocratic Kingsborough family as a governess. When Wollstonecraft got to Lon-don after her Irish year, feeling declassed and depressed, she brought home broader social knowledge and psychic freight to process. She also brought *Mary*, the first product of that processing, written while she was still a governess. Her ostensibly fictive account of a female "genius" who educates herself compensates for Wollstonecraft's humbled pride, embodies her isolation and emotional starvation, and documents a pedagogic affiliation with Rousseau. Her letters admire the French author and also criticize his *"chimerical* world" of feeling, to which she herself feels prey. "'Spite of my vexations," another letter goes, "I have lately written, a fiction . . . it is a tale, to illustrate an opinion of mine, that a genius will educate itself. I have drawn from Nature" (*Collected Letters* 145, 162). The letters and the book's motto, a quotation from Rousseau on genius, suggest the conflation of pedagogic purpose and autobiographic impulse that the "Advertisement" confirms. Her heroine is different from the generality, as Wollstonecraft instructs the reader: "The mind of a woman who has thinking powers is displayed," a protagonist drawn "from the original source." Wollstonecraft's preface shows her as both student and teacher. Adapting what she has gleaned from the French master of confession and self-creation, she will juxtapose a real-life heroine against conventional novelistic stereotypes. Renovating fiction with matter from her own experience, she moves her reader (and herself) toward a new interpretation of female life. Wollstonecraft enrolls herself with Rousseau among the "chosen few" who "wish to speak for themselves." Her practice is always grounded in the belief that experience generates knowledge, that philosophical truth is to be discovered and validated by searching into and reflecting on one's own experiences (see Nicholes 1:53). And her mentor has helped her develop a rationale for an art that does not depend on external plot, but on the expression of her own deepest feelings. "Those compositions only have power to delight . . . where the soul of the author is exhibited. . . . Lost in a pleasing dream, they live in the scenes they represent; and do not measure their steps in a beaten track."

The novel, like the "Advertisement," blends autobiography, radical literary theory, and wish fulfillment. Mary possesses all the qualities that Wollstonecraft comforted herself by cultivating—all the intelligence, the religious fervor, the intensity and discrimination of feeling summed up in the Georgian meaning of "genius." She has "strength of mind" and "sensibility," and she becomes an heiress to boot when her favored brother dies, but she, too, has been neglected by a disagreeable father and a silly mother (*Mary* 37, 5). Wollstonecraft savages the fashionable Lady Kingsborough as well as her own mother in her portrait of the heroine's "mere nothing" mama (2), just one example of the expanding social context that this novel reflects. Incisively attacking a number of feminine stereotypes, the book cannot quite bring off the revolutionary revaluation of feeling the "Advertisement" promises. Bereft of valid parental models, Mary can educate herself through Nature, native quickness, and books, but she cannot avoid reenacting family dramas. She develops a passionate romantic attachment for consumptive Ann (Fanny Blood), which matures into "an affection very like a maternal one" (19). She becomes Ann's "guardian angel" (43). The boy whom Mary's parents coerce her into marrying goes abroad to finish his education, and Mary and Ann travel to Portugal for Ann's health, as Wollstonecraft did for Fanny's. There Mary meets and gradually falls in love with Henry, an older man, also consumptive. A "man of learning," he functions first as teacher—"in his company her mind expanded"—and then, after Ann dies, as parental protector: "If I had had a father, such a father! . . . Her mind was unhinged, and passion unperceived filled her whole soul." Mary burns to be, for once, somebody's "darling child"; but as Henry's condition also worsens, she must turn solacing parent (27, 36, 35).

Mary's preface, heroine, and thematic conflicts show Wollstonecraft alert to revolutionary potentials in romantic narrative that she cannot fully realize. Initially more in control and more fully aware than Mary herself, "the Author" who composes the book's "Advertisement," the "I" who instructs the "Gentle reader" how to discriminate among varieties of heroism, eventually merges with Mary herself (3). No longer capable of distance from "our heroine," Wollstonecraft the "faithful historian" lets Mary become her own chronicler; the tale itself becomes "a transcript of her heart" (17, 24, 19). The book mingles a variety of autobiographic modes, including Mary's journal, and the exclamatory rhapsodies and fragments she inscribes in "the little book that was now her only confident" epitomize the novel's passage from oblique autobiography to raw, unmediated feeling, from ironic savoir-faire to imprisoning sensibility (46). Astutely analyzing what she cannot control, Mary lays out the oppositions that torture her. Oppressed as a girl by her parents and her society, married off to a man she doesn't even know, she seeks independence and autonomy: "I will work, she cried, do any thing rather than be a slave" (49). Yet, as a "solitary wretch" with "no social ties," she is desperate for love: throughout the book her "ardent affections" seek "an object to fix them," "one who could be all the world to me" (44, 47, 41), and she plays now soothed child, now comforting mother with Ann, with Henry, with the mothers of each, with several poor women she succors, and with the sick, old, and young in her neighborhood. Exhausted by feeling, she berates "reason, thou boasted guide," for abandoning her to her own "tumultuous passions" (52, 40). She prays to God to "compose this troubled spirit" and instantly questions, "do I indeed wish it to be composed—to forget my Henry?" (44).

Ranging from "moping melancholy" to "heroic enthusiasm" and back again, the tale more urgently replays the central drama of *Daughters* (*Mary* 42). There Wollstonecraft recognizes, in one of many generalizations from personal experience, that people of "sense and reflection" are most apt to "violent and constant passions," but she states decisively that a woman "cannot reasonably be unhappy" married to a decent man. "I am very far from thinking love irresistible, and not to be conquered," the educational persona continues firmly: painful feelings sometimes are artificially prolonged "to gratify our desire of appearing heroines" (*Thoughts* 82, 84, 86). Maybe so, but the compelling desire for love—to nurture and to be nurtured—sweeps away author and heroine together in *Mary*. Worn out by "internal struggles," neither can imagine a way out of a personal plight that is also a cultural impasse (38). The world, mourns the beleaguered heroine, "is ever hostile and armed against the feeling heart!" (41). Abandoning her pedagogical relationship with her reader and her heroine, Wollstonecraft kills off Mary's love objects, female and male alike, and leaves her stuck in a loveless marriage (we never get to know the husband), doing good around the estate and anticipating death. Benevolence affords her a tenuous connection with the social community. The fiction tries to work out the recurrent autobiographical convention of mental crisis in educative terms, but it cannot get past Mary's and Mary Wollstonecraft's dilemma: "I cannot live without loving—and love leads to madness" (62).

Like *Mary*, *Original Stories* manages to be at once radical and compensatory, but the self-dramatizations and pedagogic structures of the *Stories* tackle the conflicts that plagued Wollstonecraft in new ways. Just as, in *Mary*, she takes the romantic narrative of self-education or self-invention and forms it about the growth of a *heroine's* mind, so in the stories she converts another mutating genre—children's literature—into a woman's form, displacing the male tutors of Rousseau and Thomas Day with her female mentoria, Mrs. Mason. Like *Mary*, the book is prefaced by a rationale for the mode of education that the work portrays, and again the heroine recoups the devaluation Wollstonecraft felt as governess, this time not through "genius" or fineness of feeling, but through pedagogic and philanthropic power. Mason teaches the girls in the tale, young women readers, and also their mothers, for the progressive pedagogy that Wollstonecraft outlines in the preface depends heavily on maternal rationality and self-discipline (also central to the *Rights of Woman*). Like the later work, *Original Stories* censures fashionable mothers with "fastidious pleasures to pursue, neglecting those nature points out," because useful instruction always flows "more from example than teaching" (iv–v). As with *Mary*, Wollstonecraft once again organizes her text around parent-child, teacher-pupil relations, and once again, she seeks to reconstruct readers as well as herself through redefining the exemplary woman.

Mary opposes conventional rules against a mind's "operation of its own faculties, not subject to opinion" ("Advertisement"); it outlines an expressive theory of art whose motive force is transparently autobiographical, whose locus of reality is within. Tackling "real life" from another direction, *Original Stories* translates pedagogic theory into cultural critique, for the miscellany's "dialogues and tales are accommodated to the present state of society" that wants amendment (iii). In her preface, as in her periodical reviews of the time, Wollstonecraft takes children's literature seriously as a reformist genre: "The many ingenious works of this class, produced within the last twenty or thirty years will have a sure, though, perhaps, slow effect on the understanding of the succeeding generations," proclaims a typical notice (review of *Parent's Assistant* 428). Both *Mary* and *Original Stories* emerge from the period's interest in the processes of development and maturation and its growing awareness that childhood and education are culturally central. (The same philosophical assumptions promote the advance of autobiography.) Wollstonecraft's personal sense that childhood is the key to knowledge of self and society structures these semiautobiographical fictions in complementary ways. *Mary* turns education inward toward the observation of psychic processes. *Original Stories* situates two damaged girls in a wider social world that gradually reeducates them—and their readers.

Wollstonecraft was, of course, neither a lovelorn heiress in a marital trap nor a well-to-do village matron, but her fictional objectifications are therapeutic histories of the self nonetheless, the one claiming primacy for an individual woman's thinking and feeling mind, the other suggesting that women in their guise of mother-teachers might manage not only self-possession, but significant community impact as well. *Mary* is a metaphor for female selfhood embattled against a hostile world; the *Original Stories* offer an enabling myth.[4] Despite her rich gifts, Mary seems powerless to sustain responsibility for herself in a patriarchal world. Nor can she manage the self-mastery that *Education of*

Daughters recommends and that would ease her emotional dependence on others. With their array of self-expressive behavioral models—not just Mrs. Mason, but also other strong women like Mrs. Trueman and Anna Lofty—the *Original Stories* demonstrate through the apprenticeship of Caroline and Mary how women can school themselves toward self-command and psychic self-sufficiency, and they imply how, in the guise of mother-teachers, women can help shape the world about them. Education, then, offers women writers and female readers a way to form or reform a society as well as to fashion a self. The *Original Stories* begin to exemplify the "revolution in female manners" central to Wollstonecraft's feminist agenda in the *Rights of Woman*, showing the ways in which women must "labour by reforming themselves to reform the world" (*Rights of Woman* 84).

Just as Wollstonecraft's "Advertisement" to *Mary* insists on the book's origin in nature and in authentic psychic experience, so the subtitle of *Original Stories* claims that these fictions too are grounded in "real life." The phrase has multiple meanings. It describes an art that derives from and acts on a social world, an art that is realistically observed and socially critical. Mason, for example, recounts to her adolescent charges graphic histories of poverty and social injustice, and she takes Caroline and Mary on visits to grittily realistic ruins and slum tenements to awaken their dormant social consciences. The girls must move beyond childish egocentrism toward the book's models of educationally and charitably responsible womanhood. They hear about crazy Robin, who suffers debtor's prison and the death of all his family, or about the Bastille prisoner who befriends a spider and sees it crushed by his tyrannical keeper, and they learn that the world's suffering holds a claim on their time and pocket money. The book looks at "real life" through a woman's eyes, empathically alert to disadvantage and misery. Its dose of the reality principle, like the antinovel jibes of *Mary, A Fiction*, is meant to counter the romantic fantasies that young female readers are culturally heir to.

At the same time, use of the term *real life* hints that the *Original Stories*, too, partake of oblique autobiography. Wollstonecraft's collection of instructive tales and conversations between Mason and her pupils is based on her year as governess with the Kingsborough family, but its personal subtext goes beyond factual echoes. (She uses her real pupils' faults, for example; and the numerous scenes of distress and destitution owe much to Irish conditions.)[5] The *Original Stories* incorporate, comment on, and move beyond her prior experiments in selfhood, both lived and written. The book is reparation for the governess's "cheeks too frequently . . . flushed by a *decent* pride." "I long for a little peace and independence! . . . I am not fond of grovelling!" Wollstonecraft exclaims feelingly to publisher Joseph Johnson, who helped her establish herself in London as a full-time writer (*Collected Letters* 156, 159). Johnson, she says, "saved me from despair" and provided support for her authorial ventures: "I am then going to be the first of a new genus." Indicatively, the same letter that plans the children's book captures Wollstonecraft's energetic mental shift: "I have *done* with the delusion of fancy—I only live to be useful—benevolence must fill every void in my heart" (*Collected Letters* 164, 166).

The *Original Stories*, then, are also a constructive fantasy. Accommodating Wollstonecraft's deepest feelings and needs of the time, the work's mix of stories, dialogues, and adventures lets her criticize social conditions and cover topics central to female improvement (temper, accomplishments, beauty, and the like). The book is a way station toward the educational persona and the "enlightened maternal affection" that structure the *Rights of Woman* (*Rights of Woman* 226). Bereft of their mother, Caroline and Mary have grown up "shamefully ignorant" and chock full of prejudices (*Original Stories* vii). Under Mason's guidance, they are carefully trained toward a rational and affective awakening: "I hope you have learned to think," Mason comments, as they near the end of their tuition, "and that your hearts have felt the emotions of compassion" (168).

Mulling over Phyllis Chesler's assertion that "women are motherless children in a patriarchal society," Adrienne Rich has wondered exactly what—having neither power nor wealth—women *can* hand on to their daughters. If *Mary* seems to answer, "nothing of value," *Original Stories* reply, "virtually everything." Like the nurturing or principled or spirited female figures to whom Rich calls attention in *Jane Eyre*, Wollstonecraft's behavioral models in the *Stories* inspire daughters with a strong female tradition (Rich 91). In Wollstonecraft's novel, the badly mothered heroine more or less coaches herself toward maturity; in her tales for youth, Caroline and Mary learn not only from Mason, the book's dominating figure and narrative voice, but from alternative models of consciously designed female selfhood as well. The book includes several oblique self-representations besides Mason. Mary, the elder of the two pupils, is a partial one. She has Wollstonecraft's own hasty temper and, in contrast to her frivolous, prettier sister, she more quickly learns to exemplify the humanitarian benevolence upon which Wollstonecraft prided herself. Inculcating "fortitude of mind" as the "basis of each virtue"—"the term virtue comes from a word signifying strength," Mason informs her students—the teacher approvingly notes the elder girl's growing "strength of mind," judgment, and generosity: "There is a just pride, a noble ambition, in some minds that I greatly admire; I have seen a little of it in Mary" (156–67, 160).

The curate's wife, Mrs. Trueman, plays the bourgeois matron in the kind of domestic idyll Wollstonecraft was fond of imagining throughout her career (such idylls punctuate her letters, as well as the *Rights of Woman*). A liberally educated and talented woman, happy in her companionate marriage, Mrs. Trueman teaches her own children and voices Wollstonecraftean ideas on female accomplishments. Closer to Wollstonecraft's own situation is Anna Lofty, the village schoolmistress, whom Mrs. Mason has helped establish in a self-supporting profession. It is worth noting that Anna's is the only given name in the first edition; most adult characters bear only initials. It is also worth noting that the *Original Stories* take place in a matriarchal world. The book's men are ineffectual, vicious, absent, or working-class charitable objects who are rescued by Mason. The book rewrites Wollstonecraft's gratitude toward her mentor Johnson in the female gender, constructing a female support network through which women can advise and nurture one another: Mason helps a number of other women also, and she has adopted an orphan girl as well. Anna's "spirit of independence," her "elevated" character, and her heart "regulated by her understanding" suggest her creator's ideal self-image, as does her painful awareness of women's limited work options. She rejects physical comfort as a "humble companion," because "When I am my own mistress, the crust I earn will be sweet" (137, 132, 136, 138).

But Mason is the fullest and most complex of Wollstonecraft's educational self-productions. She is the mother-teacher in her most rigorous and revealing dress. Recalling Wollstonecraft's model of female "virtue and dignity" in the *Rights of Woman*—the widow who devotes herself wholly to molding strong citizens and whose "affection gives a sacred heroic cast to her maternal duties"—Mason embodies the emotional poise and self-dependence her creator craves. Like Wollstonecraft's exemplary widow, she too has been "raised to heroism by misfortunes" (*Rights of Woman* 90–91). At first her calm, intelligence, and authoritative command of herself and others seem scary. Knowing they have done wrong, the girls fear her "quiet steady displeasure. . . . All their consequence seemed to arise from her approbation." "I do believe," says

Mary, "that she was never angry in her life. . . . I declare I cannot go to sleep. . . . I am afraid of Mrs. Mason's eyes. . . . I wish I was as wise and as good as she is." Yet the girls also claim to be happier in their progress toward autonomous womanhood than when they were spoiled and stupid at home: "Nobody told me what it was to be good. I wish to be a woman . . . and to be like Mrs. Mason" (52–54). In the microscopic world of the *Stories*, as this example shows, Mason is all powerful, all wise, always right. She is never without an answer. She understands everything and everybody, including herself. (Her charges could never put one over on Mason, which is why some historians of children's literature have viewed her with disapproval.) Through the histories and assorted moral tales that she relates and through the educational and charitable activities she carries on, Mason interprets, orders, and heals not just the girls but the whole little community. Her hegemony caters to female fantasies of heroism. She is a dream of strength and power, even omnipotence.

But Mason is not just an embodiment of superhuman wisdom and reason—a mirror reversal of *Mary*, all passion spent. As the girls improve, she shows a softer face. She is a woman of feeling as well as of reason and religion. Within Mason's story is another autobiographical subtext. After losing her husband and daughter in one harsh winter, she reveals, she has found peace in God, nature, and fostering others; she has become "an instrument of good—I have been useful to my fellow creatures" (17). The fictional Mason can be read as embodying a wish to be cared for, a desire to control others, a self-repressive and demanding ego ideal, a walking conscience. Odd, flawed, as hyperbolic an autobiographical projection in one way as Mary is in another, Mason has much to tell about anger and deprivation, about the need for nurture and the taste for power that educating heroism conceals and reveals. In company with Wollstonecraft's other educational voices, she contributes to an ongoing self-portrayal, a succession of self-images that add up to a cumulative and multidimensional self-portrait.

Generated from mixed motives, Wollstonecraft's pedagogic exercises create and try out a plurality of selfhoods: "I am often with myself at war. . . . I cannot always feel alike," she knows, but she never gives up trying to spell out and to integrate her confusions (*Collected Letters* 110). If they are not autobiographies in the strict definition, the works I examine possess what one recent critic terms "autobiographicality" (Landow xliii). Certainly they embody myths and metaphors of the period's female selfhood, the teaching texts as much as the sentimental

fiction. Indeed, one might argue that the more distanced self-representation of overtly pedagogical genres empowers the female narrative
voice. Clearly, the preoccupation of this period's women writers with
nurture and education entails a concern with self-nurture and self-
definition as well. The self imagined as mother-teacher speaks with a
newfound confidence and moral authority.

Notes

Research for this essay was assisted by grants from the American Philosophical
Society and the National Endowment for the Humanities.

1. Jelinek's *The Tradition of Women's Autobiography* usefully expands and
exemplifies the theoretical arguments of her earlier study's introduction. Voss's
briefer overview reaches conclusions similar to those of Jelinek and Mason.

2. Although I focus here on the early works that led up to the *Rights of
Woman*, the novel Wollstonecraft left unfinished at her death and her uncom-
pleted late stories for her children are similarly informed by autobiographical
patterns. Despite Gusdorf's lack of interest in women writers, his conception of
autobiography as a drama of one "struggling to reassemble himself in his own
likeness at a certain moment of his history . . . forever adding himself to
himself," seems relevant to women's characteristic process approach to the
genre; autobiography, he argues, is a "work of enlightenment," revealing not
the actual writer but what "he believes and wishes himself to be and to have
been" (43, 45).

3. The self-referentiality of Wollstonecraft's work necessitates detailed attention to her life, as Poovey's and Ferguson and Todd's recent studies continue to
demonstrate. Fredric Jameson usefully observes that, whereas older biographical criticism read lives as causal and explanatory, newer work tends to understand the reconstruction of a life "precisely as one further text in its turn . . .
susceptible of forming a larger corpus of study" with the author's other literary
texts (340 n. 4).

4. Stories for the young, a genre as marginal and protean as autobiography
itself, have often served their authors for covert self-discovery and self-definition, as recent juvenile writers like Isabelle Holland and Philippa Pearce frankly
attest. Holland observes that such "writers write over and over about those
things that preoccupy them. In a sense, we replay our dramas to see if this time
they can come out right" (2); Pearce similarly calls attention to the juvenile
author's "peculiar relationship" with her own childhood: "In children's books
we should be prepared to find the fantasies as well as the realities of the
author's childhood" (74, 76). Nor is the practice limited to women—Twain's
Tom Sawyer is as vibrant a self-imagining as Alcott's Jo March. Yet the psychic
dynamics of mother-daughter relations and the pedagogic stance that women

writers frequently assume inform their tales with complex and troubling undercurrents. The maternal stance is culturally empowering—a way of speaking with authority—but it is also restrictive in its insistence on rational achievement and self-command for young heroines: Jo must discipline her imaginative and emotional capacities as Tom need not. Thus historians of children's literature fault Georgian mother-educators like Mrs. Mason and like Rosamond's mother in Maria Edgeworth's autobiographical juvenile *Bildungsroman* for similar reasons; my essays on Wollstonecraft and Edgeworth as writers for the young address such critiques by situating their tales within a historical context and a revisionary, explanatory framework based on contemporary feminist research on mothering. Significantly, women's autobiographical fictionalizations of childhood are usually very different from the male poetic rendering that Richard N. Coe valorizes in his recent study of autobiography and the experience of childhood.

5. McAleer's helpful study illuminates Wollstonecraft's tales, as well as detailing the later life of her favorite pupil.

Works Cited

Bloch, Ruth H. "American Feminine Ideals in Transition: The Rise of the Moral Mother, 1785–1815." *Feminist Studies* 4 (1978): 101–26.

Brody, Miriam. "Mary Wollstonecraft: Sexuality and Women's Rights (1759–1797)." In *Feminist Theorists: Three Centuries of Key Women Thinkers*. Ed. Dale Spender. New York: Pantheon, 1983. 40–59.

Chesler, Phyllis. *Women and Madness*. 1972. New York: Avon, 1973.

Coe, Richard N. *When the Grass Was Taller: Autobiography and the Experience of Childhood*. New Haven: Yale University Press, 1984.

Ferguson, Moira, and Janet Todd. *Mary Wollstonecraft*. Boston: Twayne, 1984.

Gusdorf, Georges. "Conditions and Limits of Autobiography." In *Autobiography: Essays Theoretical and Critical*. Ed. James Olney. Princeton: Princeton University Press, 1980. 28–48.

Holland, Isabelle. "The Problem with Talking about My Writing." *ALAN Review* 13.1 (Fall 1985): 1–4.

Jameson, Fredric. "Imaginary and Symbolic in Lacan: Marxism, Psychoanalytic Criticism, and the Problem of the Subject." *Yale French Studies* 56 (1977): 338–95.

Janes, R. M. "On the Reception of Mary Wollstonecraft's *A Vindication of the Rights of Woman*." *Journal of the History of Ideas* 39 (1978): 293–302.

Jelinek, Estelle C. *The Tradition of Women's Autobiography: From Antiquity to the Present*. Boston: Twayne, 1986.

———, ed. *Women's Autobiography: Essays in Criticism*. Bloomington: Indiana University Press.

Landow, George P., ed. *Approaches to Victorian Autobiography*. Athens: Ohio University Press, 1979.

McAleer, Edward C. *The Sensitive Plant: A Life Study of Lady Mount Cashell*. Chapel Hill: University of North Carolina Press, 1958.

Mason, Mary G. "The Other Voice: Autobiographies of Women Writers." In *Autobiography: Essays Theoretical and Critical*. Ed. James Olney. Princeton: Princeton University Press, 1980. 207–35.

Myers, Mitzi. "The Dilemmas of Gender as Double-Voiced Narrative; or Maria Edgeworth Mothers the *Bildungsroman*." In *The Idea of the Novel in the Eighteenth Century*. Ed. Robert W. Uphaus. East Lansing: Colleagues Press, forthcoming.

———. "Impeccable Governesses, Rational Dames, and Moral Mothers: Mary Wollstonecraft and the Female Tradition in Georgian Children's Books." In *Children's Literature*. Ed. Margaret Higonnet and Barbara Rosen. New Haven: Yale University Press, 1986. 14:31–59.

———. "Mary Wollstonecraft's *Letters Written . . . in Sweden*: Toward Romantic Autobiography." In *Studies in Eighteenth-Century Culture*. Ed. Roseann Runte. Madison: University of Wisconsin Press, 1979. 8:165–85.

———. "Reform or Ruin: 'A Revolution in Female Manners.'" In *Studies in Eighteenth-Century Culture*. Ed. Harry C. Payne. Madison: University of Wisconsin Press, 1982. 11:199–216.

Nicholes, Elenor L. "Mary Wollstonecraft." *Shelley and His Circle, 1773–1822*. Ed. Kenneth Neill Cameron. 2 vols. Cambridge: Harvard University Press, 1961. 1:39–87.

Olney, James. *Metaphors of Self: The Meaning of Autobiography*. Princeton: Princeton University Press, 1972.

Pearce, Philippa. "The Writer's View of Childhood." *Horn Book* 38.1 (Feb. 1965): 74–78.

Poovey, Mary. *The Proper Lady and the Woman Writer: Ideology as Style in the Works of Mary Wollstonecraft, Mary Shelley, and Jane Austen*. Chicago: University of Chicago Press, 1984.

"Review of *Memoirs of the Author of 'A Vindication of the Rights of Woman*,' by William Godwin." *European Magazine and London Review* 33 (1798): 246–51.

Rich, Adrienne. "Jane Eyre: The Temptations of a Motherless Woman (1973)." In *On Lies, Secrets, and Silence: Selected Prose 1966–1978*. New York: Norton, 1979. 89–106.

Sprinker, Michael. "Fictions of the Self: The End of Autobiography." In *Autobiography: Essays Theoretical and Critical*. Ed. James Olney. Princeton: Princeton University Press, 1980. 321–42.

Voss, Norine. "'Saying the Unsayable': An Introduction to Women's Autobiography." In *Gender Studies: New Directions in Feminist Criticism*. Ed. Judith

Spector. Bowling Green: Bowling Green State University Popular Press, 1986. 218–33.

Weintraub, Karl J. "Autobiography and Historical Consciousness." *Critical Inquiry* 7 (1975): 821–48.

———. *The Value of the Individual: Self and Circumstance in Autobiography*. Chicago: University of Chicago Press, 1978.

Wollstonecraft, Mary. *Collected Letters of Mary Wollstonecraft*. Ed. Ralph M. Wardle. Ithaca: Cornell University Press, 1979.

———. *Elements of Morality, for the Use of Children, with an Introductory Address to Parents*. Trans. and rev. from C. G. Salzmann. 3 vols. London: J. Johnson, 1791.

———. *The Female Reader (1790)*. Introd. Moira Ferguson. Del Mar: Scholars Facsimiles and Reprints, 1980.

———. *Letters Written during a Short Residence in Sweden, Norway and Denmark*. Introd. Sylva Norman. Boston: Branden Press, 1970.

———. *Mary, a Fiction, and the Wrongs of Woman*. Ed. Gary Kelly. London: Oxford University Press, 1976.

———. *Original Stories from Real Life; with Conversations, Calculated to Regulate the Affections, and Form the Mind to Truth and Goodness*. 2d ed. London: J. Johnson, 1791.

[———]. Review of *The Parent's Assistant*. *Analytical Review* 24 (1796): 426–28.

———. *Thoughts on the Education of Daughters: With Reflections on Female Conduct in the More Important Duties of Life*. Reprints of Economic Classics. Clifton: Augustus M. Kelley, 1972.

———. *A Vindication of the Rights of Woman, with Strictures on Political and Moral Subjects*. Ed. Charles W. Hagelman, Jr. The Norton Library. New York: Norton, 1967.

Representing Two Cultures
Jane Austen's Letters

Deborah Kaplan

Feminist historians have recently called attention to the "cultural duality" of many women's lives in the nineteenth century. Women often
participated in a general, male-dominated culture and at the same time
in a women's culture.[1] The latter, a conceptually slippery term, must be
differentiated from the traditional notion of "woman's sphere," which
names a position of subordination enforced by the dominant, patriarchal culture. "Woman's culture," by contrast, as Gerda Lerner has suggested, "is women's redefinition in their own terms" ("Politics and Culture" 52). It not only refers to a specifically female perspective; it also
demarcates women's efforts to reperceive their experiences and to find
personal meaning and satisfaction in them. Nineteenth-century women
transformed their subordination, compensating for and even valuing
differences in experiences imposed on them.

Raymond Williams would call a nineteenth-century patriarchal culture hegemonic—"the central, effective and dominant system of meanings and values, which are not merely abstract but which are organized
and lived" (38). A women's culture, again using Williams's terms, may
be identified as "alternative," but it may also be "oppositional" to the
cultural hegemony of male domination (39–40). The meanings and
values it generates may be simply different from or may be implicitly or
explicitly critical of those of a general, dominant culture. What did it
mean to participate in two different cultures simultaneously? Women
who inhabited both a general and a women's culture actively lived two
sets of values, two worldviews, which may have been compatible but
which may also have been contradictory. Focusing on the contradiction
between women's culture and the general culture, Simone de Beauvoir

has described, in her classic work *The Second Sex*, the "paradox" of women's situation: women "band together in order to establish a counter-universe, but they always set it up within the frame of the masculine universe." Women "belong at one and the same time" to a male world and to a female world in which the male world is challenged. Thus "women's docility must always be matched by a refusal, their refusal by an acceptance" (562).

Like many less famous women, Jane Austen experienced this cultural doubleness. It is not her well-known and frequently analyzed novels, however, but her often-overlooked letters that represent the experience.[2] Personal letters create their intimacy by voicing cultural identifications shared by letter writer and reader. Seven-eighths of Austen's extant letters were written to close women friends and relations, especially to Austen's sister, Cassandra, and all of these women experienced the doubleness of participation in both a women's culture and the general, gentry culture. If the letters express multiple, indeed even opposing, cultural values, they do so because this private genre has no intrinsic censoring feature which would suppress or resolve cultural contradictions. Austen's novels, by contrast, as a public and ideological form, resist expressions of cultural contradictions, and hence they do not fully convey the double nature of women's cultural lives.

To suggest, as I will in this essay, that Austen's letters do something that her novels do not is, I am aware, to reverse the priority generally accorded Austen's two main genres. Austen's letters, when they have been studied at all, have generally been judged against some standard set for us by her novels. Many readers have turned to her letters in search of a person as wise and authoritative as her novel narrators or as witty and romantic as some of her heroines, and they have been disappointed. Many have found the personality depicted in her letters—in contrast to her fictional heroines—petty, unrevealing, or ambiguous.[3] And some have insisted that the novel heroine they seek in Austen's letters *was* represented—but in those of the letters that Austen's sister destroyed after the novelist died (see Hodge 13). I want to bring the letters out of the shadow of Austen's novels and to consider them in their own terms. To do so, I offer a description of the dual cultural contexts of Austen's letters and then a reading of the letters which illuminates their stylistics of "doubleness." Finally, I compare Austen's letters and novels in order to show the unique capacity of the genre of private letters to textualize Austen's dual cultural allegiances.

"I have written to Mrs. Birch among my other writing," Jane told Cassandra in a letter in 1798, "and so I hope to have some account of all the people in that part of the world before long. I have written to Mrs. E. Leigh too, and Mrs. Heathcote has been ill-natured enough to send me a letter of inquiry; so that altogether I am tolerably tired of letter-writing, and, unless I have anything new to tell you of my mother or Mary, I shall not write again for many days; perhaps a little repose may restore my regard for a pen" (33). Jane Austen wrote letters, as this passage reveals, to provide relatives and acquaintances with news of family, friends, and neighbors. She also wrote to solicit news from others. Letter writing thus helped to develop and maintain networks among families and branches of a family. Even Austen's letters to her sister had this function. The sisters were apart when one or the other left home to visit a friend's family or, more frequently, their brother Edward's family at Godmersham in Kent or their brother Henry and his wife Eliza in London. Jane and Cassandra wrote to one another as representatives of these households.

Although the Austens were an affectionate, sociable family, we cannot overlook pragmatic motives for their development of networks. The Austens inhabited a traditional world in which, as historian Harold Perkin has suggested, "differential status was part of the given, unquestioned environment" (24). They were gentry, a social position dependent on property ownership or patronage—"the system of personal selection from amongst one's kinsmen and connections . . . by which property influenced recruitment to those positions in society which were not determined by property alone" (45). Social and kinship networks mapped out gentry communities—important because one actively experienced a social status as a member of a group—and they helped to preserve gentry status by demarcating potential relationships of patronage, of "friends."[4] Austen's own family demonstrates the importance of such networks. Her father and four of her brothers, as clergymen and naval officers, were all aided by gentry connections in securing livings and promotions. Although another brother, Edward, was not, strictly speaking, patronized, the Austens' gentry network brought him to the attention of distant relatives, the Knights, who left him large estates at Chawton and Godmersham. Austen's letter writing, then, stemmed in part from the gentry's concern with status and its underpinnings in social and kinship networks.

In listing only female correspondents, the above passage from one of

Austen's letters also suggests, accurately I believe, that Austen wrote to women more than to men. Men, too, wrote letters of "inquiry" or news in Austen's society, and Austen certainly wrote to her brothers. Her extant letters and their internal evidence show, however, that she wrote much more frequently to Cassandra, and more to her nieces than to her nephews. Moreover, they indicate that although she had several correspondences with women to whom she was not related, she almost never wrote letters of news to men who were not kin. So while Austen's letter writing reinforced gentry culture, it also became a means by which women fostered their own solidarity.

Such solidarity was possible and desirable because Austen's society was shaped by gender as well as status inequities. Although social status was crucial to this world, only men had direct access to the bases of gentry status: only men generally inherited land; only men could enter the genteel professions to which patronage gave access. To sustain their status, gentry women could marry into property or the professional roles available through patronage. Or they could become governesses—a marginally genteel female profession. Otherwise, they were forced to rely on the financial assistance of male family members. Jane Austen, her mother, and sister were in just this predicament after the death of her father. Altogether, the three women had only £210 per year. To this inadequate annual income, the Austen brothers contributed £250 more.

Given this context, it was best for women to marry. And yet, although most "lesser" gentry women consulted their feelings and not their parents when faced with a marriage proposal, a woman could only respond to, not initiate, such a proposal. The ideology of feminine propriety, which Mary Poovey has described in *The Proper Lady and the Woman Writer*, proposed modest, self-effacing behavior for women as a means of controlling their sexuality. This ideology severely circumscribed any active efforts to avoid the social stigma of spinsterhood. Austen rarely wrote letters of news to men outside her family, no doubt, because it would have been "improper." Conduct manuals and sermons of the period—vehicles of the ideology of propriety—discouraged gentry women from traveling or entering public places unchaperoned and from engaging in any assertive activity—even dancing or reading—believed capable of serving as a sexual stimulant. Efforts were made to curb women's sexuality because it was threatening to men, to the property ownership that underwrote their power. A single, secretive act of infidelity and the subsequent birth of a child, many men feared, could transfer property from one man's family to another. The ideology of feminine propriety prescribed passivity and thereby made women unequal in social as well as economic terms.

Such inequality made Austen and other women conscious of gender differences and of the subordination they experienced in common. As a consequence, female friendships were often intense, especially those among unmarried women. Again, the Austen family may serve as an example. The sisters had the closest tie. As their niece Anna remembered years after their deaths, they "were everything to each other. They seemed to lead a life to themselves within the general family life which was shared only by each other. I will not say their true, but their *full*, feelings and opinions were known only to themselves."[5] But the Austen sisters were also very attached to their nieces and to other female friends, particularly Martha Lloyd, who came to live with them and their widowed mother in 1805. When Austen and other women wrote letters to one another, they thus inevitably spoke not only as representatives of their households but as women conscious of their differences from men.[6] Letter writing helped to strengthen these female friendships, and they also promoted awareness of distinct—specifically female—experiences.

Austen's letters, then, grew out of and served her society in two ways, because she had allegiances to what were, in effect, two cultures. She shared the concerns of the male-dominated gentry society in general and her brothers in particular. She did so because her gentry status in this hierarchical world was a crucial part of her identity and because she depended on her brothers for the maintenance of her status identity. In addition, her status position—indeed the entire traditional world of which it was part—was under attack by an emerging urban, industrial, capitalist order. She responded by assuming a particularly conservative position, aligning herself with her status group against the urban industrial newcomers (see Lovell). But Austen was also part of a women's culture, which generated, out of a subordination based on gender, an acute consciousness of women's "situation," an awareness of women's common bonds, and a set of positive, specifically female values.

Austen and other gentry women knew the general culture and their women's culture as both complementary and contradictory. In her letters, Austen inscribed these two relationships. They are not highly visible in all her letters, however. Austen expressed complementary and incompatible cultural positions mainly when writing to women and especially when writing to Cassandra, with whom, as her niece Anna has already testified, she was most candid. Her letters to Cassandra best show the differing, sometimes opposing, yet intermingling discourses of women.

The intermingling of discourses is made possible by the overall character of Austen's letters—they are news—and by the stylistic features that identify news. News is indicated in her letters to Cassandra not by extended narratives, by stories, but by short, informative bursts of prose. News is also demarcated by sudden and rapid changes of direction, usually without preparatory transitions. Although not every letter employs them, the majority use dashes frequently to take the place of descriptions and transitions. They enforce the bulletinlike quality of the discourse and enable sudden shifts that obey no principles of ordering except, occasionally, chronological sequencing: "It will give me pleasure to see Lady B.—she is now quite well.—Louisa goes home on friday, & John with her; but he returns the next day. These are our engagements; make the most of them.—Mr. Waller is dead I see;—" (196).

The frequent shifts in direction may be shifts in topic, as we see above. But they may also be alterations in the communication context of a piece of news. The letters evoke writer and reader especially vividly, asserting the primacy of a verbal communication, face-to-face gossip, upon which these letters are modeled.[7] Austen herself refers to this feature of her letters in the midst of one to Cassandra: "I have now attained the true art of letter-writing, which we are always told, is to express on paper exactly what one would say to the same person by word of mouth" (102). She not only makes assertions but asks questions, makes conjectures, and provides replies, and in so doing seems to create the presence of both herself and her interlocutor. The letters are thus not only shaped by their context; they produce it. And the context of a communication changes as Austen and her sister shift back and forth from being spokeswomen for their general, gentry culture to being representatives of their women's culture.

Because Austen's—and Cassandra's—letters routinely create both contexts, the sisters' readings of the letters were a complex operation. Members of their households expected to have access to those parts of the letters that I refer to here as the gentry culture discourse. The sisters, consequently, seem to have read each other's letters privately first in order to sort out the two discourses, to determine what to share and what to withhold. They then summarized or read aloud the gentry culture news to others (although women in these households were sometimes also privy to the women's culture discourse of the letters): "I had but just time to enjoy your letter yesterday," Austen writes her sister from Godmersham in 1813, "before Edward & I set off in the Chair for Canty & I allowed him to hear the *chief of it* as we went along" (364; emphasis mine). And in response to a highly personal letter in 1814 from her niece, who had been analyzing her feelings for a suitor, Austen tells her, "I shall be most glad to hear from you again my dearest Fanny . . . and write *something* that may do to be read or told" (418–19).

What features distinguish the discourse of the women's culture from that of the general culture? Occasionally, subject matter makes for difference. Austen speaks as one member of the gentry to another when she describes the activities of a number of family members and acquaintances. Here is an example of one such wide-ranging account: "In the Evening came Mr. Moore, Mr. Toke, Dr. & Mrs. Walsby & others;— one Card Table was formed, the rest of us sat & talked, & at half after nine we came away.—Yesterday my two Brothers went to Canterbury, and J. Bridges left us for London in his way to Cambridge, where he is to take his Master's Degree.—Edward & Caroline & their Mama have all had the Godmersham Cold" (205).

By contrast, when Austen writes about balls, she usually speaks as one representative of the women's culture to another. Balls enabled men and women to meet eligible mates, but, as I have suggested, marriage— because on it depended a woman's economic support—was often more crucial to gentry women. In her enduring preoccupation with balls (accounts of them appear again and again in her letters) and in her concern with the ratio of men to women at these events, Austen voices the women's culture perspective. "Our ball was very thin," she writes Cassandra in 1798; "there were thirty-one people, and only eleven ladies out of the number, and but five single women in the room" (43). She also expresses her cultural orientation by listing her partners—a way of measuring her own popularity. "Our ball," she writes in 1799, "was chiefly made up of Jervoises and Terrys, the former of whom were apt to be vulgar, the latter to be noisy. I had an odd set of partners: Mr. Jenkins, Mr. Street, Col. Jervoise, James Digweed, J. Lyford, and Mr. Briggs, a friend of the latter" (56).

But subject matter is a good deal less important and less trustworthy as an index to the culture of Austen's discourse than the degree of interest she shows in it. The following passage, although it concerns male work—her father's farming—creates the discourse of the women's culture because Austen is here insistently vague and ignorant: "John

Bond [her father's bailiff] begins to find himself grow old," she writes in 1798, "which John Bonds ought not to do, and unequal to much hard work; a man is therefore hired to supply his place as to labour, and John himself is to have the care of the sheep. There are not more people engaged than before, I believe; only men instead of boys. I fancy so at least, but you know my stupidity as to such matters" (35–36). By contrast, Austen generates the gentry culture discourse in a treatment of the same subject—farming in general and John Bond in particular—because here she explores in some detail the fate of her father's bailiff after her father retires, even reporting Bond's own feelings:

> Mr. Holder was perfectly willing to take him on exactly the same terms with my father, & John seems exceedingly well satisfied.— The comfort of not changing his home is a very material one to him, and since such are his unnatural feelings his belonging to Mr. Holder is the everything needful; but otherwise there would have been a situation offering to him which I had thought of with particular satisfaction, viz= under Harry Digweed, who if John had quitted Cheesedown would have been eager to engage him as superintendant at Steventon, would have kept an horse for him to ride about on, would probably have supplied him with a more permanent home, & I think would certainly have been a more desirable Master altogether. (110)

Austen's letters may create the discourse of the women's culture and the general, gentry culture through demonstrations of interest or restlessness, but they may also do so through the more explicit articulation of particular attitudes toward female subordination. The gentry culture discourse accepts the subordination. In a letter to Cassandra in 1799, for example, Austen describes her plan to accompany her brother Charles part way in the coach which is to carry him to Deal. "I want to go with him," she says, "that I may explain the country to him properly between Canterbury and Rowling, but the unpleasantness of returning by myself deters me" (54). Far from minding that she must travel in the company of a male relative, she has learned to prefer this protection. She openly endorses the dominant patriarchal values of the gentry culture. She asserts those same values when she breezily acknowledges her social and economic dependence on one of her brothers. "*Our* Brother," she writes to Cassandra in 1808, "we may perhaps see in the course of a few days—& we mean to take the opportunity of his help, to go one night to the play" (233). Similarly, in the previously quoted description of an evening party, her brothers' visit to Canterbury, J. Bridges's departure for Cambridge University, and the ill health of a sister-in-law and two of her children, Austen accepts without question the comparative freedom that gentlemen possess and the exclusively male privilege of attending Cambridge.

The women's culture discourse, however, frequently calls specific attention to female subordination—to women's economic dependence and lack of social authority. Sometimes Austen finds compensations in female subordination. She prefers the companionship of her sister and friend Martha Lloyd, who are "at home," for example, over the material luxuries available at Edward's Godmersham estate:

> In another week I shall be at home—& then, my having been at Godmersham will seem like a Dream, as my visit at Brompton seems already. The Orange Wine will want our Care soon.—But in the meantime for Elegance & Ease & Luxury—; the Hattons & Milles' dine here today—& I shall eat Ice and drink French wine, & be above vulgar Economy. Luckily the pleasures of Friendship, of unreserved Conversation, of similarity of Taste & Opinions, will make good amends for Orange Wine. (209)

But the women's culture discourse can also register resentment of subordination. "I am tolerably glad to hear that Edward's income is so good a one," Austen writes in 1799, "as glad as I can be at anybody's being rich except you and me" (49). She also voices discontent at the "sacrifice" of women's interests to men's and at the propensity of men to overlook women. She writes Cassandra in 1813, for example, "we did not go to the Ball.—It was left to her [Edward's daughter Fanny] to decide, & at last she determined against it. She knew that it would be a sacrifice on the part of her Father & Brothers if they went—& I hope it will prove that *she* has not sacrificed much.—It is not likely that there sh^d have been anybody there, whom she wd care for" (349).

In the following excerpt Austen produces the discourse of the gentry culture first by taking pride in Edward as the magnanimous host, a role underwritten by his economic and social authority. Yet, by the end of this passage, she is voicing the women's culture discourse as she notes her brother James's failure to appreciate his daughter. She distances herself from, and attempts to compensate for, his obliviousness with her own recognition of the girl:

James & Edward are gone to Sandling today;—a nice scheme for
James, as it will show him a new & fine Country. Edward certainly
excels in doing the Honours to his visitors, & providing for their
amusement.—They come back this Even^g.—Elizabeth talks of
going with her three girls to Wrotham while her husband is in
Hampshire;—she is improved in looks since we first came, &
excepting a cold, does not seem at all unwell. She is considered
indeed as more than unusually active for her situation & size.—I
have tried to give James pleasure by telling him of his Daughter's
Taste, but if he felt, he did not express it.—*I* rejoice in it very
sincerely. (206)

Finally, Austen's letters may generate the discourses of gentry and
women's culture in the withholding or expression of female desires.
They textualize the gentry culture when accepting mutely or even
endorsing the priority of male desire and male convenience. In describing plans for Cassandra's return home from a visit to their brother
Henry in London, for example, Austen simply assumes that her sister
will prefer to accept the companionship of a servant, rather than both-
ering her brother James. Indeed, Austen speaks out of the gentry culture
here because she is imposing on Cassandra—and thus silencing a
woman with—the gentry culture point of view: "Henry would send you
in his carriage a stage or two, where you might be met by John, whose
protection you would we imagine think sufficient for the rest of your
Journey. . . . James has offered to meet you anywhere, but as that would
be to give him trouble without any counterpoise of convenience, as he
has no intention of going to London at present on his own account, we
suppose that you would rather accept the attentions of John" (121).
When Austen does voice wishes in opposition to her brothers' plans,
she creates the women's culture discourse. Although she conveys such
views in her letters, it is also clear that she has been silent on other
occasions, that she writes to Cassandra what cannot be said to male
authorities. In the following passage, which is dominated by Henry's
plans, intentions, requirements, wishes, presumptions, proposals, and
thoughts, Austen manages nonetheless to convey her disapproval. She
also explains her subtle efforts to fulfill Cassandra's travel needs without
opposing Henry, indeed without fully revealing to Henry what his sister
wants:

Henry's plans are not what one could wish. He does not mean to be
at Chawton till the 29th. He must be in town again by Oct. 5. His

plan is to get a couple of days of pheasant shooting and then return directly. His wish was to bring you back with him. I have told him your scruples. He wishes you to suit yourself as to time, and if you cannot come till later, will send for you at any time as far as Bagshot. He presumed you would not find difficulty in getting so far. I could not say you would. He proposed your going with him into Oxfordshire. It was his own thought at first. I could not but catch at it for you. (320)

Austen also objects to her brother Edward's behavior, though she does not tell Edward himself. "Here am I in Kent," she writes to Cassandra in 1813, "with one Brother [Charles] in the same County & another Brother's Wife [Mrs. Frank Austen], & see nothing of them—which seems unnatural. . . . I sh^d like to have Mrs. F.A. & her Children here for a week—but not a syllable of that nature is ever breathed" (346).

Some of the attitudes and experiences that shape the gentry culture and women's culture discourses are merely different, but, as we have just seen, they may also be incompatible. Austen both consents to and is critical of female subordination; she can both suppress and voice her desires. But Austen's letters are nowhere more contradictory than in their self-conscious references to news. The letters offer opposing versions of what is newsworthy. The gentry culture discourse depicts news as the creation of men acting in the public world and not of domestic women. Therefore, in a letter to her brother Frank in 1813, Austen compares the quality of her own subject matter to that of a naval captain who has seen several foreign countries: "My letter was a scratch of a note compared with yours—& then you write . . . so much to the point & give so much real intelligence that it is enough to kill one" (336). When writing to Cassandra from the perspective of the male-dominated gentry culture, Jane also refers to the domestic experience she records as "important nothings" (186) and "little events" (197). And since she doesn't live the kind of life that the gentry culture deems newsworthy, she often finds herself, when writing to Cassandra, without news. "The three days & half which have passed since my last letter was sent, have not produced many materials towards filling another sheet of paper," she apologizes to Cassandra in 1800 (95).

The women's culture, however, values the experiences of daily domestic life. The discourse of this culture often focuses enthusiastically on what Austen refers to as "particulars," the details of everyday life.[8] "I will first talk of my visit to Canterbury, as Mrs. J. A.'s letter to Anna cannot have given you every particular of it, which you are likely to wish for" (192–93), she writes to Cassandra in 1808. Austen produces this alternative, women's perspective whenever she asks questions of or makes statements to Cassandra about their home life. "I hope Martha had a pleasant visit again," she writes in 1814, "and that you and my mother could eat your beef-pudding. Depend upon my thinking of the Chimney-Sweeper as soon as I wake tomorrow" (377).

Everyday domestic occurrences are silly and trivial, *and* they are enormously interesting and significant. Austen has nothing to report, *and* she has a great many fascinating particulars. Out of these opposing, self-conscious attitudes about news, Austen generates two of the most artful, stylistic traits of her letters. First, some of their most wittily ironic moments emerge from juxtapositions of public and private, male and female, "great" and "small." Writing to her brother Frank, who was stationed in the Baltic and had been to Sweden, she remarks, for example: "I wonder whether You & the King of Sweden knew that I *was* to come to G^m [Godmersham] with my B^r. Yes, I supposed you have rec^d due notice of it by some means or other. I have not been here these 4 years, so I am sure the event deserves to be talked of before & behind as well as in the middle" (336–37). She implies that her own activities are insignificant by portraying her trip to Godmersham as known and avidly discussed by men participating in national and international events far from Britain. She creates a similar effect when she describes domestic events in language conventionally reserved for public occasions. About her mother's recovery from an illness, she writes to Cassandra, "My mother made her *entrée* into the dressing-room through crowds of admiring spectators yesterday afternoon" (34). In the following passage from a letter to her sister in 1804, she communicates her sense of the triviality of information Cassandra has recently reported to her not only by juxtaposing the royal family with the news of no ice but by offering an emotional response out of proportion to that particular news:

> Your account of Weymouth contains nothing which strikes me so forcibly as there being no ice in the town. For every other vexation I was in some measure prepared, and particularly for your disappointment in not seeing the Royal Family go on board on Tuesday, having already heard from Mr. Crawford that he had seen you in the very act of being too late, but for there being no ice what could prepare me? Weymouth is altogether a shocking place, I perceive,

without recommendation of any kind, & worthy only of being frequented by the inhabitants of Gloucester. (138–39)

Austen also sometimes corrects information she has previously transmitted in letters to Cassandra and, on one such occasion, uses an extreme diction to call attention once again to the unimportance of her news: "We drink tea tonight with Mrs. Busby.—I scandalized her nephew cruelly; he has but three children instead of Ten" (134).

But Austen could also reverse the irony in these playful passages, asserting the triviality of her actions and discourse while implying their value. She begins a letter to Cassandra in 1798, for example, by announcing that their brother Frank is to be promoted soon, and she follows that news with: "There! I may now finish my letter and go and hang myself, for I am sure I can neither write nor do anything which will not appear insipid to you after this" (42). Despite what she says, she trusts that her sister will find her day-to-day experiences compelling.

A second typical and quite appealing stylistic feature of Austen's letter writing appears repeatedly in her self-conscious treatment of "particulars." She gives weight to the supposedly unimportant domestic arena by making metonymic use of descriptive details. These metonymic instances show that, far from being trivial, the gestures, habits, dress, and decor of daily life have the capacity to convey social and moral knowledge about persons or experiences. They thereby implicitly challenge the gentry view of the quotidian as insignificant. We can see the usefulness of this technique in an 1807 letter to Cassandra that assesses their brother James's character but concludes with a series of behavioral details. These details are just as informative as the outright expression of her opinion and call attention to everyday activities as a rich and significant representational field:

I am sorry & angry that his Visits should not give one more pleasure; the company of so good & so clever a Man ought to be gratifying in itself;—but his Chat seems all forced, his Opinions on many points too much copied from his Wife's, & his time here is spent I think in walking about the House & banging the doors, or ringing the bell for a glass of water. (181)

This use of detail is a frequent feature of her letters. She communicates the superior elegance of life in her brother Edward's home with: "We had a very pleasant day, and some *liqueurs* in the evening" (10). She suggests the slick and selfish character of an acquaintance by focusing on one of his habits: "Mr. Rob. Mascall breakfasted here; he eats a great deal of Butter" (346); and she hints at the commonness of another acquaintance: "This morning we went to see Miss Chamberlayne look hot on horseback" (148). She expresses her view of contemporary fashions but, more important, of the pathetic vulnerability of single women in a letter from 1808: "The room was tolerably full, & there were perhaps thirty couple of Dancers;—the melancholy part was, to see so many dozen young Women standing by without partners, & each of them with two ugly naked shoulders!" (236). In a letter from 1807, she also conveys the conspicuous elegance of a new acquaintance, coupling metonymy with personification: "We found only Mrs. Lance at home, and whether she boasts any offspring besides a grand pianoforte did not appear" (175).

David Cecil, one of Austen's recent biographers, claims that her letters, "even if preserved in full," would not have revealed much because Austen "was by nature disinclined to talk about herself. The subject does not seem to have interested her" (9). What makes a person create self-effacing representations? Cecil suggests both that reticence is the result of pure "nature" and that Austen's letters are freely produced self-expressions. She did not *choose* herself as subject. I have tried to suggest here, instead, that Austen's letters are culture bound: her self-identity was formed through her participation in dual cultures; her self-expression delimited by that participation.

We might also ask of Cecil's modest Jane Austen, which self-representation did she wish to avoid? Her allegiances to the gentry and the women's culture and her awareness of more than one audience for her letters generated multivoiced texts with multiple values and perspectives. She speaks for the gentry, but when she can, to Cassandra, she also speaks for women. Her letters endorse female subordination, and they also challenge it. They are silent about her needs, adopting and sympathizing with the projects and wishes of gentry men, and they break that silence, expressing disagreement. Adopting the perspective of the gentry culture, they depict her life and letter writing as trivial; from the perspective of the women's culture, the letters implicitly refute this notion of triviality by describing her life and letter writing as rich and meaningful.

The multifaceted character of Austen's letters is not a trait of the genre of personal letters but of her experience. It *is* a trait of her letters, however, that they do not reduce the complexity of her cultural life but rather permit its full representation. As I have suggested, there is some evidence that representations of this complexity were sometimes minimized when the letters were read aloud—passages were censored in oral performances of the letters. But the complexity was never reduced in the texts of the letters. Their openness even to the contradictory nature of her cultural experience marks a significant difference between Austen's private and public writings, between her letters and her novels. Although I cannot consider this difference in detail here, I want to discuss it briefly because the contrast helps to illuminate Austen's letters as a genre.

Austen's novels reject neither the women's culture nor the gentry culture per se, but rather the structural relationship between them. They present worlds in which the two cultural experiences are wholly conflated. Thus, they depict a single gentry culture, but one which is feminized. Feminization is achieved by the novels' plots. They are organized around gentry women's efforts to marry, efforts made necessary in most of the novels by their propertylessness and the specter, not of destitution, but of narrow economic circumstances and the symbolic trauma of downward mobility. This feminization influences representation: male characters are fully realized in the novels only when they are participating in the novels' female plots.[9] Feminization is also indicated by the foregrounding and valorization of the events of daily and, often, domestic life. These events are the means (as they are sometimes in Austen's letters) to social and moral knowledge of others. Mr. Darcy's refusal to dance or the Crofts' carriage rides constitute key epistemological moments in the novels.

Austen's novels universalize women's experience. They portray worlds in which men act in accordance with the gentry woman's point of view. But the novels also eschew the challenge to the gentry culture generated by the women's culture. They offer weak and short-lived female friendships, which give way easily to the superior bond of husband and wife.[10] Without such friendships, of course, no alternative or oppositional values and experiences based on a consciousness of gender can be sustained. Indeed, Austen's female characters not only lack this alternative cultural experience: without men, as Nina Auerbach has shown, their experience is physically insubstantial. If we never see more than glimpses of men at work in Austen's novels, representation is also not fully bestowed on women alone together. They thus inhabit a kind of limbo. "Mrs. Bennet," as Auerbach suggests, "is perpetually begging any and all eligible males to come to a dinner we have never seen the family at Longbourn eat, as if only in their presence can nourishment present itself" (44).[11]

Unlike her letters, then, Austen's novels, through their particular conflation of gentry and women's cultures, seek to avoid contradictions. As Fredric Jameson has suggested about novels in general, they invent "imaginary or formal 'solutions' to unresolvable social contradictions," for they are ideological acts (79). But they resolve the contradictions, the oppositional elements of women's culture and gentry culture, through a trade-off that in itself has contradictory implications: the female experience in Austen's novels is both more and less powerful than in Austen's actual life. The concern with marrying and the valorization of domestic details dominate in the novels but are not shown to have an empowering source. In effect, we see women's culture perspectives without a women's culture. Nor do the novels acknowledge the criticism of power relations that a women's culture can generate. Austen's "resolution" has contradictory implications because the female viewpoint in the novels is given incomplete representation.

Perhaps because of these contradictory implications, Austen's conflations of gentry and women's cultures have often failed to persuade. Literary critics have made their own efforts not usually to resolve but to simplify her worldview. Some have argued, based on readings of her novels, that Austen was a feminist, at least a latent one, while others have insisted that she was a conservative defender of the social (and inevitably the patriarchal) status quo.[12] But Austen's "pre-ideological" private genre of letters shows us that she sustained both positions simultaneously. If Jane Austen has seemed in her letters to be elusive or contradictory, hard to find or hard to pin down, it is not her letters or their incomplete state that has made her so, but her life. It is, however, the particular value of the letters that they both represent that paradoxical life and enable us to see how her novels attempt to transform it.

Notes

My thanks to Eileen Sypher, Patricia Spacks, and Roy Rosenzweig for their helpful comments on drafts of this essay.

1. Recent studies by historians of American women have richly explored women's cultures—though, particularly before 1980, without always using that precise term (see, for example, the groundbreaking work of Cott and Smith-Rosenberg). In 1979 Gerda Lerner and in 1980 Ellen DuBois and her

coauthors offered important arguments about and clarifications of the term; these studies have influenced the work of subsequent American historians, perhaps most notably Suzanne Lebsock. The concept has had less impact on histories of British women, at least until very recently (see Vicinus). Judith Newton mentioned DuBois et al. in her 1981 study of British fiction, but Elaine Showalter's 1981 essay formally introduced the term *women's culture* into feminist literary studies, putting it forward as the model for a gynocentric literary criticism. The essay envisions women's culture as a culture of published writers and their literary relations. As will be clear, my own work diverges from Showalter's suggested applications for the model, concentrating on textualizations of cultural duality and arguing for their locus in private rather than public genres.

2. Cassandra Austen gave many of the letters she preserved to family members as keepsakes. J. E. Austen-Leigh, the son of Austen's brother James, had access to some of these when he prepared his *Memoir of Jane Austen* (1870). In 1884 Lord Brabourne published the *Letters of Jane Austen*, but he used only those which had been in the possession of his mother, Lady Knatchbull (Fanny, the eldest daughter of Austen's brother Edward). Other letters written to Frances Austen were first published in 1906 in J. H. and E. C. Hubbacks's *Jane Austen's Sailor Brothers*. R. W. Chapman collected and superbly edited all of Austen's extant letters in 1932, revising the edition in 1952 to include a few newly discovered letters. I refer to his *Jane Austen's Letters to Her Sister Cassandra and Others* throughout this study; page references for quotations from the letters are to Chapman's edition.

3. R. W. Chapman's *Jane Austen: Facts and Problems* considers many of the standard objections to Austen's letters (90–120).

4. For the uses of the term in the social context of patronage relationships, see Perkin 46–51.

5. Quoted in Hodge 114.

6. For a discussion of Austen's female friendships as they are documented in her letters, see Todd 396–402.

7. For a discussion of the relationships between gossip and personal letters, see Spacks 65–91.

8. For an account of the importance of such "particulars" in gossip, see Spacks 14–23.

9. The infrequency with which Austen represents males at work—overseeing their farms or carrying out the duties of their gentlemanly professions—has been widely noted. See, for example, Chapman 118–19 and, more recently, Newton 62–63.

10. Janet Todd has noted the discrepancy between the close female friendships depicted in Austen's letters and the "distrust of female friendship which appears in the later novels." But she offers a biographical explanation for that

discrepancy, while I argue that its source rests in generic differences between letters and novels. See Todd 401–2.

11. In the last decade several critics have commented on female friendship in Austen's novels. In addition to Auerbach and Todd, see Lanser and Perry.

12. A list of critical writings presenting either of these views is too lengthy to produce here, but the list of "conservative" readings would certainly include Duckworth, Butler, and Monaghan. The list of feminist readings would include Gilbert and Gubar.

Works Cited

Auerbach, Nina. *Communities of Women: An Idea in Fiction.* Cambridge: Harvard University Press, 1978.

Austen, Jane. *Jane Austen's Letters to Her Sister Cassandra and Others.* Ed. R. W. Chapman. Oxford: Oxford University Press, 1952.

Austen-Leigh, J. E. *Memoir of Jane Austen.* 1870. Rpt. Ed. R. W. Chapman. Oxford: Clarendon, 1926.

Beauvoir, Simone de. *The Second Sex.* Trans. H. M. Parshley. 1953. New York: Bantam, 1961.

Brabourne, Edward, ed. *Letters of Jane Austen.* London, 1884.

Butler, Marilyn. *Jane Austen and the War of Ideas.* Oxford: Clarendon, 1975.

Cecil, David. *A Portrait of Jane Austen.* New York: Hill, 1978.

Chapman, R. W. *Jane Austen: Facts and Problems.* Oxford: Oxford University Press, 1948.

Cott, Nancy. *The Bonds of Womanhood: 'Woman's Sphere' in New England, 1780–1835.* New Haven: Yale University Press, 1977.

DuBois, Ellen, Mari Jo Buhle, Temma Kaplan, Gerda Lerner, and Carroll Smith-Rosenberg. "Politics and Culture in Women's History: A Symposium." *Feminist Studies* 6 (1980): 26–64.

Duckworth, Alistair. *The Improvement of the Estate: A Study of Jane Austen's Novels.* Baltimore: Johns Hopkins University Press, 1971.

Gilbert, Sandra M., and Susan Gubar. *The Madwoman in the Attic: The Woman Writer and the Nineteenth-Century Literary Imagination.* New Haven: Yale University Press, 1979.

Hodge, Jane Aiken. *Only a Novel: The Double Life of Jane Austen.* New York: Coward, 1972.

Hubback, J. H., and E. C. Hubback. *Jane Austen's Sailor Brothers.* London: John Lane, 1906.

Jameson, Fredric. *The Political Unconscious: Narrative as a Socially Symbolic Act.* Ithaca: Cornell University Press, 1981.

Lanser, Susan. "No Connections Subsequent: Jane Austen's World of Sisterhood." In *The Sister Bond: A Feminist View of a Timeless Connection.* Ed. Toni

McNaron. New York: Pergamon, 1985. 51–67.

Lebsock, Suzanne. *The Free Women of Petersburg: Status and Culture in a Southern Town, 1784–1860*. New York: Norton, 1984.

Lerner, Gerda. "The Challenge of Women's History." In *The Majority Finds Its Past*. New York: Oxford University Press, 1979. 168–80.

———. "Placing Women in History: Definitions and Challenges." In *The Majority Finds Its Past*, 145–59.

———. "Politics and Culture in Women's History: A Symposium." In DuBois et al., 49–54.

Lovell, Terry. "Jane Austen and the Gentry: A Study in Literature and Ideology." In *The Sociology of Literature: Applied Studies*. Ed. Diana Laurenson. Keele: University of Keele, 1979. 15–37.

Monaghan, David. *Jane Austen: Structure and Social Vision*. Totowa: Barnes, 1980.

Newton, Judith Lowder. *Women, Power, and Subversion: Social Strategies in British Fiction 1778–1860*. Athens: University of Georgia Press, 1981.

Perkin, Harold. *The Origin of Modern English Society, 1780–1880*. London: Routledge and Kegan Paul, 1969.

Perry, Ruth. "Interpreted Friendships in Jane Austen's *Emma*." *Tulsa Studies in Women's Literature* 5.2 (Fall 1986): 185–202.

Poovey, Mary. *The Proper Lady and the Woman Writer: Ideology as Style in the Writings of Mary Wollstonecraft, Mary Shelley, and Jane Austen*. Chicago: University of Chicago Press, 1984.

Showalter, Elaine. "Feminist Criticism in the Wilderness." *Critical Inquiry* 8 (1981): 179–205.

Smith-Rosenberg, Carroll. "The Female World of Love and Ritual: Relations between Women in Nineteenth-Century America." *Signs* 1 (1975): 1–29.

Spacks, Patricia Meyer. *Gossip*. New York: Knopf, 1985.

Todd, Janet. *Women's Friendship in Literature*. New York: Columbia University Press, 1980.

Vicinus, Martha. *Independent Women: Work and Community for Single Women, 1850–1920*. Chicago: University of Chicago Press, 1985.

Williams, Raymond. "Base and Superstructure in Marxist Cultural Theory." In *Problems in Materialism and Culture*. London: Verso, 1980. 31–49.

Dorothy Wordsworth's Journals
Putting Herself Down

James Holt McGavran, Jr.

The "beauteous forms" of the Wye valley, which William Wordsworth simultaneously describes, remembers, and idealizes for his sister Dorothy in "Tintern Abbey," enable him through sense, emotion, and thought—blood, heart, and mind (28–29)—to discover the enlarged, powerful self, the "living soul" that can reciprocally "see into the life of things" (46, 49) and subsequently record its vision in poetry. No longer is the external world "a landscape to a blind man's eye" (24); indeed, "All which we behold / Is full of blessings" (133–34), he assures her, thus further emphasizing the crucial importance of perception in his attempts to marry the mind and nature, subject and object, in his writings. Wordsworth realized that his readers, in turn, must see his poems imaginatively if they were to behold the blessings there. Thus he succinctly challenges the reader in "Simon Lee," "Perhaps a tale you'll make it" (72), while in "Tintern Abbey" he hopes that "in after years" Dorothy may find "healing thoughts / Of tender joy" from her continuing experience of "these my exhortations" (137–46). But what tale can we make of the interlocked perceptions and expressions of the two Wordsworths, the poet of the "egotistical sublime" and the self-sacrificing diarist of the Alfoxden and Grasmere journals? And what effect did this conflation of "eyes" and "I's," these cross-readings of nature and selves and texts, have upon Dorothy Wordsworth's powers of seeing and knowing and writing?

On Christmas Day 1805, her thirty-fourth birthday, Dorothy Wordsworth wrote of her time at Grasmere, "I think these years have been the very happiest of my life" (*Letters* 1:659). She had made a choice more than a decade previously, and clearly she was pleased with it. During an adolescence spent with various, mostly sympathetic relatives, Dorothy was exposed to several of the more important religious and social conflicts of her day: the open-minded religion of the Congregationalists and Unitarians and the fervent evangelical Anglicanism of the Clapham sect; the antislavery campaign of William Wilberforce, whom Dorothy knew and with whom she was once teasingly accused of being in love; and, through Wilberforce, the eloquent moralistic writings of Sarah Trimmer (Gittings and Manton, 6–12, 22–27). Women of her time had few choices, to be sure, but nevertheless Dorothy—bright, energetic, creative—could have opted to pursue the people and the issues she had encountered, perhaps through marriage to a man active in public or ecclesiastical affairs, perhaps through work as a teacher, governess, or writer among people of sympathetic views. Instead, she eagerly chose to share her life and her talents with her brother William. First at Windy Brow, then at Racedown and Alfoxden, then at Goslar in Germany, and finally at Grasmere, the orphaned siblings tried to make up for the years of childhood lost as a result of their parents' untimely deaths. Dorothy expresses some of what she felt in another letter of Christmas 1805:

> The Day was always kept by my Brothers with rejoicing in my Father's house, but for six years (the interval between my Mother's Death and his) I was never once at home, never was for a single moment under my Father's Roof after her Death, which I cannot think of without regret for many causes, and particularly, that I have been thereby put out of the way of many recollections in common with my Brothers of that period of life. (*Letters* 1:663)

Not only were they trying to be children again; they were also reenacting their parents' sheltering and nurturing roles, since at Racedown and Alfoxden they were guardians of young Basil Montagu. If Dorothy's resentment at her father's excluding her from the family was ever transferred to William—as one of the boys who rejoiced without her, or as father-substitute in the relationship with Basil—she never gave a sign.

Besides reestablishing their interrupted family romance, there was another reason, both more compelling and more problematic, why Dorothy chose life with William—why, as Pamela Woof has written, "Dorothy's early Journals . . . offered to Wordsworth, and still offer to us, . . . a world accepted" (107). Susan Levin has wisely speculated, "Perhaps she stayed in her brother's house because of the participation in art that was allowed her there" (353). Levin continues: "The country walks, the reading and discussions, the emotional tensions which formed her life with William formed the subject of her art. Dorothy Wordsworth lived far more intensely than most of her female contemporaries" (354). It was a life of creativity. Though she remained unconscious of the reason, I believe Dorothy chose life with William less for *his* literary gifts and aspirations than for her own, which were sufficient, with help from Coleridge, to create the most powerful male poet in England since Milton and still enable her to produce the haunting beauties, sorrows, passions, and reticences of her Alfoxden and Grasmere journals. However, for all the selves that Dorothy became for William—child, parent, servant, observer, recorder, amanuensis—a terrible price was exacted: the loss of any firm sense of personal identity. Unlike Mary Wollstonecraft, Dorothy seems never to have realized that not all the enslaved of her age were American blacks. Motherless from the age of six, lacking the ebullient self-assertiveness of contemporaries otherwise as different as Wollstonecraft and Trimmer, Dorothy could not develop the collective, interdependent identity that Susan Friedman outlines earlier in this collection (see chapter 2). Giving up her sensory perceptions, her feelings, her thoughts, and her words to William, how and where could she formulate and articulate a self?

In her introductory essay to this volume, drawing on the work of Jacques Lacan, Shari Benstock points the way to an answer when she states that "language itself . . . is a defense against unconscious knowledge. . . . But it is not an altogether successful defense network," because messages from the unconscious try to break through the fence of language—just as Dorothy's conscious choice to live with William could not entirely obscure her awareness of the possibility of other ways of living. Lacan's association of language with repression applies to people of both sexes; but, as both Benstock and Friedman suggest, if one is a woman there is the enormous additional problem of having to speak or write in a society whose forms—including literary forms—systematically threaten to violate or even annihilate female selfhood. Working with these feminist concepts, and with the help of Virginia Woolf (who regarded both Dorothy Wordsworth and Mary Wollstonecraft as foremothers) as well as phenomenological insights derived from the work of Maurice Merleau-Ponty, I intend to show that Dorothy's repressed perceptions and knowledge of herself, her literary ability, and her great sacrifice *do* appear, most often indirectly, in her early journals. In the very act of "putting herself down"—which for Dorothy involved both self-deprecation and self-transcendence as methods of self-avoidance—

she cannot help also putting down on paper traces of the beautiful, relinquished psyche she never fully recognized.

That Dorothy possessed unusual gifts of observation, sensitivity, and intellect was recognized by many who knew her. De Quincey, for instance, comments, "Her manner was warm and even ardent; her sensibility seemed constitutionally deep; and some subtle fire of impassioned intellect apparently burned within her" (114). Coleridge, in an early letter, seems to have formed much the same impression:

> Her manners are simple, ardent, impressive—.
> > In every motion her most innocent soul
> > Outbeams so brightly, that who saw would say,
> > Guilt was a thing impossible in her.
> Her information various—her eye watchful in minutest observation of nature—and her taste a perfect electrometer. (1:330–31)

Much later in his life, Coleridge blends reminiscence with evocative surmise to describe Dorothy as "a Woman of Genius, as well as manifold acquirements, and but for the absorption of her whole Soul in her Brother's fame and writings would, perhaps, in a different style have been as great a Poet as Himself" (6:959). De Quincey comments more extensively on the visible effects of this discrepancy between her apparent abilities and her accomplishment, noting that her intellect,

> being alternately pushed forward into a conspicuous expression by the irrepressible instincts of her temperament, and then immediately checked, in obedience to the decorum of her sex and age, and her maidenly condition . . . , gave to her whole demeanour, and to her conversation, an air of embarrassment, and even of self-conflict, that was almost distressing to witness. (114–15)

But if De Quincey gives more detail of what appeared to him to be Dorothy's outward embarrassment, Coleridge's phrases plunge more deeply to the core of the problem: "a Woman of Genius"; "as great as Himself." Coleridge qualifies his contention carefully, but nevertheless he puts into words the socially and psychically unacceptable possibility that neither the "most innocent," unselfconscious Dorothy nor the soul-absorbing William could ever directly confront. William's hearty poetic praise for Dorothy's abilities, and her generosity in sharing these with him, begs the question of what this continued giving does to the giver—or, to be sure, the taker—in such a relationship. From early childhood on, as William gratefully acknowledges in "The Sparrow's Nest," Dorothy had given him her senses and sensibilities:

> She gave me eyes, she gave me ears:
> And humble cares, and delicate fears;
> A heart, the fountain of sweet tears;
> And love, and thought, and joy.
> (17–20)

As an adult, he makes clear, she gave him still more: after the "crisis" of his young manhood, recounted in *The Prelude*, she brought about his restoration to his younger self, to nature, and—most important—to poetry (*Prelude* XI [1850], 306, 345–48). Later, of course, while he gave her his poems to copy, she gave him her journals; even when he did not rely directly upon them for his own work, as in the creation of "A Night-Piece" and "I Wandered Lonely as a Cloud" (*Journals* 2, 109), the journals regularly afforded him their abundance of perceptions of nature, people, and events. It was not that William undervalued Dorothy's gifts; indeed, the question seems rather to have been whether he thought he could do without her. We can hear a tone of desperation, even of envy, as well as loving gratitude in his "prayer" in "Tintern Abbey": "Oh! yet a little while / May I behold in thee what I was once?" (119–20). Perhaps it would not be pressing speculation too far to see a shadow of Dorothy's own desperation, along with the joy, in the one place she could not see it for herself—"in the shooting lights / Of . . . [her] wild eyes" (118–19).[1] For William to wish, however subconsciously, to hold Dorothy's eyes and self prisoner in his own is not only to acquiesce in her arresting of her own development (Fadem 26), but also to seal her into the rural nature they both loved to read, entombing her there (Homans, *Women Writers* 20–23; Reiman 154–58).[2]

William does seem to have sensed that Dorothy was suffering and would continue to suffer, however obscurely, and that she would *need* "healing thoughts" "in after years"; perhaps, suffering himself, he thought he would need them too. In any case, his prophecy of "solitude, or fear, or pain, or grief" ("Tintern Abbey" 143) for her future came terribly true. It is difficult to imagine that in the near-total physical and mental eclipse of her later life Dorothy could have found in William's "exhortations" sufficiently abundant recompense for all she had relinquished. But she herself had willed and executed this relinquishment, directed by her love, but also "in obedience"—as De Quincey put it—

"to the decorum of her sex and age, and her maidenly condition." And thus the other part of William's prophecy also came true. Through those long, dark years, nodding and fretting by the fire, she still could hear or recite William's poetry with great feeling and joy; indeed, his words, or his presence at her side, were almost the only means by which the family was able to wake her to any semblance of her former loving, giving self, the "most innocent soul" who had so moved Coleridge years before (De Selincourt 397–98; Moorman 515, 607; Gittings and Manton 276).

Exactly how great was Dorothy's literary ability? Do her journals contain poetry "in a different style"? What were the literary costs, and what the literary profits, of being William's "dear, dear Sister" ("Tintern Abbey" 121)? Sensing that to open Dorothy Wordsworth's journals is to reenact the loving but appropriating role of her brother, yet recognizing that Dorothy herself, like William in "Simon Lee," presupposes the existence of a strong reading presence, I will look for help to perhaps the strongest revisionary reader and writer of our own century. Virginia Woolf, who hauntingly described the inevitable destruction of the sister she imagined for Shakespeare (*A Room of One's Own* 48–51), has read the journals of Wordsworth's sister with such acuteness and empathy that one must believe she saw and felt a parallel to exist, in self-destructive frustration, between Dorothy and "Judith Shakespeare." And yet, in her essay on Dorothy, written in 1929, Woolf also credits her with a literary achievement she could not even dream of for the sixteenth-century "Judith." Woolf confronts us with the central paradox at which I have already hinted: that Dorothy Wordsworth's relentless self-crippling of her powers of perception and composition is inseparable from the near-mystical self-sublimation of her best lyrical descriptive passages:

> . . . if she let "I" and its rights and its wrongs and its passions and its suffering get between her and the object, she would be calling the moon "the Queen of the Night"; . . . she would be soaring into reveries and rhapsodies and forgetting to find the exact phrase for the ripple of moonlight upon the lake. It was like "herrings in the water"—she could not have said that if she had been thinking about herself. . . .
>
> . . . But if one subdued oneself, and resigned one's private agitations, then, as if in reward, Nature would bestow an exquisite satisfaction. (*Collected Essays* 3:200, 203)

Woolf saw that Dorothy had so repressed her awareness of her own role as observer that she could actually believe it was Nature that bestowed the satisfaction. But further, Woolf must have found in Dorothy a precursor with regard to her own attempts in her fiction to escape the social, sexual, and psychic boundaries of personal identity. "But how describe the world seen without a self?" asks Bernard, Woolf's hero of expanded consciousness in *The Waves*, during his final epiphany (287); this is Woolf's authorial problem in the descriptive interludes of that fiction and in the "Time Passes" section of *To the Lighthouse* as well. Whether or not Woolf had Dorothy's descriptive style consciously in mind while writing *The Waves*,[3] seeing "without a self" was Dorothy Wordsworth's dilemma long before it was Virginia Woolf's. As we shall see, following Woolf's lead, Dorothy's self-repression leads to some profound self-revelation; conversely, Dorothy's lyricism in its finest flights attains the superpersonal, anonymous creative energy that Woolf admired in *A Room of One's Own* (102) when she echoed Coleridge's statement from the *Table Talk* that "a great mind must be androgynous."

Dorothy's unwillingness to look at herself is revealed on several levels in the Alfoxden and Grasmere journals (1798, 1800–1803), in passages that stand out against the matter-of-factness of her writing about ordinary activities. The first of these levels concerns Dorothy's use of the first person. De Quincey notes that Dorothy sometimes stammered in her speech when agitated (*Recollections* 115), and Woolf speaks of her stammering pen (*Collected Essays* 3:203). The journals show a repeated stammering use of "I," and of other first-person-singular pronouns, when Dorothy is experiencing painful feelings deriving from William's absence; she not only misses William, she misses the way he distracts her from thinking about herself.[4] Near the beginning of the Grasmere journal, for example, praising the restorative beauty of the lake, she writes:

> Grasmere was very solemn in the last glimpse of twilight it calls home the heart to quietness. I had been very melancholy in my walk back. I had many of my saddest thoughts and I could not keep the tears within me. But when I came to Grasmere I felt that it did me good. (17)

"I had," "I could," "I came," "I felt": Grasmere does Dorothy good, it seems, because her glimpse of it distracts and thus quiets the heart agitated by an unwanted self-consciousness. Ten days later, still missing William and still drawn against her will to sad introspection, she writes:

"I sate till I could hardly drag myself away I grew so sad" (21). She finds relief when she continues, not in her own voice, but rather by alluding to William's "Lines Written in Early Spring" and "that sweet mood when pleasant thoughts / Bring sad thoughts to the mind" (3–4). Nearly two years later, when William has left for a visit with Coleridge at Keswick, she still must find some distraction, something to do to fight off the melancholy self-awareness that struggles toward articulation: "Now for my walk. I *will* be busy, I *will* look well and be well when he comes back to me" (97). But then for a long moment Dorothy's eye is held by the core of an apple William had eaten before his departure—surely a symbol not just of William's absent self but also, subconsciously, of her own relinquished self. "I can hardly find in my heart to throw it into the fire," she remarks pathetically; but then, apparently, in it went, and she breaks away and flees: "I must wash myself, then off." Later, returning to her journal, she suggests once again that nature and thoughts of her brother have diverted her from self-contemplation: "I walked round the two Lakes crossed the stepping stones at Rydale Foot. Sate down where we always sit. I was full of thoughts about my darling. Blessings on him" (97).

Of course no mere temporary separation from the self she preferred to her own could threaten Dorothy so much as William's marriage to Mary Hutchinson in October 1802. Once again in the journal the stuttering "I" struggles in pain, and finally in vain, to assert itself:

> I kept myself as quiet as I could, but when I saw the two men running up the walk, coming to tell us it was over, I could stand it no longer and threw myself on the bed where I lay in stillness, neither hearing or seeing any thing, till Sara came upstairs to me and said "They are coming." This forced me from the bed where I lay and I moved I knew not how straight forward, faster than my strength could carry me till I met my beloved William and fell upon his bosom. (154)

As if she were acknowledging her identity with the dead Lucy, and again echoing her brother's words, Dorothy "neither hears nor sees" in the terrible moment when some act of self-perception or of self-assertion, however painful, should occur. Brownstein feelingly praises the "moving self-control" of this passage (61);[5] but what moves us here is precisely the impression that Dorothy is exercising a repressive power far more drastic than what is usually meant by "self-control"—almost a kind of psychic suicide. The conflict and torment in the wedding passage subside only when Dorothy, after welcoming "my dear Mary," can once again subordinate "I" to "eye," recording nature and events for William as the three of them start on the wedding trip: "It rained when we set off. Poor Mary was much agitated when she parted from her Brothers and Sisters and her home. Nothing particular occurred till we reached Kirby. We had sunshine and showers, pleasant talk, love and chearfulness [*sic*]" (154). In this way, time and again, Dorothy honored the generous and yet terrible commitment with which she had begun her task: "I resolved to write a journal of the time till W. and J.[ohn] return, and I set about keeping my resolve because I will not quarrel with myself, and because I shall give Wm Pleasure by it when he comes home again" (15–16). Refusing to quarrel with herself, to let "eye" look at "I," she sublimates that self, in a sense dying for William into the descriptions of nature, or of people and events, that so greatly pleased them both.

In Dorothy's perceptions of nature, however, as in her use of the first-person pronouns, there frequently appear further suggestions of a repressed awareness of herself, her gifts, and what she was doing with them.[6] But because the self-awareness is buried in the natural images, Dorothy can confront and describe the images themselves without the distress implicit in the jittery "I's" just noted. Repeatedly the sky above the Lake District becomes for her a dome, an image of enclosure with sepulchral implications. Early in the Alfoxden journal—in the passage that William later used for "A Night-Piece"—she describes the night sky, after the clouds have parted, as a "black-blue vault" (2). Another evening, four years later, she almost seems to pun as she writes, "it was a grave evening—there was something in the air that compelled me to serious thought. The hills were large, closed in by the sky" (104). In another entry, Dorothy uses the image of the sky-dome in revealing combination with a bird's flight and its echoing sound:

> we saw a raven very high above us—it called out and the Dome of the sky seemed to echo the sound—it called again and again as it flew onwards, and the mountains gave back the sound, seeming as if from their center a musical bell-like answering to the bird's hoarse voice. (31)

Dorothy too may yearn, however subconsciously, to escape—in an act of self-assertion or, more likely, of self-transcendence—to fly as high as the raven and send her voice, her words, echoing back; but that enclosing dome—the limit of the rural world to which, for her brother's sake, she has dedicated herself—seems to circumscribe her flight while si-multaneously providing, along with the mountains, a necessary sound-ing board.[7] Other images of flight abound in the journals, regularly linked with a limit or impediment to flight: "As I came past Rydale in the morning I saw a Heron swimming with only its neck out of water—it beat and struggled amongst the water when it flew away and was long in getting loose" (22). At this point, early in the writing of the Grasmere journal, still missing her absent brother, Dorothy is trapped not only spatially but temporally as well; she sees the heron while hurrying to Ambleside, hoping to intercept a letter from William, but "forgetting that the post does not come till the evening. How was I grieved when I was so informed" (22). Did Dorothy ever wish, even subconsciously, to rebel, to strike out, to break away from the orbit of her solitary life with William? The journals reveal very few moments of overt violence on Dorothy's part; once, however, moved by beauty and a show of bold independence, she performed an impulsive act of removal—only to repent of it immediately afterward:

> I found a strawberry blossom in a rock. The little slender flower had more courage than the green leaves, for *they* were but half expanded and half grown, but the blossom was spread full out. I uprooted it rashly, and I felt as if I had been committing an outrage, so I planted it again. It will have but a stormy life of it, but let it live if it can. (83)

In an act of relinquishment, refusing to murder and dissect, Dorothy replants the strawberry, just as it seems she reconciled herself to her situation in life without ever directly confronting it; the empathy of her final comment, "let it live if it can," is all the more touching for its show of toughness and bitterness.

Dorothy's journals suggest the presence of this subconscious empa-thy not only with the natural images of her entrapment—hills and sky, birds and plants—but also with other women she meets, especially poor women, whether Lake Country residents or travelers and beggars. Her portrayals of these women confirm Dorothy's awareness of the precar-iousness of her own social and economic position as a single woman, an orphan, living a rather irregular life in a remote district; they also hint at a deep-buried feeling of sisterhood. If we assemble them in order of the ascending age of the subjects, these descriptions provide an indirect, but still very sharp and moving, reflection of Dorothy's sense of the course of her own life—her childhood, her young womanhood, the disturbed years of her later maturity, and even her death. Early in 1802 she sees on a road a group of travelers led by a carman "talking to a little lass about 10 years of age who seemed to make him her companion." She sees the girl run ahead to fetch a large stone for blocking the wheel of the cart:

> She was a beautiful creature and there was something uncommonly impressive in the lightness and joyousness of her manner. Her business seemed to be all pleasure—pleasure in her own motions—and the man looked at her as if he too was pleased and spoke to her in the same tone in which he spoke to his horses. There was a wildness in her whole figure, not the wildness of a Mountain lass but a *Road* lass, a traveller from her Birth, who had wanted neither food nor clothes. (91)

Dorothy apparently has no conscious thought, as she describes the carman's tone of voice, that the child may be ill used or exploited for her generous spirit; instead she sees freedom, spontaneity, and courage in the girl, and perhaps she envies her nomadic existence. Her thoughts are totally different, however, upon meeting a woman traveling with her two daughters, one in her arms and the other, a four-year-old, walking with difficulty at her side in second-hand shoes:

> Alas too young for such cares and such travels. The Mother when we accosted her told us that her husband had left her and gone off with another woman and how she "*pursued*" them. Then her fury kindled and her eyes rolled about. She changed again to tears.

Next, clearly expressing her sense of relationship to this victimized woman, Dorothy reveals a peculiar coincidence: "She was a Cockermouth woman 30 years of age—a child at Cockermouth when I was. I was moved and gave her a shilling—I believe 6^d more than I ought to have given" (121). What complex feelings must have moved Dorothy to what she subsequently regarded as too great a generosity! As we read the two passages, it almost seems as if the "road lass" chattering with the carman had grown up to become this desperate, deserted wife and mother. Did Dorothy, as the time drew nearer for William's marriage to Mary Hutchinson, unconsciously feel that her own childlike wildness of eye and spirit had been ill used, and that she too was being deserted for another woman? And what lay ahead? Though Dorothy could not have been aware of it, her long years of serving in her brother's house were foreshadowed in the behavior of an old woman who served tea to

William and her one day in June 1800: "[She] was very happy to see us and we were so in the pleasure we gave. She was an affecting picture of patient disappointment, suffering under no particular affliction" (30); Dorothy herself is affectingly quick here to diagnose "patient disappointment." Perhaps a poor woman whose funeral Dorothy subsequently attended and described had also suffered under "no particular affliction" other than to have been a dependent woman living in England at the turn of the nineteenth century:

> The dead person 56 years of age buried by the parish. The coffin was neatly lettered and painted black and covered with a decent cloth. They set the corpse down at the door and while we stood within the threshold the men with their hats off sang with decent and solemn countenances a verse of a funeral psalm. The corpse was then borne down the hill and they sang till they had got past the Town-end. I was affected to tears while we stood in the house, the coffin lying before me. There were no near kindred, no children. When we got out of the dark house the sun was shining and the prospect looked so divinely beautiful as I never saw it. It seemed more sacred than I had ever seen it, and yet more allied to human life. The green fields, neighbours of the churchyard, were as green as possible and with the brightness of the sunshine looked quite gay. I thought she was going to a quiet spot and I could not help weeping very much. (38)

Dorothy continues this account by turning critical attention upon the officiating clergyman: "The priest met us—he did not look as a man ought to do on such an occasion—I had seen him half-drunk the day before in a pot-house. Before we came with the corpse one of the company observed he wondered what sort of cue 'our Parson would be in'" (38). Dorothy's indignation, following her great personal distress at the spectacle of the poor woman's funeral, suggests that she was very close to knowing and articulating her psychic kinship with the deceased as another victimized woman. No wonder, then, that "the prospect looked . . . more sacred . . . and yet more allied to human life" than ever before: in terms of Dorothy's personal involvement, her own inner need for what Virginia Woolf called an "exquisite satisfaction," it *was* more divinely beautiful—it *had* to be.[8] Nevertheless, as Woolf perceived, Dorothy could never have attained the peculiar intensity of passages like this one had she thought or spoken directly of her own feelings or of women's problems generally, as her more assertive contemporary

Mary Wollstonecraft did. The self-sublimation that kept her from becoming a strong authorial presence or a crusading feminist also produced these reticent, painful beauties in the journals.

We have found evidence of Dorothy's struggle not to see or quarrel with herself in her agitated use of personal pronouns, her repeated use of certain images from nature for which she has an unconscious affinity, and her empathic descriptions of some of the women whose lives crossed hers. But there is another, in a sense more positive, aspect of her art of repression: it is the way her rigorous denial of self can lead, as it did sometimes for Woolf and a few of her fictional characters, to an almost mystical expansion of self—the outpouring of her personal identity, with all its pain and fear, into the greater vessel of nature itself. This is the power one reads in Dorothy's most rapturous descriptions— for example, the opening entry in the Alfoxden journal:

> The green paths down the hillsides are channels for streams. The young wheat is streaked by silver lines of water running between the ridges, the sheep are gathered together on the slopes. After the wet dark days, the country seems more populous. It peoples itself in the sunbeams. The garden, mimic of spring, is gay with flowers. The purple-starred hepatica spreads itself in the sun, and the clustering snow-drops put forth their white heads, at first upright, ribbed with green, and like a rosebud; when completely opened, hanging their heads downwards, but slowly lengthening their slender stems. The slanting woods of an unvarying brown, showing the light through the thin network of their upper boughs. Upon the highest ridge of that round hill covered with planted oaks, the shafts of the trees show in the light like the columns of a ruin. (1)

Dorothy herself is not numbered as part of the rural population; she has succeeded so well in effacing herself that the sunbeams and flowers have more individual identity than she does. The reader, excited by the strange but irresistible energy of the passage, the androgynous balance of channels and sunbeams, of flowers and lengthening stems, returns to a more contemplative mood in the final image of the tree shafts, "like the columns of a ruin," with their suggestion of temples and worship. It is almost as if Dorothy had built Kubla Khan's pleasure dome in Somersetshire; as in Coleridge's dream-poem, this depersonalized but not dehumanized energy is intensely physical and sexual as well. A similar passage, written more than two years later, again contains this energy: "The air was become still the lake was of a bright slate colour, the hills darkening. The Bays shot into the low fading shores. Sheep resting all things quiet" (108). The air, the lake, the hills, and even the sheep are all quiet and yet as if electrically charged with an inner life and power that are felt all the more strongly for the surface of tranquility. "The Bays shot into the low fading shores": one feels the same sort of energy in Woolf's interludes in *The Waves*, in many of D. H. Lawrence's descriptions of rural nature, and in the remarkable early sepia paintings of the nineteenth-century British artist Samuel Palmer. Dorothy's best-known description, that of the daffodils (109) which served as the basis for William's "I Wandered Lonely as a Cloud," similarly moves the reader with its selfless synthesis of "simplicity and unity and life." Her expostulation, "I never saw daffodils so beautiful," like an earlier one in the Alfoxden journal ("I never saw such a union of earth, sky, and sea" [5]), acquires a strangely literal new dimension: the troubled and troublesome "I" really is *not* seeing the flowers, for Dorothy is beyond herself. In another unusual passage of self-transcendence, however, she and William lie "unseen by one another" "in the trench under the fence," as if "in the grave"; this passage indicates that there may be the stirrings of another sort of awareness in Dorothy, a consciousness of the power of words over passion, over change, over mortality: "There was no one waterfall above another—it was a sound of waters in the air—the voice of the air" (117). It is as if Dorothy were overhearing herself, for surely "the voice of the air," crying from nowhere and yet everywhere at once, like the echoing voice of the raven in the passage quoted earlier, is the voice Dorothy herself achieves in such moments.

Dorothy's journals seem nowhere so full of visionary literary potential, yet so pathetically unable fully to realize that potential, as in passages where the self-sublimating motion, after taking her beyond the limits of individual identity, reverts her to herself again, but with the beginnings of a stronger, more assertive power of perception and creation. In a well-known sarcastic comment on a rich man's garden, from the Alfoxden journal, Dorothy says, "Happily we cannot shape the huge hills, or carve out the valleys according to our fancy" (13), but there are indications elsewhere in the journals that she may have come close to recognizing her ability as an artist to do just that. "O thought I!" she bursts out, after two days of unseasonably cold weather in mid-May 1802, "what a beautiful thing God has made winter to be by stripping the trees and letting us see their shapes and forms. What a freedom does it seem to give to the storms!" (125). She seems not quite to realize that she too, her "eye" and "I" reconciled in the medium of language, has the godlike power, the freedom, to shape nature. Instead she seems to associate the basic "shapes and forms" of nature and the wind with a more dominant, masculine force, and to regard her own powers as secondary, comparable to the beautiful but relatively insubstantial leafing out of trees in summer. Another entry, written late in 1802, seems to confirm the presence of a constricting sense of masculine and feminine in Dorothy's view of her relationship with nature:

> I could not help observing as we went along how much more *varied* the prospects of Wensly Dale are in the summer time than I could have thought possible in the winter. This seemed to be in great measure owing to the trees being in leaf, and forming groves, and screens, and thence little openings upon recesses and concealed retreats which in winter only made a part of the one great vale The *beauty* of the summer time here as much excels that of the winter as the variety, owing to the excessive greenness of the fields, and the trees in leaf half concealing, and where they do not conceal, softening the hard bareness of the limey white Roofs. (158)

This summery aspect of nature pleases Dorothy consciously for its delicate variety, and unconsciously, it would seem, for the female energy, the hidden spatial potentiality of its "little openings," "recesses," and "concealed retreats." But the thrice-repeated use of "conceal" suggests that she associates something less admirable, something false or deceptive, with it as well, possibly relating to those images of entrapment—sky, hills, lakes—discussed earlier. It may be that her own female sexuality, imaged in these elements of nature, serves as a source of both pride and shame—as if she were both the agent and the victim of her own creative power. Later in the same passage, she complains that "even the Banks were less interesting than in winter" (159). She regrets that "Nature"—that is, this softening, beautifying, but concealing power—"had entirely got the better in her struggles against the giants who first cast the mould of these works"; continuing this surprisingly evocative passage, she writes:

> for indeed it is a place that did not in winter remind one of God, but one could not help feeling as if there had been the agency of some "Mortal Instruments" which Nature had been struggling against without making a perfect conquest. There was something so wild and new in this feeling, knowing as we did in the inner man that God alone had laid his hand upon it that I could not help

regretting the want of it, besides it is a pleasure to a real lover of Nature to give winter all the glory he can, for summer *will* make its own way, and speak its own praises. (159)

Why is nature "less interesting" in its summer greenery? Are beauty, variety, and potentiality, or the complementary qualities of conceal-ment, deception, and entrapment, so lacking in interest? How will summer "speak its own praises" if no one speaks for it? Dorothy seems here to be reiterating the familiar dichotomy of the Beautiful and the Sublime, but in conjunction with a sexual stereotyping, possibly based on an unconscious sexual envy, that robs her of power over both nature and language. Who are these "Mortal Instruments," "the giants who first cast the mould of these works," whose shaping power seems to Dorothy to rival or excel God's? If they are mortal, and not pagan gods, are they then Titans? the thinkers or prophets or poets of the past? or, closer to home, William and Coleridge? Apparently, Dorothy must stop short of considering herself one of these larger-than-life beings. She cannot imagine speaking summer's and winter's praises simultaneously, syn-thesizing the female and male aspects of nature and creativity into the sort of androgynous psychic unity that Virginia Woolf, following Cole-ridge, envisions in *A Room of One's Own*—even though, as we have seen, she sometimes achieves it in totally unselfconscious moments. Dorothy moves toward this exciting awareness of a gigantic power of creation that is both primitive and visionary, but she feels debarred from actively tapping it and using it to grow as woman and writer; she ends self-defeatingly by leaving summer to "make its own way," and lending her words "to give winter all the glory."

There is one more remarkable passage, however, in which Dorothy does appear about to effect a conscious resolution of this conflict through androgynous creativity. Walking with her brother and Cole-ridge under Nab Scar, she sees and then describes mountain scenery whose male images of upward thrust—peaks and trees—and female images of seats, bowers, and enclosing hills seem not opposing but complementary, to be shared equally by all:

It was very grand when we looked up very stony, here and there a budding tree. William observed that the umbrella Yew tree that breasts the wind had lost its character as a tree and had become something like to solid wood. Coleridge and I pushed on before. We left William sitting on the stones feasting with silence—and C.

and I sate down upon a rocky seat. . . . He was below us and we could see him. He came to us and repeated his poems while we sate beside him upon the ground. He had made himself a seat in the crumbly ground. After we had lingered long looking into the vales—Ambleside . . . Rydale . . . , and our own dear Grasmere first making a little round lake of nature's own with never a house never a green field but the copses and the bare hills enclosing it and the river flowing out of it. Above rose the Coniston Fells in their own shape and colour. Not Man's hills but all for themselves the sky and the clouds and a few wild creatures. C. went to search for something new We saw him climbing up towards a Rock. He called us and we found him in a Bower, the sweetest that was ever seen. . . . Above at the top of the Rock there is another spot—it is scarce a Bower, a little parlour on[ly] not *enclosed* by walls but shaped out for a resting place by the rocks and the ground rising about it. (114–15)

All here seems familiar yet strangely changed, re-created out of itself like the yew tree William first notices. The bowers or seats in the hills are clearly not women's prisons in any sense, nor are the hills themselves "Man's hills." The freedom, the exhilaration of this long passage are very rare in the journals. It seems that here, with the male presences of William and especially Coleridge not threatening her but supporting her, and with fond wishes for her absent female friends Mary and Sara Hutchinson as well, Dorothy is for a moment in command of her powers; she is creating the scene, making it a seat, a parlour, a containing vehicle for her self-transcendent but self-assured imagination. Her final comment suggests a moment of reconciliation with her own femininity as well: "We resolved to go and plant flowers in both these places tomorrow" (115).

These flowers are not mentioned again,[9] but as we have seen others bloom throughout the Alfoxden and Grasmere journals: flowers of beauty and fear; flowers of sympathy and repression; flowers of self-denial and occasionally of self-transcendence. Like that of the wild strawberry she first snatched up and then replanted, Dorothy Wordsworth's hold on life was uncertain, tenuous. Serving nearly all her life in dependent roles, subject to social and economic as well as psychological pressures, Dorothy had too many constraints upon her vision. In spite of her unusual gifts of observation and composition, she could not, as Virginia Woolf saw, fully assert a creative self without risking the delicate grasp of life and language she already possessed. Although he did not intend it to be so, William's seeing and writing could disastrously interrupt or interfere with her own self-creative acts of perception. One evening, Dorothy wrote in March 1802, "I looked before me and I saw a red light upon Silver How as if coming out of the vale below" (103); attempting no further description herself of this unusual light, she instead interpolates into the journal three lines her brother had written about a similar appearance:

> There was a light of most strange birth
> A Light that came out of the earth
> And spread along the dark hill-side.

She concludes this paradigmatic passage, "Thus I was going on when I saw the shape of my Beloved in the Road at a little distance—we turned back to see the light but it was fading—almost gone" (103). Indeed, the shape of her beloved—and his words, which it was so often her duty to copy—must have appeared everywhere in Dorothy's remote rural world, coming between her and the light, casting their shadows over the pages of her book. Yet the journals were expressly written for her brother's eyes, to "give Wm pleasure by it when he comes home again" (15–16). Nor can there be any question that Dorothy herself found pleasure in her life with and for her brother, in spite of all the difficulties they experienced. She describes a terrible, bone-chilling walk in January 1802 near Grisedale Tarn, through hail, snow, and disorienting mists: "We were long," she writes, "before we knew that we were in the right track but thanks to William's skill we knew it long before we could see our way before us." Having thus admired William's power of reading nature, she continues by writing of the feelings they shared upon returning home: "O how comfortable and happy we felt ourselves sitting by our own fire. . . . We talked about the Lake of Como, read in the descriptive Sketches, looked about us, and felt that we were happy" (79). True contentment could hardly be made more explicit than this.[10] Still, more than the warm fire, more even than the twenty-five pounds sterling lying on the table (she had just received her yearly allowance from her brother Christopher and five pounds from the Beaumonts), Dorothy's happiness derives from being able to write here in the first person plural, to direct her thoughts to William's travels to Como and to William's poetry, and thus once again to avoid confronting herself as a single perceiver, a subject. Without her brother, as we have seen, she could not feel free, only desolate.

Nevertheless there were moments, however brief and half-understood, of strong self-assurance. "God be thanked," she exclaims, "I want not society by a moonlight lake" (23). The moon, with its richness of mythic association, its show of power and authority, and its continuous motion and changes of appearance, seemed always unusually evocative and restorative to her. Of another experience she writes: "O the unutterable darkness of the sky and the earth below the moon! and the glorious brightness of the moon itself! . . . When I saw this lowly Building in the waters among the Dark and lofty hills, with that bright soft light upon it, it made me more than half a poet" (104). Dorothy subsequently went home and tried to write verses, about which she could say only "alas!"—but we can find poetry in the journal itself; its images of moonlight, waters, and the island house richly suggest a metaphor for the interaction of imagination, nature, and art in the creative processes of the mind. In one other moonlit passage, Dorothy is anxious for Thomas Wilkinson to leave her and let her walk home alone so she can finish reading a letter from William and Mary:

> I was glad when he left me. Then I had time to look at the moon while I was thinking over my own thoughts. The moon traveled through the clouds tinging them yellow as she passed along, with two stars near her, one larger than the other. These stars grew or diminished as they passed from or went into the clouds. (108)

The moon here seems to dominate not only the clouds but the two stars that appear to be following in its wake—just as Dorothy, holding the letter, seems to be controlling her world and her words at this moment. But of course the moon, even when reflecting splendor, cannot move the stars, nor can it break the bond of the earth's gravity or free itself from its orbit—any more than Dorothy, reading the words of William and Mary, is completely free to think her own thoughts even after Wilkinson leaves her in the road.[11]

One of the most eloquent modern writers on the powers and limitations of perception has been the French phenomenologist Maurice Merleau-Ponty. In a key statement, which the writings of both Wordsworths seem strongly to support, Merleau-Ponty asserts that "perception will . . . appear as the paradoxical phenomenon which renders being accessible to us" ("The Primacy of Perception" 52). But if perception, with its potential for both "immanence and transcendence" (51), enables us to grow both within and beyond ourselves, there is always, he tells us, also a "hidden side" (48–49): of objects only partially seen from a particular point of view; of words only partially comprehended; or perhaps, as in the case of Dorothy Wordsworth, of a creative self repressed and yet at times articulating itself in the very terms of that repression—putting herself down. Merleau-Ponty concludes a remarkable essay on Cézanne with a haunting commentary that seems in many ways applicable to Dorothy Wordsworth, in spite of the gender difference:

> Cézanne's observers did not guess the transmutations which he imposed on events and experiences; they were blind to *his* significance, to that glow from out of nowhere which surrounded him from time to time. But he himself was never at the center of himself: nine days out of ten all he saw around him was the wretchedness of his empirical life and of his unsuccessful attempts. . . . Yet it was in the world that he had to realize his freedom, with colors upon a canvas. It was on the approval of others that he had to wait for the proof of his worth. That is the reason he questioned the picture emerging beneath his hand, why he hung on the glances other people directed toward his canvas. ("Cézanne's Doubt" 251)

Of course, apart from her brother's, few glances—approving or otherwise—were ever directed at Dorothy's journals in her own lifetime. And unlike Cézanne, who continued to develop as a painter all his life, most of Dorothy's best writing seems to have been done early, in the journals we have been studying. Still, both were artists deeply and repeatedly frustrated by the circumstances of their lives, although Cézanne was evidently more conscious of the frustration than Dorothy. Both possessed profound abilities to perceive their worlds and the powers to use their respective media—what Merleau-Ponty calls the ability to impose transmutations upon events and experiences—yet both failed to understand their relationships to their worlds or to see their crafts steadily or whole. But how many artists, and how many critics, *can* see that strongly? Merleau-Ponty's final comment in "Cézanne's Doubt," with its shift to the first-person plural pronoun, implicitly links Cézanne's powers and limitations not only with Dorothy Wordsworth's, but with those of many others as well: "We never get away from our life. We never see our ideas or our freedom face to face" (251).

Notes

Parts of an earlier version of this essay were read at the Carolinas Symposium for British Studies, Appalachian State University, Boone, N.C., 10 October 1982. I am grateful to the Foundation of the University of North Carolina at Charlotte and to the University of North Carolina for the grant which enabled me to write the essay. Parenthetical numbers following quotations from William Wordsworth's poetry are line references from the Stillinger edition cited below; numbers following quotations from Dorothy Wordsworth's journals are page references to the Moorman edition cited below.

1. According to De Quincey, Dorothy's eyes were "not soft, as Mrs. Wordsworth's, nor were they fierce or bold; but they were wild and startling, and hurried in their motion" (114). Influenced by De Quincey's descriptions of Dorothy, Elizabeth Hardwick senses fright or panic in her manner and behavior (148, 156).

2. Richard Fadem speaks of Dorothy's arrested development; Fadem and I share many areas of concern, but I challenge his thesis that Dorothy's writing is not "in any sustained way interesting as literature" (17). Margaret Homans and Donald Reiman associate Lucy's death with Dorothy's ambivalent position in her brother's life and writing. Homans's approach to Dorothy Wordsworth in *Women Writers and Poetic Identity* is more compatible with mine than Fadem's; her thesis about "poetic identity," however, requires her to concentrate on Dorothy's attempts to write in verse, and while this concentration produces some brilliant readings, the journals do not receive all the attention they deserve. In *Bearing the Word*, Homans argues—mistakenly, I believe—that Dorothy "self-consciously literalizes several of her brother's most important figures for sublimity and transcendence" (16); for me, Dorothy is prewriting, not rewriting, William. Donald Reiman essentially supports the argument about a "tragic intensification" in the relationship between William and Dorothy first advanced by F. W. Bateson (see 153–54). I have learned from these scholars and also from Rachel Mayer Brownstein, Susan Levin, and Pamela Woof. Susan Levin's much-needed book, *Dorothy Wordsworth and Romanticism* (New Brunswick: Rutgers University Press, 1987), appeared too late for me to use it in this article. Although I speak of Dorothy Wordsworth as a repressed person, it is her buried awareness of her own self as a writer, and how that buried awareness manifests itself in her journals, that primarily concern me, not the question of a passionate involvement with her brother.

3. See McGavran 276–77, where this possibility is explored.

4. Homans (*Women Writers and Poetic Identity* 71–73) has observed in Dorothy the converse tendency to *avoid* the use of the first-person pronoun and suggests there is more to this than the old custom of dropping "I" from hurried personal correspondence; but clearly both the stammerings and the omissions suggest Dorothy's discomfort at the prospect of self-contemplation.

5. Bateson (157) unaccountably describes this passage as having "level unemotional tones," perhaps in reaction to the paralysis which was the *result* of Dorothy's terrible emotions; but surely her tone is "level" only in the sense that it is the tone of a mentally exhausted woman lying prostrate on a bed.

6. For some of the images of entrapment and attempted flight which follow, I am indebted to my former student, Susanne Felton, whose paper, "Dorothy Wordsworth: A Study in Contrasts," won an award as the best undergraduate submission to the Carolinas Symposium for British Studies in 1981, and was read at the symposium at Wake Forest University, Winston-Salem, N.C., 10 October 1981.

7. She notes elsewhere William's much more strongly negative reaction to a similar sensation of enclosure in nature: "He had been surprized [sic] and terrified by a sudden rushing of winds which seemed to bring earth sky and lake together, as if the whole were going to enclose him in—he was glad he was in a high Road" (62). Evidently, Dorothy was more used to coping with such feelings than her brother.

8. Fadem recognizes the intensity of this passage, but we completely disagree on its significance. "Dorothy," he writes, "is clearly not interested in death in general or even this particular death. . . . On the contrary, her weeping is really an excess of joy at the dauntless beauty of nature" (23).

9. Brownstein concludes her essay with a fine commentary upon the personal significance to Dorothy of a wild columbine she described as "a graceful slender creature, a female seeking retirement and growing freest and most graceful where it is most alone" (Moorman 129).

10. Woolf—evidently struck by this passage—chose the last part of it as a conclusion for her essay (*Collected Essays* 3:206); it may have seemed to Woolf that Dorothy's "eye" had finally triumphed over her "I."

11. See Levin (349–50). Brownstein strongly argues that the moon here is William, the stars Mary and Dorothy, and that "Dorothy sketches her terrible, probably true perception of the shiftings and measurings that were going on as her brother made his choice" in April 1802 (52). Dorothy uses the feminine pronoun, however, and I feel that she had reason to identify herself, too, with both the powers and the limitations of the moon.

Works Cited

Bateson, F. W. *Wordsworth: A Re-Interpretation.* 2d ed. London: Longmans, 1956.

Brownstein, Rachel Mayer. "The Private Life: Dorothy Wordsworth's Journals." *Modern Language Quarterly* 34 (1973): 48–63.

Coleridge, Samuel Taylor. *Collected Letters of Samuel Taylor Coleridge.* Ed. Earl Leslie Griggs. 6 vols. Oxford: Clarendon, 1956–71.

De Quincey, Thomas. *Recollections of the Lake Poets.* Ed. Edward Sackville-West. London: John Lehmann, 1948.

De Selincourt, Ernest. *Dorothy Wordsworth: A Biography* [1933]. Oxford: Clarendon, 1965.

Fadem, Richard. "Dorothy Wordsworth: A View from 'Tintern Abbey.'" *The Wordsworth Circle* 9 (1978): 17–32.

Felton, Susanne. "Dorothy Wordsworth: A Study in Contrasts." Carolinas Symposium for British Studies, Wake Forest University, Winston-Salem, N.C., 10 October 1981.

Gittings, Robert, and Jo Manton. *Dorothy Wordsworth.* Oxford: Clarendon, 1985.

Hardwick, Elizabeth. *Seduction and Betrayal: Women and Literature.* New York: Random, 1974.

Homans, Margaret. *Bearing the Word: Language and Female Experience in Nineteenth-Century Women's Writing.* Chicago: University of Chicago Press, 1986.

———. *Women Writers and Poetic Identity: Dorothy Wordsworth, Emily Brontë, and Emily Dickinson.* Princeton: Princeton University Press, 1980.

Levin, Susan M. "Subtle Fire: Dorothy Wordsworth's Prose and Poetry." *Massachusetts Review* 21 (1980): 345–63.

McGavran, James Holt, Jr. "'Alone Seeking the Visible World': The Wordsworths, Virginia Woolf, and *The Waves.*" *Modern Language Quarterly* 42 (1981): 265–91.

Merleau-Ponty, Maurice. "Cézanne's Doubt." Trans. Hubert L. Dreyfuss and Patricia Allen Dreyfuss. In *The Essential Writings of Merleau-Ponty.* Ed. Alden L. Fisher. New York: Harcourt, 1969. 233–51.

———. "The Primacy of Perception and Its Philosophical Consequences." Trans. James M. Edie. In *The Essential Writings of Merleau-Ponty.* Ed. Alden L. Fisher. New York: Harcourt, 1969. 47–63.

Moorman, Mary. *William Wordsworth: A Biography; The Later Years, 1803–1850.* New York: Oxford University Press, 1965.

Reiman, Donald H. "Poetry of Familiarity: Wordsworth, Dorothy, and Mary Hutchinson." In *The Evidence of the Imagination: Studies of Interactions Between Life and Art in English Romantic Literature.* Ed. Donald H. Reiman, Michael C. Jaye, and Betty T. Bennett. New York: New York University Press, 1978. 142–77.

Woof, Pamela. "Dorothy Wordsworth, Writer." *The Wordsworth Circle* 17 (1986): 95–110.

Woolf, Virginia. *Collected Essays.* 4 vols. New York: Harcourt Brace Jovanovich, 1967.

———. *A Room of One's Own.* New York: Harcourt Brace Jovanovich, 1957.

———. *To the Lighthouse.* New York: Harcourt Brace Jovanovich, 1964.

———. *The Waves.* New York: Harcourt Brace Jovanovich, 1978.

Wordsworth, Dorothy. *Journals of Dorothy Wordsworth: The Alfoxden Journal, 1798; The Grasmere Journals, 1800–1803.* 2d ed. Ed. Mary Moorman. New York: Oxford University Press, 1971.

Wordsworth, William. *Selected Poems and Prefaces.* Ed. Jack Stillinger. Boston: Houghton Mifflin, 1965.

Wordsworth, William, and Dorothy Wordsworth. *Letters of William and Dorothy Wordsworth.* Ed. Ernest De Selincourt. 2d ed. Vol. 1, *The Early Years, 1787–1805.* Ed. Chester L. Shaver. Oxford: Clarendon, 1967.

Charlotte Forten Grimké and the Search for a Public Voice

Joanne M. Braxton

To be burned in case of my death immediately.
He who dares read what here is written.
Woe be to him.
——Unpublished pencil inscription, diary 2

In the earnest path of duty
    With the high hopes and hearts sincere,
We, to useful lives aspiring
    Daily meet to labor here.

No vain dreams of earthly glory
    Urge us onward to explore
Far-extending realms of knowledge
    With the rich and varied store;

But with hope of aiding others,
    Gladly we perform our part;
Nor forget, the mind, while storing,
    We must educate the heart,——
    ——"Poem" (1856)

Charlotte Forten Grimké (1837–1914), turn-of-the-century black woman poet, scholar, teacher and translator, is remembered chiefly for a version of four of her five manuscript diaries edited by Ray Allen Billington and published as *The Journal of Charlotte L. Forten, 1854–1862*.[1] As a young black woman poet reading the *Journal* in the early

1970s, I was put off by the diarist's romantic language, as well as her class pretensions, and I resisted all identification with her.

Years later, when I read Anna Julia Cooper's typed transcriptions of all five diaries, I began to see their nature as a series of interrelated texts sustaining progression and development.[2] Restoring Billington's editorial omissions presented a more rounded view of Charlotte Forten's day-to-day life, beyond her commentary on matters of political and historical significance; I began to view the published edition of the diaries as a mutilated text. Yet even when I read the typed copy with omissions restored, Forten seemed aloof and distant; she refused to speak with me.

In the hope of improving my relationship with the subject of my interest, I began to read what Forten read: Shakespeare, Blake, Keats, Wordsworth, Lydia Maria Child, Emerson, the Brownings, and the Brontës. And I read what she wrote: her "Life on the Sea Islands," her "Personal Recollections of Whittier," the dozen or so poems published during her lifetime, and *Madame Therese, or the Volunteers of '92*, a novel by Emilie Erckmann and Alexander Chartrian, which Forten translated from the French for Scribners.[3]

When I returned to the Moorland-Spingarn Research Center at Howard University to read the original handwritten manuscript diaries for possible omissions, Charlotte began to smile on me. And when I held the slender, leather-bound volumes, each covered with a graceful marble paper, and when I read the delicate, faded black ink handwriting, I could feel the tension of pen against paper, and I could hear a voice. It was, unmistakably, the voice of a poet, struggling to be heard—the voice of Charlotte Forten.

Forten's first and second diaries cover the periods from 24 May 1854 to 31 December 1856 and from 1 January 1857 to 27 January 1858. These diaries, which Forten kept between the ages of seventeen and twenty-one, describe her life as a schoolgirl in Salem, Massachusetts, as a young abolitionist, and as an aspiring poet and writer. The third and fourth diaries cover the span from January 1858 to February 1863 and from February 1863 to May 1864, respectively. In these Forten records her continuing personal development and her participation in the historic "Port Royal Experiment" on the South Carolina Sea Islands during the Civil War. Forten began her fifth diary in November 1885 and made her final entry in July 1892, twenty-two years before her death in 1914. The final diary, which remains unpublished, presents a view of Forten's thirty-five-year marriage to the Reverend Francis J. Grimké, a distinguished black Presbyterian minister, who was also the nephew of white feminist abolitionists Sarah and Angelina Grimké Weld, the son of their brother and a slave woman, Nancy Weston (Billington 29).

Forten's five manuscript diaries show an intelligent black and female cultural sensibility struggling to balance political, intellectual, and emotional conflicts and to forge a public voice. Although Forten intended her diaries as a private record, her private autobiographical act relates to the development of a public voice in the move to objectify and take control of experience through the writer's craft; in the pages of her diaries, she gains distance between herself as subject and as object. This essay examines Forten's use of the diary as a tool for the development of her political and artistic consciousness and as a means of self-evaluation; for Forten, the diaries also represent a retreat from potentially shattering encounters with racism and a vehicle for the development of a black and female poetic identity, a place of restoration and self-healing.

The product of an environment that was both abolitionist and feminist in nature, Charlotte Forten grew up in the Philadelphia home of her paternal grandfather, James Forten, a wealthy and respected free black who advocated abolition and women's rights. In 1837, the year Charlotte was born, her aunts Sarah and Margaretta Forten, both active in the Philadelphia Female Anti-Slavery Society, organized a national convention of black women abolitionists (Billington 13).

The Fortens were cultured and well-educated, yet, like other free blacks in the "city of brotherly love," they found themselves excluded from museums, stores, ice-cream parlors, and restaurants. Predictably, the Fortens chose a private tutor over a segregated public school education for Charlotte. Stifled by years of living primarily in her grandfather's house and by being shut out from much of the typical social routine in which other girls participated, Charlotte Forten grew into an intensely introspective adolescent, continually examining and reexamining her intellectual and literary development. Thus she grew up separated from the dominant culture by race, and from much of the black community by economic and educational privilege, or by class and culture.

In 1854, Robert Bridges Forten responded to his daughter's developing isolation by sending her to the Higginson Grammar School in Salem, Massachusetts, where she lived with the Charles Lenox Remond family. Significantly, Forten began her first diary with the advent of her stay in Salem, marking the initial separation from her home and Philadelphia.

But even in "free" Massachusetts, Forten felt the sting of white racism:

> I wonder that every colored person is not a misanthrope. Surely, we have everything to make us hate mankind. I have met girls in the classroom—they have been thoroughly kind and cordial to me,—perhaps the next day met them in the street—they feared to recognize me; these I can but regard now with scorn and contempt. (12 Sept. 1854)

When encounters such as these threatened her sense of self, Forten sought refuge in the pages of her diary, looking back on the incidents from her own perspective and laying claim to her experience in the language of her private diary. Here, Forten confronted the dominant white culture in small, homeopathic doses, analyzing and gaining psychological distance. On 17 July 1854, Forten entered: "I am hated and oppressed because God gave me a *dark skin*. How did this cruel, this absurd prejudice ever come to exist? When I think of it, a feeling of indignation rises in my soul too deep for utterance." For Charlotte Forten, the diary became a private (and therefore defensible) "territory" of the mind and a retreat from the racism and sexism of the dominant culture.

Forten's first and second diaries also demonstrate her quest for literary models. In Salem, she read voraciously and attended an impressive number of readings, lectures, and antislavery fairs. Caught in the 1850s surge of politics and romanticism, she found Hawthorne's Gothic tales "thrilling" and enjoyed walks by the sea and in the moonlight. On Christmas Day 1858, she came away from Ralph Waldo Emerson's lecture "On Beauty" feeling "much pleased" (25 Dec. 1858, diary 3). Quaker poet John Greenleaf Whittier, a special friend, sought Forten out for nature walks and for talks on farming and spiritual development.

Among Forten's favorite writers were Blake, Keats, Wordsworth, Emerson, the Brontës, and Lydia Maria Child. Forten apparently accepted Child's promotion of "a love of reading as an unspeakable blessing for the American female."[4] Engaged in the quest for literacy and self-respect, Forten found books a means of knowing a world from which she felt excluded, a route to transcendence of her perceived cultural isolation:

> And hence are *books* to us a treasure and a blessing unspeakable.
> And they are doubly this when one is shut out of society as I am,
> and has not opportunities of studying those living, breathing,
> *human* books, which are, I doubt not, after all, the most pro-
> foundly interesting and useful study. (1 Jan. 1860, diary 3)

Forten, as a young abolitionist in 1854, read and reread Elizabeth
Barrett Browning's powerful feminist-abolitionist polemic, "The Fugitive
Slave at Pilgrim's Point," as "most suitable to my feelings and the times."
On 30 May 1854, she added this commentary to the diary: "How
earnestly and touching does the writer portray the bitter anguish of the
poor fugitive as she thinks over all the wrongs and sufferings that she
has endured, and of the sin the tyrants have driven her but which they
alone must answer for!" (diary 1). Hence, the young black writer identified both with the literary sensibility of the white author of the poem
and with the feminine heroism of its narrator, an outraged mother who
rebels against her rapist master by murdering the child she has borne
him.

Naturally, Forten's heroes and heroines included the fugitive slaves
whose experiences were beginning to come to light, not only through
polemical poetry and fiction, but through first-hand narratives and the
camera. One entry in her second diary describes her reactions on being
shown:

> a daguerreotype of a young slave girl who escaped in a box. . . . My
> heart was full as I gazed at it; full of admiration for the heroic girl,
> who risked all for freedom; full of bitter indignation that in this
> boasted land of liberty such a thing *could occur*. Were she of any
> other nation her heroism would receive all due honor from these
> Americans, *but as it is*, there is not even a single spot in this broad
> land, where her rights can be protected,—not one. (5 July 1857,
> diary 2)

Perhaps there is a sense in which the girl in the box can be viewed as a
metaphor for Forten's own experience of separateness from and of
isolation within the dominant culture, for although she herself was free,
Forten recognized the interrelatedness of her oppression with the bond-
age of the slave woman.

Determined to live a full and expansive life, to *live out* herself, Forten
responds to a feeling of restlessness which portends the rise of modernism in black women's writing. "I wonder," she wrote in her third manu-

script diary on 2 January 1858, "why it is that I have this strange feeling of not *living out myself*. My existence seems not nearly full or expansive enough—This longing for—something, I know not what?" What Forten seeks, without her conscious knowledge, is, in the words of critic Margaret Homans, "a return to her proper origins," the place where her identity (and her own subjective voice) reside (Homans 17).

Like other black women writing autobiography in nineteenth-century America, Forten discusses family, society, her profession, and her duty to her race; she also writes of her longing for an image of her deceased mother. "How I love to hear of her," Forten wrote. "What a pleasure it would be if I had an image of her, my own dear mother!" (15 Apr. 1858, diary 2). Lacking such a portrait, Forten set out to paint her own, and she would create her images with words.

Forten's poetry, noted for "its quiet simplicity and controlled tension," might well qualify her as a "literary lady." Although she never published more than a handful of poems, some of these received critical acclaim. Praising Forten's "The Angel's Visit" (1860), William Wells Brown wrote: "For style and poetic diction, it is not surpassed by anything in the English language (475). "Were she white," Brown commented, "America would recognize her as one of its brightest gems."[5] Although minor in the dominant tradition, Forten's poetry possesses rich descriptive imagery, intense lyricism, and sheer dramatic power.

Given the choice of a public voice and a private one, Forten, in a different time and in a culture where she did not bear the dual stigma of race and gender difference, might have blossomed as a poet. In Forten's third and fourth diaries, she gains the desired distance between self as subject and object, making a clearer distinction between the public and the private voice. During these years, Forten published more actively than at any other period, placing "Two Voices" (1858), "The Wind among the Poplars," "The Slave Girl's Prayer," and "The Angel's Visit" (all ca. 1860) in the *National Anti-Slavery Standard* and *The Liberator* (Sherman, "Afro-American Women" 254). In "The Angel's Visit," the poet's angel-mother/muse returns to plant the kiss of tradition and restore a childhood sense of wholeness threatened by the "cruel wrongs" which might destroy the motherless child who drifts from her roots:

> A sudden flood of rosy light
> Filled all the dusky wood,
> And, clad in shining robes of white,
> My angel mother stood.

She gently drew me to her side,
  She pressed her lips to mine,
And softly said, "Grieve not, my child"
  A mother's love is thine.

I know the cruel wrongs that crush
  The young and ardent heart;
But falter not; keep bravely on,
  And nobly bear thy part.
                              (Brown 475–76)

In this public creative act Forten, as the motherless speaker of the poem, claims the identity of both poet and daughter, still attempting to come to terms with the vocation of poethood as well as her experience of race and gender difference. In "The Angel's Visit," the speaker of the poem recovers the "maternal origins" of her "feminine creativity" and creates a vehicle for the potential realization of her black and female poetic identity. That Charlotte Forten never realized her literary goals may be attributed, in part, to what Margaret Homans has called a pressure "to conform to certain ideas of ideal womanhood, none of which included a poet's vocation" (5). To add that racial conflicts intensified Forten's confusion may be redundant, for as Claudia Tate has written, "Nowhere in America is the social terrain more rugged than where a social minority and a 'weaker' gender intersect" (1).

Providing a testing ground for the development of Forten's poetic identity and her public voice, diaries three and four also narrate her participation in the "Port Royal Experiment" during the Civil War. Forten's attraction to this experiment, designed to prove the fitness of former slaves for freedom, may be explained in part by her strong sense of duty to her race. Early in 1862, U.S. general Rufus Saxton, commander of the military district comprised of Port Royal and the South Carolina Sea Islands, wrote to the War Department to request instructors to teach former slaves. Forten answered the call immediately but was turned away, ostensibly because she was a woman.[6]

Despite her disappointment, Forten showed her determination to go to Port Royal. Refused in Boston, she applied to the Philadelphia Port Royal Relief Association, where she was again discouraged because of the dangers facing a woman working in a war zone. However, John Greenleaf Whittier interceded in Forten's behalf, and on 27 May 1862 she sailed from New York aboard the steamship *United States* as an accredited agent of the Philadelphia Port Royal Relief Association (27 May 1862, diary 3).[7]

In terms of her inner life, the experiment, viewed romantically as part of her duty to her race (and her transcendental or higher purpose), promised a partial solution to her predicament of isolation, a reconciling of intellect and a sense of Christian duty with the so-called cult of true womanhood. An inscription written in pencil inside the front cover of diary four confirms this interpretation. Speaking of her experience as a teacher at Port Royal, Forten comments: "This is what the women of this country need—healthful and not too fatiguing outdoor work in which are blended the usefulness and beauty I have never seen in women."[8] Forten speaks of her labor as "healthful"; it might also be viewed as *health-building* in that it offered her opportunities to work for the sublime balance between usefulness and beauty.

Forten's diaries modify the impulse toward self-sufficiency with the Christian ideal of duty and service. On her twenty-fifth birthday, Forten made this reflective entry:

> The accomplishments, the society, the delights of travel which I have dreamed of and longed for all my life, I am now convinced can never be mine. If I can go to Port Royal, I will try to forget all these desires. I will pray that God in his goodness will make me noble enough to find my happiness in doing my duty. (17 Aug. 1862, diary 3)

Always something of a self-apologist, Forten makes use of the apology as a type of literary strategy, for she does not wish to appear presumptuous or self-serving. Moreover, doing one's Christian duty absolves a woman of the need to conform to the cult of true womanhood and opens up new avenues of identity.

Many entries in diaries three and four have a lyrical, poetic quality. Forten describes her romantic vision of the voyage to Port Royal in an entry written on white letter paper and headed by the title "At Sea—1862":

> Oh, how beautiful those great waves were as they broke upon the sides of the vessel, into foam and spray, pure and white as new fallen snow. People talk of the monotony of the sea. I have not found it monotonous for a moment, since I have been well. To me there is "infinite variety," constant enjoyment about it. . . . One of

the most beautiful sights I have yet seen is the phosphorescence in the water at night—the long line of light in the wake of the steamer, and the stars, and sometimes balls of fire that rise so magically out of the water. It is most strange and beautiful. (12 Oct. 1862)[9]

Here, once again, the diary becomes a testing ground for the development of Forten's poetic identity, as she explores her experience in language.

Simultaneously, Forten continues her use of the diary as a tool of personal restoration and self-healing. An entry made on her arrival at Port Royal provides an example of this use. Here Forten "overheard" a conversation between two white Union officers, a conversation she judges deliberately calculated to disturb her: "The word 'nigger' was plentifully used, where upon set them down as *not* gentlemen. Then they talked a great deal about rebel attacks and yellow fever, and other alarming things. We saw through them at once" (28 Oct. 1862, diary 3). Maintaining an admirable detachment, Forten finds refuge in the pages of her diary, balancing her encounter with these racists with a lyrical description of the singing black boatmen who rowed her from St. Helena to Port Royal:

The row was delightful. It was just at sunset—a grand Southern sunset; and the glamorous clouds of crimson and gold were reflected in the waters below, which were as smooth and calm as a mirror. Then as we glided along, the rich sonorous tones of the boatmen broke upon the evening stillness. The singing impressed me very much. It was so sweet and strange and somber. (28 Oct. 1862, diary 3)

Transforming and transcending, Forten brings the values of romantic poetry to her text as she comments on the power of black spirituals to "lift [her] out of [her]self."

A parallel between the diarist's romantic mode of self-expression and the "transcendental present" of the slave spiritual emerges here, and Forten responds to both oral and literary traditions as she seeks her own voice: "The singing was very beautiful. I sat there in a kind of trance and listened to it, and while I listened looked through the open windows into the grove of oaks with their moss drapery. 'Ah w'ld that my tongue c'ld utter the thoughts that arise in me'" (2 Nov. 1862, diary 3).[10] Yet, despite a sensitivity to black communication styles and the language of feeling, Forten remained an outsider. From the viewpoint of her own standard English voice, the lyrical orality of the slave spiritual was still foreign to the New England–educated diarist; she stood outside the veil of the black folk experience.

Although Forten generally reserved her diary entries as a record of the growth of her own mind, she did send an excerpt to John Greenleaf Whittier "for private perusal." Whittier submitted "Life on the Sea Islands" to the *Atlantic Monthly*, where it was published in two segments in May and June 1864.[11] The published article, subtly different from the form of the private journal entries, displays more thematic and topical development than the strictly chronological diaries. Likewise, this account shows more detailed analysis and seems more publicly autobiographical, giving focused attention to Forten's role as a teacher of former slaves. Significantly, she refers to her young scholars as "my children," seeking a public persona that would redeem her in the eyes of the "cult of true womanhood."

By the time Forten comes to the end of her fourth and final Port Royal diary, the entries have become less frequent; however, they display the thematic and topical development which distinguishes diary four from the earlier diaries. Thus diary four is more reflective and coherent and adheres more closely to the form of what has traditionally been called a journal than any of the earlier diary texts, where organization is strictly chronological and sometimes fragmentary. Oddly, diary four omits Forten's reaction to her father's death in April 1864. (James Forten died in Maryland, where he was recruiting black troops for the Union army.)[12] Although the completion of the fourth diary coincides roughly with her father's death, Forten makes no comment about it—a very curious omission indeed. After her father's death, Forten returned to Philadelphia, where she remained for seven years before moving to Washington, D.C.

An interruption of twenty-two years ensues between the fourth and fifth diaries. During most of these years, Forten attempted to support herself as a writer of children's stories and as a translator of novels from the French and German. It was a point of honor with her to support herself solely by her own efforts—literary efforts. In these years, Whittier played an active role as Forten's mentor and protector, but her requests for help of various kinds eventually exhausted him. After one of Forten's continuing bouts with illness, Whittier wrote: "I am pained to hear of Charlotte Forten's illness. I wish the poor girl could be better situated—the wife of some good, true man who could appreciate her as she deserves."[13]

In 1878 Forten married such a man. After moving to Washington, Forten taught for a year at the Summer School and later worked as a clerk in the U.S. Treasury Department; she also joined the Fifteenth Street Presbyterian Church and later married its pastor, the Rev. Francis James Grimké. Called the "black Puritan," Grimké upheld ideals of black womanhood as well as black manhood, exposing the sexual double standard of the South and attacking it in his sermons.[14] As the son of a slave woman and her white master, he was well qualified to do so.

Despite the fact that Charlotte Forten was thirteen years older than her husband, the two were drawn together by the magnetism of like minds: both Francis Grimké and Charlotte Forten were isolated by the tensions of race and intellect; both faced the "crisis of confidence" confronting ministers and literary women in mid-nineteenth-century America and as defined by Ann Douglas in *The Feminization of American Culture*. According to Douglas, both literary women and ministers shared a feminizing "impulse toward articulation and change," but they were "confined to the kitchen and the pulpit" and "forbidden to compete in the markets of the masculine world." In reaction, Douglas argues, these ministers and literary women often stressed illness "as a way . . . to dramatize their anxiety that their culture found them useless and wished them no good." They also used their illnesses "as a means of getting attention, of obtaining psychological and emotional power even while apparently acknowledging the biological correlatives of their social and political unimportance" (92). Perhaps this parallel development explains, in part, Forten's life-long invalidism as well as the continual ill health of her beloved husband Francis; in this sense, Forten's experience reflects that of other literary women of nineteenth-century America who chose to marry ministers.

During the years of her marriage, Charlotte Forten continued to write poetry, but although her craft improved, her perspective changed substantially with age. Gone is the rebellion and conflict of the early poems, replaced by a tone of reflection and contemplation, as seen in her poem "Wordsworth," stylistically reminiscent of that poet's "Prelude":

> In youth's fair dawn, when the soul, still untired,
> Longs for life's conflicts, and seeks restlessly

Food for its cravings in the stirring songs,
The thrilling strains of more impassioned bards;
Or, eager for fresh joys, culls with delight
The flowers that bloom in fancy's fair realm—
We may not prize the mild and steadfast ray
That streams from thy pure soul in tranquil song
But, in our riper years, when through the heat
And burden of the day we struggle on,
Breasting the stream upon whose shores we dreamed.

No longer the dreaming youth, the poet has entered "the riper years," "breasting the stream" of the dominant tradition, meeting, opposing, and balancing against it at the crest. She has grown, in her own words, "Weary of all the turmoil and the din / Which drowns the finer voices of the soul;" and weary of her struggle against the tide. Seeking now "the finer voices of the soul" she turns to the hierophant in his temple, speaking in a neutral voice but embracing symbolic polarities she avoided in her earlier poems.

We turn to thee, true priest of Nature's fane,
And find the rest our fainting spirits need,—
The calm, more ardent singers cannot give;
As in the glare intense of tropic days,
Gladly we turn from the sun's radiant beams,
And grateful hail fair Luna's tender light.[15]

Associating the sun with the active "masculine" principle and the glaring heat of the struggle, the poet seeks a retreat into a "feminine" radiance symbolized by "fair Luna's tender light." Charlotte Forten retreated into the inner solaces of a marriage that would be, for her, a source of renewal and rejuvenation.

Together, the Grimkés braced each other, finding in their marriage a retreat from the anxieties of constant confrontation with the dominant culture. Here she found the balance, the communion she had achieved earlier only in the pages of her diary. Charlotte Forten found love, not the glaring love of subordination and domination that passes with the day, but a radiant, tender, and enduring one—a higher marriage.

Although Forten maintained diary five in a bound notebook of 140 pages, she apparently used only 43. Pages 44 to 100 are empty and unfortunately, pages 1 and 2 have been lost. Had they not been, they might have furnished insight into the reasons that Forten returned to keeping her diary. We may speculate that she found life with Mr. Grimké in "The High Ranks of Afro-America" to be another adventure, or that she may have been influenced by watching the reverend keep his own diary.[16] On the other hand, it is possible that Forten returned to diary keeping to objectify her many personal losses and the separations from her husband occasioned by her ill health. Although the diary includes the years January 1885 to July 1892, there are fewer and fewer entries as Forten's health worsens. Most of the entries occur between 1885 and 1889. There are no entries for 1890 or 1891 and only one for 1892.

The fifth and final diary has a very different character from that of the first four. This diary represents the work of a mature woman who has become a chronic invalid, but one who has also found personal happiness in her marriage with Francis Grimké—a noble man who apparently possessed all of the gentleness and kindness of his slave mother and none of the faults of his white master/father. In this as yet unpublished diary, Forten writes of her 1885 move to Florida and her desire "to accomplish something" in "missionary labor" as well as to "direct church work . . . among the lower classes" (29 Nov. 1885). For although the Grimkés clearly saw themselves as part of a black elite, they must set an example.

Although the Grimkés held themselves a bit above many of the less fortunate in the small town in which they lived, they were warmly received into the new parish. One evening while they were still living at a boarding house, they were asked to come to church and were then escorted to their new home, provided by the congregation. The Grimkés found the cottage "beautifully lighted," with a "sitting room and bedroom very comfortably furnished . . . besides a handsome writing table for F's study, and a kitchen table, plates, and other useful articles." Their home, the classic "dog-trot" of southern architecture, had been built with "a hall through the center,—a style," Forten remarked, "I have always liked,—a study and a bedroom on one side, sitting room and kitchen on the other. Our pictures and books make the place very homelike" (15 Nov. 1885). But there was no study for Charlotte Forten, and no desk either.

The idealized view of her marriage that Forten presents in diary five may be justifiable, but the critic must ask why, as the wife of Francis Grimké, Forten never found fulfillment in her own work. Perhaps the answer lies in the restrictions placed on her as a minister's wife and in her reluctance to assume a public voice.

Greatest among the losses sustained by the Grimkés—including the deteriorating health of Whittier and the death of family members and other friends from the old abolitionist network—was the death of their only child, a daughter, Theodora Cornelia, who died less than a year after she was born (Logan 233). On 19 December 1885, Forten made this reflective entry:

> We have been married seven years today,—they would have been seven happy hears had it not been for that one great sorrow! Oh my darling, what unspeakable happiness it would have been to have her with us to-day. She would be nearly six years old, our precious New Year's gift, how lovely and companionable I know she would have been. But I must not mourn. Father, it was Thy will. It *must* be for the best. I must wait.

Forten, already cut off from her primary link to black women's culture through the early death of her mother, was further separated from that tradition because the loss of her daughter denied her the possibility of acting out the role of mother. Her reflections centered on the idea that Theodora would have been "lovely and companionable," a creature balanced in beauty and intellect, another potential source of identity for the mother herself. When she writes "I must wait," Forten— already nearing the end of her biological generativity and still child-less—probably does not mean that she must wait for another child. Rather, she must wait *on the Lord* for an understanding of the inherent ironies of her life. She continues to use her diary for restoration and self-healing, a tool for readjusting her psychic balance.

During the Grimké's many separations, Charlotte's diary was still her best companion and possibly her only confidant. During the spring and summer of 1887, she found it necessary to go north "for her health," spending May in Washington and June and July at Newport. "Beautiful, beautiful Newport!" she wrote in July 1887. "In spite of illness I enjoy the sea and the rocks." "If my dear, dear F. were only here to share the happiness with me," she added. The next entry, dated October 1887, begins: "Back home with my dearest F. How glad I am to see him and find him well. I hope we shall not be separated again."

In several entries, Forten notes that she was "too unwell" to attend evening service. In fact, her illness prevented her from maintaining her diary with any regularity. "I having been able to write only at long intervals in my journal. My head and eyes are so bad that I can't use them much of the time" (October 1887). In April 1888 she suffered in the Florida heat, complaining of mosquitoes and fleas. "If one could only spend six months here, and the remainder of the year at the North! Sometimes I become dismayed at my almost continual ill health. It unfits me for work, and there is so much to be done here."

Although a physician examined Forten in Newport in July 1888, "he could find no organic disease,—only weakness." This diagnosis reminds us of Ann Douglas's discussion of the "cultural uses of sickness for the nineteenth century minister and lady" (92). Certainly it could be argued that Forten, the invalid, used her ill health to dramatize her anxiety over a culture that found her useless (as the very appellation *invalid* implies). Francis Grimké was affected to a lesser degree; he developed a competent public voice in his highly articulate sermons. His wife, on the other hand, became more and more retiring, publishing less and less and making fewer entries in her diaries as her headaches increased and her vision dimmed.

There are few entries for 1889, the year Grimké resumed his ministry of the Fifteenth Street Presbyterian Church in Washington, and none for 1890 or 1891. In 1892 Forten made only one entry, in Lenox, Massachusetts, during the month of July. "The last three years have been full of work and of changes, but on the whole, happy ones," she wrote. "The greatest drawback has been constant ill health, which seemed to culminate this summer, and I was obliged to leave [W]ashington with its intense heat, sewer gas, and malaria, before it was time for Frank to. I was sorry to leave him, but hope he will join me next week." This entry, typical of those made by Forten during the years of her declining health, proved to be her last. She died of a cerebral embolism in Washington, D.C., on 23 July 1914, twenty-two years after her last entry (Logan 233).

On his wife's death, Francis Grimké wrote a testament of praise for the years of their marriage. "Not only my love for her, but my highest respect for her remained to the very last," he wrote shakily. "I have always felt that I was very fortunate in being thrown into such close and intimate company with so rare and beautiful a spirit." In thirty-five years of marriage, he wrote, he had never been able to detect anything "little, mean, contemptible, or unbecoming about her." He found his wife "an unusual woman, not only of great strength and character, but also sweet of temper, gentle, loving, full of the milk of human kindness."[17]

Poet Angelina Weld Grimké, daughter of Francis Grimké's brother Archibald, remembered her "Aunt Lottie" with a poem entitled "To Keep the Memory of Charlotte Forten Grimké." The Grimké poem attempts to place Forten's "gentle spirit" in the stream of eternity:

> Where has she gone? And who is to say?
> But this we know: her gentle spirit moves
> And is where beauty never wanes,
> Perchance by other streams, mid other groves;
> And to us here, ah! She remains
> A lovely memory
> Until eternity.
> She came, she loved, and then she went away.
> (*The Crisis*, 9 Jan. 1915)

Wherever she has gone, Charlotte Forten Grimké did not die without leaving her mark on a tradition of black women's writing. Her private autobiographical act portends the rise of literary forms less restrictive than most nineteenth-century narratives by black American women, and the diaries themselves offer untold insight into one black woman's search for a poetic identity and a public voice. In her own words:

> Knowing this, toil we unwearied.
>   With true hearts and purpose high;—
> We would win a wreath immortal.
>   Whose bright flowers ne'er fade and die.
> ("Poem," *The Liberator* 23 [24 August 1856])

Notes

1. Billington omits the fifth and final diary, as well as large sections of the first three diaries describing "the weather, family affairs, and other matters of purely local interest."

2. All five of the original manuscript diaries, along with the typewritten copies transcribed by Anna Julia Cooper, are located in the Grimké Papers, Moorland-Spingarn Research Center, Howard University. They are used here by permission.

3. Forten's published works include poetry, articles, and autobiography. The most complete bibliographies of Forten's work are found in Sherman, "Afro-American Women," and Stetson.

4. Lydia Maria Child, quoted in Douglas 62.

5. William Wells Brown, quoted in Sherman, *Invisible Poets* 95.

6. "I got little satisfaction from the B[oston] Com[mission]," Forten wrote. "They were not sending women at present, etc." (14 Sept. 1862, diary 3).

7. Charlotte Forten and John Greenleaf Whittier visited each other frequently during the 1850s and 1860s and maintained an active correspondence through the 1870s. Forten was one of many women writers Whittier assisted in the mid-nineteenth century; he edited her work, helped her find jobs, and acted as her unofficial literary agent, making contacts with publishers and occasionally receiving funds on her behalf.

8. Inscription in pencil on the cover of diary 4.

9. An undated note, handwritten on the stationery of Anna Julia Cooper and found in the Francis Grimké papers, reads in part: "Nobody wants to take a pig in a poke. Here are two 'samples'—may they help to 'sell' the job. The 'At Sea 1862' is not in the notebooks, and it has not been typed." Thus it would appear that "At Sea—1862," an entry written in Forten's hand on white letter paper, was not included in the original notebook manuscript. Cooper apparently made the decision to add this entry to the typewritten fair-copy text in an attempt to help sell the manuscript to potential publishers. Cooper's letter carries no date.

10. For a discussion of the "transcendent present" in slave spirituals, see Cone 92–97.

11. See Whittier, editor's note to Forten's "Life on the Sea Islands."

12. Billington, introduction to *Journal* 14. See also *The Liberator* 31 (13 May 1864) for the obituary of Robert Bridges Forten.

13. Whittier, *Letters* 8:278, no. 1198. When Forten married Francis J. Grimké in 1878, Whittier sent a wedding gift of fifty dollars.

14. Simmons 612. Grimké's sermons are located in the Grimké Papers, Moorland-Spingarn Research Center, Howard University.

15. Charlotte Forten Grimké, "Wordsworth," undated. Anna Julia Cooper Papers, Moorland-Spingarn Research Center, Howard University.

16. Francis J. Grimké's diaries and notebooks are located in the Grimké Papers, Moorland-Spingarn Research Center, Howard University.

17. Undated, typed copy of Francis J. Grimké's testimonial to the memory of his wife, on the occasion of her death. Grimké Papers, Moorland-Spingarn Research Center, Howard University.

Works Cited

Billington, Ray Allen, ed. *The Journal of Charlotte L. Forten.* New York: Dryden, 1953.

Brown, William Wells. *The Rising Sun, or the Antecedents and Advancements of the Colored Race.* Boston: n.p., 1874.

Cone, James A. *The Spirituals and the Blues.* New York: Seabury, 1972.

Douglas, Ann. *The Feminization of American Culture*. New York: Knopf, 1977.

Erckmann, Emilie, and Alexander Chartrian. *Madame Therese; or the Volunteers of '92*. Trans. Charlotte L. Forten. 13th ed. New York: Scribners, 1869.

Forten, Charlotte L. Diaries 1–5. Grimké Papers. Moorland-Spingarn Research Center. Howard University, Washington, D.C. Used by permission.

———. "Interesting Letter from Charlotte L. Forten." With editor's note by John Greenleaf Whittier. *The Liberator* 19 (12 December 1862): 7.

———. "Life on the Sea Islands." *Atlantic Monthly* (May/June 1864): 11.

———. "Personal Recollections of Whittier." *New England Magazine* 8 (June 1893): 472.

Homans, Margaret. *Women Writers and Poetic Identity*. Princeton: Princeton University Press, 1979.

Hull, Gloria T., Patricia Bell Scott, and Barbara Smith, eds. *But Some of Us Are Brave*. New York: Feminist Press, 1982.

Logan, Rayford W., and Michael R. Winston, eds. *Dictionary of American Negro Biography*. New York: Norton, 1982.

Sherman, Joan R. "Afro-American Women of the Nineteenth Century: A Guide to Research and Bio-Bibliographies of the Poets." In Hull, 254.

———. *Invisible Poets*. Urbana: University of Illinois Press, 1974.

Simmons, William. *Men of Mark*. 1887. Salem: Arno, 1968.

Stetson, Erlene. *Black Sister: Poetry by Black American Women, 1746–1980*. Bloomington: Indiana University Press, 1981.

Tate, Claudia. *Black Women Writers at Work*. New York: Crossroad, 1983.

Whittier, John Greenleaf. *The Letters of John Greenleaf Whittier*. Ed. John B. Picard. 8 vols. Cambridge: Belknap, 1975.

CHAPTER TWELVE

"Wider Than the Sky"
Public Presence and Private Self in Dickinson, James, and Woolf

Nancy Walker

This is my letter to the World—
—Emily Dickinson

My mind is great!
—Alice James

Whom do I tell when I tell a blank page?
—Virginia Woolf

The "I" and the "Other"

The quotation in the title of this essay is part of the first line of Emily Dickinson's poem "The Brain—is wider than the sky."[1] Dickinson claims that the mind is infinitely larger than the physical spaces of sky and sea, which seem so vast. The brain, she says, can "contain" the sky "with ease," and with room to spare; it can "absorb" the sea as can a sponge. That Dickinson lived what could be called "the life of the mind" is concomitant with the extreme privacy in which she lived most of her life; she demonstrated a preference for thought as opposed to action, for seclusion rather than society. That she exercised this preference as a positive, conscious choice instead of as a retreat from "real life" is the thesis of Suzanne Juhasz's study of Dickinson's poetry, *The Undiscovered Continent*. Juhasz explains that for Dickinson the mind held "supremacy" over physical space: "By conceiving of the mind as a world, by conceiving of the exploration of the mind as ultimate experience, she provides both a rationale and an apologia for her chosen lifestyle. To live in the mind is to be most thoroughly alive" (26).

Yet there is a point at which a life lived primarily in the mind or imagination encounters and must be translated for the world outside the mind, for other people—a public, however limited. The medium of this encounter, if one is a writer, is words. For Emily Dickinson, words meant poetry, in sharp contradistinction to prose, as she explains in another poem:

> I dwell in Possibility—
> A fairer house than Prose—
> More numerous of Windows—
> Superior—for Doors—
>
> (*CP* no. 657)

Poetry is equated with "Possibility," "Prose" with that which is limiting, confining, predictable. Poetry offers a way to bend language to suit the vision of the mind's exploration; it need not conform to the expectations of a "prosaic" reader. Indeed, so unique and personal is Dickinson's poetry that it did not find an appreciative audience until many years after her death. Even now, feminist analysis is just beginning to reveal the extent to which Dickinson's poetry may constitute a record of her thoughts, an "autobiography" of a poet for whom the private though all-encompassing life of the intellect was far richer than the public life of social encounter.

If poetry—or, for other writers, fiction or drama—may be considered autobiographical in the sense that it reveals a vision unique to the individual writer, other forms of writing not traditionally considered "literature" may be equally revealing of the writer's vision and relation to the world. Such forms as letters, journals, and diaries are at once more private and more accessible than poetry or fiction that is intended for direct exposure to the eyes of strangers. The distance between writer and reader afforded by the artifices of poetry and fiction—devices such as metaphoric and symbolic structures—is nominally absent, and the writer translates thought into direct dialogue with self or specific others. When the writer is a woman, such overtly autobiographical forms provide insight into the tensions between private and public, "self" and "other," that have been especially problematic for women.

As both Shari Benstock and Susan Friedman argue elsewhere in this volume, the very concept of an individual identity—an "I" that is central to any text purporting to be "about" the "self"—raises different issues for women than it does for men. Whereas the white, male, heterosexual "I" can assert that it is somehow *impersonal*, that it represents cultural and aesthetic values, the female "I" reflects instead the instability of the "self," as the woman occupies the marginal position of "other."[2] Further, as Friedman points out, the concept of individualism is counterbalanced in women's consciousness by an "awareness of group identity": "Instead of seeing themselves as solely unique, women often explore their sense of shared identity with other women, an aspect of identity that exists in tension with a sense of their own uniqueness."[3] In the autobiographical writings of Emily Dickinson, Alice James, and Virginia Woolf, both the search for—rather than the certainty of—the "self" and the sense of "shared identity with other women" are strikingly evident. Each seeks in different ways to assert an individuality by rejecting the "normal" role of women (a rejection that results in mental and/or physical anguish); each addresses the page/reader from behind a series of identities or "masks"; and each makes clear that her "private" writing is addressed to some "public" with which she has an uneasy relationship.

To some extent, a study of letters, journals, and diaries—whether written by men or by women—can, unless one is writing a biography of the author, seem a curious form of voyeurism. If such forms of writing are in fact regarded as private, as in the case of diaries, or intended for a limited, specific audience, as with letters, does not the very publication of them amount to an invasion of privacy? That Emily Dickinson intended her poetry to be published in some form seems clear from her careful binding of the majority of her poems in small bundles, or "fascicles." Her letters, on the other hand, were retrieved (except in the case of some rough copies she retained) from their recipients, to whom she had tacitly given ownership of them and their contents. Yet there is a long tradition in Western culture of the publication of letters and journals, often as a posthumous act intended to give the public a glimpse of the daily life and thought of the great or near-great. In some ways, then, such personal forms as diaries and letters satisfy our curiosity about the everyday private lives of public figures, and they differ markedly from the autobiography.

In *The House by the Sea*, May Sarton speaks of the "huge difference" between the autobiography and the journal: "Autobiography is the story of a life or a childhood written, summoned back, long after its events took place. Autobiography is 'what I remember,' whereas a journal has to do with 'what I am now, at this instant'" (79). Sarton claims more certainty about what one "is" at a given moment than do the writers under consideration here. Nevertheless, it is the immediacy of the letter or journal entry that engages us; we feel closer to the humanity of the writer as she or he records the minutiae of life, and are better able to surmise the influences on more formal and public utterances. It is this sense of immediacy that Virginia Woolf, in the midst of writing a biography of Roger Fry, almost despairs of capturing as she speaks of the "invisible presences" that affect each individual life: "Consider what immense forces society brings to play upon each of us, how that society changes from decade to decade; and also from class to class; well, if we cannot analyze these invisible presences, we know very little of the subject of the memoir" (*Moments of Being* 80). The letter or the diary can bring us closer to these "invisible presences" than can the autobiography or the memoir.

Furthermore, authors of letters, diaries, and journals have often displayed a consciousness that these documents would eventually be in some way public—that posterity would have an interest in these ostensibly private forms.[4] Each of the women whose personal, autobiographical writing is considered here makes it clear in one way or another that she feels some ultimate public eye upon her as she writes. In the case of Emily Dickinson, the evidence is indirect but compelling and consists primarily of the fact that her letters often accompanied or included poems. The letters function as settings or contexts for the poems. Early in Dickinson's career, Susan Gilbert, her childhood friend and later the wife of Emily's brother, Austin, was a frequent recipient of her poems. The most famous instance of this pattern—inasmuch as it proved how deficient Susan was as a critic of Dickinson's poetry—is her exchange with Dickinson about the poem "Safe in their Alabaster Chambers" (*CP* no. 238). In response to Susan's dissatisfaction with the second stanza of the poem, Dickinson submitted to her two other versions, and in her note accompanying the second of these revisions she says, "Could I make you and Austin—proud—sometime—a great way off—'would give me taller feet—."[5] Susan and Austin constituted an early "public" for Dickinson's writing even if they were not able to understand her genius. As she matured as a poet, Dickinson's letters increasingly employ the style of her poetry, until the two are finally almost indistinguishable except by arrangement on the page. Further linking the poems and the letters as "public" writing is Dickinson's well-known poem "This is my letter to the World," in which the poet becomes the medium for telling "the simple News that Nature told—." In one of her most direct addresses to some future reading public, Dickinson asks her "countrymen" to "Judge tenderly—of Me" (*CP* no. 441).

With a similar sense that she would one day be "judged" on the basis of her writing, Alice James, invalid sister of Henry and William James, carefully composed the diary she kept from May 1889 until her death in March 1892. This brief account of the last few years of her life is the only "literature" that Alice James produced in a short life overshadowed by the powerful figures of her two oldest brothers. She appears to have taken to heart the realization of her youth, that to survive the repressions of Victorian society, "the better part is to clothe oneself in neutral tints, walk by still waters, and possess one's soul in silence" (95). Yet once she broke that silence in the "private" form of a diary, she obviously imagined readers other than herself. On several occasions she refers to the reader as "you" and at one point addresses "dear Inconnu" (129). In the 1 December 1889 entry she notes that a joke she has told in another entry also appears in a book by Oliver Wendell Holmes, but she insists that she did not take the joke from his book—"lest unborn generations should think me a plagiarist" (61). When James became too ill to write, she dictated entries to her companion, Katharine P. Loring. In a postscript to the diary, Loring notes that the day before she died Alice requested that wording be altered in her last diary entry:

> One of the last things she said to me was to make a correction in the sentence of March 4th "moral discords and nervous horrors."
>
> This dictation of March 4th was rushing about in her brain all day, and although she was very weak and it tired her much to dictate, she could not get her head quiet until she had it written. (232–33)

Such dedication to precise wording suggests strongly that James realized—even wished—that her private diary would one day become public.[6]

Far more certain than Alice James that "unborn generations" would be interested in her private writing was Virginia Woolf, whose collected letters fill six volumes and whose diaries fill five. In contrast to Emily Dickinson and Alice James, Woolf was a public personality and more traditionally ambitious. Unlike either Dickinson or James, Woolf became a well-known literary figure during her lifetime, and her letters and diaries are filled with comments about the shape or fate of these documents. Typical is a passage in the third volume of the diaries, in the entry dated 20 March 1926:

> But what is to become of these diaries, I asked myself yesterday. If I died, what would Leo [Leonard] make of them? He would be disinclined to burn them; he could not publish them. Well, he should make up a book from them, I think; and then burn the body. I dare-say there is a little book in them: if the scraps and scratches were straightened out a little. (67)

Woolf intended her diaries as notes for an ultimate autobiography or memoir. She even knew when she would begin such a work:

> At 60 I am to sit down & write my life. As rough material for that masterpiece—and knowing the caprice of my own brain as record reader for I never know what will take my fancy, I here record that I come in to find the following letters waiting me. . . . (3:58)

Despite the tongue-in-cheek tone of this passage, it is clear that Woolf felt that her life would be of sufficient interest to the public to warrant publication of her memoirs (which her suicide at age fifty-nine prevented) and parts of her diaries.[7] Even more revealing is Woolf's perception that *all* writing is a form of communication, as when, on 7 November 1928, she begins a diary entry by saying, "And this shall be written for my own pleasure,—" but stops abruptly to add: "But that phrase inhibits me: for if one writes only for one's own pleasure,—I dont [sic] know what it is that happens. I suppose the convention of writing is destroyed; therefore one does not write at all" (3:201). Woolf acknowledges that any form of writing is intended to communicate—not merely to oneself, but to an assumed reader; the "convention of writing" itself requires an audience.

Woolf's assurance, by her mid-forties, that her life and career would be sufficiently auspicious to merit the interest of strangers in bookstores is in sharp contrast to the reticent hinting of Dickinson and James. Yet the substance of the autobiographical writing of these three women has marked similarities. Most obviously, these are the letters and diaries of women, and even though these women do not share a common generation or nationality, their most personal writing nevertheless reveals common concerns and devices that set it apart from similar writing by men. Traditionally, the published letters or journals of male figures have been intended as records of "great lives," and their autobiographies have served as guides or cautionary tales. Thus Benjamin Franklin detailed his rise to prominence in his *Autobiography* so that his descendants might see how such success properly takes place, and Virginia Woolf's great-grandfather wrote his memoirs for the same purpose.[8] The tone of women's autobiographical writing is both more diffident and more intimate: insecurities and failures are part of the record, as are, usually, the details of domestic life—the private arena in which so much of women's lives has been played out. In her introduction to *Ariadne's Thread*, Lyn Lifshin quotes Maxine Kumin on her interest in women's journals:

> Women's journals perforce record more domestic details than men's—possibly this is why they also seem more interesting, certainly more pertinent. I think women are always curious to discover how one or another of us handles the delicate balance between the personal and public life. (15)

It is this balance, or more often a tension, between the personal and public lives that determines both the tone and the substance of autobiographical writing by Dickinson, James, and Woolf. All three women found the writing of diaries and letters a way of defining and presenting themselves to a world outside the self—a world that they could suppose to be alien or hostile to their experiences and aspirations. Woolf and Dickinson have in common a devotion to artistic creation and a concomitant fear that their efforts will be unworthy; therefore Woolf quails before the judgment of Leonard and the *Times Literary Supplement*, and Dickinson presents herself as a "Humble Scholar" to Thomas Wentworth Higginson. Alice James, having decided to "possess [her] soul in silence," fears not her reputation as a writer, but her worth as a person who has to be continually cared for. At one point in her diary James records her realization that "*my* glorious role was to stand for *Sick headaches* to mankind!" (48). This acute consciousness of judgment by others is a distinguishing characteristic of women's autobiographical writing. So, too, is the variety of roles or poses women adopt in an apparent effort to find one that fits both the self and the public. As women, Dickinson, James, and Woolf were subjected to sets of expectations that they in various ways denied but that continued to affect their sense of identity. As writers, particularly in the cases of Woolf and Dickinson, they risked rejection on professional grounds. And all three suffered "nervous disorders" that seem linked to the struggle for control over their lives. An examination of theme and style in the letters and diaries of these three women allows us to see patterns and correspondences that suggest the extent to which such writing records the search for identity.

The differences among the lives of these three women make the commonalities in their autobiographical writings all the more striking. As a first consideration, they belong to different generations. Emily Dickinson (1830–1886) and Alice James (1848–1892) inhabited quite another world from Virginia Woolf (1882–1941). In addition to being nineteenth-century Americans (though the nationality of the James family is always a debatable point) rather than twentieth-century Britons, Dickinson and James were fully subject to Victorian ideals of womanhood. Indeed, Dickinson's reclusiveness and James's illness (another form of removal) may be seen as real if indirect responses to white, middle-class, nineteenth-century requirements for female piety and submissiveness. Woolf, on the other hand, shared in the sensibility of the twentieth century, not only in the conscious experimentalism of her own art, but also in the angst of skepticism and world conflict. As a matter both of era and of personality, Woolf was engaged in social and political movements—including feminism—whereas Dickinson and James inhabited the traditionally private sphere of women. Yet neither Dickinson nor James ever married, and so were not involved in "normal" family life; Woolf, though she did not have children, had an enduring if unconventional marriage and frequent contact with close family members, and she was the only one of the three to manage her own household.

Perhaps most important, these three women had very different relations to the world of writing and literature. Alice James lived on the periphery of some of the most intense intellectual activity of late-nineteenth-century America, but did not, herself, contribute to it during her life. Her diary, published posthumously, affords one of the few glimpses we have of her intellect at work. To the world around her, Emily Dickinson would have been perceived as being on the fringe of the intellectual ferment of Amherst and Boston, but her poems and letters convey a deep immersion in her career as a writer, as well as the struggle to balance her ambitions with what she saw as her subordinate status. Virginia Woolf, on the other hand, was both publicly and privately engaged in the literary life—as publisher, critic, and novelist—and writing was, with her, a constant activity. In "A Sketch of the Past," Woolf reports that she was "born into a very communicative, literate, letter writing, visiting, articulate, late nineteenth century world" (*Moments of Being* 65), and she enlarged upon the traditions of her forebears.

Defining a Self Apart: Rejection

Despite great differences in the outward conduct of their lives, Dickinson, James, and Woolf share a sense of alienation from the expectations of "normal" womanhood that involved marriage and motherhood. Both James and Dickinson express the feelings of outsiders to these experiences, alternating awe with skepticism. James's health was too precarious for marriage to be a serious consideration, and Dickinson chose "single blessedness" as part of her commitment to the "wider" life of the mind. In one diary entry, Alice James reveals her conviction that women have a propensity to subjugate themselves to others: "When will women begin to have the first glimmer that above all other loyalties is the loyalty to Truth, i.e., to yourself, that husband, children, friends and country are nothing to that" (60). In one of many witty passages, she comments on the tendency of Englishwomen to remarry: "'Tis always a surprise, not that I have any foolish young inflexibility about it, for I am only too glad to see creatures grasp at anything, outside murder, theft or intoxication, from which they fancy they may extract happiness" (102). It is not really marriage itself that James finds amusing, but the repetition of it; "you would suppose," she continues, "that the wife part of you had been sufficiently developed in one experiment" (103). Yet despite her flippant tone, James yearned for a stable, caring relationship, and her friendship with Katharine Loring helped to fill a void in her life. After one of Katharine's visits to England, where James lived during the last few years of her life, James expresses her sense of loss at Katharine's departure, and continues:

> My soul will never stretch itself to allowing that it is anything else than a cruel and unnatural fate for a woman to live alone, to have no one to care and "do for" daily is not only a sorrow, but a sterilizing process. This is a scientific statement, not a lament. (57)

Because Alice James was the one who required others to "do for" her, this statement is especially poignant; she feels cut off from the "natural" state of womanhood, but wishes the readers of her diary to perceive her views as "scientific" rather than as a "lament." The pose of scientific objectivity is necessary to her self-esteem.

Emily Dickinson's attitudes toward marriage remain enigmatic, despite the frequent use of marriage as a metaphor in her poems and letters. Her insistence on telling the truth "slant" has evoked much critical detective work to determine the extent of her emotional or physical relationships with supposed lovers. The latest effort to solve the mystery is William H. Shurr's *The Marriage of Emily Dickinson*. Shurr's determination to "prove" that the Rev. Charles Wadsworth was indeed the object of Dickinson's affections, and that many of her poems detail the stages of courtship and marriage, represents a misguided effort to see Dickinson as a "normal" woman. Such an argument makes the poetry a response to emotional dependence and psychological disturbance instead of the work of a fine poet. According to Shurr's analysis, "the canons of esthetics still apply, but now as secondary to the canons of correspondence and autobiography. . . . [The poems] were sent as private communications to one beloved person" (10). Whether Dickinson pined for Wadsworth or for someone else or for no one at all is less important than the fact that she had an uneasy relationship with domesticity that grows out of the tension between her work as a poet and her role as a mid-nineteenth-century New England woman.

Marriage itself is seldom a topic in Dickinson's letters. Even as a young woman, in letters to close friends such as Abiah Root and Susan Gilbert, she dwells on the friendship they share rather than on actual or anticipated relationships with men. The few extant Valentine's Day letters she wrote to male friends employ the same teasing tone she uses in her letters to her brother Austin. In one of these Valentine letters, written in 1850 when she was twenty, she mocks the language of the love letter:

> Our friendship, sir, shall endure till sun and moon shall wane no more, till stars shall set, and victims rise to grace the final sacrifice. We'll be instant, in season, out of season, minister, take care of, cherish, sooth, watch, wait, doubt, refrain, reform, elevate, instruct. . . . I am Judith the heroine of the Apocrypha, and you the orator of Ephesus.
> That's what they call a metaphor in our country. (*SL* no. 34)

The last line of this passage, like Alice James's claim to be making a "scientific statement," is a conventional disclaimer to avoid being taken seriously.

That Dickinson's bantering tone, in addition to being part of the convention of such Valentine messages, may have also masked serious reservations about marriage and sexuality is suggested by a letter to Susan Gilbert more than two years later. In this letter Dickinson first refers to a conversation with another friend about "those unions . . . by which two lives are one, this sweet and strange adoption wherein we can but look, and are not yet admitted." In the next paragraph, however, such "unions" become threatening for women, whom they overpower and reduce:

> How dull our lives must seem to the bride, and the plighted maiden, whose days are filled with gold, and who gather pearls every evening, but to the *wife*, Susie, sometimes the *wife forgotten*, our lives seem dearer than all others in the world. . . . Oh, Susie, it is dangerous, and it is all too dear, these simple trusting spirits, and the spirits mightier, which we cannot resist! . . . I tremble lest at sometime I, too, am yielded up. (*SL* no. 93)

The sense is inescapable here that Dickinson perceived marriage as a "dangerous" relation in which the "trusting" bride must succumb to the "spirits mightier" that now possess her.

Indeed, Dickinson may have been correct in assuming that love would cause her to be "yielded up"—to lose herself in another person. In this same letter to Susan Gilbert she uses the common metaphor of flowers to represent women in order to explain the point she has made. Young unmarried women are like "flowers at morning, *satisfied* with the dew," whereas wives are "those same sweet flowers at noon with their heads bowed in anguish before the mighty sun; . . . the man of noon, is *mightier* than the morning and their life is henceforth to him" (*SL* no. 93). The same image of the woman as flower is used in Dickinson's "Master" letters—abject love letters to an unidentified recipient, real or imaginary—but here, instead of speaking of the woman *as* flower, the speaker *is* the flower, both in reference to herself and in the signature "Daisy." The language of the "Master" letters, apparently written about ten years after the above letter to Susan, articulates the dependence that she had earlier described. In one of these letters Daisy "bends her smaller life to his . . . meeker every day." The love that Daisy feels is "so big it scares her, rushing among her small heart—." There is no sense of irony or flippancy in this letter; Dickinson describes herself as emotionally "yielded up" to her "Lord" and "Master" (*SL* no. 248). So strongly could Dickinson feel love, so fearful was she of "yielding up" her own identity to another, that she made a conscious choice to live without marriage.[9]

Virginia Woolf maintained her distance from conventional womanhood in different ways. Though her marriage to Leonard Woolf seems in some ways to have been the anchor of her life from 1912 until her death in 1941, their relationship was at least as much an intellectual and business partnership as it was an emotional commitment. Even the suicide note she left for Leonard on 28 March 1941 posits the interference of her periodic madness with his work as a major reason for her decision to end her own life. The letter reads in part: "I am wasting your life. It is this madness. . . . You can work, and you will be much better without me. . . . Until this disease came on we were perfectly happy. It was all due to you. No one could have been so good as you have been, from the very first day till now" (*Letters* 6:487). The genteel culture in which Woolf was raised, though very different from that of Dickinson and James, certainly encouraged home and family as the center of a woman's life. As Quentin Bell says in his introduction to the first volume of Woolf's diaries:

> A lady was, in a refined way, a domestic animal; it was her duty to devote herself to the home and to her relations, to be an obedient child, an unpaid companion, an amateur nurse and, in effect, a kind of upper servant. Marriage was the grand aim of her youth, it enabled her to escape from the tyranny of the home and to exchange a lower for a higher form of servitude. (xix)

This idea of marriage as "servitude" was one that Woolf endorsed; she, like Dickinson, resisted succumbing to "powers mightier," and this resistance lies behind her negative reaction to the marriage ceremony itself. In a letter to Shena, Lady Simon, in 1937, Woolf expresses her views: "As for thinking that I should have exhorted you to go to a marriage service, I can only say last time I went to one I had much ado not to stand up and cry out on the disgusting nature of it. So next time you go, do this—One doesn't, of course, through sheer cowardice" (*Letters* 6:115).

Woolf resisted identification with the typical, conventional woman in both small and large ways. In 1915 she wrote in her diary, "I dislike the sight of women shopping. They take it so seriously" (1:8). She admired strong women and disdained those she perceived as weak and indecisive. In a 1930 diary entry she presents a scathing portrait of Margaret Snowden. Snowden's face, Woolf observes, "has a curious preserved innocency which makes it hard to think that she is 50. . . . The preserved look seems to indicate lack of experience; as if life had put her in a refrigerator" (3:289). Woolf compares her own boldness to Snowden's ineffectuality:

Lord, how I praise God that I had a bent strong enough to coerce every moment of my life since I was born! This fiddling & drifting & not impressing oneself upon anything—this always refraining & fingering & cutting things up into little jokes and facetiousness— thats whats [*sic*] so annihilating. (290)

Women to whom Woolf was attracted were those who were in control of their own lives rather than being tentative and dependent. Such a woman was Vita Sackville-West, with whom she began an intense relationship in the mid-1920s. Woolf describes Vita as "recalling some image of a ship breasting a sea, nobly, magnificently, with all sails spread" (*Diary* 3:146). One of the unconventional aspects of Woolf's marriage to Leonard was that for the most part he accepted her relationship with Vita, apparently recognizing that it was necessary to her precarious emotional well-being.[10] In a diary entry in 1926, Woolf refers to both the affair with Vita and Leonard's reaction to it: "She had come up to see me—so we go on—a spirited creditable affair, I think, innocent (spiritually) & all gain, I think; rather a bore for Leonard, but not enought [*sic*] to worry him. The truth is one has room for a good many relationships" (3:117).

Despite her determination not to succumb to conventional ideas of female fulfillment, Woolf felt the pull of tradition sufficiently to be competitive with her sister Vanessa, who married Clive Bell and had three children. In a letter written to Vanessa after the latter had praised her biography of Roger Fry, Woolf sounds much like Emily Dickinson telling Susan how much her and Austin's opinion means to her:

Your letter has made me so happy. I've been so haunted by the fear that you wouldn't like it [*Roger Fry*]. I never wrote a word without thinking of you and Julian and I have so longed to do something that you'd both like. As for thanking me—well, when you've given me Julian and Quentin and Angelica—. (*Letters* 6:385)

Just as Dickinson sought the approval of her brother and sister-in-law, so Woolf expresses her fear that Vanessa would not be pleased with *Roger Fry*. Julian, Quentin, and Angelica were Vanessa's children, and Woolf reveals at several points in her letters, and especially in her diaries, that she felt Vanessa had made a contribution to the world by having children that Virginia herself could only hope to equal by writing books. Vanessa's achievement, in other words, was the "normal" one for a woman, whereas her own was odd and perhaps inadequate. This sense is sometimes conveyed obliquely, as in the almost stream-of-consciousness diary entry of 15 September 1926, in which Woolf describes the horror of one of her depressions:

> Oh its [*sic*] beginning its coming—the horror—physically like a painful wave swelling about the breast. . . . God, I wish I were dead. Pause. But why am I feeling this? Let me watch the wave rise. I watch. Vanessa. Children. Failure. Yes; I detect that. (3:110)

As she describes the return to a calmer emotional state, Woolf makes it clear that it is *she* who is the failure—"the irrational pain: the sense of failure"—and the connection of that sense with "Vanessa" and "children" suggests a comparison with Vanessa's "success" and Virginia's "failure."

More overt evidence that the bearing of children was a focal point for Woolf's feelings of competition with her sister occurs in two closely spaced diary entries from December 1927. On 20 December, the day after a party for Vanessa's children, Woolf speaks of the "infinitely sentimental" feeling she has for them. Yet although she can "dramatize" herself as a parent, she has decided she does not want children, in part because of her resistance to sexuality: "I don't like the physicalness of having children of one's own." Writing has obviously become a substitute for bearing children: "This insatiable desire to write something before I die, this ravaging sense of the shortness & feverishness of life, make me cling, like a man on a rock, to my own anchor" (3:167). Two days later, after berating herself for behaving in a self-centered manner at a party, Woolf returns to the theme of Vanessa, children, and competition:

> So· easily might I have become a hare brained egotistic woman, exacting compliments, arrogant, narrow, withered. Nessa's children (I always measure myself against her, & find her much the largest, most humane of the two of us . . . as she [battles?] her way so nonchalantly modestly, almost anonymously past the goal, with her children round her. (168)

The sentence beginning "Nessa's children" is never completed in this entry. Instead, that phrase triggers the closely related thought of Woolf "measuring" herself against her sister, and the rest of the passage conveys the traditional idea that the woman with children is more "humane," more generous than the childless woman, even to the point of becoming "anonymous." Woolf's coming to terms with the fact that she would remain childless did not exempt her from the culturally imposed notion that the childless state made a woman more prone to selfishness, or was in fact a *form* of selfishness. Woolf's most succinct statement of the tension between motherhood and professional ambition occurs in a letter to Quentin Bell in 1930: "How any woman with a family ever put pen to paper I cannot fathom" (*Letters* 4:176).

The rejection or avoidance of conventional wife- and motherhood is only one way these women claim individuality. Another is their skepticism about or rejection of organized religion. Part of women's conformity to societal expectations in Western culture has involved their role as moral exemplars. In Western Christian tradition, piety and virtue have been inextricably linked as requirements for female behavior, as if women were to atone perpetually for the sin of Eve. For women raised in a strict religious tradition, such as Emily Dickinson, anything short of full acceptance of religious doctrine put both the soul and one's earthly reputation in jeopardy. For those of later generations who could enjoy an intellectual climate more attuned to human than to divine control of the world, such rejection involved less personal risk and represented a commitment to seeing oneself as unique and powerful. It is this commitment that Virginia Woolf expresses eloquently in "A Sketch of the Past" when she speaks of the "rapture" she feels when, in writing, she "seem[s] to be discovering what belongs to what":

> Behind the cotton wool [of everyday life] is hidden a pattern; that we—I mean all human beings—are connected with this; that the whole world is a work of art; that we are the parts of the work of art. *Hamlet* or a Beethoven quartet is the truth about this vast mass that we call the world. But there is no Shakespeare, there is no Beethoven, certainly and emphatically there is no God; we are the words; we are the music; we are the thing itself. (*Moments of Being* 72)

This almost pantheistic view moves art and the creators of art to the center of human consciousness and experience, and denies the presence of God, replacing that presence with the human imagination. Religion as a topic of interest is conspicuous by its absence in most of Woolf's autobiographical writing. She typically mentions it briefly and ironically, in statements that reveal her distance from its influence. In a 1936 letter to Ethel Smyth, for example, she interrupts a discussion of Wordsworth to write: "Now theyre [sic] mending the church. Tap tap

tap . . . it drives me wild, the care of your religion. As irony would have it, my garden room is immediately below the spire" (*Letters* 6:73).

With similar wit, Alice James expresses her skepticism about the efficacy of religious belief. James's comments about herself in her diary frequently reveal a sense of good and evil that are derived from religious belief but transformed into secular behavior—especially her behavior as a woman. At one point she bursts out, "how sick one gets of being 'good'" (64). After a particularly trying day she reports that Katharine has said to her, "What an awful pity it is that you can't say *damn.*" James continues: "I agreed with her from my heart. It is an immense loss to have all robust and sustaining expletives refined away from one! at such moments of trial refinement is a feeble reed to lean upon" (66). It is the clash between Christianity and humane and sensible behavior that most often perplexes James, and she is quick to point out instances in which organized religion requires people to behave in what she feels to be absurd or inhumane ways. Referring to an incident that she does not detail, James comments on the irony of Christianity's treatment of women:

> Two thousand years of Christianity, as interpreted by the pious of all nations, necessitates that when a poor girl goes wrong she should be ejected from all Societies to which she belongs, *instituted* for the purpose of keeping her in the straight path! (84)

The issue on which James takes the most firm stand against the teachings of conventional religion is the individual's right to terminate her own life. Although she did not, like Virginia Woolf, commit suicide, she often considered it the logical end to her suffering. In the diary entry dated 5 August 1889, James pits logic against religious doctrine:

> How heroic to be able to suppress one's vanity to the extent of confessing that the game is too hard. The most comic and apparently the chief argument used against [suicide] is that because you were born without being consulted, you would be very sinfull should you cut short your blissfull career! (52)

James's attitude toward religious and moral issues may be summed up by a statement she made less than a year later: "Every hour I live I become an intenser devotee to *common-sense!*" (125).

Because Alice James did not begin her diary until she was forty, we have little direct evidence of what early struggles she might have had to reach her ironic detachment from religious conventions; but the intellectual atmosphere in which the James family moved was vastly more receptive to religious skepticism than was the New England environment of her contemporary, Emily Dickinson. By the time Dickinson was forty, she had come to terms with her own resistance to the religion of her forefathers. As Wendy Martin puts it in *An American Triptych*, when Dickinson "rejected the certainties of patriarchal religion, she accepted the risk of independence and the burden of being in charge of her own life" (9). But this rejection was not easy in a community in which Protestantism had a strong Puritan heritage, especially when one was a member of one of Amherst's most prominent families. By the time Dickinson wrote "Some keep the Sabbath going to Church— / I keep it, staying at Home" (*CP* no. 324) when she was about thirty, she had been subjected to the pressures of family, peers, and the Mt. Holyoke Seminary to accept fully the doctrines of the First Church of Amherst. Inasmuch as those doctrines required an admission of her own sinful nature, Dickinson could not comply and submit her fate to the will of God. When she was about twenty, in the midst of revivalistic fervor in Amherst, she wrote to her friend Abiah Root of her sense of guilt at not being "saved":

> [T]he place is very solemn, and sacred, and the bad ones slink away, and are sorrowful. . . . I am one of the lingering *bad* ones, and so do *I* slink away, and pause, and ponder . . . and do work without knowing why—not surely for *this* brief world, and more sure it is not for Heaven. (*SL* no. 36)

Even in what was surely a state of agitation about her lack of complete faith, Dickinson employs a certain irony or flippancy in this letter, especially as she goes on to say that with her mother ill and in "invalid" status, "Father and Austin still clamor for food, and I, like a martyr am feeding them"—her characteristic tone when speaking of her reluctance to perform household tasks. Yet she asks for Abiah's prayers so that "the Father may bless one more!"

About a year later, in July 1851, Dickinson again uses an ironic tone—one that emerges also in many of her poems about religion—when writing to Austin about a church service: "I have just come in from Church very hot, and faded, having witnessed a couple of Baptisms, three admissions to church, a Supper of the Lord, and some other minor transactions time fails me to record" (*SL* no. 46). Her sense of having "witnessed" rather than participated in these "transactions" at church distinguishes her from Austin, to whom she refers as a "'Lamb' unto [the reverend Colton's] fold." By February 1852 Dickinson had begun to move toward keeping the Sabbath "at home," as when she writes to Susan Gilbert not to go to "*their* meeting," but to "come with me this morning to the church within our hearts, where the bells are always ringing" (*SL* no. 77). The "church within our hearts" was the one Dickinson ultimately chose in preference to an external, physical church representing rules and doctrines. Earth itself, and the life of the imagination possible on it, were Heaven enough for her. Dickinson's final stance on organized religion was one that she initially took when she was sixteen, writing to Abiah Root that she feels "the world holds a predominant place in my affections. I do not feel that I could give up all for Christ were I called to die" (*SL* no. 13). Her last known letter, written to her Norcross cousins, reads in its entirety "Called back," but to what or where she felt she had been called remained a mystery to her, as it does to her readers.

Defining a Self Apart: Roles

As surely as their diaries and letters reveal these writers' alienation from the conventions of traditional womanhood, they also demonstrate the strategies by which each sought a means of mediating between private and public worlds. Having resisted or avoided some common measures of a woman's worth, each was forced to find alternate forms of self-definition. One of these, particularly for women in the nineteenth century, was illness—physical or mental. Numerous women responded to repression and a sense of uselessness by developing or exaggerating physical or psychological maladies that defied diagnosis by doctors of the day. Dickinson's emotional anguish, James's invalidism, and Woolf's recurring madness can all be viewed as unconscious responses to the tension between the desire for autonomy and independence and the reality of subordinate status. Rather than indicating weakness, such strategies exerted a subversive power over the women's immediate environments, and granted them a measure of freedom from ordinary demands. Another strategy was the conscious playing of roles—presenting a variety of faces and personalities to the outside world, as if to challenge the very notion of a fixed identity that could be too confining. Instead of masks to hide behind, these various roles—child, lover, tease, intellectual—mirrored the variety of selves involved in the individual identity and demonstrated the ability to select consciously a presentation of self. Thus Emily Dickinson could be "Daisy" or "Emilie," and Virginia Woolf was adept at addressing a variety of publics, including unknown readers of her diary. The two sets of strategies—one an apparent withdrawal, the other a deliberate confrontation—are related in the sense that both resist classification of the self by others, reserving that option for the women themselves.

Dickinson's poem, "I'm Nobody! Who are you?" is emblematic of the merging of the two strategies. Using the bantering tone she sometimes employed in her letters, Dickinson proposes that the lack of a specified identity is better than to be "Somebody," which is "dreary":

> To tell one's name—the livelong June—
> To an admiring Bog! (no. 288)

Isolation, whether by means of illness or the physical solitude that Dickinson chose, provides mental and emotional "space" that prevents limitation by the "Bog" of humanity. Near the end of her diary Alice James quotes the second stanza of this poem, concurring with Dickinson's sentiments and stating that the poem "expresses the highest point of view of the aspiring soul . . . completely" (227).[11]

The fact of illness or physical removal from ordinary society is linked by these three writers to the concept of place, which is in turn related to the mind and the process of thought. Alice James identifies her struggle as a fight between body and mind. When she first became ill at the age of nineteen, with "violent turns of hysteria," she remembers: "I saw so distinctly that it was a fight simply between my body and my will, a battle in which the former was to be triumphant to the end. . . . I had to 'abandon' my brain, as it were" (149). To "abandon" one's brain means to cease to think, and James's comment recalls the sort of treatment usually recommended in the nineteenth century for women with "nervous disorders": total inactivity, especially an avoidance of reading, writing, or any other mental involvement. As Charlotte Perkins Gilman describes this treatment in her story "The Yellow Wallpaper," its effect was often to increase rather than decrease the symptoms it sought to alleviate. Virginia Woolf recalls that during an illness she used to "hook" a piece of paper "out of the nurse's eye"—"what a tremendous desire to write I had" (Diary 3:315).

Alice James's description of her initial illness as caused by mental activity, leading her to "abandon" her brain so as not to upset her body, suggests that she effectively gave up the "life of the mind" to her oldest brothers and adopted illness as her form of distinction. This reading is substantiated by her response to her doctor when he asked whether she, like they, had "written for the press": "I vehemently disclaimed the imputation. How sad it is that the purely innocuous should always be supposed to have the trail of the family serpent upon them. The domestic muse isn't considered very original" (227–28). The role that James adopts here is that of the "innocuous" person, the one with nothing to offer intellectually. Yet her ironic tone suggests that she did not consider herself "innocuous" at all, and the next statement makes plain that her gender, complicated by her illness, has forced her into the "domestic" life that is not considered "original" enough to inspire literature.

Although Alice James seems to have acquiesced to the idea that as a woman she was unfit for the intellectual life, she lived an active mental existence and, like Dickinson, conceived the mind as a place to inhabit. Just as Dickinson could see all of eternity mirrored in her limited physical environment, so James experienced life widely from her invalid's bed. In 1889 she notes:

> It's amusing to see how, even on my microscopic field, minute events are perpetually taking place illustrative of the broadest facts of human nature. . . . . Lying in this room, with the resistance of a thistle-down, having illusory moments of throbbing with the pulse of the Race. (48–49)

The mind was for James not merely a place to record or store observations, but the creative source of ideas. At one point she speaks of herself as a "coral insect building up my various reefs of theory by microscopic additions drawn from observation, or my inner consciousness, mostly" (109). Isolation from normal social life could be a blessing for thought: "I have seen so little that my memory is packed with little bits which have not been wiped out by great ones" (34). When James refers to her "centimetre of observation," as contrasted with her brother Henry's "wider and varied field" (97–98), she takes the pose of the younger sister adopting a subordinate stance. But when she is not viewing herself in relation to those who, by virtue of gender, health, and productivity, overshadow her, she does not feel the same need to be coy. In a passage written about six months before her death, when she was in great pain from a malignant tumor, she conveys an urgency to share her ideas before it is too late. On 3 September 1891, after a six-week lapse in the diary, she writes: "These long pauses don't point to any mental aridity, my 'roomy forehead' is as full as ever of germinating thoughts, but alas the machinery is more and more out of kilter. I am sorry for you all, for I feel as if I hadn't even yet given my message" (218).

The phrase "you all" in the last sentence refers to the large public with whom James wished to communicate, though the nature of her "message" is not clear. This passage recalls Dickinson's "letter to the World," containing the "message" of nature (no. 441), and both authors' direct address to the reader is similar to Woolf's statement after completing *The Waves*: "And I think to myself as I walk down Southhampton Row 'And I have given you a new book'" (*Diary* 3:302)—the "you" referring to the world outside her mind with which she communicated all the time.

Virginia Woolf's consciousness of a specific "you" or public for whom she wrote is far greater than that of James or Dickinson; she was a prolific and widely published author. Yet she used the strategies of retreat and role-playing, as did they, as a means of claiming space for herself. As the author of *A Room of One's Own*, in which she argues clearly that women who wish to be professionals must have space and time belonging only to themselves, she struggled continually with this need. The Woolfs' constant movement back and forth from London to the appropriately named Monk's House in Sussex, as well as her recurring bouts of madness, are motifs of engagement and removal in her life, and her diaries and letters frequently reflect these motifs. London social life was a magnet she could not resist, yet comments such as "I feel more and more inhibited and irritated by London life: I feel its meshes closing in—" reveal her need for the peace of Monk's House, where "one can sit on the fender and read" (*Letters* 4:119). Similarly, she vacillated between intense mental activity and periods during which, like Alice James, she had to "abandon" her brain because of severe headaches or depression. But whereas James saw her mind as dominant over her body, Woolf gradually came to see her periods of illness as times of incubation for ideas. In a 1930 diary entry, Woolf comes to the conclusion that her "mind works in idleness. To do nothing is often my most profitable way." She uses the analogy of a chrysalis to describe this productive dormant state:

> I believe these illnesses are in my case—how shall I express it?— partly mystical. Something happens in my mind. It refuses to go on registering impressions. It shuts itself up. It becomes chrysalis. I lie quite torpid, often with acute physical pain. . . . Then suddenly something springs. (3:287)

Woolf sees herself as apart from her mind, and watches as it gathers strength to "spring" into activity again. Illness was, for Woolf, a form of enforced solitude, but solitude could also be sought consciously, and she frequently equates isolation and thought with a sense of confronting the most important things in life. In a diary passage that approaches stream-of-consciousness in style, Woolf connects "interruption" with "children," and says that she has stopped wanting children since "my ideas so possess me." A life of solitude, without interruptions, allows her to "get my utmost fill of the marrow, the essence" (3:189).

Although Woolf is conscious of an audience or reader for her diary, she is less prone in it to adopt specific roles than she is in her letters. The more than 3,700 of her letters that have been collected are addressed to a wide variety of people with whom she had vastly differing relationships, and it is natural that she would use different tones and styles when writing to family, friends, social acquaintances, and other writers. Yet even in letters to those closest to her, Woolf alters her expression to accord with the presentation of self required by the relationship. For example, letters written on the same day in 1929 to her sister Vanessa and to Vita Sackville-West refer quite differently to one of her debilitating headaches. To Vita, with whom she had an intense relationship, apparently threatened at this point by Vita's friendship with another woman, Woolf writes that she has had to "retire to bed with the usual old pain," and the letter hints strongly that Vita's relationship with Hilda Matheson is partly responsible for her discomfort. The letter ends playfully as she attempts to reassure Vita that their relationship is still sound; she uses the nickname "Potto"—a pet name for herself that marks her intimacy with Vita: "I feel very happy about Virginia and Potto and dear old Vita" (*Letters* 4:77). Her relationship with Vanessa was at this point secure; there was no need for roles or games.

That Woolf was conscious of human role-playing—of the deliberate selection of a self to present to others—is clear from numerous comments in her letters and diaries. In her worst moments, she felt that all life was a facade. She records in her diary in 1929: "I shall make myself face the fact that there is nothing—nothing for any of us. Work, reading, writing are all disguises; & relationships with people. Yes, even having children would be useless" (3:235). In more positive moods, she played with the idea of identity, especially as identity is assumed to be conferred by names. In correspondence with several people she uses nicknames for them and/or for herself; most are names of animals. Leonard she addresses as "Mongoose," signing her letters to him "M." for "Mandril." Vanessa is addressed as "Dolphin," and Woolf characteristically signs these letters "B." for "Billy," because Vanessa's childhood nickname for her had been "goat." With Vanessa's children Woolf is usually playful in her letters. She addresses Angelica, the youngest, as "Pixie" or "Pixy," and signs herself variously "Old Aunt V," "V." or "Witcherina Maxima." The letters themselves are lighthearted and fanciful. Her favorite name for her nephew Quentin Bell was "Claudian," one of the names given him at birth, and in one letter to him she explains that she wishes to give him a new identity. Following the salutation "Claudian," she writes parenthetically, "I am going to call you this, in order to give you another start in life." Later in the same letter she explores the concept of identity as suggested by names:

> Please write again and let us go at some length into the question of your new character. Quentin was an adorable creature and I'm sorry he's been sloughed (sluffed) like the gold and orange skin of the rare Mexican tsee-tsee snake. Why not be him and Claudian on alternate days? Claudian is a secretive, marble-faced, steady-eyed deliberate villain. That is what his name indicates. (*Letters* 4:24–25)

Just as she could be both Virginia and "Potto," so she imagined that Quentin could change his identity at will.

For all that Woolf could play with the concept of names and identity, she remained skeptical about an ultimate essence and meaning, of either life or the individual. As a fiction writer, she was acutely conscious of the attempt to capture a human being in words that such writing requires. Her books she conceived as "spaces" allowing the author to try the experiment. In a 1930 diary entry she remarks: "The test of a book (to a writer) [is] if it makes a space in which, quite naturally, you can say what you want to say" (3:297). But Woolf always has the sense that words are finally inadequate to convey what the mind thinks—that the distance between self and reader through the medium of words on paper has a tendency to distort or to miss the point. In a letter to Gerald Brenan in 1929, she expresses doubt that one's essential self can ever be presented to another person:

> Suppose one could really communicate, how exciting it would be! Here I have covered one entire blue page and said nothing. One

can at most hope to suggest something. Suppose you are in the mood, when this letter comes, and read it in precisely the right light, by your Brazier in your big room, then by some accident there may be roused in you some understanding of what I, sitting over my log fire in Monk's House, am or feel, or think. It all seems infinitely chancy and infinitely humbugging—. (*Letters* 4:97)

Almost ten years later, attempting to patch up a misunderstanding with Vita, Woolf returns to this theme: "I suspect that anything written acquires meanings and both the writers [sic] mood and the reader's mood queer the pitch" (*Letters* 6:257). So deeply did Woolf live in her own thoughts that not even the medium of words could convey the person she knew herself to be. If Alice James displayed some certainty about presenting herself to an "inconnu," Woolf found such presentation only an effective strategy for dealing with the world, not an accurate measure of identity.

More than either James or Woolf, Emily Dickinson consistently used the strategy of roles to explore her relation to the world. Her letters as well as her poems display a wide variety of tones and voices; her "nobody" is multifaceted. Just as she physically removed herself from the world, she speaks as if from behind the closed door of her room, delighting in the fact that only her voice can be heard—a voice she could alter to reveal parts of her personality at will. Caught by the camera only once, she describes herself to T. W. Higginson by means of simile: "[I] am small, like the Wren, and my Hair is bold, like the Chestnut Bur [sic]—and my eyes, like the Sherry in the Glass, that the Guest leaves—" (*SL* no. 268). There is, she says in the same letter, no "mold" or portrait of her, and one expects that she has chosen the word "mold" deliberately, for its suggestion of her uniqueness: just as she is unduplicated by another human being, her image exists only as she chooses to render it in words. Living in a mind that is "wider than the sky," she has control over how and when she chooses to allow others into the place where she lives.

Other than the deep feeling that characterizes both her letters and her poetry, there is little evidence that Dickinson suffered from either physical or mental problems to the extent that James and Woolf did; these do not explain her solitude. In his biography of Dickinson, Richard Sewall quotes a portion of the obituary that Susan Gilbert Dickinson wrote for the *Springfield Republican* a few days after Dickinson's death. With more accuracy than apology, Susan describes her as having a "sensitive nature" but responds to likely suppositions about her reclusiveness by saying:

> Not disappointed with the world, not an invalid until within the past two years, not from any lack of sympathy, not because she was insufficient for any mental work or social career . . . but the "mesh of her soul," as Browning calls the body, was too rare, and the sacred quiet of her home proved the fit atmosphere for her worth and work. (228)

Susan's poetic language, expressing her insistence on Dickinson's general health, seems borne out by what we know of her life. Certainly her letters do not often mention illness, except that of others. Toward the end of Dickinson's life, she several times suffered nervous collapses, but these have specific origins in the deaths of loved ones. Following the death of her nephew Gilbert, she wrote to Mrs. J. G. Holland that "the Physician says I have 'Nervous prostration.'. . . The Crisis of the sorrow of so many years is all that tires me" (SL no. 873). After the death of Otis Lord the following year she again was prostrated, as she tells Louise and Frances Norcross: "The doctor calls it 'revenge of the nerves'; but who but Death had wronged them?" (SL no. 907). Gilbert had been a particular favorite of hers, and there is some evidence that she was in love with Otis Lord; little wonder, then, that she reacted so strongly to their deaths.

It was the attraction of home and thought, rather than frequent illness or madness, that fed Dickinson's need for solitude. Within the walls of her own house she was free to explore the wideness of her mind and come to understand the multifaceted "self" that she chose to conceal from or reveal to others. "Home," for Dickinson, was as much a concept as it was a physical place; it represented a center or base from which the consciousness could reach out to wider understanding and experience. "Home" and "mind" are almost interchangeable terms in her letters, suggesting that both refer to the most private and intimate parts of life. Writing to Austin from Mt. Holyoke in 1848, she sounds like any homesick schoolgirl when she says, "Home was always dear to me . . . but never did it seem so dear as now." Everyone is kind to her, but "their countenances meet mine not like home faces" (SL no. 22). Yet as she matured, home took on a far deeper meaning and came to be a metaphor for the innermost life. Writing to Abiah Root in 1854, Dickinson explains her reluctance to leave what has become her defined

world: "I don' [*sic*] go from home, unless emergency leads me by the
hand, and then I do it obstinately, and draw back if I can." A few
sentences later, she suggests that leaving home can mean taking on a
different identity, perhaps considering marriage, as Abiah was doing:
"*Do* you think it my *duty* to leave?" (*SL* no. 166). Whether Abiah or
anyone else considered it her "duty" to leave home, she did not adopt
the new identity that such leaving might signify; home, instead, increasingly stood for that which was most essential to her. T. W. Higginson,
after first meeting her, reported in a letter to his wife that Dickinson
asked him, "could you tell me what home is" (*SL* no. 342b), and several
years later, in 1876, she ended a letter to him by saying, "I often go
Home in thought to you" (*SL* no. 450). Higginson represented an
intellectual "home" to Dickinson, even if he was finally unable to appreciate and encourage her art on its own terms.

Within the compass of home and mind were all that Dickinson
required. "To shut our eyes is Travel," she writes to Elizabeth Holland
(*SL* no. 354). Thought rather than action was so necessary to her that
she could not understand how people lived differently than she did.
Higginson reports her comments from his meeting with her: "How do
most people live without any thoughts. There are many people in the
world (you must have noticed them in the street) How do they live.
How do they get strength to put on their clothes in the morning" (*SL*
no. 324a; punctuation Higginson's). Yet despite the in-dwelling of the
life of the mind—or perhaps because of it—Dickinson depended upon
friendships to help sustain her emotionally. "My friends are my 'estate,'"
she writes to Samuel Bowles in 1858; "Forgive me then the avarice to
hoard them!" (*SL* no. 193). Again to Bowles she writes, "Friends are
gems—infrequent" (*SL* no. 205). Letters were by far Dickinson's most
common means of communication with her friends, and though not as
prolific a correspondent as Virginia Woolf (somewhat more than one
thousand of Dickinson's letter are extant), she used them for much the
same purpose: to maintain a social network that could allow expression
of her many personalities.

In letters written before she reached her late twenties, Dickinson's
tone tends to be either teasing, as in her letters to Austin, or warmly
affectionate, as in her letters to Abiah Root and Susan Gilbert. Although
with Austin she is frequently the fond younger sister, concerned about
his health and happiness, she also betrays a competitive spirit, especially when Austin tries his hand at writing, a province she already—in
1853—considers her own:

And Austin is a Poet, Austin writes a psalm. . . . Now Brother Pegasus, I'll tell you what it is—I've been in the habit *myself* of writing some few things, and it rather appears to me that you're getting away my patent, so you'd better be somewhat careful, or I'll call the police! (*SL* no. 110)

Though the tone of the letter is flippant, and she refers in the next sentence to the "folly" of what she has written, Dickinson's comments have an undercurrent of seriousness. Austin did not, in fact, become a writer, and her sense of competition was not an enduring one, as was Woolf's with her sister Vanessa, but it marks Dickinson's need for an identity separate from her brother. This letter and most of those to her female friends Dickinson signed "Emilie" rather than "Emily"—the altered spelling is a common indication of youthful desire to name the self. To her female friends Dickinson writes of her need for their friendship; the tone is less flippant, sometimes even ardent, as when she writes to Susan: "Oh my darling one, how long you wander from me, how weary I grow of waiting and looking, and calling for you" (*SL* no. 73). The language of such letters is to some extent formulaic, inspired by romantic literary models, but it nonetheless suggests a dependence on friendship that caused Dickinson to retain close ties with others through words if not through physical contact.[12]

About 1858, Dickinson's letters change rather abruptly from the long, bantering or loving missives that characterized her youth to the short, epigrammatic letters of her maturity. Gone is the "Emilie" of the earlier letters; the selves that Dickinson presents in the later letters are various, but the style is consistently cryptic, the meaning often enigmatic to all but the recipient. Instead of the polite introduction, such as "It is Sunday, and I am here alone" (*SL* no. 125), the later letters begin without preamble, and paragraphs frequently consist of a single sentence. Like Dickinson's poetry, these letters are highly metaphoric and aphoristic, the more so as she deliberately selects a self to present to her reader. The most extreme examples of role-playing are the "Master" letters, addressed to an unknown recipient and unsigned, although she clearly refers to herself as "Daisy." These abject love letters present a persona overwhelmed by her dependence on another's approbation, and they form a sharp contrast to the control over self and language that she otherwise manifests.

This control is seen most clearly in her letters to Higginson; though dependent upon him for artistic guidance, she carefully manipulates his image of her by presenting herself sometimes as "Your Scholar" and at other times as the matter-of-fact "E. Dickinson." On one occasion she signs herself "Your Gnome," presumably a response to his characterization of her poetry as "gnomic"; the signature suggests that she is willing to accept this description of her work only if she is permitted to have fun with its implications. In fact, other than in the "Master" letters and those which express grief or sympathy, Dickinson is quite clearly playing a kind of hide-and-seek with her correspondents, allowing only partial access to her private world. This limited access to the "self" behind the words is concomitant with her perception of the poet's relationship to the speaker in the poem, articulated in a letter to Higginson: "When I state myself, as the Representative of the Verse—it does not mean—me—but a supposed person" (*SL* no. 268). In her letters, as in her poetry, writing is a form of art that can conceal, not reveal, the artist.

Messages

In "Reminiscences" Virginia Woolf writes: "Written words of a person who is dead or still alive tend most unfortunately to drape themselves in smooth folds annulling all evidence of life" (*Moments of Being* 36). As both fiction writer and biographer, Woolf was acutely aware that words are inadequate to capture or convey the essence of an individual, fictional or actual. Yet constantly, in her own diaries and letters, she attempted to communicate her thoughts, feelings, preferences, and fears, as though words could lend reality to experience that was always fleeting. Though most alive and fulfilled when exploring her own imagination, Woolf was compelled to transform her thoughts into words that could potentially "annul" the very reality they were intended to preserve. Similarly, Emily Dickinson and Alice James felt it necessary to commit to paper their private thoughts—ostensibly for themselves, but also for readers who might come to an understanding, albeit an imperfect one, of another human life. Whatever "message" James wished desperately to send us will remain obscure; more important is her desire to send one, even in the private form of a diary entry. For Dickinson the word, once written, had a magic, if unpredictable, power. As she writes to Higginson in 1869: "A Letter always feels to me like immortality because it is the mind alone without corporeal friend. Indebted in our talk to attitude and accent, there seems a spectral power in thought that walks alone—" (*SL* no. 330). The "spectral power" derives both from the writer's inability to capture thought with precision and the chance that the reader, unassisted by "attitude and accent," may misinterpret the words; communication becomes, as Woolf puts it, "infinitely chancy and infinitely humbugging."

Yet the autobiographical writing of these three women—and many others—is obviously intended to communicate to someone, to leave a record of life beneath the "smooth folds" that more formal language can create. In writing for an unknown future reader—James's "inconnu"—they have left candid and often painful evidence of what life was like for relatively privileged white women in the Victorian and post-Victorian periods. Specifically, they tell of the effort to free themselves of the constraints of "true womanhood" in order to participate in the life of the intellect. By most measures, Alice James failed in this struggle: confined by invalidism for most of her life, she had neither family nor career. But her diary is a testament to her intelligence and perception—perhaps her message is that even within her "centimetre of observation" was an unsuspected richness of thought and feeling. By any measure, Emily Dickinson is a successful poet, but her success was achieved only after her death; during her lifetime she pursued her career more or less in secret, misunderstood by her few critics and thought to be eccentric, at best, by those around her. Like Alice James, however, Dickinson lived more fully in her solitude than many people who live "normal" lives. Virginia Woolf achieved her "room of one's own" and wide public acclaim for her work, but she was haunted by the fear that perhaps motherhood would have been a more important contribution to society. Despite her successes, she was plagued by madness and ended her own life.

The diaries, letters, journals, and memoirs of women are properly of increasing interest to scholars. Not only are these often the only kinds of writing women have produced, as in the case of Alice James, but they also illuminate the lives and concerns of women generally in their recording of small as well as large—"public"—moments. It is less important to know with whom, if anyone, Emily Dickinson was in love than to know what relationships with men and women meant to women of her time and place, and how these meanings became transformed into art. If the brain is indeed "wider than the sky," autobiographical records such as these can give us access to some of its vastness, and can help to recreate women's history as a significant factor in women's art.

Notes

1. Dickinson, *Complete Poems* no. 632. Hereafter referred to in the text as *CP*.

2. There is currently a great deal of interest in the relationship between women and the "minority" or "ethnic" experience. One example is Mary V. Dearborn's *Pocahontas's Daughters*, which argues that ethnicity is related to power and powerlessness more than to shared cultural characteristics, and that women writers have had to challenge the notion of genre in order to speak from their own hidden, marginal experience.

3. Women's humorous writing displays a strong sense of sharing a common experience with other women, even though the individual voice expresses great isolation. See Nancy Walker, *"A Very Serious Thing": Women's Humor and American Culture* (Minneapolis: University of Minnesota Press, 1988).

4. Indeed, much of early American literature is composed of such private/public documents. Such colonial leaders as William Bradford, Samuel Sewall, and William Byrd commented on the affairs of their day as well as their own personal lives in such a way as to blend the private with the public.

5. Dickinson, *Selected Letters* no. 163. Hereafter referred to in the text as *SL*.

6. Indeed her diary was, in a sense, "published" shortly after Alice James died. Before her death, James had requested that the diary be typewritten, and in 1894 Katharine Loring had four copies privately printed, one for herself and one for each of the surviving James brothers (Yeazell 5).

7. That is, Woolf did not sit down at sixty and write her life. She did, however, leave several autobiographical fragments, especially "A Sketch of the Past," written in 1939–40 and collected in *Moments of Being*.

8. In "Reminiscences," collected in *Moments of Being*, Woolf ostensibly follows in the tradition of her male ancestors: the sketch is addressed to her nephew Julian Bell, but the memories here are more about her mother and her sister Vanessa (Julian's mother) than about herself.

9. If Emily Dickinson was, as has been suggested for years, involved—however distantly—with Charles Wadsworth, Samuel Bowles, or Otis Lord, she could on some level have been taking the "safe" course of being involved with married, and therefore unavailable, men. However, her brother Austin's all-consuming thirteen-year affair with Mabel Loomis Todd—an affair with which Dickinson was quite familiar—would have demonstrated that married men were not always merely worshiped from afar. The suggestion that Dickinson was lesbian in inclination if not in experience has been posited as another explanation for her remaining single, and there is ample evidence in her poems and letters of strong emotional attachments to other women, especially during her adolescence and young adulthood. Whatever Dickinson's sexual preference, it is clear that she had a strong resistance to being subsumed by a relationship with another person.

10. Leonard was not so accepting of relationships that Virginia had with

other women, in particular with Ethel Smyth, an older woman who was unabashedly in love with her. In a letter to Ethel in 1941, Woolf says:

> Never mind Leonard. He is a good man: in his heart he respects my friends. But as for *my* staying with *you*, for some occult reason, he cries No no No. I think it is a bad thing that we're so inseparable. But how, in this world of separation, does one break it? (*Letters* 6:460)

Apparently, Leonard admired Vita, and so could comprehend Virginia's affection for her, but he did not feel the same about Ethel. In other words, his resistance to Ethel was a matter of taste rather than jealousy.

11. Alice James seems to have been a great admirer of Dickinson's work, which she would have read in one or both of the two volumes of poems edited by Mabel Loomis Todd and Thomas Wentworth Higginson in 1890 and 1891. James was one of the earliest readers to recognize that Dickinson was undervalued as a poet and also that Higginson was not the most sympathetic editor her poems could have had. In a diary entry dated 6 January 1892, she says:

> It is reassuring to hear the English pronouncement that Emily Dickinson is fifth-rate, they have such a capacity for missing quality; the robust evades them equally with the subtle. Her being sicklied [sic] o'er with T. W. Higginson makes one quake lest there be a latent flaw which escapes one's vision. (227)

12. Many have suggested that Dickinson's emotional dependence on Susan—and other women—is evidence of latent homosexuality. A sensitive discussion of this point is found in Vivian R. Pollak's *Dickinson*. A similar suggestion has been made about Alice James's relationship with Katharine Loring, and there was definitely an intimate relationship between Virginia Woolf and Vita Sackville-West. While this certainly does not argue that lesbianism is essential to female intellectual maturity, it does point to the struggle each of these women had to define herself in relation to a male-dominated society.

Works Cited

Dearborn, Mary V. *Pocahontas's Daughters: Gender and Ethnicity in American Culture*. New York: Oxford University Press, 1986.

Dickinson, Emily. *The Complete Poems of Emily Dickinson*. Ed. Thomas H. Johnson. Boston: Little, Brown, 1955.

———. *Selected Letters*. Ed. Thomas H. Johnson. Cambridge: Belknap, 1971.

James, Alice. *The Diary of Alice James*. Ed. Leon Edel. New York: Penguin, 1982.

Juhasz, Suzanne. *The Undiscovered Continent*. Bloomington: Indiana University Press, 1983.

Lifshin, Lyn. *Ariadne's Thread: A Collection of Contemporary Women's Journals*. New York: Harper and Row, 1982.

Martin, Wendy. *An American Triptych: Anne Bradstreet, Emily Dickinson, Adrienne Rich*. Chapel Hill: University of North Carolina Press, 1984.

Pollak, Vivian R. *Dickinson: The Anxiety of Gender*. Ithaca: Cornell University Press, 1984.

Sarton, May. *The House by the Sea*. New York: Norton, 1977.

Sewall, Richard B. *The Life of Emily Dickinson*. New York: Farrar, Straus and Giroux, 1980.

Shurr, William H. *The Marriage of Emily Dickinson*. Lexington: University Press of Kentucky, 1983.

Woolf, Virginia. *The Diary of Virginia Woolf*. Ed. Anne Olivier Bell. 5 vols. New York: Harcourt Brace Jovanovich, 1977–84.

————. *The Letters of Virginia Woolf*. Ed. Nigel Nicolson and Joanne Trautmann. 6 vols. New York: Harcourt Brace Jovanovich, 1975–80.

————. *Moments of Being*. Ed. Jeanne Schulkind. New York: Harcourt Brace Jovanovich, 1976.

Yeazell, Ruth Bernard, ed. *The Death and Letters of Alice James*. Berkeley: University of California Press, 1981.

NOTE ON THE CONTRIBUTORS

Shari Benstock is professor of English at the University of Miami, Coral Gables. She is author of *Women of the Left Bank: Paris, 1900–1940* (translated into French as *Femmes de la rive gauche*). She is also editor of *Feminist Issues in Literary Scholarship*, a collection of essays first published in *Tulsa Studies in Women's Literature* and winner of the 1985 Conference of Editors of Learned Journals award for best special issue of a scholarly journal. She is currently at work on *Textualizing the Feminine: Essays on the Limits of Genre*, a collection of her own essays, and *Modernism Made Manifest: The Ideologies of Periodical Publication*, a two-volume study that reads Modernism through the journals and reviews that published its manifestos and representative texts. She is coeditor, with Celeste Schenck, of the feminist book series "Reading Women Writing" at Cornell University Press.

Joanne M. Braxton is associate professor of English at the College of William and Mary. She is the author of a forthcoming book entitled *Autobiography by Black American Women: A Tradition within a Tradition* and coeditor, with Andree N. McLaughlin, of *Wild Women in the Whirlwind: Culture and Politics in the Renaissance of Afro-American Writing*. Her essay in this collection was previously published in the Wellesley College Center for Research on Women Working Papers Series (Fall 1985).

Elizabeth Fox-Genovese is professor of history and director of women's studies at Emory University. She is author of *Within the Plantation Household: Black and White Women of the Old South* and *The Origins of Physiocracy*, editor and translator of *The Autobiography of P. S. DuPont de Nemours*, and coauthor of *Fruits of Merchant Capital*. Her essay, "Zora Neale Hurston as Exile," appeared in *Signs* (Spring 1987).

Susan Stanford Friedman is professor of English and women's studies at the University of Wisconsin–Madison. She is the author of *Psyche Reborn: The Emergence of H.D.* and coauthor of *A Woman's Guide to Therapy*, and she has two books forthcoming: *Penelope's Web: H.D.'s Fictions and the Gendering of Modernism* and *Portrait of an Analysis with Freud: The Letters of H.D. and Bryher, 1933–1934*. Among her many articles on women's writing is "Theories of Autobiography and Fictions of the Self in H.D.'s Canon," forthcoming in *Self-Representations: Autobiographical Writing in the Nineteenth and Twentieth Centuries*, edited by Thomas Smith. She has coedited, with Rachel Blau DuPlessis, a special issue of *Contemporary Literature* on H.D.

Deborah Kaplan is associate professor of English at George Mason University. She is completing a feminist biographical and critical study of Jane Austen. Her published articles on Austen include "Achieving Authority: Jane Austen's First Published Novel," *Nineteenth-Century Fiction* (1983); "The Disappearance of the Woman Writer: Jane Austen and Her Biographers," *Prose Studies* (1984); and "Female Friendship and Epistolary Form: *Lady Susan* and the Development of Jane Austen's Fiction," *Criticism* (1987).

James Holt McGavran, Jr., is associate professor of English at the University of North Carolina, Charlotte. He is the author of "'Alone Seeking the Visible World': The Wordsworths, Virginia Woolf, and *The Waves*," *Modern Language Quarterly* (1981); "The Wordsworths and the Writing Process: Towards an Androgynous Rhetoric," *CEA Forum* (1987–88); and "Coleridge, the Wordsworths, and Androgyny: A Reading of 'The Nightingale,'" *South Atlantic Review* (1988). He is currently editing an anthology entitled *Romanticism and Children's Literature*.

Jane Marcus is professor of English at the City University of New York Graduate Center and the City College of New York. She is the editor of several books on Virginia Woolf and Rebecca West and the author of dozens of articles on twentieth-century women's writings and feminist critical theory. Her most recent publications include *Art and Anger: Reading Like a Woman*, and *Virginia Woolf and the Languages of Patriarchy*, and she is the editor of *Virginia Woolf and Bloomsbury: Centenary Celebration* and *Suffrage and the Pankhursts*.

Mitzi Myers teaches children's literature, women's literature, and writing at the University of California, Los Angeles, and at Scripps College. She has published essays on Mary Wollstonecraft in *Studies in Eighteenth-Century Culture*

and *Studies in Romanticism* and in *Children's Literature*, edited by Margaret Higonnet and Barbara Rosen. She is presently writing essays on Hannah More, Maria Edgeworth, and Sarah Trimmer, all of which are part of a larger investigation of Georgian women writers of children's and educational books. Central to that study is the notion, explored in her essay in this volume, that writing for the young offers psychic benefits for the woman writer.

Felicity A. Nussbaum is professor of English at Syracuse University. She is author of *The Brink of All We Hate: English Satires on Women, 1660–1750* and *Three Seventeenth-Century Satires* and editor, with Laura Brown, of *The New Eighteenth-Century: Theory/Politics/English Literature*. Her essay "Toward Conceptualizing Diary" appears in *Studies in Autobiography*, edited by James Olney, and she is completing a book entitled *Rethinking Eighteenth-Century Autobiography: Gendered Subjects*.

Patricia Meyer Spacks is professor of English at Yale University. She is author of *Imagining a Self, The Female Imagination, The Adolescent Idea*, and *Gossip*. Her essays on women's autobiographical forms have appeared in *Harvard Library Bulletin, Yale Review, Hudson Review*, and *Boston University Journal*.

Nancy Walker teaches at Stephens College, where she is chair of languages and literature. She is author of *The Tradition of Women's Humor in America* and of a forthcoming book, *"A Very Serious Thing": Women's Humor and American Culture*. Her essays on women's writing have appeared in *American Quarterly, Denver Quarterly*, and *Tulsa Studies in Women's Literature*.

Kathleen Woodward is director of the Center for Twentieth Century Studies and associate professor of English at the University of Wisconsin–Milwaukee. She is author of *At Last, the Real Distinguished Thing: The Late Poems of Eliot, Pound, Stevens, and Williams* and coeditor of *Memory and Desire: Aging—Literature—Psychoanalysis, Aging and Elderly: Humanistic Perspectives in Geron-* tology, and *The Technological Imagination: Theories and Fictions.* She is general editor of the book series "Theories of Contemporary Culture" at Indiana University Press. Her essays have appeared in *Kenyon Review, Contemporary Literature, Women and Literature,* and *North Dakota Quarterly,* among others.

INDEX